War and the Media

War and the Media

*Essays on News Reporting,
Propaganda and
Popular Culture*

Edited by
PAUL M. HARIDAKIS,
BARBARA S. HUGENBERG *and*
STANLEY T. WEARDEN

McFarland & Company, Inc., Publishers
Jefferson, North Carolina, and London

ALSO OF INTEREST: *Sports Mania: Essays on Fandom and the Media in the 21st Century.* Edited by Lawrence W. Hugenberg, Paul M. Haridakis and Adam C. Earnheardt (McFarland, 2008)

LIBRARY OF CONGRESS ONLINE CATALOG DATA

War and the media : essays on news reporting, propaganda and popular culture / edited by Paul M. Haridakis, Barbara S. Hugenberg and Stanley T. Wearden.
    p.   cm.
    Includes bibliographical references and index.

    ISBN 978-0-7864-4607-0
    softcover : 50# alkaline paper ∞

    1. Mass media and war — United States. 2. War in mass media. 3. Popular culture — United States. 4. Mass media and public opinion — United States. 5. Mass media and propaganda — United States. I. Title. II. Haridakis, Paul M., 1957– III. Hugenberg, Barbara S., 1954– IV. Wearden, Stanley T.
P96.W352U5585   2009
070.4'4935502 — dc22   2009030616

British Library cataloguing data are available

©2009 Paul M. Haridakis, Barbara S. Hugenberg and Stanley T. Wearden. All rights reserved

No part of this book may be reproduced or transmitted in any form or by any means, electronic or mechanical, including photocopying or recording, or by any information storage and retrieval system, without permission in writing from the publisher.

Cover images ©2009 Shutterstock

Manufactured in the United States of America

McFarland & Company, Inc., Publishers
  Box 611, Jefferson, North Carolina 28640
    www.mcfarlandpub.com

Table of Contents

Preface 1

Introduction: The Impact of War on Communication Theory, Research, and the Field of Communication
The Editors 3

Part I: Images in Popular Culture

Protest Music as Alternative Media During the Vietnam War Era
    Richard A. Lee   24

Created Heroes, Humanized Soldiers, and Superior Western Values: Fantasy Theme Analysis of *Flags of Our Fathers* and *Letters from Iwo Jima*
    Koji Fuse and James E. Mueller   41

Ghosts of Vietnam: Filmic Representations of Unconsummated American Heroism in the Beginning of the Twenty-First Century
    Wesley J. O'Brien   57

Drawn-Out Battles: Exploring War-Related Messages in Animated Cartoons
    Rekha Sharma   75

Part II: Institutional Propaganda Messages

Economic Convergence and the Celebration of Mass Production: The World War II Advertising Campaign to Sell Jeeps
    Kathleen German   92

"You Boys and Girls Can Be the Minute Men of Today": Narrative Possibility and Normative Appeal in the U.S. Treasury's 1942 *War Victory Comics*
    James J. Kimble and Trischa Goodnow   112

Inspecting the Rhetorical Arsenal: The War Frame in Nazi Germany's
der Kampf and America's War on Terror
  Roy Schwartzman 126
An Enduring Legacy of World War I: Propaganda, Journalism and
the Domestic Struggle over the Commodification of Truth
  Burton St. John III 147

Part III: Effects of News Coverage

Coverage of the Iraq and Afghanistan Wars in Business Magazines:
The Profit and Economy of U.S. War and Policy
  Karen Rohrbauck Stout 164

"New Mexico's Always Been Patriotic and Loyal to the Country":
Uncritical Journalistic Patriotism in Wartime
  David Weiss 183

Embedded Reporting and Audience Response: Parasocial
Interaction and Perceived Realism in Embedded Reporting
from the Iraq War on Television News
  M. F. Casper and *Jeffrey T. Child* 205

Prince Harry and the Afghanistan Media Blackout
  Terri Toles Patkin 222

Part IV: Future

Cyberwar: The Future of War?
  Brett Lunceford 238

About the Contributors 253

Index 257

Preface

At first blush the relationship between media and war is obvious and transparent. Media cover war, mass communication is used by governments to support the respective war efforts, and media images are created or manipulated to inform, persuade, or otherwise guide interpretations of those images. The connection between war and wartime communication research and the field of communication studies is equally obvious. In fact, individuals widely recognized as the founders of the field of communication studies — Harold Lasswell, Paul Lazarsfeld, Kurt Lewin, and Wilbur Schramm — all conducted wartime-related research. Since then, communication scholars have played an integral role in each war in which the United States has been involved.

But the goal of this book is to look beyond the obvious. The contributors examine specific historical and contemporary examples of war-related communication that reflect the role of the media and/or mass communication during wartime. Together, the chapters suggest that the symbiotic relationship between communication and war is as important to understand as war itself. They highlight the centrality of communication to the perpetuation of war and the resolution of it. The various types of media and mass communication efforts examined suggest further that as each new media technology emerges, it is enlisted during wartime. As a result, each new medium shapes in unique ways how communication is used and war is portrayed and interpreted.

While the breadth of wartime research cannot be covered in a single book, we hope that this volume can serve as a way to reflect upon prior research and serve as a guide for continued exploration and future inquiry. The contributors review prior actions, consider present practices, and contemplate future efforts. The chapters focus on both negative uses and effects of communication and positive uses and effects, recognizing that complete understanding comes from considering both communication successes and failures.

In the same way that the research is illustrative of a wide body of social science research devoted to advancing understanding wartime media use and effects, the contributors to this book are representative of the numerous social scientists devoted to the study of wartime communication who came before them and others who will come after them.

They examine propaganda and public opinion; mass communication campaigns and persuasion; rhetorical uses of communication; pro-war and anti-war communication; how news organizations and popular media such as magazines, movies, and music frame and communicate wartime images; and potential media effects on audiences. The war-related communication examined ranges from World War I to the current wars in Iraq and Afghanistan, to speculation about the role of media in future wartime.

The contributors' research evidences the sheer importance of the role of war-related communication and campaigns. It also highlights that researchers must remain vigilant in scrutiny of the media's role in war and utilizing lessons from the past to inform the future. This inquiry suggests the need to increase wartime communication literacy to avoid past failures and build upon past successes. It represents perhaps one of the most important areas of media effects research — how communication works during times when a nation is most vulnerable — times of societal conflict and war.

It is our hope, then, that this book serves as an outline for the interested reader to find further information on the subjects and research areas referenced and that the authors' contributions stimulate interest in the exploration of the wider body of wartime social science research the chapters represent.

We hope you find the book enjoyable *and* enlightening. Most importantly, we hope it stimulates you to join the community of scholars who are dedicated to enhancing understanding of wartime media use and effects. Historically, the power of communication during times of military conflict has been harnessed and directed toward productive *and* destructive ends. Unfortunately, strife and violent conflicts will always be with us. Our hope is that research efforts in this very important area contribute to the use of more humane wartime communication behaviors.

Paul M. Haridakis • Barbara S. Hugenberg • Stanley T. Wearden

Introduction: The Impact of War on Communication Theory, Research, and the Field of Communication

The Editors

The importance of communication, particularly mass communication, during times of war is well recognized. The government needs to mobilize the citizenry and respond to the crisis. Citizens need information, assurances that the government is responding effectively, and connection and support from each other. The media serve as conduits of necessary and desired information. Accordingly, dependence on the media is heightened during times of war.

Examples of the important wartime role of the media in the United States predate the foundation of the republic. These include publication of Paul Revere's famous engraving depicting the Boston Massacre and Benjamin Franklin's depiction of a snake separated into eight pieces to represent each of the colonies (Jowett & O'Donnell, 2006). Following the war for U.S. independence, newspapers were used to publish the federalist papers (Hamilton, Madison, & Jay, 1788/1996), a post-war communication campaign to persuade the states to ratify the new U.S. Constitution.

It is not surprising that, historically, times of such intense societal conflict have generated research interest in the critical role of mass communication during wartime. At times the focus of scrutiny has been on the potential for negative effects such as misinformation, propaganda, and communication activities that may undermine the war effort. At other times researchers have focused on prosocial effects such as aiding interpretation of war effort, providing factual knowledge, mobilization, and preparedness.

In short, war intensifies awareness of the power of communication for positive and negative outcomes. This fact leads to attempts to control access to information, harness the power of communication for persuasion, and, at times, to manipulate its power for propagandistic ends.

Regardless of the particular focus of attention, the study of the uses and effects of communication during wartime has played an integral role in advancing the legitimacy of Communication Studies as a field of study, and the advancement of communication theory and scholarship.

The extent of the research generated cannot be covered comprehensively (even superficially) in a single essay. In this chapter, our aims are modest. We provide a representation of significant wartime scholarship/research in the U.S. during the twentieth century that has shaped and advanced theoretical development in the field of communication studies and added to our contemporary understanding of communication, particularly mass communication, media use and effects, and persuasion.

We focus predominantly on U.S.-based research conducted during wars in which the United States has been involved. We have elected to review it chronologically, as we feel that presents a clearer picture of the progression of both thought and efforts with the use of communication. While our review is necessarily brief and illustrative of a wide body of research conducted during wartime, we hope that it can serve as an outline for the interested reader to find further information on each of the subjects and research areas referenced.

World War I and Its Aftermath

Fears that led to concerns about propaganda and the need to maintain support for the war effort in the U.S. were evidenced clearly during World War I, when the government passed the Espionage Act of 1917. Communication was the specific emphasis of a 1918 amendment to this law, the Sedition Act. It provided, in part,

> Whoever ... shall willfully utter, print, write, or publish any disloyal, profane, scurrilous, or abusive language about the form of government of the United States, or the Constitution of the United States, or the military or naval forces of the United States, shall be punished by a fine of not more than $10,000 or imprisonment for not more than twenty years, or both.

This statute, in essence, criminalized any communication that could undermine the war effort. For example, speakers who were critical of the nation's entry into the war or the conscription of soldiers into it were prosecuted for their antiwar rhetoric. This included German (*Frohwerk v. United States*, 1919), Socialist (*Debs v. United States*, 1919), and Russian (*Abrams v. United States*, 1919) sympathizers. Such prosecutions were often focused on those who used or attempted to use mass media (e.g., leaflets, newspapers) to propagate their message. While deemed necessary at the time to curtail antiwar sentiment, today scholars point to the actions of the government to control such communication as notorious examples of assaults on the First Amendment during wartime (Tedford & Herbeck, 2005).

Fear of the power of mass communication was stimulated specifically by the perceived effective use of propaganda by both allied and axis powers during the war. Although major research on this subject influential to the development of mass communication inquiry was not conducted during the war, the relative effectiveness of wartime communication, particularly enemy and allied propaganda, stimulated and influenced mass communication research conducted in the 1920s and 1930s (Cmiel, 1996; Sproule, 1991).

Some scholars such as political scientist and mass communication scholar, Harold Lasswell (1927), emphasized the centrality of propaganda for mobilizing public opinion during wartime. Others emphasized its dangers and the need to be aware of it (Lumley, 1933). At the same time, scholars and journalists, such as John Dewey (1927) and Walter Lippmann (1922), speculated about the function of public opinion in twentieth century society and the role of the mass media in shaping it. On balance, there was a clear post-war growth in interest in how to use propaganda and mass communication productively to meet government ends and garner public support, particularly during wartime.

In the late 1930s mass communication scholars found a benefactor for their research in the Rockefeller Foundation. The Foundation funded various social science research projects and institutes devoted to the study of mass communication. Too numerous to detail here, they included Paul Lazarsfeld's Columbia radio research project, Hadley Cantril's and Frank Stanton's Princeton radio research project, and Lasswell's work at the Library of Congress. The social scientific approach to communication undertaken by these Foundation-funded projects was instrumental to the field's development (Gary, 1996). The Foundation's support of a new journal, *Public Opinion Quarterly*, provided a valuable new outlet for the publication of research.

By the late 1930s and the spectre of World War II looming, social scientists began turning their attention to the potential new wartime threat. After Germany invaded Poland in 1939, the Rockefeller Foundation sponsored a series of communications seminars that called together several mass communication scholars and other social scientists who had received Foundation funding (Gary, 1996; Rogers, 2004). These seminars were dedicated to addressing numerous issues including how to utilize effectively communication for mobilizing public opinion and preparing the government and country for war and combating propaganda.

Meeting over the next 15 months the group prepared several papers and a culminating report entitled *Needed Research in Mass Communications* (cited in Gary, 1996, p. 133). One paradigm shifting outcome of this group was an overarching conceptualization of the communication process that influenced the field for decades. Articulated later by Lasswell (1948), it described the communication process as focusing on who says what to whom in which channel with what effects (p. 37). Given Lasswell's focus on mass communication and propaganda, his model directed scholars to research designed to address media effects.

World War II

Many prominent social scientists in the United States served in the armed services or as consultants to the military during World War II. For example, Lazarsfeld and Stanton conducted research and/or consulted for the Office of War Information. Lasswell worked for the War Communication Division at the Library of Congress. Ithiel de Sola Pool, today widely recognized for his new media text, *Technologies of Freedom* (1983), contributed to Lasswell's project. Wilber Schramm worked for the Office of War Information (for further discussion see Jowett & O'Donnell, 2006; Simpson, 1994).

The war gave communication scholars, in particular, the opportunity to engage in applied communication research pertaining to topics such as the effects of fear appeals, persuasive arguments and campaigns, propaganda, the mobilization of public support, readying the United States for a wartime economy and production, indoctrination of soldiers, building and maintaining troop morale, and the collection of intelligence. In one of the seminal media effects studies, psychologist Carl Hovland and his wartime colleagues studied the effectiveness of Frank Capra's *Why We Fight* Army training films. The researchers' findings suggested that these training efforts were good at providing information and increasing factual knowledge, but less effective at attitude change (Hovland, Lumsdaine, & Sheffield, 1949).

While much of the research conducted during the war was instrumental in advancing empirical research methodology for examining media use and effects, research using critical cultural (e.g., Frankfurt School) (see, e.g., Horkheimer & Adorno, 1972) and other qualitative methods also were important. These included Kenneth Burke's critical rhetorical analysis of Hitler's use of propaganda (for a review see Weiser, 2007), content analysis of German radio propaganda and it's attempt to terrorize (Speier & Otis, 1944), and using interviews to collect intelligence from civilian populations regarding possible allied landings (Cantril, 1965).

Some research conducted during the war challenged theoretical notions of direct media effects and fostered a paradigm shift that stimulated a limited media effects research tradition for some time. This research included Cantril's (1940) consideration of the influence of social and psychological factors in inducing panic among listeners of the radio broadcast of H. G. Wells' *The War of the Worlds*; Merton and Lazarsfeld's analysis of responses to radio programs and other media (cited in Merton, 1968), the Lazarsfeld, Berelson, & Gaudet (1944) assessment of a two-step flow of communication (i.e., the role of interpersonal influence in the dissemination of media messages), and Kurt Lewin's examination of the importance of group discussion in wartime decision making (see Jowett & O'Donnell, 2006, p. 170; Rogers, 1994, pp. 335–336).

Much of what we know about this wartime research was published in the decade after the war and provided a body of research on which to build the field of communication. For example, after the war, the results of analysis of Frank Capra's army training films were published (Hovland et al., 1949). This and other wartime research conducted by Hovland and his associates stimulated scrutiny of the effects of fear appeals, the relative effectiveness of two-sided vs. one-sided arguments on attitude change, the importance of source credibility, and a host of other groundbreaking persuasion studies at Yale University in the late 1940s and 1950s (e.g., Hovland, Janis, & Kelly, 1953; Kelman & Hovland, 1953).

More broadly, scholars published theoretical models of the communication process. For example, during the war, Claude Shannon worked on a mathematical or transmission model of communication. It depicted a linear model of the communication process (Shannon & Weaver, 1949), as did Lasswell's (1948) model referenced above.

Thus, the importance of research conducted during World War II continued to shape communication studies after the war. Many mass communication scholars drew on their applied and research experiences during the war. This wartime research provided opportunities for researchers to not only study the practical effects of communication campaigns, but also to articulate theoretical explanations for understanding them.

Korean War and Early Cold-War Era

The Cold War that began in the immediate aftermath of World War II was closely intertwined with the Korean and Vietnam conflicts. These were conflicts in which the overarching ideological battle between democracy (embodied in the United States and its allies) and communism (embodied most visibly in the Soviet Union and China) were manifested in wars in which the U.S. effort was to contain the spread of communism — and by extension, the threat of nuclear warfare. The threat was perceived as acute. After World War II the Soviet Union immediately assumed control of Eastern Europe and East Germany. Its control of the latter led to the U.S. airlifting food and supplies to that city. In 1949, the Communist regime headed by Mao Tse-tung assumed control of China. China began supplying troops and aid to the communist regime in North Korea that invaded South Korea and triggered U.S. entry into the war.

At the same time, the U.S. government was extremely vigilant in combating the perceived threat of the spread of communism within the U.S. This led to the establishment of the House Un-American Activities Committee, the use of the Alien Registration Act of 1940 (a law that criminalized seditious and antiwar communication) to target and prosecute communists (see, e.g., *Dennis v. United States*, 1951), and the onslaught of "McCarthyism."

This atmosphere proved to be a boon for communication research. As Cmiel (1996) put it, how communication could be used to "build loyalty at home and stable, new, non-communist nations around the globe became critically important to the field" (p. 95). Some researchers turned their attention to studying and understanding the use and form of communication within communist nations (e.g., Schramm & Riley, 1951). Other scholars focused on how mass communication could build consensus and lead people to work together (e.g., Smith, Lasswell, & Casey, 1946; Wirth, 1948).

One ambitious series of studies conducted during this time period evaluated the effectiveness of leaflets dropped by aircraft. Patriotically coined "Project Revere," researchers examined the effectiveness of the leaflets' message on target populations and how the messages spread interpersonally (for a review of some studies, see DeFleur & Larson, 1958). One of the principal findings of this military-sponsored project was that as the messages spread interpersonally there was significant distortion and misinformation (Lowery & DeFleur, 1988).

Of course, leafleting is a very specific form of non-electronic mass communication. A more practical and large-scale application of mass communication involved using the electronic media, particularly radio, to influence those in other nations of the advantages of democracy and, often, U.S. values.

For example, the Voice of America (VOA) was established in the U.S. during World War II and began international broadcasts under the auspices of the Office of War Information. In 1948, the VOA was placed under the authority of the U.S. State Department. By the late 1950s the VOA was broadcasting around the world in numerous languages. Broadcasts often were, and continue to be, targeted to specific nations. For example, targeted broadcasts to Cuba were conducted by Radio Marti, and later by TV Marti. Government agencies established to coordinate international information flow and development were created in the 1950s and early 1960s. These included the United States Information Agency (USIA) and the United States Aid for International Development (USAID) (for a brief review of this history see Jowett & McDonnell, 2006).

As a result, communication and other social science research aimed at developing third world nations began to expand. UNESCO, for example, funded some of Schramm's (1964) research on the role of mass communication on development of Third World Nations. There was an increase in efforts and research designed to foster and/or study the diffusion of various innovations aimed at aiding in the development of third world nations (see, e.g., Rogers, 1962). The U.S. government also consulted with mass communication scholars to address early anti-capitalistic Cold War propaganda (Rogers, 1994).

By the early 1960s, with the Cold War in full vigor and the United States on the brink of war in Vietnam, mass communication and media effects research had a firm foundation in communication studies. Beginning with Schramm's establishment of the first Ph.D. programs in Mass Communication at Iowa and the University of Illinois in the 1940s, numerous universities now offered Ph.D. degrees in communication. Research conducted during the 1940s and 1950s had refined understanding of the influence of the media on their audience. Summarizing some of this early research, Klapper (1960) suggested that rather than leading to direct effects, media effects were mediated by a host of individual differences such as existing attitudes and beliefs, group influence, and the like. When such mediating factors were not present, however, the influence of the media was more powerful. According to Katz (1959), there was growing recognition that people construct their perceptions based on their own values, beliefs, and experiences. With this view, the social milieu during times of military conflict, and individuals' political ideologies, has an impact on how consumers use media and the impact media have on them.

Early two-step flow research suggested that people often received information not from the media directly, but from others in their social circles who attended to the media (e.g., Katz & Lazarsfeld, 1955). Theories such as diffusion of innovations theory (Rogers, 1962) suggested that there is a multi-step flow of communication within society or a given social system. In general, it was suggested that the media were rather effective at disseminating information, but that interpersonal communication was more effective at attitude change (Rogers, 1973, 2003). Accordingly, the important role of opinion leaders and change agents in disseminating media content interpersonally was getting attention by scholars.

The functionalist tradition that emerged in mass communication research in the 1940s (e.g., Herzog, 1944; Lasswell, 1948) suggested people turn to the media because of the functions media serve for the audience. This notion spawned new audience-centered theories such as uses and gratifications that directed research attention away from a focus on what the media do to people and toward inquiry about what people do with the media (Klapper, 1963).

Post-World War II persuasion studies popularized at Yale by Hovland and his colleagues spawned a rich tradition. New theories emerged, such as balance theory (Heider, 1956) and cognitive dissonance theory (Festinger, 1957) that suggested that people seek cognitive consistency when interpreting and accepting or rejecting media messages. Researchers also addressed how to counteract persuasive effects (McGuire, 1964). Root notions of how persuasion works derived from this body of research can still be found in persuasion theories such as social judgment theory (Sherif & Hovland, 1961), the elaboration likelihood model (Petty & Cacioppo, 1986) and the extended parallel process model (fear appeals) (Witte, 1994).

Researchers also became increasingly interested in effects of media and their content on susceptible audiences such as children. Media violence and advertising were major areas of concern (e.g., Himmelweit, Oppenheim, & Vince, 1958; Schramm, Lyle, & Parker, 1960; Wertham, 1954).

Even though persuasion researchers turned their attention to the use of persuasion by corporate advertisers, rather than government institutions, and media effects researchers were concerned with the influence of popular media content on audiences, the Korean conflict in the 1950s, the Vietnam conflict in the 1960s and 1970s, and the overarching psychological doom of the Cold War continued to stimulate research, policy, and public attention to wartime communication.

Vietnam War Era

Vietnam, in particular, posed unique communication issues for the government. Unlike World War II, for example, the United States was not attacked. In addition, the war was the longest in U.S. history. Therefore, the government was faced with a situation in which it had to garner and maintain support for the war effort over a long period of time from a population that was never faced directly with an attack at home.

As in prior wars, information was manipulated. In the early days of the war the government was secretive about the extent of U.S. involvement and military activities in Vietnam (Hammond, 1988). Accordingly, early press reports generally were supportive of the U.S. position (Hallin, 1986). However, at least in comparison to strict controls on the media in later wars, there does not appear to have been a uniform military policy restricting the movement of media in Vietnam (Barber & Weir, 2002). Somewhat free to cover events, media coverage increased as the war wore on. Some media coverage also became more critical of official government positions and competence over time. Criticism seems to have become more intense toward the end of the 1960s, when coverage of precipitous events such as the Tet Offensive and the Mai Lai massacre made it glaringly obvious that the U.S. public had not been made aware of the difficulty encountered by U.S. troops or the toll on civilians.

In addition to the relative lax controls on the media, there was less rigid enforcement of anti-speech initiatives such as those reflected in the Espionage Act during World War I and the Alien Registration Act passed during World War II and enforced during the early days of the Cold War. Accordingly, antiwar protest activities increased as the war wore on (see, e.g., Gitlin, 1980).

Communication scholars played a vital role in examining war-related communication issues. Studies of media coverage of the war and war-related protest, in particular, became prominent during and after the Vietnam War era. Some focused on media coverage of the war (Patterson, 1984; Russo, 1971) and of protesters (Gitlin, 1980; Singer, 1970–71). Other research addressed specific issues such as rhetorical acts of protesters (Cox, 1974; Gustainis, 1983; Gustainis & Hahn, 1988) and presidents and/or their administrations (King & Anderson, 1971; Logue & Patton, 1982; Newman, 1970; Smith, 1972), protesters' motives and perceptions (Flacks, 1967; Morse, & Peele, 1971), deviance or violence by protesters (Murdock, 1981; Unger, 1988) and against protesters (Rudwick & Meier, 1972; Walker, 1968), flag desecration (Goodman & Gorden, 1971), and the impact of protest activities on public opinion (Berkowitz, 1973). Others focused on broad issues such as the history behind the conflict in Vietnam (Carver, 1965), freedom of speech issues related to civil disobedience and other expressive activities (Haiman, 1967), the growth of social movements such as the free speech movement on college campuses (Gitlin, 1980), and putting in historical perspective portrayals of the enemy (Ivie, 1980).

Antiwar protests and conflict related to the growing unrest pertaining to the war was only part of a broader social milieu of conflict during the Vietnam War years. The 1960s was a tumultuous decade. In addition to the war itself, conflict revolved around a host of social issues such as the rise in student activism, urban strife, the environment, civil rights, rising crime, and the like. In addition, it was a decidedly violent decade. Images of the confrontation between demonstrators, many protesting the war, at the 1968 Democratic National Convention shocked the nation. So did the growing number of urban riots across the country. But, perhaps nothing shook up the nation as much as the assassinations of John F. Kennedy, Malcolm X, Martin Luther King, and Robert Kennedy.

The proliferation of unrest and violence during the 1960s led President Lyndon Johnson to impanel the President's Commission on the Causes and Prevention of Violence. Established by executive order, the commission's charge was to examine the causes of societal violence and to advise the president on matters requiring policy attention.

One focus of the commission was the role of the media in the perpetration of violence. With government funding, several communication scholars contributed to this research project. The overarching conclusions suggested by the many studies included in the final report on mass media and violence was that exposure to media violence (particularly television) was linked to violent behavior and perceptions of violence (Baker & Ball, 1969).

These concerns led to more government funding of research devoted to exploring links between televised violence and violence in society. The most well known of these follow-up efforts included those of the Surgeon General's Scientific Advisory Committee on Television and Social Behavior (1972), and the 10-year follow-up to that study sponsored by the National Institute of Mental Health (Pearl, Bouthilet, & Lazar, 1982). Once again, much of the research focused on the harmful effects associated with exposure to violent media fare. This research focus remains one of the most consistent lines of research in the field today (e.g., National Television Violence Study, 1998).

Clearly, the war-related and domestic tumult in the U.S. that marked the Vietnam War era spurred much research and commentary on the role of the media in this conflict laden period in U.S. history. Concern about the role of the media in perpetuating societal violence was coupled with concern about the media's role in adversely affecting support for the war. Lessons learned from research conducted during the Vietnam War and its immediate aftermath have impacted how communication is used and controlled in post–Vietnam War conflicts in which the United States has been involved.

Post-Vietnam and Cold War Years

It has been noted that there has been an assumption that cynical media coverage adversely impacted U.S. success in the Vietnam War (Gilboa, 2005; McLaughlin, 2002). Whether that assumption is correct or not, significant controls have been placed on the media during military conflicts in which the United States has been involved after Vietnam (Barber & Weir, 2002). The

United States has been involved in numerous significant military operations since the early 1980s. These include conflicts in Grenada, Lebanon, Panama, Libya, the Persian Gulf, Somalia, Bosnia, Afghanistan, and Iraq. The military has limited media coverage significantly. Sometimes, as in the case of the Grenada conflict, the press has been banned from the battlefield. In other war zones reporters have been organized into pools or embedded with and escorted by military personnel (for a discussion of recent military practices, see Middleton & Lee, 2006). Consequently, televised coverage of actual fighting in these military actions generally has been far less extensive than was the case in the latter years of the Vietnam War.

Such government controls, however, have not dampened the tradition of wartime-related communication research. Studies of media coverage of various wars involving the United States over the last 25 years have been extensive. There have been studies of the coverage by specific media such as TV (Gilboa, 2005; Mermin, 1997), newspapers (Hertog, 2000; King & Lester, 2005; Ryan, 2004), and newer media such as the Internet (Dimitrova, Kaid, Williams, & Trammell, 2005; Jha, 2007; Randle, Davenport, & Bossen, 2003). There have been critiques of coverage of specific conflicts in Nicaragua (Dickson, 1992), Libya (Hertog, 2000), the Persian Gulf (Reese & Buckalew, 1995), Panama (Dickson, 1994; Mermin, 1996), Afghanistan (Ryan, 2004), and Iraq (Kumar, 2006), as well as assessment of coverage across wars (King & Lester, 2005; Mermin, 1996). There also has been comparative analysis of differences in war coverage by media in different countries (Herber & Filak, 2007; McLaughlin, 2002).

Some research has focused on specific war-related communication issues such as the use of propaganda (Kellner, 1992; Kumar, 2006; Palmer & Carter, 2006), media coverage of protest (Boyle, McCluskey, McLeod, & Stein, 2005; Dardis, 2006; Jha, 2007), the war rhetoric of presidents and justification for war (Bates, 2004; Birdsell, 1987; Kumar, 2006; Olson, 1991), government control of information (Haridakis, 2005, 2006; Hickey, 2002) as well as the media's role in the control of information (Kumar, 2006), and the impact of the media on public opinion (Eveland, McLeod, & Signorielli, 1995; McLeod, Eveland, & Signorielli, 1994).

In addition to studies of media coverage of issues specific to particular wars, researchers have examined the influence of media coverage on more global issues. For example, there has been comparative content analyses of pre–and post–Cold War coverage of international affairs (Norris, 1995), and the impact of media coverage on international relations (Gilboa, 2005). In addition to studies of protest specific to particular wars, researchers have examined coverage of protest activities related to issues such as nuclear weapons and nuclear power (Hartz & Gubin, 2007; Meyer, 1995), world trade (Jha,

2007), peace movements (Meyer, 1993; Vasi, 2006), and other social movements (Johnston & Klandermans, 1995; Meyer & Tarrow, 1998).

Recent studies such as those referenced above are informed by research conducted during prior wars. They draw on prior research to critique and assess topics ranging from how administrations justify war, to how the media frame their stories in challenging or supporting the government or opponents of the war, to journalistic practices during wartime, and the handling of protest and propaganda. In short, the tradition of examining uses and effects of communication in war-related contexts continues to emerge with each war. Lessons from the past and theoretical frameworks developed over the years have been applied during recent wars to study uses and effects of media during these many military conflicts.

The War on Terrorism

Currently, the United States is involved in wars in Iraq and Afghanistan, as well as an overarching war on terrorism. In the same way that fear of communism hung over the Korean and Vietnam wars, fear of terrorism is inextricably linked to the wars in Iraq and Afghanistan. Communication-related issues pertaining to how terrorism is being addressed by the government and covered by the media, and the role new media such as the Internet are playing in current conflicts have received considerable research attention in the twenty-first century. The breadth and scope of research topics are too broad to detail here. But, representative examples of research suggest that the tradition of wartime communication research is still a vital area of scholarly inquiry.

Recent research has been grounded in communication research and theory, much of it informed by research conducted during earlier wars. For example, the information diffusion process, which was a focus of the "Project Revere" studies during the Korean War and was influential in Cold-War era development communication studies, also has been assessed in the study of the diffusion of information after 9/11 (Kanihan & Gale, 2003). The application of cultivation theory, the genesis of which was applied in research conducted as part of the President's Commission on the Causes and Prevention of Violence (see Gerbner, 1998), has been applied to study whether media coverage of 9/11 news stories has led to fear and perceptions of a lack of safety (Rubin, Haridakis, Hullman, Sun, Chikombero, & Pornsakulvanich, 2003). Media framing analysis, which became a popular framework for assessing the media's role in supporting or marginalizing governmental actions or antiwar groups, has continued to undergird analyses of media coverage of terrorism (e.g., Norris, Kern, & Just, 2003). The tradition of examination of war-related protest activities and media coverage of them that was pronounced during the Vietnam War years also has remained a vital area of communication research during current wars (e.g., Dardis, 2006; Vasi, 2006).

Newer theories also have guided contemporary wartime communication research. For example, the third-person effect hypothesis has been applied to explore whether terrorist-related news stories leads to support for policies aimed at combating terrorism (Haridakis & Rubin, 2005). Communication infrastructure theory has been used to examine dependence on media after 9/11 (Kim, Jung, Cohen, & Ball-Rokeach, 2004). Some have suggested combining theoretical frameworks to assess media use and effects processes in an atmosphere of threat and fear similar to that in the United States, after the terrorist attacks of 9/11 (Haridakis & Rubin, 2005; Matsaganis & Payne, 2005; Rubin et al., 2003).

In addition to theory developed over the years, researchers also are armed with past experience and practices of media and government during prior war years. Prosecutions under the Espionage and Alien Registration Acts, activities on the part of the House Un-American Activities Committee during the Korean War and early Cold-War years, and confrontations of civil rights and antiwar activists during the Vietnam War, have heightened sensitivity to constraints on civil liberties that often are imposed during times of war. Accordingly, in recent years scholars have been scrutinizing government activities such as electronic surveillance (Fitsanakis, 2003), constraints on media and citizen access to information (Haridakis, 2006; Kumar, 2006), controls on media coverage of deportation hearings and terrorist-related trials (Haridakis, 2004; Olson, 2003), and restrictions on protest and other expressive activities (Knicely & Whitehead, 2005).

The growth in the number of media available today has intensified interest in the importance of newer media during wartime. Whereas some of the research referenced above has examined how people are using newer media such as the Internet to get information and connect with each other (e.g., Kim et al., 2004; Randle et al., 2003), there also has been research concern focused on terrorists use of newer online and wireless media for terrorist activities and terrorist-related communication (Weimann, 2008). On the other end of the spectrum has been examination of governmental attempts to use newer media technologies to combat terrorism (Winseck, 2008). There also has been critical assessment of the state of security of computer networks (Lewis, 2005), and the need to adapt wartime policies to adapt to changing media environments. For example, concerns have been raised as to whether the traditional model used by the USIA and VOA for handling propaganda is still effective in newer media environments (e.g., Palmer & Carter, 2006).

Accordingly, today, communication research is applied to a diverse array of contexts to assess the wartime role of communication in traditional and changing media environments. The research highlights what has always been the case: the centrality of the media in the conduct and coverage of war.

Conclusion

Today, communication studies is a mature discipline. We've attempted to highlight some of the important research conducted in the United States during wartime that contributed to the field's theoretical development. As stressed at the outset, however, this was just an overview. It is hard to stress all the ramifications of wartime on social science research and the development of the field of communication specifically. The sheer scale of World War II, in particular, demanded the attention of researchers and affected post-war academic thought and inquiry immeasurably. Fear of communism that dominated the Cold-War years and precipitated the Korean and Vietnam wars affected the thinking of multiple generations of Americans and scholars. The turmoil of the 1960s, a decade enveloped by the Vietnam War, changed the way Americans and scholars think about civil rights and liberties, and highlighted schisms in society that we are still grappling to understand and put into perspective.

Experience gleaned from prior wars, the media's role in them, and a large body of research on wartime communication is being applied to study wartime communication today. We have learned so much. Times of crises are when communication is its most potent. The severity of war, in particular, demands effective communication to confront and eliminate the threat to society the crises imposes. Thus, the need for information and informed civic debate and participation are at their highest.

Yet, we cannot be content with our current state of knowledge. We must continue to build on it. Each war brings new issues and new challenges to understand how communication is being applied as we apply and adapt our theories to assess the role of communication in traditional and ever changing media environments. Today, for example, the fear of terrorism is not unlike the fear of communism that garnered public and research attention in prior decades. Yet, it is different, too. Today, a plethora of media (many of which were not available during prior wars) are being used to both foster and combat terrorism. In this atmosphere there are unanswered questions that researchers are being drawn to assess. What is the proper balance between freedom of speech and national security? Are restrictions on expressive activities too stringent or not stringent enough? Is domestic electronic surveillance of citizens constitutional? Is it ethical? Is the current practice of embedded reporters a beneficial control of battlefield reporting, or does it compromise citizen's access to information and the objectivity of the media? Are the activities of the USIA and propagandistic activities of media such as the VOA still proper, and if yes, are they effective? What role are newer communication vehicles such as cell phones, text messaging, websites, and online social networking activities playing, in wartime communication-related activities?

These are just a few communication-related issues that need to continue to be addressed as we seek to understand how media are being used in current wartime contexts. Prior and ongoing wartime communication research highlights the need to continue to study wartime expressive activities, controls on communication, and the various roles of the media by citizens and governmental actors during wartime.

It is in the spirit of that inquiry and placing such activities in historical perspective that the chapters in this volume are devoted. It is our hope that this book stimulates future research that will continue to advance our understanding so that past mistakes can be avoided and society benefits from continued exploration. Much of the research that continues to be conducted during wartime is done in the quest to learn, reflect and make our society better. The latter, arguably, is the ultimate goal of social science inquiry—and, hopefully, of human nature.

REFERENCES

Abrams v. United States, 250 U.S. 616 (1919).
Baker, R. K., and S. J. Ball (Eds.) (1969). *Mass Media and Violence: A Staff Report to the National Commission on the Causes and Prevention of Violence.* Washington, DC: Government Printing Office.
Barber, R., and T. Weir (2002). Vietnam to Desert Storm: Topics, sources change. *Newspaper Research Journal, 23,* 88–98.
Bates, B. R. (2004). Audiences, metaphors, and the Persian Gulf War. *Communication Studies, 55,* 447–463.
Berkowitz, W. R. (1973). The impact of anti–Vietnam demonstrations upon national public opinion and military indicators. *Social Science Research 2,* 1–14.
Birdsell, D. S. (1987). Ronald Reagan on Lebanon and Grenada: Flexibility and interpretation in the application of Kenneth Burke's pentad. *Quarterly Journal of Speech, 73,* 267–279.
Boyle, M. P., M. R. McCluskey, D. M. McLeod, and S. E. Stein (2005). Newspapers and protest: An examination of protest coverage from 1960-1999. *Journalism & Mass Communication Quarterly, 82,* 638–653.
Cantril, H. (1940). *The Invasion from Mars: A Study in the Psychology of Panic.* Princeton, NJ: Princeton University Press.
_____. (1965). Evaluating the probable reactions to the landing in North Africa in 1942: A case study. *Public Opinion Quarterly, 29,* 400–410.
Carver, G. A., Jr. (1965). The real revolution in South Vietnam. *Foreign Affairs, 43,* 387–408.
Cmiel, K. (1996). On cynicism, evil, and the discovery of communication in the 1940s. *Journal of Communication, 46*(3), 88–107.

Cox, J. R. (1974). Perspectives on rhetorical criticism of movements: Antiwar dissent, 1964–1970. *Western Speech, 38,* 254–268.

Dardis, F. E. (2006). Marginalization devices in U.S. press coverage of Iraq war protest: A content analysis. *Mass Communication & Society, 9,* 117–135.

Debs v. United States, 249 U.S. 211 (1919).

DeFleur, M. L., and O. N. Larson (1958). *The Flow of Information: An Experiment in Mass Communication.* New York: Harper.

Dennis v. United States, 341 U.S. 494 (1951).

Dewey, J. (1927). *The Public and Its Problems.* Chicago: Swallow.

Dickson, S. H. (1992). Press and U.S. policy toward Nicaragua, 1983–1987: A study of the *New York Times* and *Washington Post. Journalism Quarterly, 69,* 562–571.

———. (1994). Understanding media bias: The press and the U.S. invasion of Panama. *Journalism Quarterly, 71,* 809–819.

Dimitrova, D. V., L. L. Kaid, A. P. Williams, and K. D. Trammell (2005). War on the web: The immediate news framing of Gulf War II. *Harvard International Journal of Press/Politics, 10,* 22–44.

Eveland, W. P., Jr., D. M. McLeod, and N. Signorielli (1995). Actual and perceived U.S. public opinion: The spiral of silence during the Persian Gulf War. *International Journal of Public Opinion Research, 7,* 91–109.

Festinger, L. (1957). *A Theory of Cognitive Dissonance.* Stanford, CA: Stanford University Press.

Fitsanakis, J. (2003). State-sponsored communications interception: Facilitating illegality. *Information, Communication & Society, 6,* 404–429.

Flacks, R. (1967). The liberated generation: An exploration of the roots of student protest. *Journal of Social Issues, 23*(3), 52–75.

Frowerk v. United States, 249 U.S. 204 (1919).

Gary, B. (1996). Communication research, the Rockefeller Foundation and mobilization for the war on words, 1938–1944. *Journal of Communication, 46*(3), 124–147.

Gerbner, G. (1998). Cultivation analysis: An overview. *Mass Communication & Society, 1,* 175–194.

Gilboa, E. (2005). The CNN effect: The search for a communication theory of international relations. *Political Communication, 22,* 27–44.

Gitlin, T. (1980). *The Whole World is Watching: Mass Media in the Making and Unmaking of the New Left.* Berkeley: University of California Press.

Goodman, R. J., and W. I. Gorden (1971). The rhetoric of desecration. *Quarterly Journal of Speech, 57,* 23–31.

Gustainis, J. J. (1983). The Catholic ultra-resistance: Rhetorical strategies of anti-war protest. *The Communicator, 13,* 37–50.

———, and D. F. Hahn (1988). While the whole world watched: Rhetorical failures of anti-war protest. *Communication Quarterly, 36,* 203–216.

Haiman, F. S. (1967). The rhetoric of the streets: Some legal and ethical considerations. *Quarterly Journal of Speech, 53,* 99–114.

Hallin, D. C. (1986). *The "Uncensored War": The Media and Vietnam.* New York: Oxford University Press.

Hamilton, A., J. Madison, and J. Jay (1996). In B. F. Wright (Ed.), *The Federalist.* New York: Barnes & Noble. (Original work published 1788.)

Hammond, W. M. (1988). *Public Affairs: The Military and the Media, 1962–1968.* Washington, DC: United States Army Center of Military History.

Haridakis, P. M. (2004). The war on terrorism: Military tribunals and the First Amendment. *Communication Law & Policy, 9,* 317–349.

———. (2005). The tension between national/homeland security and the first amendment in the new century. *Temple University Political & Civil Rights Law Review, 14,* 433–454.

_____. (2006). Citizen access and government secrecy. *Saint Louis University Public Law Review, 25*, 3–32.

_____, and A. M. Rubin (2005). Third-person effects in the aftermath of terrorism. *Mass Communication & Society, 8*, 39–59.

Hartz, C. E., and O. Gubin (2007, August). *Antinuclear Power Movement: Paradigm Shifts and Social Networks*. Paper presented at the annual meeting of the American Sociological Association.

Heider, F. (1946). Attitudes and cognitive organizations. *Journal of Psychology, 21*, 107–112.

Herber, L., and V. F. Filak (2007). Iraq war coverage differs in U.S., German papers. *Newspaper Research Journal, 28*, 37–51.

Hertog, J. K. (2000). Elite press coverage of the 1986 U.S.-Libya conflict: A case study of tactical and strategic critique. *Journalism & Mass Communication Quarterly, 77*, 612–627.

Herzog, H. (1944). What do we really know about daytime serial listeners? In P. F. Lazarsfeld and F. Stanton (Eds.), *Radio research 1942–1943* (pp. 3–33). New York: Duell, Sloan & Pearce.

Hickey, N. (2002, Jan/Feb). Access denied: Pentagon's war reporting rules are toughest ever. *Columbia Journalism Review*, pp. 26–31.

Himmelweit, H. T., A. N. Oppenheim, and P. Vince (1958). *Television and the Child: An Empirical Study of the Effect of Television on the Young*. London: Oxford University Press.

Horkheimer, M., and T. W. Adorno (1972). *Dialectics of Enlightenment*. New York: Herder & Herder.

Hovland, C. I., I. L. Janis, and H. H. Kelly (1953). *Communication and Persuasion: Psychological Studies of Opinion Change*. New Haven, CT: Yale University Press.

Hovland, C. I., A. A. Lumsdaine, and F. D. Sheffield (1949). *Experiments on Mass Communication*. Princeton, NJ: Princeton University Press.

Ivie, R. L. (1980). Images of savagery in American justifications for war. *Communication Monographs, 47*, 279–291.

Jha, S. (2007). Exploring Internet influence on the coverage of social protest: Content analysis comparing protest coverage in 1967 and 1999. *Journalism & Mass Communication Quarterly, 84*, 40–57.

Johnston, H., and B. Klandermans (Eds.) (1995). *Social Movement and Culture*. Minneapolis: University of Minnesota Press.

Jowett, G. S., and O'Donnell (2006). *Propaganda and Persuasion* (4th). Thousand Oaks, CA: Sage.

Kanihan, S. F., and K. L. Gale (2003). Within 3 hours, 97 percent learn about 9/11 attacks. *Newspaper Research Journal, 24*, 78–91.

Katz, E. (1959). Mass communication research and the study of culture. *Studies in Public Communication, 2*, 1–6.

_____, and P. F. Lazarsfeld (1955). *Personal Influence: The Part Played by People in the Flow of Mass Communications*. New York: Free Press.

Kelman, H. C., and C. I. Hovland (1953). Reinstatement of the communicator in delayed measurement of opinion change. *Journal of Abnormal and Social Psychology, 48*, 337–335.

Kellner, D. (1992). *The Persian Gulf TV War*. Boulder, CO: Westview.

Kim, Y-C, J-Y Jung, E. L. Cohen, and S. J. Ball-Rokeach (2004). Internet connectedness before and after September 11 2001. *New Media & Society, 6*, 611–631.

King, A. A., and F. D. Anderson (1971). Nixon, Agnew, and the "silent majority": A case study in the rhetoric of polarization. *Western Speech, 35*, 243–255.

King, C., and P. M. Lester (2005). Photographic coverage during the Persian Gulf and Iraqi wars in three U.S. newspapers. *Journalism & Mass Communication Quarterly, 82*, 623–637.

Klapper, J. T. (1960). *The Effects of Mass Communication*. Glencoe, IL: Free Press.
_____. (1963). Mass communication research: An old road resurveyed. *Public Opinion Quarterly, 27*, 515–525.
Knicely, J. J., and J. W. Whitehead (2005). The caging of free speech in America. *Temple Political & Civil Rights Law Review, 14*, 455–493.
Kumar, D. (2006). Media, war, and propaganda: Strategies of information management during the 2003 Iraq War. *Communication and Critical/Cultural Studies, 3*, 48–69.
Lasswell, H. D. (1927). *Propaganda Technique in the World War*. New York: Knopf.
_____. (1948). The structure and function of communication in society. In L. Bryson (Ed.), *The Communication of Ideas* (pp. 37–51). New York: Harper.
Lazarsfeld, P. F., B. Berelson, and H. Gaudet (1944). *The People's Choice: How the Voter Makes Up His Mind in a Presidential Campaign*. New York: Duell, Sloan, and Pearce.
Lewis, J. A. (2005). Aux armies, citoyens: Cyber security and regulation in the United States. *Telecommunications Policy, 29*, 821–830.
Lippmann, W. (1922). *Public Opinion*. New York: Macmillan.
Logue, C. M., and J. H. Patton (1982). From ambiguity to dogma: The rhetorical symbols of Lyndon B. Johnson on Vietnam. *Southern Speech Communication Journal, 47*, 310–329.
Lowery, S. A., and M. L. DeFleur (1988). *Milestones in Mass Communication Research*. New York: Longman.
Lumley, F. (1933). *The Propaganda Menace*. New York: Century.
Matsaganis, M. D., and J. G. Payne (2005). Agenda setting in a culture of fear: The lasting effects of September 11 on American politics and journalism. *American Behavioral Scientist, 49*, 379–392.
McGuire, W. J. (1964). Inducing resistance to persuasion: Some contemporary approaches. In L. Berkowitz (Ed.), *Advances in Experimental Social Psychology* (Vol. 1, pp. 124–139). New York: Academic.
McLaughlin, G. (2002). Rules of engagement: Television journalism and NATO's "faith in bombing" during the Kosovo crisis, 1999. *Journalism Studies, 3*, 257–266.
McLeod, D. M., W. P. Eveland, and N. Signorielli (1994). Conflict and public opinion: Rallying effects of the Persian Gulf war. *Journalism Quarterly, 77*, 20–31.
Mermin, J. (1996). Conflict in the sphere of consensus? Critical reporting on the Panama invasion and the Gulf War. *Political Communication, 13*, 181–194.
_____. (1997). Television news and American intervention in Somalia: The myth of a media-driven foreign policy. *Political Science Quarterly, 112*, 385–403.
Merton, R. K. (1968). *Social Theory and Social Structure* (3rd ed.). New York: Free Press.
Meyer, D. S. (1993). Protest cycles and political process: American peace movements in the nuclear age. *Political Research Quarterly, 46*, 451–479.
_____. (1995). Framing national security: Elite public discourse on nuclear weapons during the cold war. *Political Communication, 12*, 173–192.
_____, and S. Tarrow (Eds.) (1998). *The Social Movement Society: Contentious Politics for a New Century*. Lanham, MD: Rowan & Littlefield.
Middleton, K. R., and W. E. Lee (2006). *The Law of Public Communication* (2006 ed.). Boston: Pearson Education.
Morse, S. J., and S. Peele (1971). A study of participants in an anti–Vietnam war demonstration. *Journal of Social Issues, 27*(4), 113–136.
Murdock, G. (1981). Political deviance: The press presentation of a militant mass demonstration. In S. Cohen and J. Young (Eds.), *The Manufacture of News: Deviance, Social Problems and the Mass Media* (pp. 206–225). Beverly Hills, CA: Sage.
National Television Violence Study, vol. 3 (1998). Thousand Oaks, CA: Sage.
Newman, R. P. (1970). Under the veneer: Nixon's Vietnam speech of November 3, 1969. *Quarterly Journal of Speech, 56*, 168–178.

Norris, P. (1995). The restless searchlight: Network news framing of the post-cold war world. *Political Communication, 12*, 357–370.

———, M. Kern, and M. Just (Eds.) (2003). *Framing Terrorism: The News Media, the Government, and the Public.* New York: Routledge.

Olson, K. M. (1991). Constraining open deliberation in times of war: Presidential war justifications for Grenada and the Persian Gulf. *Argumentation & Advocacy, 28*, 64–79.

———. (2003). Courtroom access principles apply to deportation hearings. *Newspaper Research Journal, 24*, 152–165.

Palmer, A. W., and E. L. Carter (2006). The Smith-Mundt Act's ban on domestic propaganda: An analysis of the cold war statute limiting access to public diplomacy. *Communication Law & Policy, 11*, 1–34.

Patterson, O. (1984). Television's living room war in print: Vietnam in the news magazines. *Journalism Quarterly, 61*, 35–39.

Pearl, D., L. Bouthilet, and J. Lazar (Eds.) (1982). *Television and Behavior: Ten Years of Scientific Progress and Implications for the Eighties: Summary Report.* Washington, DC: Government Printing Office.

Petty, R. E., and J. T. Cacioppo (1986). The elaboration likelihood model of persuasion. *Advanced Experimental Psychology, 19*, 123–205.

Pool, I. de Sola. (1983). *Technologies of Freedom.* Cambridge, MA: Belknap.

Randle, Q., L. D. Davenport, and H. Bossen (2003). Newspapers slow to use web sites for 9/11 coverage. *Newspaper Research Journal, 24*, 58–71.

Reese, S. D., and B. Buckalew (1995). The militarism of local television: The routine framing of the Persian Gulf war. *Critical Studies in Mass Communication, 12*, 40–59.

Rogers, E. M. (1962). *Diffusion of Innovations.* New York: Free Press.

———. (1973). Mass media and interpersonal communication. In I. de S. Pool & W. Schramm (Eds.), *Handbook of Communication* (pp. 290–310).

———. (1994). *A History of Communication Study: A Biographical Approach.* New York: Free Press.

———. (2003). *Diffusion of Innovations* (5th ed.). New York: Free Press.

———. (2004). Theoretical diversity in political communication. In L. L. Kaid (Ed.). *Handbook of Political Communication Research* (pp. 3–16). Maweh: NJ: Erlbaum.

Rubin, A. M., P. M. Haridakis, G. Hullman, S. Sun, P. Chikombero, and V. Pornsakulvanich (2003). The aftermath of September 11th: Has television contributed to a culture of fright? *Newspaper Research Journal, 24*, 128–145.

Rudwick, E., and A. Meier (1972). The Kent State affair: Social control of a putative value-oriented movement. *Sociological Inquiry, 42*(2), 81–86.

Russo, F. (1971). A study of bias in TV coverage of the Vietnam War: 1969 and 1970. *Public Opinion Quarterly, 35*, 539–543.

Ryan, M. (2004). Framing the war against terrorism: U.S. newspaper editorials and military action in Afghanistan. *Gazette: International Journal for Communication Studies, 66*, 363–382.

Schramm, W. (1964). *Mass Media and National Development: The Role of Information in the Developing Countries.* Stanford, CA: Stanford University Press.

———, J. Lyle, and E. B. Parker (1961). *Television in the Lives of Our Children.* Stanford, CA: Stanford University Press.

Schramm, W., and J. W. Riley, Jr. (1951). Communication in the Sovietized state, as demonstrated in Korea. *American Sociological Review, 16*, 757–766.

Shannon, C. E., and W. Weaver (1949). *The Mathematical Theory of Communication.* Urbana: University of Illinois Press.

Sherif, M., and C. I. Hovland (1961). *Social Judgment: Assimilation and Contrast Effects in Communication and Attitude Change.* New Haven, CT: Yale University Press.

Simpson, C. (1994). *Science of Coercion: Communications Research and Psychological Warfare, 1945–1960*. New York: Oxford University Press.
Singer, B. D. (1970–71). Violence, protest, and war in television news: The U.S. and Canada compared. *Public Opinion Quarterly, 34*, 611–616.
Smith, B., H. Lasswell, and R. Casey (1946). *Propaganda, Communication, and Public Opinion: A Comprehensive Guide*. Princeton, NJ: Princeton University Press.
Smith, F. M. (1972). Rhetorical implications of the "aggression" thesis in the Johnson administration's Vietnam argumentation. *Central States Speech Journal, 23*, 217–224.
Speier, H., and M. Otis (1944). German radio propaganda in France during the Battle of France. In P. Lazarsfeld and F. Stanton (Eds.), *Radio Research, 1942–1943* (pp. 208–247). New York: Duell, Sloan, & Pearce.
Sproule, J. M. (1991). Propaganda and American ideological critique. *Communication Yearbook, 14*, 211–238.
Surgeon General's Scientific Advisory Committee on Television and Social Behavior. (1972). *Television and Growing Up: The Impact of Televised Violence*. (Report to the Surgeon General United States Public Health Service). Washington, DC: Government Printing Office.
Tedford, T. L., and D. A. Herbeck (2005). *Freedom of Speech in the United States* (5th ed.). State College, PA: Strata.
Unger, I. (1988). *The Movement: A History of the American New Left 1959–1972*. Lanham MD: University Press of America.
Vasi, I. B. (2006). The new anti-war protests and miscible mobilizations. *Social Movement Studies, 5*, 137–153.
Walker, D. (1968). *Rights in Conflict: The Violent Confrontation of Demonstrators and Police in the Parks and Streets of Chicago During the Week of the Democratic National Convention of 1968*. New York: E. P. Dutton.
Weimann, G. (2008). The psychology of mass-mediated terrorism. *American Behavioral Scientist, 52*, 69–86.
Weiser, M. E. (2007). Burke and war: Rhetoricizing the theory of dramatism. *Rhetoric Review, 26*, 286–302.
Wertham, F. (1954). *Seduction of the Innocent*. New York: Rinehart.
Winseck, D. (2008). Information operations "blowback": Communication, propaganda and surveillance in the global war on terrorism. *International Communication Gazette, 70*(6), 419–441.
Wirth, L. (1948). Consensus and mass communication. *American Sociological Review, 13*, 1–15.
Witte, K. (1994). Fear control and danger control: An empirical test of the extended parallel process model. *Communication Monographs, 61*, 113–134.

Part I:
Images in Popular Culture

Protest Music as Alternative Media During the Vietnam War Era

Richard A. Lee

More than 30 years after the war in Vietnam came to a formal close with the unconditional surrender of South Vietnamese President Duong Van Minh, it remains an emotional, divisive and controversial issue in America. The war still surfaces as a campaign issue in presidential elections. For example, Bill Clinton had to fend off charges that he dodged the draft, George W. Bush was accused of using family connections to gain entrance into the National Guard to avoid combat in the war, and political opponents raised questions about the medals awarded to John Kerry for his service in Vietnam. During the 2008 campaign, John McCain's experience as a POW during the war was a frequent topic, as was the extent of Barack Obama's relationship with a 1960s anti-war activist.

In addition, Vietnam veterans continue to suffer from emotional and physical wounds, and the war has become a part of popular culture through films, books and plays. As former *NBC Nightly News* anchor Tom Brokaw (2007) observed, "Vietnam — as a war, as a political issue, and as a deeply significant personal experience for many — continues to occupy a central role in our collective memory" (p. 430).

Among the many topics that continue to spark debate and discussion is the news media's coverage of the war. According to Taylor (1985), "In no other war have journalists played so important a role in recording events and shaping public opinion" (p. 460). Critics contend that the media were responsible for eroding public support for U.S. involvement in Vietnam by presenting a negative picture of the war through news accounts that included — for the first time in U.S. history — graphic images of death and destruction that were broadcast on nightly newscasts that families watched in their living rooms. Studies on news coverage during the Vietnam War, however, fail to support this argument. In fact, research has shown that news reports usually echoed the party line, whether it was being delivered by generals in Vietnam or government officials in Washington, D.C. This was especially true during the early years of the war (Hallin, 1986; Herman & Chomsky, 1988).

How then and why did opposition to the war among the American public grow if the news reports from Vietnam were largely positive? There is no single answer. In part, as Herman and Chomsky (1988) related, it was the stories told by servicemen and women returning to the United States — stories with stark differences from what was being reported. Occasionally, there were news accounts that ran counter to the government's positive storyline, such as Morley Safer's 1966 television report showing U.S. Marines burning down the homes of Vietnamese civilians (Herman & Chomsky, 1988). In addition, there was a growing underground press that provided an alternative to mainstream media, offering different perspectives not only on the war, but also on lifestyle issues such as sex and drugs.

In this chapter, I posit that protest music played a significant role in strengthening opposition to the war by functioning as alternative media that provided a different (and arguably more accurate) picture of U.S. involvement in Vietnam. Specifically, I suggest that protest music raised issues and asked questions that were absent from — or overlooked or downplayed by — the mainstream media, a sentiment shared by some of the artists who wrote and performed anti-war songs during the Vietnam War era. For example, Buffy Sainte-Marie, who has labeled protest music an alternative news outlet, said, "I wrote 'Universal Soldier' when they were still saying that we weren't having a war in Vietnam. Mainstream media were reporting a party line, even while our generation was being drafted" (personal communication, July 11, 2008). Singer/songwriter Tom Paxton said protest music filled a void. "These were songs that had to be written. They were expressing a deeply held anger in a strong segment of the population about this war," he said (personal communication, August 19, 2008).

Defining Protest Music

"Protest music" is a broad term that conjures up an image of a solitary singer with an acoustic guitar. While this image often is an accurate one, protest music comes in many forms and varieties. Several powerful protest songs from the Vietnam War era were written and performed by rock and folk-rock bands, such as The Byrds; Steppenwolf; and Crosby, Stills, Nash and

Young (Arnold, 1991b). Others were popularized by African-American artists such as Marvin Gaye and Edwin Starr (Smith, 1999). Occasionally, songs written without the war in mind took on new meanings, such as the Animals' "We Gotta Get Out of This Place," the Rolling Stones' "2000 Light Years from Home," and the Box Tops' "The Letter," all of which became popular among U.S. soldiers in Vietnam (James, 1989).

For purposes of this chapter, the term "protest music" will be applied broadly to encompass those songs that opposed war, specifically U.S. involvement in Vietnam. Within this broad parameter, I will focus on songs written during the early years of the war. This was a period in which many Americans were either supportive of the nation's involvement in Vietnam or still forming opinions about it, so there was considerable opportunity for protest music to influence public opinion and increase opposition to the war.

The Songs

When Americans began questioning the wisdom of the nation's involvement in Vietnam, the foundation for the early protests had already been built by folksingers who challenged the status quo with songs about justice, civil rights and other social issues. As Arnold (1991b) explained, "The social protest song quickly became the anti-war protest song" (p. 320). Years before Vietnam became a topic for national debate, Pete Seeger had been singing about labor unions and the civil rights movement. Peter, Paul and Mary had been performing as a trio since 1961, singing traditional folk songs as well as their own versions of compositions with socially conscious messages by new artists such as Bob Dylan. Dylan himself had already released four albums by 1964. Seeger; Peter, Paul and Mary; and Dylan, along with singer-songwriters such as Phil Ochs and Joan Baez were part of an emerging folk music scene in New York's Greenwich Village (George-Warren & Romanski, 2001).

Although the songs touched on a variety of social issues that were developing in the 1960s, the references to war generally were not to specific conflicts. Rather, they were characterized by rhetorical questions such as those posed by the title of Pete Seeger's "Where Have All the Flowers Gone?" and the lyrics of Dylan's "Blowin' in the Wind" in 1963. As U.S. involvement in Vietnam grew with the start of bombing raids on North Vietnam and the arrival of the first combat troops, the music began to zero in on the war in Southeast Asia, raising questions and issues that were absent from mainstream media. According to James (1989), "A movement, associated especially with Phil Ochs, to replace this unspecific and therefore sentimental and/or collusive protest music with more precise topical reference made consideration of Vietnam possible" (p. 128).

To support the argument that protest music functioned as alternative media, I will examine the manner in which several issues involving the war were reported by mainstream media outlets and compare the coverage with how these same issues were described in popular protest songs. The songs selected for analysis were chosen based upon my personal recollection of that era and my experience as a music critic. All are from the early years of the war. Characterization of the news media was based upon numerous secondary sources, most notably *The Uncensored War* (1986) by Daniel Hallin, in which he conducted extensive content analyses of news coverage of the war, and *The Military and the Media 1962–1968* by William Hammond (1988), a book that was published by the Center of Military History and describes media coverage of the war from the perspective of the military. In addition to these and other secondary sources, I read news accounts of the war that were published in *The New York Times* and *Time* magazine between 1964 and 1967. I also found valuable first-hand material in *Reporting Vietnam: American Journalism, 1959–1975*, an anthology of news and magazine stories written about — and during — the war.

The Description of America's Early Military Involvement

In the early years of the Vietnam War (before August 7, 1964, when the Gulf of Tonkin Resolution authorized President Lyndon B. Johnson to use military force in Southeast Asia), it was U.S. policy to deny that military personnel were engaged in active combat, even though journalists in Vietnam knew from their firsthand observations that this was not the case (Hallin, 1986). Nevertheless, the U.S. government described members of its armed forces as "advisors" or "trainers" for the South Vietnamese. According to Hammond (1988), "American officials in both Saigon and Washington saw no reason to tell the press that American pilots were flying combat missions for the South Vietnamese" (p. 17). A February 21, 1962, directive issued by the U.S. Information Agency and the State and Defense Departments Cable "stressed the need to reinforce the idea that the war was essentially a South Vietnamese affair" (Hammond, 1988, p. 17). The directive, issued to the U.S. mission in Saigon, stated that it was not in America's best interest "to have stories indicating that Americans are leading and directing combat missions against the Viet Cong" (Hammond, 1988, p. 15).

This policy was practiced at the highest levels of government. For example, *New York Times* reporter Tom Wicker (1978) described a January 15, 1962, press conference during which he asked President John F. Kennedy if American troops were involved in combat in Vietnam. According to Wicker,

"Kennedy looked at me — six feet away and slightly beneath his elevated lectern — as if he thought I might be crazy. 'No,' he said crisply — not another word — and pointed at someone else for the next question" (p. 92).

Despite journalists' apprehensions, the situation in Vietnam during this period generally was characterized in the manner in which the U.S. government wished. As Herman and Chomsky (1988) related, "It was standard practice during the Indochina war for journalists to report Washington pronouncements as fact, even in the extreme case when official statements were known to be false" (pp. 176–177). For example, an October 11, 1963, *Time* magazine story on Vietnam described the war as "South Vietnam's political war" and quoted (but did not question) a U.S. policy statement characterizing U.S. involvement as "working with the people and government of South Viet Nam to deny this country to Communism." The article also indicated that the government's policy statement predicted that the U.S. "training" program would progress to the point where 1,000 United States military personnel assigned to Vietnam could be withdrawn by the end of 1963, and the United States military task could be completed by the end of 1965.

One individual who refused to accept the government's pronouncements was songwriter Phil Ochs (George-Warren & Romanski, 2001). A former journalism student who believed a folksinger was a "walking newspaper" (James, 1989, p. 127), Ochs drew many parallels between journalism and protest music. His first album, released in 1964, was titled *All the News That's Fit to Sing*, a play on the words "All the News That's Fit to Print," the well-known motto of *The New York Times*. That album included a song called "Talking Vietnam," one of the first compositions written specifically about Vietnam. In the song, Ochs suggested that American military involvement was being described as a training mission in order to avoid embarrassment should the U.S. lose the war. According to James (1989), "Talking Vietnam" exposed "American military intervention and its domestic implication" and showed tremendous prescience and acumen on the part of Ochs, since he wrote the song at a time when American involvement totaled only 15,000 troops (pp. 128–129). The lyrics also expressed mock chagrin that the enemy in Vietnam failed to recognize the (false) claim that Americans were only offering assistance and not engaging in combat.

The Possibility That the United States Might Lose

Prior to Vietnam, the United States had won every war it entered. In the early 1960s, the memory of major victories on two fronts in World War II was still fresh in the minds of the American public, as was the belief that the U.S. had a global responsibility to mankind that included opposing Communist aggression (Herman & Chomsky, 1988). Hallin (1986) wrote that winning the war was one of several "unspoken propositions" underlying media coverage of Vietnam (p. 142), an issue that Ochs addressed in "Talking Vietnam."

The positive spin that U.S. military and government officials put on the war generally was reflected in early news accounts from Vietnam. As Hallin (1986) explained, "There was no need for high-level meetings of network executives when it was a question of reporting a claim of victory from an official briefing in Saigon or a story of American heroism" (p. 133). Not until the Tet offensive in early 1968 did major journalists such as *CBS Evening News* anchor Walter Cronkite acknowledge on the air or in print that the U.S. might not win (Herman & Chomsky, 1988). According to Taylor (1985), "American journalists did not immediately recognize the pitfalls of their nation's most recent Asian war. The old 'Asia hands' who reported the conflict in the decade before it became front page news generally supported the policy of helping an Asian nation withstand Communist aggression" (p. 454).

Folksinger Pete Seeger also raised the specter that America might be in over its head — literally — in the song "Waist Deep in the Big Muddy." On the surface, the song tells the story of a platoon leader relentlessly ordering his troops to cross a raging river, even though they kept falling deeper and deeper into the water. In reality, "The Big Muddy" was a metaphor for U.S. involvement in Vietnam. The platoon leader, described as a fool in Seeger's (1967) lyrics, represented President Lyndon Johnson.

The Characterization of the Enemy as Savage and Faceless

Ivie (1980) contends that as far back as the Revolutionary War, America has perpetuated an image of its enemies as savage and ruthless, and that during the Vietnam War, creation of such an image was especially important for the U.S. government. He suggests that in order to gain support for the war, the government needed the American public to perceive the North Vietnamese as the aggressor and the cause for the war: "Close inspection of the administration's efforts reveals that the enemy is portrayed as a savage, i.e., as an aggressor, driven by irrational desires for conquest, who is seeking to subjugate others by force of arms. This image of the enemy is intensified by a contrasting image of the United States as a representative of civilization who is rational, tolerant of diversity, and pacific" (Ivie, 1980, p. 281).

By and large, the mainstream American press portrayed the enemy in the same terms as the government did. Even in the context of war (in which soldiers of both sides attempt to kill each other), the North Vietnamese were described as assassins, guerillas and snipers in news accounts (Bates, 1998). Typical of this reporting was an October 6, 1965, *New York Times* story labeling a North Vietnamese attack as an "ambush" by "guerillas" who used "ferocious" gunfire to kill and wound American soldiers (Mohr, 1965b, p. 1).

As Herman and Chomsky (1988) observed, "Only rarely did U.S. reporters make any effort to see the war from the point of view of 'the enemy'" (p. 177). The two authors also noted that "Vietcong," the name used to describe the enemy by the media and the government, was actually a derogatory term created by American and Saigon propaganda. Rarely were they referred to as the "National Liberation Front," the name they used for themselves. Reflecting on the overall tone of the manner in which enemy forces were depicted, Hallin (1986) said, "Television painted an almost perfectly one-dimensional image of the North Vietnamese and Vietcong as cruel, ruthless, and fanatical" (p. 148).

By contrast, folksinger Tom Paxton (1967) described the "enemy" in more human terms in "Talking Vietnam Potluck Blues." In the song, a group of U.S. servicemen wandering the jungle while high on marijuana come across a band of young North Vietnamese soldiers who share their penchant for the drug and offer to share their special brand of "Hanoi Gold."

The Killing of Civilians and Destruction of Villages by U.S. Troops

Reporting of the My Lai massacre, in which several hundred unarmed civilians were killed by U.S. soldiers, focused public attention on civilian casualties (Hallin, 1986). However, before My Lai took place in 1968 and was reported by the media in 1969, the war had been claiming the lives of civilians. Herman and Chomsky (1988) contend that prior to My Lai the media downplayed civilian casualties and regarded them as unavoidable consequences of war, at least in the instances in which the U.S. was the perpetrator. "Reporters often did not conceal atrocities committed by the U.S. military forces, although they did not appear to perceive them as atrocities and surely did not express the horror and outrage that would have been manifest if others were the perpetrators, and the United States or its clients the victims," they wrote (p. 193). News accounts of atrocities also were couched in vague, non-descriptive terms that belied the actual horrors of death and destruction. Such terms were used by military officials and "parroted by the press" (James, 1990, p. 84). Furthermore, the reasons cited for General William Westmoreland's 1965 order directing U.S. troops to take special care to avoid civilian casualties were not humanitarian, but rather tactical and strategic. Mohr

(1965a) reported that "The use of unnecessary force would embitter the population and drive them into the arms of the Vietcong guerillas" (p. 1).

Folk artist Arlo Guthrie put civilian casualties into context in "Alice's Restaurant," an 18-minute musical narrative from 1967 that begins with the story of his arrest for littering and concludes when he reports for a physical examination to determine if he is fit to serve in the military. Upon learning of Guthrie's arrest, a Sergeant asks if he has rehabilitated himself. Guthrie's response includes elements of sarcasm, irony, and outrage.

America's Motives for Entering and Escalating the War

Protest songs questioned the need for the war at a time when U.S. intervention enjoyed widespread media support because it was seen as part of what Herman and Chomsky (1988) characterized as a noble effort to protect the free world against Communism. An example of how differently protest singers addressed this issue can found in the lyrics of Country Joe McDonald's "I-Feel-Like-I'm-Fixin'-to-Die Rag."

In "The Rag," not only did McDonald (1965) question why the U.S. was in Vietnam, he also suggested that the nation's motives—rather than being noble—were militaristic Writing about the song on his website, McDonald (2000a) said, "The song attempts to put blame for the war upon the politicians and leaders of the U.S. military and upon the industry that makes its money from war, but not upon those who had to fight the war—the soldiers." Evidence of the fiscal benefits of U.S. involvement in Vietnam can be found in news accounts from the early years of the war. For example, *The New York Times* reported that increased earnings from gold, copper and grains all were tied to positive reports on U.S. military activities in Vietnam. However, this information was published in the business section of the newspaper—far beyond the front page—and the relationship of the market conditions to the war in Vietnam was not highlighted. Rather, it generally was included near the end of the reports (Fowler, 1965; Frost, 1964).

How the Music Spread

Media scholars have found that when the press places attention on an issue, the result is increased public attention (McCombs & Shaw, 1972), and that that heavy news coverage of a particular issue makes that issue more salient for readers and viewers (Erbring, Goldenberg, & Miller, 1980). Therefore, in order to demonstrate that protest music functioned as alternative media which strengthened opposition to the Vietnam War, one must show that the anti-war messages contained in the music were delivered with frequency to large groups of people. On the surface, this appears unlikely in light of conditions in the music industry at the time. In contrast to today's superstars, the artists who wrote and sang protest songs did not routinely sell millions of records or play to huge audiences in stadiums and arenas. They were not promoted by the massive publicity campaigns employed today nor could they benefit from the resources and support of the mega-transnational corporations that control the modern music industry. In addition, the popular radio and television programs of the time were unlikely to play protest music because of its subject matter and its anti-war (and hence anti-government) message. As Phillips (1967) explained in an article written during this period, "At this point, none of the songs is widely known, largely because most radio and TV stations will not touch this kind of material" (p. 12).

Even when artists were given opportunities to appear on popular radio and television programs, there were restrictions. After Buffy Sainte-Marie's love song "Until It's Time for You to Go" was recorded by Barbara Streisand, Neil Diamond and the Boston Pops Orchestra, she was invited to appear on the *Tonight Show* and other major television programs. However, she was prohibited from performing her anti-war compositions. Sainte-Marie said, "In dealing with the big time shows, I discovered their reluctance to let me sing any protest songs or speak about anything controversial. The real action happened outside of the show biz construct. The established media were still living in the Eisenhower generation and acted as if this must be stopped" (personal communication, July 11, 2008).

But as Pete Seeger (1983) discovered, there were other means for protest music to reach people across the nation. "Most of my life I have assumed that the kind of songs I sing would not normally get played on the airwaves. I pointed to examples like Woody Guthrie's song, 'This Land Is Your Land' to show that they don't have to get played on the airwaves. If it's a real good song, it will get spread around anyway" Seeger said.

Indeed, protest songs became a fixture among American youth, who were exposed to them in coffeehouses on college campuses, at protest marches, and on freeform, underground radio stations playing music that commercial radio would not dare to touch. James (1989) said group singing at coffeehouses, marches and demonstrations produced social bonding as well as a small star system for protest singers. Sainte-Marie noted that "In the early 1960s coffeehouses were the student meeting grounds, caffeinated discussion and networking were expected, and singers and songwriters were the troubadours spreading/generating the news" (personal communication, July 11, 2008). Tom Paxton said much of the music spread through simple word of mouth among a growing number of Americans who shared a disdain for the war. Paxton said FM radio also played an instrumental role. "They had what nowadays would be considered unbelievable autonomy; they played whatever they wanted they wanted to play" (personal communication, August 19, 2008). Two New York–based magazines—*Broadside* and *Sing Out!*—also helped spread protest music by printing song lyrics in their publications (Phillips, 1967). Pop music critic Ralph Gleason (1969) wrote that songs with an anti-war message resonated all across the country "for kids in remote towns who wouldn't otherwise know they are part of a vast movement or wouldn't connect their discontent to its source in our social-political setup (pp. 160–161). He used Country Joe McDonald's "I-Feel-Like-I'm-Fixin'-to-Die Rag" as an example: "That song has been heard and understood by millions. It is heard by someone every day in all probability. Is there any comparable medium? In Iowa and Minnesota, in Arizona and Florida and Washington—as well as in Central Park—Country Joe and the Fish sing that song" (p. 162).

The music was not the only means by which singers helped spread the anti-war message across the nation. Arnold (1991b) explained that "Many pop singers actively protested the war as well, and not only in their music, but through their arrests during peace marches and public protests. Popular protest songs gained momentum as the war prolonged. Phil Ochs, Joan Baez, Joe McDonald, Bob Dylan, and many others actively protested the war" (p. 320). Controversy also helped to spread the message. "The Big Muddy" received national attention in 1967 and 1968 after CBS removed Seeger's performance of the song from *The Smothers Brothers Comedy Hour*, igniting a controversy that sparked widespread media coverage and eventually led the network to reconsider its decision and allow Seeger to perform the entire song on the show several months later. According to Seeger (1983), "The Smothers Brothers did a clever thing. They took their argument to the newspapers and they got lots of free publicity. They said, 'CBS censors our best jokes, they censored Seeger's best song. It ain't fair.'" By the time CBS relented and agreed to broadcast the song in full, the publicity had increased interest in "The Big Muddy" throughout the country, resulting in more viewers (an estimated seven million) for Seeger's televised performance (Seeger, 1983).

Gleason (1969) said that because record companies recognized the potential for large profits from protest music, they willingly provided funds and other resources to promote recording artists, even if they disagreed with the message. "In order to make money, corporate America will, in a kind of autolysis, allow its destruction to be preached via a product that is profitable," he wrote (p. 165). Country Joe McDonald's recollection of the era supports Gleason's argument: "We did play the largest arenas there were at that time. The record companies did PR campaigns then just like now. Of course there was no Internet, but there were other media forms" (personal communication, July 28, 2008). McDonald did in fact perform for large crowds. He sang "The

Rag" for 500,000 people at the Woodstock Music and Arts Festival in 1969, and his rendition of the song became one of the highlights of the record and film versions of the festival (George-Warren & Romanski, 2001, p. 216). And corporate America was willing to support him as long as the dollars kept coming in. As Gleason (1969) explained, although McDonald's penchant for leading his audiences in the chanting of an obscenity at the start of "The Rag" ruffled feathers at the band's booking agency, the company never stopped arranging money-making concerts for the group.

Similarly, Hollywood saw the potential to profit from the popularity of the anti-war sentiment and turned Arlo Guthrie's "Alice's Restaurant" into a major motion picture. "Alice's Restaurant" also provides a good example of how quickly songs spread without the benefit of airplay on commercial radio or television. Guthrie originally performed the song in February 1967 on WBAI, a non-commercial, listener-supported radio station in New York City. In August of that year, he sang it for a small group of people at a workshop at the Newport Folk Festival. Later in the festival, he performed it before a crowd of 3,500 as part of the afternoon session. The audience reaction was so positive that he was added to the festival's evening lineup and performed the song for nearly 10,000 people (Goldstein, 1967; Wilson, 1967).

Pete Seeger related a similar experience about singing John Lennon's "Give Peace A Chance" at the Washington Monument. "After two minutes, thousands were singing. After three minutes, four minutes, a hundred thousand were singing. At the end of eight minutes, all five hundred thousand were singing," he said (Seeger, quoted in Gaffney, 2008, p. 26). Likewise, when the Daughters of the American Revolution refused to allow Joan Baez to perform in its Constitution Hall in Washington, D.C., because of her views on the war, she moved the concert outside, where there was an instant audience of 30,000 (Phillips, 1967).

The popularity of protest music in the 1960s also was fueled by the massive social change that evolved from the Civil Rights movement, the rise of feminism, and more liberal attitudes on sex and drugs. As Hopkins (1970) related, "The lifestyle was against Vietnam and for marijuana, against Lyndon Johnson and for dancing, against hypocrisy and for ecstasy, against the draft and for meditation, against police and for sex, and on and on and on" (p. 95).

Influencing Public Opinion

Did protest music make a difference? Scholars and performers generally believe it did. According to Chomsky, "There's no doubt that music played a very substantial role in the protest movements of the 1960s" (personal communication, July 12, 2008). Hallin contends the impact of protest music was an indirect one: "I don't think it's primarily the effect of lyrics that refer directly to the war, as the more general way music in that era reinforced a culture of opposition to authority that was important" (personal communication, July 16, 2008). McDonald expressed a similar view, explaining that music and songs validate existing feelings and thoughts: "In this sense, the anti war music/songs did that" (personal communication, July 28, 2008). Seeger (1983) was somewhat non-committal about the impact of "The Big Muddy" when he asked, "Did the song do any good? No one can prove a damned thing. It took tens of millions of people speaking out, before the Vietnam War was over." On the other hand, Graham Nash, who composed "Chicago" about the anti-war protests at the 1968 Democratic National Convention, was more definitive. Asked if the song's refrain, "We can change the world, rearrange the world" (Nash, 1971) had come true, he answered, "Absolutely, the war ain't there anymore. I rest my case" (Nash, quoted in Lee, p. 44)

These comments, however, are just opinions. Demonstrating that agenda setting has taken place is an inexact science, especially when it comes to political movements. According to Small (1994), "One of the most difficult problems confronting a historian interested in the media's relationship to a political movement involves the assessment of the impact of the media on their various audiences" (p. 10). What is clear is that opposition to the war in Vietnam among the American public increased substantially during the 1960s. In a series of Gallup polls, the percentage of respondents who said it was a mistake to send troops to Vietnam rose from 24 percent in 1965 to 55 percent in 1969. Hundreds of thousands of Americans took part in marches and rallies to end the war, and Lyndon Johnson's decision not to seek reelection to the presidency in 1968 has been attributed to public dissatisfaction with his policies on Vietnam. As Arnold (1991) wrote, "The American public also became disillusioned as the war grew increasingly unpopular. Nightly on the television news, the public observed for itself the horrors taking place on a continent far away" (p. 318).

As more Americans, particularly young people, raised questions about the war, racism, sexism and other social issues, the messages conveyed in protest music started to resonate with larger segments of the U.S. population and eventually entered the mainstream. Nowhere was this more evident than in the music industry. Entertainers who had been reluctant to touch controversial topics for fear of losing their popularity began to embrace what heretofore had been a counter-culture — and they did so with great commercial success (Lee, 2008):

- Although the Beatles already had extended their repertoire beyond love songs, they took even bolder steps in 1968 by releasing "Revolution." The following year John Lennon recorded "Give Peace a Chance," a song that quickly became an anthem for the anti-war movement (George-Warren & Romanski, 2001).

• The Young Rascals, one of America's most popular bands during the late 1960s, dropped "young" from their name and made peace and freedom their focus in "People Got to Be Free." Lest there be any doubt the public was ready for their message, the song became one of the biggest hits of 1968 (Whitburn, 1983).

• Dion DiMucci, the lead singer of a 1950s doo-wop group called Dion and the Belmonts, shifted to a folksier sound and had a top-selling record with "Abraham, Martin and John," which dealt with the assassinations of U.S. leaders (George-Warren & Romanski, 2001).

• African-American groups began to focus on social issues with songs such as Marvin Gaye's "What's Going On" and the Temptations' "Ball of Confusion." The songs reached Numbers 2 and 3 on the *Billboard* charts, respectively. The Supremes, instead of recording another love song, had a big hit with "Love Child" a song about the difficulties of growing up as an illegitimate child (Whitburn, 1983).

• Not to be outdone, Frank Sinatra released *Cycles*, an album that included songs by young composers such as Joni Mitchell's "Both Sides Now" and John Hartford's "Gentle on My Mind" (George-Warren & Romanski, 2001). These, as well as other selections on the album, are not what one would consider protest music. But the fact that they were recorded by Sinatra — an artist whose identity was closely intertwined with the older, established ruling class — was significant. It was one of many signs that a new era had arrived.

The infusion of protest music into the mainstream culture is well-illustrated by the manner in which most Americans first heard songs from *Hair*, a musical about hippies, war, and America in the 1960s. When the play began its off–Broadway run in 1967, it was a raw and shocking production that featured nudity, profanity and desecration of the American flag on-stage. By 1969, the songs of *Hair* were among the most popular in the nation due largely to cover versions by the Fifth Dimension, a pop-soul quintet known for easy-listening ballads and the Cowsills, a real-life musical family that provided the inspiration for *The Partridge Family* television program (George-Warren & Romanski, 2001).

Not everyone was happy with this turn of events. Ochs worried that the movement was being compromised and he viewed the 1968 Chicago Convention and the Kent State shootings as the final nails in the coffin (Bragg 1990). "The radical political will was beaten out of the anti-war movement, and any belief that music would change the world was crushed," Bragg (1990) wrote. Nor was everyone enamored with protest music. After McDonald sang "The Rag" on prime time coast-to-coast television on *The David Frost Show* in 1969, the program was besieged with letters from angry viewers (McDonald, 2000b). There even were musical responses from those who disagreed with the messages contained in protest songs. "The Ballad of the Green Berets," a patriotic tribute to American soldiers, was the number-one record in the country in 1966 (Whitburn, 1983). In a hit 1969 song, country music artist Merle Haggard boasted that he was proud to be an "Okie from Muskogee," a place where people don't burn draft cards or grow their hair long (Burris & Haggard, 1969). "The Battle Hymn of Lt. Calley," a song written in support of Lieutenant William Calley while he was on trial for his role in the My Lai Massacre, reached number 37 on the Billboard charts in 1971 (Whitburn, 1983).

Conclusion

I have provided examples that suggest protest music provided the American public with information about the Vietnam War that was not being reported on a regular basis. I also have discussed how protest songs spread rapidly throughout the nation without heavy airplay on commercial radio or exposure on popular television programs. The final piece of the triad — demonstrating that protest music influenced public opinion — is difficult to prove, although it is clear that opposition to the war increased immensely at a time when protest music was popular throughout the nation. In addition, those who related their own personal recollections for this chapter generally agreed that there was a nexus between protest songs and the shift in public opinion about the war.

As Small (1994) suggests, demonstrating that agenda setting has taken place is an inexact science. This is especially true when it comes to political movements — and even more so with music. By its very nature, a song has different characteristics than a news account. A news account is published, broadcast or (in today's world) posted at a specific date and time. At best, it rarely has a lifetime of more than a few days. In addition, a good news report tells a story supported by facts; its meaning should not be left to interpretation by the audience. On the other hand, the lifetime of a song is ongoing. It reaches people when it is released, when it is played on radio and television, and when it is performed in concert. It may resonate with the public and even take on new meanings years after it was written. As Seeger (1983) explained, "A song is not a speech. It reflects new meanings as one's life's experiences shine new light upon it. Often a song will reappear several different times in history or in one's life as there seems to be an appropriate time for it."

All this makes a song a powerful tool to influence public opinion. Arnold (1991a) contends that "Music in general can certainly appeal to the emotions and express the general atmosphere of anger, anxiety and fear" (p. 26). During the Vietnam War era, the power of song was stronger than ever. As Gleason (1969) wrote at the time, "As I see it, the situation is plain, if you want to reach young people in this country (and revolutions are made by the young; the old make counter-revolution) then write a song, don't buy an ad or issue a statement" (p. 162).

Speaking in a broader context, Sainte-Marie said, "I believe that the art of the three-minute song is very special and can sometimes do what a censored newspaper article or a fat book might not be able to accomplish in spotlighting an issue. A good song is immediate, small, easy to remember, makes a point quickly and strategically, and is portable, flexible, replicable, transferable to other people and other languages, and can last for generations. A song never goes out of print" (personal communication, July 11, 2008).

While it may not be possible to prove conclusively that protest music influenced public opinion, the words of Gleason, Sainte-Marie, Seeger and others who lived through the Vietnam War era attest to the power of the music and the critical role it played in American society during the 1960s. Perhaps the power of song was best described by Joe Hill, an early twentieth century labor organizer and songwriter, when he said, "A pamphlet, no matter how good, is never read more than once, but a song is learned by heart and repeated over and over" (Hill, quoted in Bragg, 1990).

REFERENCES

Arnold, B. (1991a, June). Music, meaning, and war: The titles of war compositions [Electronic version]. *International Review of the Aesthetics and Sociology of Music, 22*, 19–28.
_____. (1991b, Autumn). War music and the American composer during the Vietnam era [Electronic version]. *The Musical Quarterly, 75*, 316–335.
Bates, M. (Ed.) (1998). *Reporting Vietnam: American Journalism, 1959–1975*. New York: Library of America.
Bragg, B. (1990). [Liner notes to CD] *There and Now: Phil Ochs Live in Vancouver 1968*. Santa Monica, CA: Rhino Records.
Brokaw, T. (2007). *Boom*. New York: Random House.
Burris, R., and M. Haggard (1969). Okie from Muskogee. On *Okie from Muskogee* (record). New York: Capital Records.
Dylan, B. (1963) Blowin' in the Wind. On *The Freewheelin' Bob Dylan* (record). New York: Columbia Records.
Erbring, L., E. Goldenberg, and A. Miller (1980). Front-page news and real-world cues: a new look at agenda-setting by the media. *American Journal of Political Science, 24*, 16–49.
Fowler, E. (1965, October 14). Commodities: Sugar futures trading bolstered by Brazilian sale of 30,000 tons. [Electronic version]. *The New York Times*, p. 78.
Frost, R. (1964, October 30). Commodities: Prices of copper futures reverse trends and climb in brisk trading. [Electronic version]. *The New York Times*, p. 58.

Gaffney, D. (2008, June 22). Familiar voice of protest keeps a roadside vigil. *The New York Times*, p. 26.
George-Warren, H., and P. Romanowski (Eds.) (2001). *The Rolling Stone Encyclopedia of Rock & Roll*. New York: Fireside.
Gleason, R. (1969, Summer). The greater sound [Electronic version]. *The Drama Review: TDR, 13*, 160–166.
Goldstein, R. (1967, Nov. 5). Arlo takes a giant step. *The New York Times*, p. D22.
Guthrie, A. (1967). Alice's Restaurant. On *Alice's Restaurant* (record). Burbank: Reprise Records.
Hallin. D. (1986). *The "Uncensored War": The Media and Vietnam*. Berkeley: University of California Press.
Hammond, W. (1988). *Public Affairs: The Military and the Media, 1962–1968*. Washington, D.C.: Center for Military History, United States Army.
Herman, E., and N. Chomsky (1988). *Manufacturing Consent*. New York: Pantheon.
Hopkins, J. (1970). *The Rock Story*. New York: Signet.
Ivie, R. (1980). Images of savagery in American justification for war [Electronic version]. *Communication Monographs, 47*, 279–291.
James, D. (1989, Autumn-Winter). The Vietnam war and American music [Electronic version]. *Social Text, 23*, 122–143.
_____. (1990, Winter). Rock and roll in representations of the invasion of Vietnam [Electronic version]. *Representations, 29*, 78–98.
Lee, R. (1992, September 15). The world may have changed, but the song remains the same. *The Aquarian Weekly*, 44.
_____. (2008, Spring). The Music Was More Than Just a Soundtrack for the Events of 1968. *Asociacion de la Historia Actual Bulletin, 14*, 20–21
McCombs, M., and D. Shaw (1972). The agenda-setting function of mass media. *The Public Opinion Quarterly, 36*, 176–187.
McDonald, J. (1965). I-feel-like-I'm fixin'-to-die rag. On *Rag Baby Talking Issue No. 1* (record). Berkeley: Rag Baby Records.
_____. (2000a). How I wrote the rag. Retrieved July 28, 2008, from http://www.countryjoe.com/howrag.htm.
_____. (2000b). America Meets the "Rag." Retrieved November 15, 2008, from http://www.countryjoe.com/frost.htm.
Mohr, C. (1965a, September 18). Care in attacks ordered [Electronic version]. *The New York Times*, p. 1.
_____. (1965b, October 6). G.I. patrol decimated by a Vietcong ambush [Electronic version]. *The New York Times*, p. 1.
Nash, G. (1971). Chicago. On *Songs for Beginners* (record). New York: Atlantic Records.
Ochs, P. (1964). Talking Vietnam. On *All the News That's Fit to Sing* (record). New York: Elektra Records.
Paxton, T. (1967). *Talking Vietnam Potluck Blues*. On *Morning Again* (record). New York: Elektra Records.
Perone, J. (2004). *Music of the Counterculture Era*. Westport, CT: Greenwood.
Phillips, T. (1967, October 8). Vietnam blues [Electronic version]. *The New York Times*, p. SM7.
Seeger, P. (1967). Waist deep in the big muddy. On *Waist Deep in the Big Muddy and Other Love Songs* (record). New York: Columbia Records.
_____. (1983). How waist deep in the big muddy finally got on network television in 1968. Retrieved July 28, 2008, from http://www.peteseeger.net/givepeacechance.htm.
Small, M. (1994). *Covering Dissent: The Media and the Anti-Vietnam War Movement*. New Brunswick, N.J.: Rutgers University Press.

Smith, S. (1999). *Dancing in the Street: Motown and the Cultural Politics of Detroit.* Cambridge, MA: Harvard University Press.
Taylor, S. (1985, September). Reporting history: Journalists and the Vietnam war [Electronic version; review of the books *Without Honor: Defeat in Vietnam and Cambodia* and *Vietnam: A History*]. *Reviews in American History, 13,* 451–461.
Unclouded judgment [Electronic version]. (1963, October 11). *Time.* Retrieved July 30, 2008, from http://www.time.com/time/magazine/article/0,9171,873074,00.html.
Whitburn, J. (Ed.) (1983). *The Billboard Book of Top 40 Hits.* New York: Billboard.
Wilson, J. (1967, July 18). Newport is his just for a song [Electronic version]. *The New York Times,* p. 30.
Wicker, T. (1978). *On Press.* New York: Viking.

CREATED HEROES, HUMANIZED SOLDIERS, AND SUPERIOR WESTERN VALUES: FANTASY THEME ANALYSIS OF *FLAGS OF OUR FATHERS* AND *LETTERS FROM IWO JIMA*

Koji Fuse and *James E. Mueller*

Preceded by a few days of heavy naval and aerial bombardment, the U.S. ground invasion of Iwo Jima commenced when the first Marines landed on a beach of the tiny island located about 660 miles south of Tokyo on February 19, 1945. They expected Japanese troops to commence firing immediately or to conduct *banzai* charges, but what awaited them instead was a tactical trap — minimal resistance. When the Marines filled the beach afterward, Japanese artillery, mortars, machine guns, and rifles took a devastating toll (Newcomb, 1965; Wheeler, 1980).

However, the Marines advanced steadily in the next several days, and as a result, Associated Press photographer Joe Rosenthal captured the famous image of five Marines and one Navy corpsman raising the U.S. flag on Mount Suribachi on February 23. But fierce fighting went on until May, killing about 20,000 Japanese and 7,000 Americans. Fewer than 1,000 Japanese were captured (Lofgren, 1995; Newcomb, 1965).

Six decades later, Clint Eastwood directed two films, *Flags of Our Fathers* and *Letters from Iwo Jima*. *Flags* depicted the battle from the American side and *Letters* depicted the Japanese side. Eastwood wanted to avoid the jingoistic tone of John Wayne's 1949 film, *Sands of Iwo Jima*. In this classic, four members of the flag-raising detail recreated their own actions during the battle, describing it as literal representations of the battle and the Marine Corps (Marling & Wetenhall, 1991; Suid, 1978). But Eastwood wanted to make a movie that did not focus on the "gung-ho heroics" often portrayed in classic Hollywood war films (Rickey, 2006). Moreover, Eastwood strived to re-evaluate the one-dimensional characterization of the Japanese in many Hollywood World War II films. "There were good guys on one side. Life isn't like that.... It's not about winning or losing, but mostly about the interrupted lives of young people. These men deserve to be seen, and heard from," Eastwood said (quoted in McCurry, 2006).

Did Eastwood succeed in presenting each side's perspective? How do the films differ in their presentations of each country's collective memories? Analysis of the two films demonstrates how all fantasy themes embedded in the films develop into rhetorical visions. First, however, it is important to understand the history of the battle as it relates to the films.

The Battle of Iwo Jima and the Eastwood Films

Based on James Bradley's and Ron Powers' (2006) book of the same name, the film sheds light on how the lives of the three survivors of the flag raisers were embroiled in a government publicity campaign designed to capitalize on Rosenthal's photograph.

Rosenthal's photograph was actually of the second flag-raising on Iwo Jima. The secretary of the Navy wanted the original flag as a souvenir, but the commander of the 2nd Battalion of the 28th Marine Regiment wanted the flag for his unit and ordered a small group to replace the first flag. Rosenthal happened to photograph the second flag-raising, which featured a larger Stars and Stripes than the original. This photograph was widely published throughout the United States and instantly became a symbol of American patriotism. President Franklin D. Roosevelt saw immense morale value in the photograph and ordered all the surviving second flag-raisers to be shipped back to the United States for "public relations duties" (Bradley & Powers, 2006; Haynes & Warren, 2008; Marling & Wetenhall, 1991).

Although the photograph symbolized American victory, the fighting continued after the capture of Mount Suribachi and left an indelible mark on the surviving flag-raisers. Bradley continued to be haunted by nightmares of the battle. His best friend had been severely tortured and brutally murdered by Japanese soldiers. Pfc. Rene Gagnon initially liked the showering of national attention on him but became bitter when his fame did not help him land a good job. Pfc. Ira Hayes suffered post–traumatic stress syndrome and eventually died of complications related to alcohol abuse (Bradley & Powers, 2006; Marling & Wetenhall, 1991).

On the other hand, *Letters from Iwo Jima* focuses primarily on the courageous acts of two Japanese high-ranking commanders, Kuribayashi and Nishi, the survival of Private Saigo and the death of Private Shimizu who was killed while a POW. Eastwood decided to produce this companion film after learning about Kuribayashi and reading his letters to his family while on Iwo Jima (Rickey, 2006). The letters, which provide a monologue for the film, show Kuribayashi to be a caring man devoted to his family (Kakehashi, 2007).

Both Kuribayashi and Nishi had spent time in the United States before the war. Kuribayashi had been a deputy attaché in Washington, D.C., and Nishi had won a gold medal in an equestrian event in the1932 Olympics in Los Angeles (Wheeler, 1980). Kuribayashi, who was the descendant of 16th Century samurais, became "a cult figure among the Japanese people" after the war (Kakehashi, 2007, p. 199). Kuribayashi did not fit the image of the fanatical Japanese commander ordering futile banzai charges but instead conducted a campaign noted for its strategic brilliance in delaying the inevitable American victory (Haynes & Warren, 2008).

Two competing forces are portrayed in these films, and the application of fantasy theme analysis reveals the construction of disparate *and* common rhetorical visions.

Fantasy Theme Analysis

Fantasy theme analysis, originally introduced in the area of small group communication by Ernest G. Bormann (1972), seeks to discover how members of a group come to create and share a symbolic reality for themselves. However, the term "fantasy" does not mean something imaginary but refers to "the creative and imaginative interpretation of events that fulfills a psychological or rhetorical need" (Bormann, 2001, p. 5). Rhetorical fantasies "may include fanciful and fictitious scripts of imaginary characters, but they often deal with things that have actually happened to members of the community or that are reported in authenticated works of history, in the news media, or in the oral history and folklore of the group" (Bormann, 2001, p. 5).

The content of the dramatizing message that chains out stories from person to person and group to group is called a fantasy theme, which can range from a word to a paragraph in length (Bormann, Cragan, & Shields, 2001, p. 282). Hierarchically above fantasy themes is a rhetorical vision, which is a "unified putting-together of the various scripts which gives the participants a broader view of things" (Bormann, 2001, p. 8). In other words, "A rhetorical vision is constructed from fantasy themes that chain out in face-to-face interacting groups, in speaker-audience transactions, in viewers of television broadcasts, in listeners to radio programs, and in all the diverse settings for public and intimate communication in a given society" (Bormann, 1972, p. 398). The so-called "symbolic convergence theory" of communication attempts to explain the dynamic processes that fantasy themes chain out within a given communication context as well as to different contexts (Bormann, 2001; Bormann et al., 2001).

Communicators weave fantasy themes into a rhetorical vision's substructural elements that include "*dramatis personae* or characters, *plot lines* or action, elements of the *scene* or setting, and *sanctioning agent* or legitimizer for the rhetorical vision" (Bormann et al., 2001, p. 285). "Without protagonists (heroes) and antagonists (villains), there is little drama" (Bormann, 1986, p. 226). The characters can also include other supporting players. The plot line refers to various actions and the development of the story, and the scene is the story's tangible and intangible setting, such as actual locations, properties, and sociocultural surroundings. Finally, the sanctioning agent is a story-legitimizing source, which may be "an authority who lends credibility to the story or authorizes its telling" or "a common belief in God, a commitment to justice or democracy, or even a belief in a shared enemy" (Littlejohn & Foss, 2008, p. 163).

Some fantasy themes attain a high degree of familiarity because of repetition, which can be triggered by symbolic cues such as inside jokes. They are called fantasy types. Bormann (2001) defines a fantasy type as "a stock scenario repeated again and again by the same characters or by similar characters" (p. 7).

Fantasy theme analysis follows the tradition of dramatism. Because "The drama frame is well suited for studies concerned with communication as performance" (Lindlof & Taylor, 2002, p. 236), Bormann's method can be applied to media products such as films. In addition, it is intended to investigate the manifest content of messages, which contains "the conscious, intentional, and rational elements that a rhetorical dimension would imply" (Bormann, 1982, p. 291).

However, applications of fantasy theme analysis do not represent one uniform, standardized procedure to analyze a text or discourse. Some researchers (e.g., Crouse-Dick, 2002; Marambio & Tew, 2006) presented their analytic narratives in a discursive manner, and others (e.g., Benoit, Klyukovski, McHale, & Airne, 2001; Duffy, 2003; Yergensen, 2006) showed fairly systematic analyses. Still others (e.g., Foss & Littlejohn, 1986) produced quantitative data to tally the number of occurrences for each fantasy theme or rhetorical vision.

Criticizing Bormann for taking repetition of a fantasy theme as evidence for its existence and significance, Mohrmann (1982a) contends that the "presence [of a dramatistic entity such as a fantasy theme] alone may be of no special significance, and presence hardly permits a carte blanche imputation of importance" (p. 123). To Mohrmann (1982a, 1982b), mechanical counting of fantasy themes is atheoretical to the tradition of rhetorical criticism; everything comes down to a trained critic's argument and interpretation, which constitute evidence for significant meanings of a text.

Because pop culture reflects to some extent the outside reality that has positioned Japan as an important postwar U.S. ally, we can easily predict that Hollywood's Pacific War films produced in the new millennium, including *Flags of Our Fathers* and *Letters from Iwo Jima*, will reconstruct the U.S. discourse on the Pacific War to question some fundamental assumptions about the war and depict Japanese people as human. However, how is wartime heroism being questioned? In what ways are the Japanese "human"? Are there any themes repeatedly presented to conform to the "normal" interpretation of history? In short, did Eastwood succeed in what he promised to deliver in his films?

The first author, Koji Fuse, is Japanese, and he analyzed *Letters from Iwo Jima*. The second author, James Mueller, an American, examined *Flags of Our Fathers*. After conducting individual analyses, the authors watched each other's assigned films and read each other's analyses to resolve disagreements, eliminate ambiguities, and identify the rhetorical visions that permeated each film. The authors' different cultural affiliations allowed them to bring cultural knowledge to the analysis.

This research took a middle-ground approach that avoids simplistic counting of rhetorical cues but incorporates the hierarchical structure of fantasy themes and rhetorical visions to analyze the Eastwood films. First, while watching the films and taking notes, we identified major protagonists and antagonists — dramatis personae — in each film. Certain individuals were singled out for their heroic, vicious or otherwise prototypically ordinary acts performed in a particular setting. In short, it was most appropriate to focus on and analyze (1) heroes, villains and other symbolically meaningful participants who created human dramas in each film, and (2) their actions in given settings. Second, we extracted and named fantasy themes that cut across the individuals, actions, and settings in each movie. Third, we attempted to search for a sanctioning agent or legitimizer for the story. Finally, we attempted to discover a rhetorical vision that pulled together all the fantasy themes embedded in each film. This research examined the issue of symbolic convergence that extends beyond the films.

Flags of Our Fathers—Themes and Visions

Fantasy Theme 1: We Are All Fallible

The film consistently emphasized that all of the flag-raisers made mistakes or had significant character flaws. Gagnon, perhaps the least heroic of the Marines, is presented as the vainest. In one scene, early in the movie before the battle, he is shown getting a haircut and fussing over the results. When another Marine asks Gagnon if he enlisted in the Marines because their uniforms looked good, he replies, "No sense being a hero if you don't look like one." Gagnon does look like a hero throughout the film, always standing in erect, military posture with a neat uniform and perfectly coiffed hair, which contrasts with the often disheveled Hayes and more casual Bradley.

But Gagnon's bearing and looks mask an unheroic nature. At the beginning of the battle, he is assigned as a runner—a Marine who carries messages—because his sergeant has doubts about how Gagnon will perform in combat. His assignment as a runner leads to Gagnon being ordered to carry the replacement flag to the infantrymen at the top of Mount Suribachi so that it seems almost accidental that he is involved in the flag-raising. After Rosenthal's photo is published, American officials order the Marine commanders to find the flag-raisers and send them home for public relations duty. But the flag-raisers are not easily identified from the photo and some have been killed in battle. When Gagnon learns the military is looking for the flag-raisers, he immediately wants to take advantage of his fame and leave Iwo Jima. But Ira Hayes does not want to abandon his comrades on Iwo Jima and tells Gagnon keep Hayes' identity as a flag-raiser secret. But when officials threaten to remove Gagnon from public relations duty unless he identifies the other flag-raisers, he betrays Hayes' confidence. The three surviving flag-raisers—Bradley, Gagnon and Hayes—join the bond drive across America, but Hayes and Gagnon remain enemies for most of the movie. Gagnon often berates Hayes for drinking too much and ruining the experience of the bond drive for all of them.

Hayes' alcoholism is an obvious character flaw. The film portrays Hayes' drinking bouts in detail, showing a man who cannot face the horrors he saw in the war nor deal with the guilt of surviving. In one scene, Hayes vomits violently while the flag-raisers are riding on a train during the bond drive. Bradley holds him while he leans over the side. A blubbering Hayes then recalls his fellow soldiers who died on Iwo Jima and says they should be on the bond tour instead. Later, when he meets the mother of one of the dead flag-raisers at a public event, Hayes almost collapses in her arms, sobbing so dramatically that the mother is compelled to comfort *him*. He becomes so much trouble that the government decides to grant his request to leave the bond tour. While he is a sympathetic character, bearing numerous slights against his Indian heritage with dignity, his portrayal is the antithesis of the classic hero. Hayes is a broken man.

Bradley, too, suffers intense survivor's guilt after the war, but he usually keeps it hidden; only letting the emotions escape in dreams. In scenes showing Bradley as an older veteran, he refuses to talk about the war, hiding his medals and records in a box. He tells his children to lie for him and to tell reporters he is on a fishing trip. His humility, while in some ways laudable, is also a mistake because he does not share his experiences with his fellow citizens or to his family. Bradley seems to sense this mistake at the end of his life when he tells his son he wishes he has been a better father and talked with him more.

But his most poignant mistake — if it can be called one — occurred during the battle. A scene on Iwo Jima shows Bradley abandoning his panicked friend to treat a wounded Marine. The Marine is beyond help, and when Bradley returns to the shell hole, his friend has disappeared. Later, Bradley and some other Marines find his friend's body. He was captured, tortured, and killed. Although Bradley's duty as a corpsman was to treat the wounded Marine, he dreams about the disappearance of his dead buddy for the rest of his life. A traditional movie hero would be able to save both men. Bradley could save neither.

Fantasy Theme 2: Images Are Only Part of Realty

Bradley's memories of the events are told in jarring, teasing flashbacks. At various times during the film, it is uncertain whether a given scene is a dream, a memory, a recreation of the flag-raising or the actual battle. Perhaps the most confusing scene depicts Marines struggling in the dark to climb the mountain with deafening canon fire and exploding shells in the background. Eventually the scene expands to show that the men are actually recreating the event on a mockup mountain in a sports stadium, and the artillery fire is really fireworks.

Throughout the film, first impressions often betray the truths. For example, when Gagnon and other Marines are getting their haircut by Bradley while relaxing in their tent, they assume he knows how to cut hair because was training to be a barber before the war. They find out to their surprise he was training to be an undertaker and has practiced cutting hair on corpses. The barber scene is a small moment of a wrong first impression, but the entire film is based on a grand event — the flag-raising — that is not entirely what it seems to be. As was stated earlier and as the film makes clear for the many viewers who are unfamiliar with the flag-raising story, Rosenthal's iconic photograph is a portrayal of the second flag-raising on Mount Suribachi. It does not mark the end of the battle but only the capture of the mountain. In addition, one of the flag-raisers who were killed in the battle was misidentified. The real identities of all the participants emerged years afterward.

Fantasy Theme 3: Individual Is Insignificant Compared to the Mission

The film makes this theme explicit in a number of ways. One of the most striking is by the callous disregard for life compared to the group goals. While the Marines are sailing for Iwo Jima, one falls overboard. The rest mock him, tossing him a life preserver and assuming one of the many ships that fill the scene will pick him up. But they learn the ships have orders not to stop; they cannot delay the whole convoy and put many men and the mission at risk in order to save one man. On the island, the Marines die by the score. Bradley struggles to save as many wounded men as he can, but it is often futile. One camera shot focuses on two men straining to carry an injured Marine to safety. Gradually the background shows the beach, then the ocean, filled with U.S. ships shelling the island or bringing more men to fight and die until the battle is won.

Toward the end of the film, a wounded Bradley sees a smoking B-29 bomber land on the island, justifying the high cost in capturing it. The main purpose for taking the island is to use it as an emergency airfield for bombers damaged while raiding Japan. As one former Marine says to Bradley's son years after the war, "That island saved a lot of lives." Of course the island did save a number of airmen, but the saving of those airmen aided the U.S. bombing campaigns, which killed a number of Japanese civilians while also damaging Japan's military. The individual suffering on Iwo Jima and in the bombing of Japan was horrific, but it contributed to the group mission — to end the war as quickly as possible.

Rhetorical Vision: The American Flag Represents a Nation of Ordinary People, Not Created Heroes

The sanctioning agent that legitimizes the story is the belief in American democracy as symbolized by the American flag. Throughout the film, the flag is cheered. At times the cheering may seem illegitimate, because it is done by crowds of people who are unaware of the suffering of the flag-raisers and their real-life flaws and see only a recreation of the Iwo Jima flag-raising. But when the original flag is raised, weary servicemen all over the island enthusiastically raise their helmets and rifles and shout for joy. The people back home are not necessarily weary from combat, but they are war-weary and anxiously awaiting the return of their loved ones. They cheer the faux flag-raisings and the guilt-ridden flag-raisers because they symbolize a victorious end of the war.

The men who brought the war to a successful end are not movie heroes. They are shown, as Eastwood has intended, to be the opposite of John Wayne–style action heroes. They have personal flaws, they have survivor's guilt, and they make mistakes.

In the film's conclusion, Bradley's son muses: "Maybe there's no such thing as heroes. Maybe there are just people like my dad." He says heroes are created by society as a way to understand how soldiers can sacrifice so much for the country. But the soldiers fought for the country and died for their friends, their buddies, and they were uncomfortable in the role of hero, he concluded.

But whatever their individual motivations and whatever their individual flaws, the flag-raisers and the rest of the men who fought on Iwo Jima collectively did achieve something heroic. Their achievement is shown clearly in the final vision of the movie: A shot from the top of Mount Suribachi showing the Stars and Stripes waving over a beautiful ocean background, now clear of the implements of war. The terrible fighting is over; the battle is a memory. The mountain, impassive, remains beautiful and indifferent to the ravages of war. So, too, does the American flag, which continues to arouse patriotism and symbolize the triumph not of cartoon heroes but of ordinary Americans who rose to the challenge when faced with a war for survival.

Letters from Iwo Jima — Themes and Visions

Fantasy Theme 1: Japanese Are Also Human

Two fictional characters are used to demonstrate Japanese soldiers as ordinary people who worried about their families and wanted to survive the war. They are not extraordinarily "humane," but their narratives are as a counterpoint to the savage imagery of Japanese soldiers that Hollywood promoted in many movies about World War II.

The movie shows Pfc. Saigo digging holes on Iwo Jima before the battle. Saigo curses the island and says, "We should just give the island to the Americans ... and then we can go home." A flashback shows his shock and sorrow on the day he was drafted. He feebly says what he is supposed to say: "Thank you very much. I'm happy to serve the country." He tries to comfort his pregnant wife, who is pessimistic about his fate. Saigo, talking to their unborn child in her swollen belly, says: "Can you hear me? It's Dad. Listen. Don't tell anyone what I'm telling you now. It's a secret. Your dad ... is going to come home for you." Then he hugs his wife.

The human side of another soldier was shown through his affection for dogs. Superior Pvt. Shimizu had been a military policeman before the battle. A flashback scene shows him disobeying his commander's order to kill a barking dog. When the officer found out, he beat Shimizu severely, discharged him from the military police for insubordination and ordered him sent to Iwo Jima.

During the battle on Iwo Jima, when Mount Suribachi is about to be captured, a Japanese officer orders everyone, including Saigo and Shimizu, to commit suicide with grenades. The soldiers who kill themselves sob all day before committing suicide. Saigo and Shimizu decide to escape to join Japanese forces on another part of the island and ultimately attempt to surrender.

One real-life character who did not surrender, Kuribayashi, is nevertheless often shown as a humane man with tender feelings for children. The movie quotes tender letters he sent to his family from Iwo Jima. And in one scene he cries when he hears Japanese children singing on the radio for the soldiers on the island. *Letters from Iwo Jima* contains many similar scenes that portray Japanese not as suicidal fanatics but human beings with the same emotions as Americans.

Fantasy Theme 2: Those Japanese Who Have Experience in the United States Are Benevolent and Civilized

Contrary to the stereotypically savage images of Japanese soldiers in many Hollywood movies, Kuribayashi and Nishi are shown as beacons of humane generosity. Kuribayashi is portrayed as a gentleman comfortable at formal dinners and humane toward his troops. One flashback scene depicts Kuribayashi having a dinner conversation with American generals while he is visiting the United States. Back on the island, he is a tolerant leader who thinks banzai charges are ineffective. In fact, he dismisses a bellicose high-ranking commander who believes all soldiers should die on the island. Kuribayashi also stops his officers from using corporal punishment on their troops.

When Nishi arrives on Iwo Jima, Kuribayashi invites him to dinner and drinks. Their conversation demonstrates that Nishi is also is a rational military officer, not a savage fanatic. Nishi tells Kuribayashi, "If you want my honest opinion, General ... the best thing to do ... would be to sink the island to the bottom of the sea."

During the battle, a badly wounded American was brought to Nishi's headquarters. Nishi orders his subordinates to treat the critically wounded soldier. When one of his men says, "Sir, the Americans would not treat a wounded Japanese soldier," Nishi immediately replies: "Son, have you ever met one? Treat him." Nishi smiles and treats the American kindly even while he is trying to interrogate him.

However, both Nishi and Kuribayashi are severely wounded in battle and decide to commit suicide. Nishi, blinded in an explosion, orders his soldiers to escape to another part of the island, then shoots himself with a rifle. Kuribayashi, wounded while leading a charge, asks his aide to cut off his head. When his aide is killed by an American sniper, Kuribayashi shoots himself with a pistol. By committing suicide, the two officers were following the Japanese military code of bushido, which required that high-ranking officers die rather than surrender. In reality, no one knows for sure how the two men died. The suicides depicted in the movie reflect a more "civilized" death than the indescribable suffering of barbarian hara-kiri — ritual disembowelment. Even in death, the Japanese officers who had visited America were depicted as rational, civilized men following their own honor code.

Fantasy Theme 3: Only Japanese Who Are Indoctrinated by Japanese Propaganda Are Suicidal Maniacs

In the early part of the film, a group of high-ranking officers disagree with Kuribayashi. In line with Japanese propaganda, they insist their soldiers should die honorably in suicidal banzai charges. Kuribayashi, on the other hand, decides to use patient tactics that would tie down the American troops to delay them as long as possible from invading Japan. Despite Kuribayashi's decision, one officer orders a banzai charge. The movie shows Kuribayashi's anger over the officer's actions, which were born of indoctrination from propaganda.

The power of indoctrination was also shown when Saigo and Shimizu observe a group of Japanese soldiers capture, beat up and use their bayonets to murder an American solider. The scene is much more dramatic and barbaric than another scene during which an American soldier uses a rifle to kill two Japanese prisoners-of-war.

When Saigo and Shimizu retreat from Mount Suribachi and report for duty on another part of the island, the fictitious bloodthirsty officer, Navy Lt. Ito, also influenced by indoctrination, tries to execute them by sword. He says, "It was your duty to stay in your position until death. You should have died ... with your fellow troop members. You are both a disgrace." Ito insists that Mount Suribachi must be recaptured. He even has a direct verbal and physical confrontation with his superior, Nishi. Eventually, Eastwood's film shows Ito's disgrace when he does not commit suicide but instead becomes a prisoner-of-war.

Kuribayashi's last charge is dramatized by Eastwood as a banzai attack. But the attack is made as a last resort when the battle is lost, in contrast to his fanatic subordinates who wanted suicidal missions at the beginning of the battle. Holding his Japanese sword and leading his men quietly on the battleground, he suddenly shouts "Attack!" in front of the American barracks, leading his men in a heroic last-ditch effort.

Kuribayashi and Nishi reveal noble characteristics like benevolence throughout the movie. The negative actions like those of Ito resonate with Americans' existing beliefs about wartime Japanese soldiers. This fantasy theme is demonstrated by the negative actions of Japanese soldiers who follow standard wartime propaganda.

Rhetorical Vision: War Is Futile

Who remains alive in the end? Interestingly enough, only two among the major Japanese characters survive the battle. An ordinary young man, who has always wanted to go home, Saigo, is eventually captured by American soldiers. The other is Ito, who represents stereotypically fanatic Japanese. All others, including Kuribayashi and Nishi, are dead.

Eastwood chose to spotlight Kuribayashi and Nishi, and this is significant. The sanctioning agent in *Letters from Iwo Jima* is "Western rationality" embodied by Kuribayashi and Nishi, but their deaths indicate the war's destruction of Western rationality. Therefore, the film attempts to demonstrate how futile any war is.

Moreover, many young and ordinary soldiers lose their lives, and this adds to the rhetorical vision. Killing savages or beasts is not a problem, but when Japanese soldiers are perceived as human beings, it becomes increasingly difficult to justify a war as moral or necessary. The same also applies to American soldiers who are seen as ordinary human beings. If we continue to see all groups of people as equally human, we must conclude that all wars are insupportable. The perceived futility of war is the larger and more complex drama, or rhetorical vision, of *Letters from Iwo Jima*. This vision supports the Japanese "victim mentality" that since the end of the war has tried to conceal many Japanese war crimes such as the Bataan Death March, Unit 731, and the use of non–Japanese civilians as "comfort women."

Conclusion

This chapter presented a fantasy theme analysis of Eastwood's films about the Battle of Iwo Jima. He directed them for two culturally different audiences, and the films' rhetorical visions — the nation of ordinary people for *Flags of Our Fathers* and the futility of war for *Letters from Iwo Jima*—indicate one vision for the winner and the other for the loser. He successfully depicted the suffering of both sides by dramatizing the "interrupted lives of young people," who he argues "deserve to be seen, and heard from" (quoted in McCurry, 2006). Yet, *Flags* projects more redeeming, positive values of America because of the "mission accomplished" by ordinary folks. *Letters,* on the other hand, is rather bleak with only two fictitious major characters alive at the end of the war. The American flag shown at the end of *Flags* represents the protection of democracy and freedom by ordinary Americans. The American experiences of Kuribayashi and Nishi depicted in *Letters* underlies their benevolence and rationalism. Thus both films support the idea that American or Western values are superior to Japanese values.

Acknowledging that World War II is a delicate issue, Tokyo's conservative governor, Shintaro Ishihara, gave Eastwood permission to film *Letters from Iwo Jima* on the island after the latter agreed never to stamp on "Japanese sensitivities" (McCurry, 2006). The reality of rage and racism, demonstrated by Japanese soldiers' brutal mutilation of an American soldier (Bradley & Powers, 2000), is hinted at in *Flags,* but the Americans' practice of making desk ornaments or ashtrays out of Japanese skulls (Weingartner, 1992) are conveniently ignored. Those historical facts must be brought into an analysis of popular war films that their directors frequently make palatable to the target audiences.

Several theoretical and methodological avenues exist for future research. First, fantasy theme analysis may or may not successfully delve into the deep meaning structure of a media text because it primarily dissects the structure of existing elements in the text. For example, Foss and Littlejohn's (1986) research demonstrates rather mundane, predictable fantasy themes that are part of a larger rhetorical vision of nuclear war. No one critically questioned which country had used atomic bombs on humans and contributed to accelerating the worldwide nuclear race. By the same token, the present research debunked the deep meaning structure of the films that covertly and hegemonically approve the supremacy of American values over others only because it included historical facts and explored meta-text ideological issues while also applying critical oppositional reading (Hall, 1980). In *Letters,* Kuribayashi and Nishi maintain disproportionate prominence precisely because they had previous experience in the United States. In short, good officers espoused American values. By positioning them as the two main protagonists in *Letters,* Eastwood paradoxically projected the American viewpoint in disguise of a Japanese one. If not critical enough, we could have identified the sanctioning agent in *Letters* as generic "humanism," instead of "Western rationality."

A meta-text fantasy theme could be that Japan would have avoided war if it had more cosmopolitan people like Kuribayashi and Nishi? An example of this meta-text fantasy theme could be when Japanese and some Americans praise Harvard-educated Admiral Isoroku Yamamoto for his strong opposition to entering into war with the United States while contrasting him with other Japanese high-ranking commanders whom they characterize as unintelligent and belligerent savages. This concealed fantasy theme is used by some Japanese to dodge all war responsibility on certain Japanese individuals like Hideki Tojo and to disregard the tremendous sufferings of non–Japanese Asians caused by Japanese imperialism. Therefore, complementing fantasy theme analysis with social, political, economic, and historical facts is necessary to accommodate a critical approach to media texts.

Moreover, one of Mohrmann's (1982a, 1982b) works is directed at the chaining out of fantasy themes to other contexts beyond the original piece being analyzed. How, for example, do the books written about the Battle of Iwo Jima after the release of the films differ from the previous ones? Although *Letters* centers on Kuribayashi and Nishi, some books published after the film present rather different and unspeakable truths. As an Iwo Jima survivor, Akikusa (2006) mounts his criticism against Kuribayashi in that he ordered soldiers to hold out without sufficient food and water (p. 193). In addition, he discloses brutal facts about killing fellow soldiers, the mountains of decaying and odiferous corpses, and the burning alive of Japanese soldiers by Americans. All of this occurred inside underground tunnels after Kuribayashi died. In a sense, those books provide oppositional readings of the film, disrupting the chaining out of fantasy themes.

Another application of symbolic convergence theory, an analysis of movie reviews posted online, could elicit how viewers have interacted with a media text. Online reviews are not the outcome of simultaneous communication among users, but extracting fantasy themes and rhetorical visions in the reviews will help us discover if two types of discourse correspond or diverge.

Finally, focus groups must be conducted to determine if symbolic convergence occurs by observing how people construct a symbolic reality of World War II for themselves. The focus groups must allow for many possible cross-cultural comparisons: (1) intracultural gender comparison (2) U.S.–Japan comparison, and (3) multinational comparisons that also include non–Japanese Asian nations. In addition, comparing two types of discourse, the films and focus groups, will illuminate the process of symbolic convergence between group and mass communication.

Author note: The original form of this paper was presented at a poster session of the Association for Education in Journalism and Mass Communication conference August 8, 2008, in Chicago, IL.

REFERENCES

Akikusa, T. (2006). *Junanasai no Iwoto* [A 17-year-old's Iwo Jima]. Tokyo: Bungei-shunju.
Benoit, W. L., A. A. Klyukovski, J. P. McHale, and D. Airne (2001). A fantasy theme analysis of political cartoons on the Clinton-Lewinsky-Starr affair. *Critical Studies in Media Communication, 18,* 377–394.
Bormann, E. G. (1972). Fantasy and rhetorical vision: The rhetorical criticism of social reality. *Quarterly Journal of Speech, 58,* 396–407.
_____. (1982). Fantasy and rhetorical vision: Ten years later. *Quarterly Journal of Speech, 68,* 288–305.
_____. (1986). Symbolic convergence theory and communication in group decision-making. In R. Y. Hirokawa & M. S. Poole (Eds.), *Communication and Group Decision-Making* (pp. 219–236). Beverly Hills, CA: Sage Publications.
_____. (2001). *The Force of Fantasy: Restoring the American Dream.* Carbondale, IL: Southern Illinois University Press.
_____, Cragan, J. F., and D. C. Shields (2001). Three decades of developing, grounding, and using symbolic convergence theory (SCT). In W. B. Gudykunst (Ed.), *Communication Yearbook 25* (pp. 271–313). Mahwah, NJ: Lawrence Erlbaum.
Bradley, J., and R. Powers (2006). *Flags of Our Fathers.* New York: Bantam.
Crouse-Dick, C. E. (2002). She designed: Deciphering messages targeting women in commercials aired during *Ally McBeal. Women and Language, 25,* 18–28.
Duffy, M. E. (2003). Web of hate: A fantasy theme analysis of the rhetorical vision of hate groups online. *Journal of Communication Inquiry, 27,* 291–312.
Eastwood, C. (Producer/Director), S. Spielberg (Producer), and R. Lorenz (Producer). (2006a). *Flags of Our Fathers* [Motion picture]. United States: DreamWorks Pictures & Warner Bros. Pictures.
Eastwood, C. (Producer/Director), S. Spielberg (Producer), and R. Lorenz (Producer). (2006b). *Letters from Iwo Jima* [Motion picture]. United States: Warner Bros. Pictures & DreamWorks Pictures.
Foss, K. A., and S. W. Littlejohn (1986). The Day After: Rhetorical vision in an ironic frame. *Critical Studies in Mass Communication, 3,* 317–336.
Hall, S. (1980). Encoding/decoding. In S. Hall, D. Hobson, A. Lowe, & P. Willis (Eds.), *Culture, Media, Language: Working Papers in Cultural Studies, 1972–79* (pp. 128–138). London: Unwin Hyman.
Haynes, F., and J. A. Warren (2008). *The Lions of Iwo Jima.* New York: Henry Holt.
Kakehashi, K. (2007). *So Sad to Fall in Battle: An Account of War Based on General Tadamichi Kuribayashi's Letters from Iwo Jima.* New York: Ballantine.
Lindlof, T. R., and B. C. Taylor (2002). *Qualitative Communication Research Methods* (2nd ed.). Thousand Oaks, CA: Sage.
Littlejohn, S. W., and K. A. Foss (2008). *Theories of Human Communication* (9th ed.). Belmont, CA: Thomson Wadsworth.
Lofgren, S. J. (1995). Diary of First Lieutenant Sugihara Kinryu: Iwo Jima, January-February 1945. *Journal of Military History, 59,* 97–133.
Marambio, J. L., and C. Tew (2006). Clash in paradise: A fantasy theme analysis of *A Day Without a Mexican. Journal of American Culture, 29,* 475–492.
Marling, K. A., and J. Wetenhall (1991). *Iwo Jima: Monuments, Memories, and the American Hero.* Cambridge, MA: Harvard University Press.
McCurry, J. (2006, May 28). Eastwood attacks Japan war myths. *The Observer* (Great Britain). Retrieved March 22, 2008, from LexisNexis Academic database.
Mohrmann, G. P. (1982a). An essay on fantasy theme criticism. *Quarterly Journal of Speech, 68,* 109–132.

_____ (1982b). Fantasy theme criticism: A peroration. *Quarterly Journal of Speech, 68,* 306–313.

Newcomb, R. F. (1965). *Iwo Jima: The Dramatic Account of the Epic Battle That Turned the Tide of World War II.* New York: Henry Holt.

Rickey, C. (2006, October 15). Eastwood's Iwo Jima. *The Philadelphia Inquirer.* Retrieved March 22, 2008, from LexisNexis Academic database.

Suid, L. (1978). *The Sands of Iwo Jima*: The United States Marines, and the screen image of John Wayne. *Film & History, 8*(2), 25–32, 41. Retrieved March 22, 2008, from the Communication & Mass Media Complete database.

Terkel, S. (1984). *"The Good War": An Oral History of World War Two.* New York: Pantheon.

Weingartner, J. J. (1992). Trophies of war: U.S. troops and the mutilation of Japanese war dead, 1941–1945. *Pacific Historical Review, 61,* 53–67.

Wheeler, R. (1980). *Iwo.* New York: Lippincott & Crowell.

Yergensen, B. (2006). Cultural interpretations of fantasy film: *The Lord of the Rings* as Christian "equipment for living." *Ohio Communication Journal, 44,* 151–171.

GHOSTS OF VIETNAM: FILMIC REPRESENTATIONS OF UNCONSUMMATED AMERICAN HEROISM IN THE BEGINNING OF THE TWENTY-FIRST CENTURY

Wesley J. O'Brien

Writing at the end of the last century, Ralph Donald (1992) suggested that representations of war (and Western) heroes were "essentially melodramatic portrayals of men performing virile, courageous deeds designed to protect helpless civilians from some sort of aggressor. Whether these villains are land-hungry cattle barons, rampaging Indians, or rapacious Nazis, Japanese and Viet Cong, the outcomes (good triumphs over evil) are the same" (p. 126). With this in mind, the following discussion addresses questions posed by departures from such soldierly cinematic representations and investigates the extent to which popular cinema of the last decade subverts this myth of the American soldier and the nature of good and evil over which he does or does not triumph. What happens, in other words, when one replaces the mix of Nazis, Japanese, and Viet Cong, with the Iraqi Republican Guard, Sunni and Shiite insurgents, Al-Qaeda, and the United States Government?

Even at the time it was published, Donald's description was more accurate for some wars, and for some times, than for others. While it is true that most (though clearly not all) classic Hollywood World War II films of the 1940s and 1950s demonized the enemy while glorifying American soldiers, thus presenting a categorical ideology of good and evil, it also is true that once one moves beyond John Wayne performing John Wayne in *The Green Berets* (Wayne & Kellogg, 1968), a preponderance of post–Vietnam representations from approximately the mid–1970s through the 1980s are relatively unencumbered by definitive statements about good and evil. Indeed, such statements are steeped in ambiguity, blurring the lines between good, evil, oppression, and protectionism. In Nick's self-imposed exile and suicide and the heartbreaking ambivalence of "America the Beautiful" as sung at the close of *The Deer Hunter* (Cimino, 1978); in the surreal departure of Capt. Willard from Col. Kurt's bizarre compound in *Apocalypse Now* (Coppola, 1979); in Joker's display of "Born To Kill" on his helmet and peace button on his uniform, his execution of the praying female sniper, and the march of the Lusthogs through the hellish, fire-bathed mise-en-scène singing the Mickey Mouse theme song in *Full Metal Jacket* (Kubrick, 1987) — in these images and others of their ilk, one is hard pressed to identify virile and courageous deeds through which good has triumphed.

But these observations are not new. Such anti-heroic, post–Vietnam filmic representations have been discussed often in terms contrary to Donald's (1992) description. John Newsinger (1993), for example, has pointed to a "fractured masculinity, a masculinity that is under pressure, that has been found wanting" (p. 126); and Rasmussen and Downey (1991) wrote, "Although critics differ in their interpretation and assessment of these films, most would agree that they offer a disturbing vision of war as destructive, of its rituals as hollow, and of human actions in war as morally ambiguous" (p. 177).

Revisiting such observations is appropriate now, because some 35 years later, the ghost of Vietnam still haunts TV sets and multiplex cinemas regardless of the war being represented and despite the once-clear moral outrage precipitated by 9/11. Although films of the last decade representing World War II seemed, for a time at least, to leave behind representations containing the destructive and hollow rituals identified above, even "the good war" provides no unequivocal return to motivation based upon God and country. *Saving Private Ryan's* Captain John Miller (Bryce & Spielberg, 1998), for example, asserts that his only purpose is to earn the right to return to his wife, and the ensemble of self-serving, cynical or chronically AWOL soldiers in *The Thin Red Line* (Stephens & Malick 1998) leaves little room for even a Captain Miller, let alone a John Wayne. A more recent debunking of the heroic myth is *Flags of Our Fathers* (Eastwood, 2006), which reveals its central image (raising the U.S. flag over Iwo Jima) as a simulacrum, using it to de-mythologize the heroic myth — to point to its fabrication as a comfortable though non-existent fiction, rendering the "heroes" themselves uncomfortable. Aided by Eastwood's child-like score, the film's final sequence suggest that we remember American World War II soldiers, not as valorous fighting men but as little boys splashing about in the ocean.

What these World War II films of the last decade share are protagonists in search of a moral compass to inform their heroism (a heroism based upon familial or fraternal fidelity rather than patriotic fervor), and a tendency to grapple with what it means to earn the designation "hero." Even in depictions of "the good war," then, one cannot help but suspect, given a collective disillusionment of the American soldierly myth precipitated by the tragedy of Vietnam, that the gears of popular culture were casting about for the mechanism through which an American audience could once again identify with its war film protagonists — a formula by which we could, in the popular parlance, "support the troops" despite being disillusioned with recent wars in which they fought. As evidenced by the films mentioned above, it seemed to have found such a formula by personalizing the soldiers' quest — by collapsing the larger concerns of a nation at war into the smaller, personal and sentimental concerns of the individual soldiers who fight for it.

But the ghost of Vietnam has been summoned by the tragedy of Iraq, and as a result, the personalized representations of the American heroic myth give way to an ongoing, incremental devolution. What follows is an examination of a series of combat films released on or after the turn of this century that demonstrate a progression from personalized heroism to heroism thwarted and finally to heroism destroyed.

Greed, Moral Awakening, and Un-pledging Allegiance

Three Kings (Goodman & Russell, 1999) is set during the inconclusive conclusion to the 1991 Gulf War. The protagonists ultimately exemplify Donald's (1992) "men performing virile, courageous deeds designed to protect helpless civilians from some sort of aggressor" (p. 126). Here, however, the "aggressor" turns out to be both warring parties — the Iraqi Army and the U.S. Army. What begins as a self-serving plan to pilfer Kuwaiti gold from Saddam's secret bunkers aided by a hand-drawn map discovered in the anus of a captured Iraqi soldier (an interesting metaphor for the road to wealth), becomes a mission to rescue a band of Shiite resisters from imprisonment, torture, and death by facilitating their flight across the Iranian border. To do so, the intentions of both the Iraqi and the American military must be circumvented. Thus the battle does not pit one nation against another, but individual soldiers against both. The protagonists, Staff Sergeant Chief Elgin, Sergeant First Class Troy Barlow and Major Archie Gates (Ice Cube, Mark Wahlberg and George Clooney, respectively) cannot hope to gain from their final act of charity, which ultimately requires that they return the pilfered gold to the U.S. Military. Further, because the war has "ended," the aid they provide violates the U.S. agreement of non-interference. Thus the three men not only relinquish their chance for wealth but also risk court martial. The victory they achieve is not military, but moral—a victory meant not only (in the films own words) to "exorcize the ghost of Vietnam" but also to expose the negative impact of American consumerism, imperialism, and corporate greed on non–Western cultures. While their actions reflect traditional tenets of heroism, the allegiance that traditionally underpins such heroism is subverted.

An illustration of this questioned allegiance is Gates' description of the damage done by gunshot wounds. "Know anything about gunshot wounds?" he asks. "The worst thing about a gunshot wound ... is something called sepsis. Say a bullet tears into your gut. It creates a cavity of dead tissue. That cavity fills up with bile and bacteria. You're fucked" (Goodman & Russell, 1999). Illustrating Gates' words, the camera tracks an extreme close-up of a bullet entering a man's flesh, creating a pocket that fills with green bile. The suggestion is that the U.S. invasion of Iraq has had similar consequences— that the American military has, in effect, given sepsis to an entire nation.

Mark Lacy (2003) identified *Three Kings* as a film that represents "war at a distance" (p. 630), suggesting that warfare technology and the saturation of mediated images of death have detached those who fight the war (and those who watch it) from the larger moral issues regarding its effects on the populations left behind. Lacy argues that as the narrative proceeds, it forces the protagonists, through proximity, to appreciate the misery the war has created, thus precipitating the desire for moral good.

Troy offers the most dramatic example of this moral awakening. Despite his encounters with senseless killing, despite the pleas of Iraqi civilians that they not be abandoned to Saddam's soldiers, despite witnessing an Iraqi mother shot in the head before her adolescent daughter and husband, he maintains his singular resolve to secure Saddam's gold. Yet after he is forced by his Republican Guard interrogator to envision his own family destroyed by bombs as the interrogator's has been, Troy emerges morally reborn, determined to facilitate the Iraqi civilians' escape. In so doing, he sabotages the agenda of the country to which he has sworn allegiance.

In the final moments of the film, as Elgin, Troy and Gates escort the Iraqi refugees across the Iranian border to freedom, an American chopper lands. American soldiers arrest Elgin, Troy and Gates and surrender the refugees to Iraqi border guards, thus ensuring their torture and imprisonment. America has withdrawn support, and rescuing the refugees violates the American-Iraqi cease-fire. In effect, the impending oppression of Iraqi civilians by Saddam's army is facilitated by U.S. policy. At the last moment, however, the protagonists surrender the gold in exchange for the refugees' free passage.

Heroism, here, is not predicated upon national allegiance. Morality occurs on a personal level. Freedom, that time-honored tenet of the American heroic myth, is championed *despite* the U.S. military, not because of it, and we identify with the individual troopers while remaining skeptical with regard to the conflict itself. The ghost of Vietnam is exorcized, not by way of a Rambo-like military victory but by way of an ethical victory that indicts both sides while simultaneously "supporting the troops."

The question of whether or not the wounds of Vietnam were still fresh enough in 1999 to prevent an American audience from reaffirming the chest-thumping, flag-waving values that drove many classical war films remains rhetorical — certainly one or two examples of popular cinema cannot affirm or deny such a question. But one would not be stretching the imagination to suggest that the events of 9/11 might have precipitated such a return. One could assume that when the nation is attacked, the resulting patriotic fervor would move beyond affixing Chinese-made American flags to car antennae and would emerge within the context of popular culture. One also could wonder if such an attack might mitigate populist cynicism regarding Vietnam and rekindle a taste for patriotic zeal. Perhaps to some degree *We Were Soldiers* (Lemley & Wallace, 2002) could be read thus, yet the protagonists embody a number of characteristics that oppose that reading.

For Family and Brother, Not Flag and Country

Like *Three Kings, We Were Soldiers* also works to reposition the hero's allegiance. It does so by foregrounding familial and fraternal bonds. While allegiance to family and comrade is by no means unique to soldierly representations, here, the degree to which it overshadows allegiance to country is noteworthy.

The film follows Lt. Col. Hal Moore (Mel Gibson) as he leads the 1st Battalion, 7th Cavalry in the first major engagement of United States forces with the North Vietnamese Army. Preceding and then cross-cut with combat sequences depicting the 1965 battle in the Ia Drang Valley are those set in Fort Benning, Georgia, where Moore's wife Julie (Madeleine Stowe) and his five children live. Thus the narrative is divided between two settings, and we see Moore interacting with his men and his family in concurrent representations of the military and the domestic.

Questions of allegiance precipitated by conflict between domestic and military responsibilities emerge in an early sequence in the hospital chapel. As Moore congratulates one of his young lieutenants, Jack Geoghegan (Chris Klein), on the birth of his daughter, the conflicted lieutenant asks Moore, "What do you think about being a soldier *and* a father?" Moore replies, "I hope that being good at the one makes me better at the other." Geoghegan is troubled by events he and his wife witnessed as Peace Corp volunteers in

Africa where a tribal war left children without parents. "I know God has a plan for me," he tells Moore. "I just hope it's to help protect orphans, not make any."

"Let's go ask him," Moore replies, and he and Geoghegan kneel to pray. Immediately, the lushly scored, hymn-like theme, "What Is War" enters and is thus baptized as a leitmotif, hereafter informing the film's frequent sequences representing soldiers questioning their role: how they will engage the enemy, how they will face mortal danger, and how they can justify killing.

Joe Galloway (Barry Pepper), a UPI reporter and photographer, also gives voice to such questions. It is not unusual for the combat correspondent or the embedded journalist to build a close relationship with the main protagonist in American combat films (e.g., Ernie Pyle with Capt. Bill Walker in *The Story of G.I. Joe* [Cowan & Wellman, 1945]; George Beckworth with Col. Mike Kirby in *The Green Berets*). The confidences established through such relationships provide a dramatic vehicle for one or the other character to be candid about his responses to war. The following sequence provides a significant example.

As Moore prays over the casualties, Galloway approaches. Moore asks, "Why aren't you a soldier? You got the guts for it." Galloway replies that his family has a long history of fighting his country's wars. "When it came to this one," he says, "I didn't think I could stop a war. Just thought I could maybe try and understand one. Maybe help folks back home understand. I just figure I could do that better shooting a camera than I could shooting a rifle." But while Galloway's purpose is clear, his questions remain unanswered. In the chapel sequence described above, Geoghegan asks Moore why he is a soldier; here, Moore asks Galloway why he *isn't* one. "You got the guts for it," he says, as if the only reason to not be a soldier is lack of courage. In neither case is a reason provided. In the first sequence, Moore prays with Geoghegan for guidance, and in the second, he simply wishes Galloway well. He does not try to explain to Galloway why wars are fought.

Classic World War II films such as *Bataan* (Schary & Garnett, 1943), *Gung Ho!* (Wanger & Enright, 1943), and *Wake Island* (Sistrom & Farrow, 1942) initiated the convention of the commanding officer explaining war based upon the American myth — the call of duty, the quest for freedom, etc. Moore's failure to explain is a significant departure from that convention and therefore subsumes a questionable ideology beneath personal integrity. The quest for understanding is an individual one, just as the reason for fighting is personal. In Galloway's final voice-over, he says, "They went to war because their country ordered them to. But in the end they fought not for their country or their flag. They fought for each other."

Clearly, representations such as Moore's depart from the stoic, courageous and virile fighting men depicted in war films of the 1940s and 1950s. Some have suggested that such representations are commiserate with an overall softening of masculine representations in general, a movement from the hard-bodied representations of the Reagan era (Jeffords, 1994) to a more conflicted masculinity that emerged during the Clinton era (Malin, 2005). Indeed, we would be hard pressed to imagine Robert Mitchum, John Wayne, Humphrey Bogart, or any number of yesterday's matinee idols sobbing openly for lost troopers as Moore does in a final sequence. They would alibi a single sniffle to a cold or a misty eye to an errant cinder. But genre films could not remain vital if their narrative patterns did not change according to the dictates of culture, and I suspect that changing representations such as Hal Moore, Joe Galloway, and Troy Barlow are precisely what Malin had in mind when he wrote: "If the masculine hero of the '90s offered a conflicted blend of hypermasculine toughness and new age sensitivity, the September 11 hero is still more profoundly conflicted, eminently heroic and eminently vulnerable" (p. 146). I would add that his heroism also is unconsummated, i.e., we have representations of the capacity for heroism, the capacity for greatness, but this capacity is often subverted by a context in which it cannot flourish.

In a 2004 *New York Times* article by Sharon Waxman, New York University cinema studies professor Robert Sklar responded to the suggestion of softening masculine representations:

> It's certainly possible that the second gulf war is going to turn the cultural definition of masculinity in new ways. We're seeing a kind of sacrifice and heroism by young people that we haven't seen in a long time in this country. That's going to impact on the kinds of stories screenwriters write, and the kind of actors we need to play them [quoted on p. E1].

Sklar's prediction provides an appropriate segue into the rest of this essay, which considers representations of soldiers after the beginning of the Second Persian Gulf War. Although Sklar did not elaborate precisely on the impact he expected, it seems that the damaged and often morally bankrupt representations we have seen since the beginning of that war do not reflect the "sacrifice and heroism" that he had in mind.

Tension

While Sam Mendes's *Jarhead* (Mercer, 2005) depicts the 1991 Persian Gulf War, it was released during the Second Persian Gulf War, and makes clear reference to the ongoing conflict. The film's protagonist Anthony Swofford (Jake Gyllenhaal) is not morally heroic as are the three kings, not introspective as are Moore and Galloway, and not self-consciously ambiguous or psychologically perverted as are the representations in the post–Vietnam films of the late 1970s and early 1980s. Mostly, he's just frustrated.

Jarhead follows Swofford through basic training and deployment in Saudi Arabia and Iraq. Visually and dialogically the opening references the training sequence in *Full Metal Jacket*. Thus, the ghost is summoned, and we are invited to compare Swofford's plight to that of *Jacket*'s Private Joker. The drill instructor asks Swofford if his father served in Vietnam, if he "had the balls to die there." As was true of *Three Kings*, in which embedded journalist Adriana Cruz (Nora Dunn) asks a group of soldiers if they feel they have "exorcized the ghost of Vietnam with a clear moral imperative," the immediate reference to Vietnam in *Jarhead* is explicit, positioning the film as a direct comment on previous representations of that war.

Despite his initial fear that enlistment was a mistake, Swofford eventually joins the elite sniper platoon, Surveillance and Target Acquisition (STA) and becomes obsessed with the "pink mist"—a combination of blood and brain matter that explodes from the head of an enemy struck by a sniper's bullet. In terms of the traditional patriarchal narrative pattern of tension and release (McClary, 1991), the pink mist as metaphor for ejaculation is unmistakable: the climactic moment following the discharge of the phallic rifle. This pattern is significant because reference to sexual tension and masturbation permeates the film. The phrase "getting some" (a colloquialism for having sex) is synonymous with killing Iraqis, but no one ever gets any. Thus masturbation — sexual release without purpose — becomes a key metaphor for unconsummated heroism.

The conflation of unconsummated sex and unconsummated heroism is imaged clearly at the film's end. Swofford and his partner Troy (Peter Sarsgaard) have won a mission to kill two high-ranking Iraqis stationed in an airfield control tower. But just as they are about to fire, bombers destroy the target. As the demoralized men return to base, they hear screaming and suspect a Republican Guard attack. Their excitement at the prospect of action is dashed, however, when they discover that the screaming comes from their own squad celebrating the war's end. "I never shot my rifle," says Swofford. "You do it now," replies Troy. He does, and the he squad follows suit. We see the entire group of shirtless soldiers with their automatic weapons braced waist-high against their bodies at forty-five degree angles firing into the air in one, massive, military circle-jerk.

In the film's penultimate sequence, the marines bus through a celebratory welcome-home parade. Here, the ghost of Vietnam is made flesh in the person of a bedraggled Vietnam veteran, who boards the bus to congratulate the returning heroes. He is unshaven, his hair disheveled and greasy, and his open fatigue shirt is soiled and tattered. "Semper-fi, Marines. Ooh-rah" he says. We read in the faces of Swofford and the others a mixture of concern and repulsion borne of fear that they are perhaps his legacy. The veteran sits as Tom Waits' plaintive "Soldier's Things" plays, a song about a veteran selling wartime memorabilia — his boots and medals — from a box for a dollar.

Thus, just as the film opens with reference to Vietnam, so too does it close. It does so without reference to triumph of good over evil; without reference to virile, courageous deeds designed to protect helpless civilians. The veteran's presence undermines the victory celebration, and as "Soldier's Things" plays, a montage reveals Swofford's squad members in their various post–Desert Storm lives: stocking grocery shelves, attending a fair, fighting the current insurgency, drunk in an empty bar with a prostitute, delivering a board-room presentation. We see Swofford rejected by his girlfriend. We see him attend Troy's funeral. In contrast to the convention of closing, triumphal voice-overs or rolling copy common in classic war films, Swofford's final voice-over does not speak of heroism. It speaks of the inability to transcend the experience of war. It speaks of frustration. It speaks of non-resolution: "Every war is different," he says. "Every war is the same." And in an unambiguous reference to the current Iraq War, the closing words are: "And all the jarheads killing and dying, they will always be me. We are still in the desert." Thus the myth of the American soldier becomes the reality of unconsummated heroism.

Despite the absence of heroic closure, despite the implicit prediction of quagmire and the disturbing implications associated with protagonists obsessed with killing for its own sake, *Jarhead* is not overtly negative about the American presence in, or motivation for, Desert Storm. While they may not sport a John Wayne brand of heroism, Mendes's protagonists also do not actively subvert such heroism as did so many representations in post–Vietnam films such as *Platoon* (Golden & Stone, 1986), *Apocalypse Now, Full Metal Jacket, Casualties of War* (Engelen & De Palma, 1989) and *Deer Hunter*. In ways conventional to classical examples of the combat genre, Mendes's protagonists share stories and pictures of girlfriends or wives, support each other during crises, monitor each other's behavior when it is inappropriate or dangerous, and are generally representations of likeable men honoring a contract. While the protagonists are mindful of the ghost of Vietnam (particularly in the person of the veteran who rides their bus), it has not yet possessed them entirely. To digress briefly, the same can be said for the protagonists in *Three Kings*. Although *Three Kings* represented the U.S. Military as unprincipled and willing to sacrifice innocent civilians for political ends, the protagonists themselves experience moral awakening that engenders humanitarian selflessness.

With this in mind, it is hard to miss the representational shift of seismic proportions in films depicting the Second Persian Gulf War (also called the Iraq War) released in the last two years: *Redacted* (Wagner & De Palma, 2007), *In the Valley of Elah* (Haggis, 2007), and *Stop-Loss* (Pierce, 2008). In these, heroism is not only unconsummated. It is impossible.

The Man in the Gray Cotton T-shirt

Redacted, Brian DePalma's controversial jeremiad that transplants the events of his 1989 film *Casualties of War* from Vietnam to Iraq, recounts the pre-meditated rape, murder and immolation of a 15-year-old Iraqi girl and the murder of her family by two soldiers, Reno Flake (Patrick Carroll) and B.B. Rush (Daniel Sherman), part of a squad operating a checkpoint at an entrance to Samarra.

The protagonist Lawyer McCoy hopes to prevent the crime. Hence, he begins with heroic intentions. However, he is outnumbered and intimidated. Flake and Rush ignore his repeated pleas to stop and subsequently bully him into silence. The crime creates an international scandal, which forces an investigation during which the interrogators question McCoy's credibility.

The main narrative ends in an American restaurant with a celebration of McCoy's "heroic" homecoming. His friends insist that he share a "war story." In tears, he recounts the crime, confessing his shame at not having prevented it. His friends, unwilling or unable to validate his feelings or respond in some appropriate way, gloss over the confession by seeking to reestablish the celebratory atmosphere, reminding everyone that they are honoring "a war hero." Thus, the term *hero* itself is drained of meaning, and we are left with a protagonist whose only reward for his service is self-loathing. *Redacted*, then, reverses Donald's (1992) definition of the war hero as one who protects innocent civilians, and presents, instead, soldiers who abuse them — either directly or through inaction.

During the celebration, McCoy confesses his inability to live with his memories. His statement recalls (as do Swofford's final words in *Jarhead*) earlier filmic representations of damaged masculinities' difficulties re-assimilating to civilian life — difficulties that work to complicate the myth of the "returning hero." Such representations were prevalent in depictions of World War II (Cohen 1997) (e.g., *The Best Years of Our Lives* [Goldwyn & Wyler, 1946]; *The Man in the Gray Flannel Suit* [Zanuck & Johnson, 1956]). Though different in kind, they also are present in films about Vietnam such as *Coming Home* (Hellman & Ashby, 1978) and *Born on the Fourth of July* (Stone, 1989).

Protagonists of the 1940s and 1950s recognized the conflict between their soldier-selves and their social-selves. For example, Tom Rath (Gregory Peck) says in *Suit*, "One day a man's catching the 8:26, and then suddenly he's killing people. Then a few weeks later he's catching the 8:26 again." Al Stephenson (Fredric March) comments similarly in *The Best Years of our Lives*: "Last year it was killing; this year it's making money." Nonetheless, these protagonist accepted the contradiction as necessary and in many cases looked nostalgically upon their soldier-selves amidst the confusing new world with which they must now cope. And although previous filmic examples sometimes represent secondary characters who ultimately are destroyed by their war experiences, the protagonists nearly always discover pathways to reintegration. In the end of *The Best Years of our Lives* and *The Man in the Gray Flannel Suit*, for example, the protagonists are "rescued" — re-civilized, so to speak — by the imposed constraint of domestic life (usually via a new or a revitalized marriage).

As one might expect, redemption differs somewhat in depictions of returning Vietnam soldiers. Nonetheless, there is redemption of a kind. Constrained by popular sentiment, representations of soldiers returning from Vietnam cannot discover self-esteem in the knowledge of a "just cause." Paradoxically, they often find it in precisely the reverse — in the epiphany that the cause was unjust. In *Born on the Fourth of July*, Ron Kovic (Tom Cruise) finds his pathway to redemption and re-assimilation through political activism. Just as he is about to deliver an antiwar message to a large audience, he closes the film with the words "I'm home; maybe we're home"; and in *Coming Home*, Luke Martin (Jon Voight) finds redemption in much the same way.

But for *Redacted*'s protagonist Lawyer McCoy there is no such pathway. As he shares his shame with his friends, one of them takes his photograph. The main narrative closes with this static, tearful image of McCoy and his wife looking into the lens (and directly at the viewing subject). The static image, then, becomes a metaphor for his inability to overcome his pain. The pain is frozen in time just as the image is frozen in pixels.

Brotherhood Betrayed

In many ways, the chances for rehabilitation and re-assimilation, indeed, for hope itself, are even bleaker in *In the Valley of Elah*. The film follows Vietnam veteran Hank Deerfield (Tommy Lee Jones) as he discovers the moral, emotional, and physical destruction of his son, Mike Deerfield (Jonathan Tucker), who has been reported AWOL upon his return from Iraq. Mike is subsequently found dead — stabbed, butchered and burnt — in a field near his stateside Army base. What began as Hank's search for his son, then, becomes a search for his son's killers. Through the father's eyes we learn of Mike's emotionally debilitating tour of duty, witness the chilling disregard for life and suffering that it engenders, and learn how it sets the stage for his murder at the hands of a close friend and fellow soldier.

A comparison between old and new, between Vietnam and Iraq, between father and son, is unavoidable here. Hank Deerfield represents a version of traditional masculinity reminiscent of that identified by Susan Jeffords (1994) as prevalent in representations from the Reagan era. He is quick and proficient with his fists (or car doors, or baseball bats); he is stoic (barely able to say thank you to Emily Sanders (Charlize Theron), the detective who helps him bring his son's killers to justice); he is uncomfortable with emotion ("I can't stand here and listen to you cry," he tells his wife as she sobs into the phone at the news of her murdered son); and he moves effortlessly through traditional male spaces such as military bases, barracks locker rooms, and strip clubs.

But this world and the soldiers who inhabit it have changed. A key theme here is Hank's inability to understand what has happened to the military code he lives by ("You do not fight beside a man and then do that to him," he tells Sanders) and to his son upon whom service has taken such a profound and destructive toll. Via a video recorded on Mike's cell phone, Hank learns that Mike was traumatized by killing an Iraqi child with his Humvee. This key transformative event is responsible for turning Mike into someone his father can no longer recognize. And without delving too deeply into Freudian psychology, it is important to note that it is Mike's desire to please the Father that makes him suppress his "feminine" response to the incident. Thus he is transformed from a sensitive son crying out for help into a callous, cold-blooded killer. He tortures wounded captives for pleasure and for the amusement of his "brothers," whose gleeful response indicates their own, similar moral bankruptcy. Finally, this loss of a moral compass, precipitated by his orders (whether those orders come from the Father or his surrogate, the military) leads to Mike's murder at the hands of one of his own "brothers."

With this in mind, it is significant that Detective Emily Sanders, the leading female role, most accurately characterizes the loss of moral constraint that allows Corporal Steve Penning (Wes Chatham) to murder Mike Deerfield during a drunken brawl not long after they return from Iraq. Note the similarity of her assessment of the crime as she interrogates Penning and the words of Tom Rath (see above) in *The Man in the Gray Flannel Suit* despite the 51-year separation. She says, "I guess back in Iraq things are different. I mean, somebody makes you mad you can deal with it, right?... React or die; react or die. Isn't that what they say?... You're there one day, back here another. I gotta tell you, somebody comes charging at me, I'd reach for my weapon."

Although Sanders' statement echoes the assimilation theme seen in *The*

Man in the Gray Flannel Suit and *The Best Years of Our Lives*, here, the returning soldier's destructive tendencies are so exacerbated by military policy that he is unable to reconcile his training with the constraints imposed by civilized society. And the fact that one of Mike's "brothers" who fought beside him later kills him in cold blood and watches while another "brother" butchers his body, sets it on fire, and then goes to a local greasy spoon for a chicken dinner, is a stunning departure from previous representations of American soldiers. It represents the complete breakdown of the mechanism identified above, whereby repositioning allegiance from country to comrade preserves the possibility of heroism despite a negative attitude toward the war.

The departure leaves Hank (and the viewer) with the profoundly bleak assessment that closes the film. In an early sequence, as Hank travels to find his son, he sees the American flag flying upside down in front of a local school. He stops to right the flag and instructs the custodian, who is from El Salvador: "You know what it means when a flag flies upside down?... It's an international distress signal.... It means we're in a whole lot of trouble so come save our ass 'cause we don't have a prayer in hell of saving ourselves." When he learns the details of his son's murder, Hank returns to the school. He replaces its flag with one that his son had sent him from Iraq with a photo of himself and his squad posing in front of it. This time, however, Hank flies the flag upside-down, duct-tapes its ropes to the flagpole, and instructs the custodian to "leave it like that." Thus the mythology customarily evoked by the flag, like that of the American soldier, is subverted — literally turned upside-down. A conventional symbol of freedom, patriotism, and of American heroism, has become a bleak and fervent plea for help — a symbol of desperation.

Identity Lost

Of all the representations of unconsummated heroism discussed here, Brandon King's (Ryan Phillippe) is perhaps the most complicated, made so by the fact that King's behavior presents an utter paradox. On the one hand, we are introduced to a protagonist who is the image of homespun, patriotic fervor. The film opens on King and his men singing Toby Keith's anthem to 9/11 retribution "Courtesy of the Red White and Blue," with its chest-thumping references to sacrifice for "ol' glory" and "the land of the free." The song accompanies a montage sequence that includes soldiers readying their weapons and practicing hand-to-hand combat, the words *Death before Dishonor* tattooed on a soldier's back, and a soldier being baptized. Shortly following these images is King's homecoming parade. Flanked by cheerleaders marching to a hometown brass band playing "Stars and Stripes Forever," King and his friend Sergeant Steve Shriver (Channing Tatum) ride a cherry-red Cadillac convertible through a cheering throng as blue-eyed blond girls bat their eyes and townspeople shower them with accolades.

Such images notwithstanding, upon learning that he has been stop-lossed, King challenges his commanding officer with the words "Fuck the President." This is a stunning blasphemy with regard to the American soldierly myth, and by the end of the film, this true-blue, hard-fighting, "good-ole-boy" from the heart of Texas has purchased a new identity and comes within moments of crossing the Mexican border to leave the United States behind forever. Having been disillusioned by the psychological and physical toll the war has taken on his friends and comrades, and having been stop-lossed into more of the same, he is ready to deny his identity rather than continue serving what he has come to believe is an unjust cause for a country that has betrayed his trust. But just as he is about to cross the border, love for his hometown and devotion to family stop him, and herein lies the paradox: the characteristics of the country to which he nearly disavows allegiance are what keep him from disavowing that allegiance.

King returns to Iraq having lost the love of country and the devotion to duty foundational to the heroic myth. To keep his identity, he must forfeit his self. In forcing him to return to service, by reneging on the contract he willingly fulfilled, the United States has coercively appropriated his body, but in so doing, has lost his heart.

There's Somethin' Happenin' Here

In sum, this discussion suggests that the myth of the American soldier as described by Donald (1992) has departed markedly from previous cinematic representations that have informed it. While there are still representations that cling to the exceptionalism of the individual American warrior (e.g., *Rambo*; Lerner & Stallone, 2008), even positive representations of the twenty-first century soldier have become more vulnerable, more human, and more humble than his mid–twentieth-century counterpart. Hal Moore is in tears at having survived his troops; John Miller wants only to return to his wife and the life of a small town schoolteacher. Such representations are very different in kind from John Wayne's Sergeant Stryker sacrificing his life to plant a flag on Iwo Jima or Robert Taylor's Sergeant Bill Dane sacrificing his as he empties a machine gun into a demonized Japanese hoard. Even *The Story of G.I. Joe*, which boasted a departure from guts and glory, could not resist at least one larger-than-life heroic image — that of Robert Mitchum gesturing his troops onward with bayoneted rifle held aggressively overhead. But this century has seen heroism recast. Note, again, the striking example of Eastwood's *Flags of our Fathers*, a film that redefines heroism as an unwanted ideograph thrust upon unremarkable men unwilling to accept it. For them, it is the men with whom they sacrifice and the occasion to which they rise rather than the fact of their rising that makes them heroic.

Further, beyond such generally sympathetic representations, I have identified a recent devolution of American soldierly representations. It moves from patriotic heroism based upon love of country to personal heroism based upon charity and love for one's fellow soldiers. It moves to unconsummated heroism through which individual exceptionalism is denied by technology. It finally culminates in the destruction of all things heroic due to the loss of moral compass on the part of the nation and its military policies.

Suggesting that this shift in war film discourse represents an ongoing trend is clearly premature, and the most recent examples discussed here are not enough to establish a new generic pattern. Nonetheless, I would suggest that they posit the possibility of notable change, probably seeded by post–Vietnam representations of moral ambiguity and outright disillusionment found in the films of the late 1970s and 1980s. Despite a brief interruption of such ambiguity and disillusionment at the turn of this century with films such as *Saving Private Ryan*, *We Were Soldiers* and *Black Hawk Down* (Bruckheimer & Scott, 2001), we have seen in recent representations of the Iraq War, very specific and very damning indictments of the United States Military and the United States Government, and their culpability in creating the debilitated, and at times perverted, masculinities they limn. Just as the war itself has become wildly unpopular, so too have the representations of the men who fight it become wildly un-heroic. Thus Solomon's (1976) assertion that "[The war] film tends to take its theme ready-made from the prevailing public view of war at the time of its production" (p. 246) is confirmed.

It is remarkable — indeed unprecedented — that such consistent and intense filmic criticism should occur while the war represented is being waged. Consider Schatz's (1981) statement that "[I]n the war genre, the prosocial aspects of supporting a war effort directly ruled out any subversion of even the serious questioning of the hero's attitudes. War films that did question values were made after the war and generally are considered as a subgenre" (p. 40). Writing about World War II combat films, Casper (2007, p. 332) makes a similar point when he suggests that an "anti-military stance, especially in regard to leaders" did not become common until the late '50s. Note, too, that Hollywood did not begin its invective against the war in Vietnam — arguably the most unpopular, devastating and divisive war in our history — for five years after troop withdrawal, and the only combat narrative film made about Vietnam *during* the war, *The Green Berets,* was nothing short of a chest-thumping, flag waving homage, despite the country's burgeoning anti-war sentiment.

Thus, current negative representations of the soldiers fighting our most recent and ongoing war move beyond the usual rhetoric of traditional anti-war subgenre with regard to their temporal placement and their intensity. *Redacted* and *In the Valley of Elah* offer an unprecedented indictment of the represented soldiers' most basic humanity, while *Stop-Loss* provides an unprecedented representation of righteous insubordination and loss of self. If Braudy (2003) is correct when he suggests that in the years during and following World War II America's "search for models of social behavior ... focused, as it never had before, on the examples the movies furnished" (p. 514), and if Solomon (1976) is correct when he writes, "In time of war ... the motion picture industry recognizes a certain moral duty ... and is, so to speak, drafted into the war effort" (p. 245), then it is clear that something has happened here — not only to Hollywood's recognition of a certain moral duty, but to popular notions of what is and is not acceptable as popular entertainment (and social comment) during the time of war. In *Redacted, Elah,* and *Stop-Loss* we have witnessed a new kind of American soldier: his is potential heroism made impotent — bereft of purpose and without moral compass. "They shouldn't send heroes to places like Iraq," says Bonner (Jake McLaughlin) of his murdered friend in *In the Valley of Elah*. "Everything there is fucked-up."

It is this perception of everything — the military, the government, the Iraqis, the strategy, the motives, etc. — being irreparably "fucked up" that denies the protagonists their heroism. Despite the popular rhetoric "support the troops," the message here is that if the endeavor is not underpinned by the same traditional values that informed classical war films, then heroism is not possible. Hence, these representations have moved beyond patriotic and personal heroism, beyond unconsummated heroism to empty heroism — to a point at which the heroic signifier itself is drained of meaning by the nature and purpose of the war and the powers that wage it.

References

Auster, A. (2002). *Saving Private Ryan* and American triumphalism. *Journal of Popular Film and Television, 30*(2), 98–104.

Bruady, L. (2003). *From Chivalry to Terrorism: War and the Changing Nature of Masculinity*. New York: Vintage.

Bruckheimer, J. (Producer), R. Scott (Producer/Director). (2001). *Black Hawk Down* [Motion picture]. United States: Columbia Pictures.

Bryce, I., and A.L. Segan (Producers), S. Spielberg (Director). (1998). *Saving Private Ryan* [Motion picture]. United States: DreamWorks.

Casper, D. (2007). *Postwar Hollywood: 1946–1962*. Malden, MA: Blackwell.

Cimino, M. (Producer/Director). (1978). *The Deer Hunter* [Motion picture]. United States: EMI Films.

Cohan, L. (Producer), W. Wellman (Director) (1945). *The Story of G.I. Joe* [Motion picture]. United States: Lester Cowan Productions.
Cohen, S. (1997). *Masked Men: Masculinity and the Movies in the Fifties*. Bloomington: Indiana University Press.
Coppola, F. F. (Producer/Director). (1979). *Apocalypse Now* [Motion picture]. United States: Zoetrope Studios.
Donald, R. R. (1992). Masculinity and machismo in Hollywood's war films. In S. Craig (Ed.) *Men, Masculinity, and the Media* (124–136). Newbury Park, CA: Sage.
Eastwood, C. (Producer/Director). (2006). *Flags of Our Fathers* [Motion picture]. United States: DreamWorks SKG.
Engelen, P., and E. Morricone (Producers), B. De Palma (Director). (1989). *Casualties of War* [Motion picture]. United States: Columbia Pictures.
Golden, P. (Producer), O. Stone (Director/Writer). (1986). *Platoon* [Motion picture]. United States: Cinema 86.
Goldwyn, S. (Producer), W. Wyler (Director). (1946). *The Best Years of Our Lives* [Motion picture]. United States: Samuel Goldwyn Company.
Goodman, G. (Producer), D. O. Russell (Director). (1999). *Three Kings* [Motion picture]. United States: Warner Bros. Pictures.
Haggis, P. (Director/Producer). (2007). *In the Valley of Elah* [Motion picture]. United States: Blackfriars Bridge Films.
Hellman, J. (Producer), H. Ashby (Director). (1978). *Coming Home* [Motion picture]. United States: Jerome Hellman Productions.
Jeffords, S. (1994). *Hard Bodies: American Masculinity in the Reagan Era*. New Brunswick, NJ: Rutgers University Press.
Kotcheff, K. (Director). (1982). *First Blood* [Motion picture]. United States: Anabasis.
Kubrick, S. (Producer/Director). (1987). *Full Metal Jacket* [Motion picture]. United States: Warner Bros.
Lacy, M. (2003). War, cinema, and moral anxiety. *Alternatives 28*, 611–636.
Lemley, J., and A. L. Schmidt (Producers), R. Wallace (Director). (2002). *We Were Soldiers* [Motion picture]. United States: Paramount.
Lerner, A. (Producer), S. Stallone (Director). (2008). *Rambo* [Motion picture]. United States: Lionsgate.
Malin, B. J. (2005). *American Masculinity Under Clinton*. New York: Peter Lang.
McClary, S. (1991). *Feminine Endings: Music, Gender and Sexuality*. Minneapolis: Minnesota University Press.
Mercer, S. (Producer), S. Mendes (Director) (2005). *Jarhead* [Motion picture]. United States: Universal Pictures.
Newsinger, J. (1993). "Do you walk the walk?": Aspects of masculinity in some Vietnam war films. In P. Kirkham and J. Thumim (Eds.), *You Tarzan: Masculinity, Movies and Men* (126–136). London: Lawrence & Wishart.
Pierce, K. (Producer/Director). (2008). *Stop-loss* [Motion picture]. United States: Paramount Pictures.
Rasmussen, K., and S. D. Downey (1991). Dialectical disorientation in Vietnam war films: Subversion of the mythology of war. *Quarterly Journal of Speech, 77*, 176–195.
Schary, D. (Producer), T. Garnett (Director). (1943). *Bataan* [Motion picture]. United States: Metro-Goldwyn-Mayer.
Schatz, T. (1981). *Hollywood Genres: Formulas, Filmmaking, and the Studio System*. Boston: McGraw Hill.
Sistrom, J. (Producer), J. Farrow (Director). (1942). *Wake Island* [Motion picture]. United States: Paramount Pictures.
Solomon, S. J. (1976). *Beyond Formula: American Film Genres*. San Diego, CA: Harcourt Brace Jovanovich.

Stephens, M. M. (Producer), T. Malick (Director). (1998). *The Thin Red Line* [Motion picture]. United States: Fox 2000 Pictures.

Stone, O. (Producer/Director). (1989). *Born on the Fourth of July* [Motion picture]. United States: Universal Pictures.

Wagner, T. (Producer), B. De Palma (Director/Writer). (2007). *Redacted* [Motion picture]. United States: The Film Farm.

Wanger, W. (Producer), R. Enright (Director). (1943). *Gung Ho!: The Story of Carlson's Making Island Raiders* [Motion picture]. United States: Universal Pictures.

Waxman, S. (2004, July 1). Hollywood's he-men are bumped by sensitive guys; six-pack abs not required for new masculine ideal. *The New York Times*, p. E1.

Wayne, M. (Producer), R. Kellogg & J. Wayne (Directors) (1968). *The Green Berets* [Motion picture]. United States: Warner Bros./Seven Arts.

Zanuck, D. (Producer), N. Johnson (Director). (1956). *The Man in the Gray Flannel Suit* [Motion picture]. United States: 20th Century–Fox.

DRAWN-OUT BATTLES: EXPLORING WAR-RELATED MESSAGES IN ANIMATED CARTOONS

Rekha Sharma

Although political cartoons in newspapers and magazines have served to convey political meaning with the still image for hundreds of years, much less research has focused on messages within animated cartoons. This is perhaps because scholars have discounted animated cartoons as a simplistic type of content aimed only at children, ignoring allegorical meanings, literary allusions, and political references (Chapman, 2001; Knapp, 1996; Van Buren, 2006). In their research review focusing on preschoolers' perceptions of cartoon violence, Peters and Blumberg (2002) discussed the value of applying communication theories such as Cultivation, Social Learning, Excitation Transfer/Arousal, and Cue Theory. Their review did not reveal much about how adults might interact with or consume political meanings in animated cartoons except to state that co-viewing with parents and educators could help children form impressions about the morality of using violence to solve conflicts. The bulk of insights regarding animation, propaganda, and political commentary have emerged from a critical-cultural tradition that has produced rich descriptive data and insightful interpretations.

This chapter provides an overview of representative research related to messages about war in animated cartoons. First, I explore the research literature pertaining to overt political propaganda in animated cartoons produced during the First and Second World Wars. Second, I look at the more subtle — albeit incisive — messages in animated cartoons created during the decades of the Cold War. Third, I will discuss the commentary and themes of animated cartoons that were developed near the end of the Cold War and into the 1990s. Fourth, I describe contemporary trends in animation, specifically as they relate to cartoons about the September 11, 2001, terrorist attacks and the War in Iraq. I conclude with suggestions for future research of war-related messages in animated cartoons.

The Overt Propaganda of World War I and World War II

During the First and Second World Wars, animated cartoons were employed strategically to convey political messages about patriotic behavior and the necessity of maintaining national allegiances to resist immoral enemies. Ward (2005) noted that scholars have concentrated their research on live-action films and newsreels, but they overlooked the accompanying animated cartoons that audiences watched in theaters. Some disagreement exists over whether these types of cartoons might best be categorized by their aesthetics (e.g., animation as a production technique) or in terms of content (e.g., political satire or propaganda) (Ward, 2005). Extending the definition of propaganda beyond government-funded cartoons to include those created by private companies; Ward estimated that 95 percent of the British animated films produced between 1914 and 1918 could be classified as World War I propaganda. Ward noted the themes of these films centered on the simplicity of helping the war effort. Additionally, satirical illustrators and comic strip artists in Great Britain began creating animated films to ridicule Germany and the Kaiser, and to raise the morale of soldiers and people on the home front (Bendazzi, 1994). The animation techniques, exaggerated actions and imagery, and child-like rhymes reinforced the function of these propaganda films, which was to reduce complex issues into partisan arguments, sometimes sacrificing accuracy for impact or audiences' ease of comprehension (Ward, 2005).

Prior to the entry of the United States into World War I, American animated cartoon serials depicted the European war as adventurous and soldiers as valiant and daring (Kornhaber, 2007). But in 1917, U.S. animated shorts fell into two camps: Some presented the war in graphic detail as animated documentaries geared to adults, while others depicted the war in sanitized, unrealistic, comedic ways that were less traumatic for audiences of children (Kornhaber). According to Kornhaber, in the years after the armistice, animation tended to combine elements of realism with fantastical abstractions. Unlike earlier animators, artists such as Otto Messmer and Walt Disney had direct experience with war. Messmer's cartoons about Felix the Cat combined gruesome violence with physical elasticity and imperviousness to death and deformity. In these cartoons, war was depicted as a game in which death was commonplace but impermanent, and personal determination was the key to victory. In this way, Kornhaber continued, animated cartoons helped naturalize the unnatural experience of war.

It also should be noted that Messmer's *Felix the Cat* cartoons influenced Japanese and Korean animators in the 1930s (Kim, 2006). For example, Japanese filmmaker Mitsuyo Seo made a series of animated movies about a monkey named Sankichi, one of which was set during the Chinese-Japanese war and "featured the Imperial Army efficiently attacking a fortress which was poorly protected by Chinese Pandas" (Bendazzi, 1994, p. 105). The theme of Japanese militarism was embedded in the country's educational, documentary, and propaganda films from the start of the war with China in 1933 and persisted throughout the Second World War, Bendazzi noted. Just as it did in the United States, animation also played an important role in the military action taking place in the Pacific region during World War II. Strict controls of the Japanese military over filmmaking and the difficulty of finding employment due to discrimination led some Korean animators to join Japanese film companies to create fascist propaganda (Kim, 2006). These animated films, concluded Kim, attempted to justify Imperialist Japan's colonization of other Asian countries, including those on the Korean peninsula, and to liberate them from Western forces.

Moreover, during World War II, Theodor Seuss Geisel ("Dr. Seuss"), Philip D. Eastman, and Munro Leaf—who would later be known for their children's books—were recruited to work in the animation branch of the U.S. Army's Information and Education Division to make educational films for American troops (Nel, 2007). Reasoning that the soldiers would only pay attention and learn if they could also be entertained, Geisel, Eastman, and Leaf created the character of Private SNAFU, a negative example of behaviors soldiers should avoid. The *Private SNAFU* training films were classified by the government as "Top Secret," and even the workers in the ink and paint departments at the animation studios were only able to view a limited number of cells without wordage so they would not be able to discern the content of the cartoons (Sigall, 2005).

The *Private SNAFU* films educated servicemen about topics such as the dangers of malaria and fascism, the importance of patriotism and obeying authority, and the need to preserve military intelligence and American ideals. But Nel (2007) pointed out that the films propagated sexist and racist attitudes about women and Japanese people as well. The films' creators purposely depicted women as prostitutes, strippers, and spies to make the films racy enough to hold soldiers' attention while illustrating the dangers of venereal disease and general indiscretion. But, argued Nel, their use of negative Asian stereotypes contradicted their condemnation of prejudice against Black and

Jewish people, rendering otherwise progressive propaganda latently oppressive. Arguably, according to Nel, some of the positive and negative themes and narrative styles from the *Private SNAFU* films influenced the creators' later literary messages about good behavior, racial diversity, and the consequences of war. What remains significant, Nel concluded, was that the fathers who may have watched the *SNAFU* films could have read books by the same authors to their children, contributing to the younger generation's ideas about American cultural identity and the nature of war.

Portrayals of the Other

American animation during World War II not only cultivated attitudes about nationalism and the patriotic duty to serve in the U.S. military or assist in supportive activities on the home front, but it inspired the creation of racist or xenophobic messages about ethnic groups perceived as the enemy — on both sides of the conflict. Germans under the Third Reich were displeased with their own animated features and preferred the movement, colors, and overall quality of Disney films produced in the United States. So when the Dutch National-Socialists in the Department van Volksvoorlichting en Kunsten (the equivalent of Joseph Goebbels' Propaganda Ministry) decided to produce an animated anti–Semitic film advocating racial purity, they hoped to increase the prestige of the Dutch film industry (Barten & Groeneveld, 1994). In the film, a rhinoceros arrives in a kingdom, preaching liberty and promoting cross-species procreation to the other animals. The animal miscegenation leads to chaos, and the rhino becomes drunk with power and greed, appointing his relatives as tax collectors. The other animals eventually become dissatisfied and kill the rhino and his kin. Although the eugenic message of the film was a far cry from the Mickey Mouse movies that the Nazi leaders envied, the film was praised as advancement in Dutch animation (Barten & Groeneveld).

Although American animators at Disney, MGM, and other studios criticized and satirized Adolph Hitler's plans for creating a "master race," they continued to characterize African Americans in stereotypical ways (Lehman, 2001). During the 1940s, Lehman observed, Black servicemen were portrayed as either musically inclined or inept at their duties, and they were often drawn with excessively large lips and eyes. Following the attack on Pearl Harbor, the paradox of American racism in a war against the Nazis extended to portrayals of Imperial Japan, Nazi Germany, and the Communist Soviet Union, respectively dubbed the Yellow, Brown, and Red Perils (MacDougall, 1999). Although several animated cartoons depicted the Nazis and the Communists in negative ways, MacDougall argued that portrayals of the Japanese were especially vicious (buck teeth, slanted eyes, and thick glasses), and Japanese people were likened to apes, mad dogs, vipers, and "an octopus stretching its tentacles across the Pacific" (p. 62).

But as the wartime alliance between the United States and Russia gave way to Cold War tensions, animated films were used to shift the negative sentiments about the Japanese and the Nazis onto the lurking threat of Communist domination: "The bestial savagery and mindless obedience that had been associated with the Japanese, and the mad ambition and diabolical cunning assigned to the Nazis, were now united in America's nightmare image of Soviet Communism" (MacDougall, 1999, p. 68). The Cold War, Vietnam, and Subversive Political Commentary following World War II, the perceived Communist threat to the United States was manifested in a series of political and military actions that led to hostilities in the 1950s and tension that extended well into the 1980s. American and British animators addressed the simmering conflict and hysteria about possible infiltration by Communist forces as well as worries about the dangers of escalation into an all-out nuclear war.

As part of its covert methods to wage psychological warfare against the Soviets, the U.S. Central Intelligence Agency hired American filmmaker Louis de Rochemont and British animators John Halas and Joy Batchelor to make an animated film based on George Orwell's *Animal Farm*, a satirical allegory of the Bolshevik Revolution (Leab, 2005). However, the U.S. government ignored likely interpretations that Orwell, a Socialist, was actually criticizing both capitalist totalitarianism and Communism. Rather, they conceived of *Animal Farm* as an anti–Communist text that would work effectively as propaganda against Communist tyranny and corruption (Leab).

But in the 1950s, animated cartoons about war and politics were moving away from movie theaters and into living rooms due to the proliferation of the television. Chapman (2001) argued that animator Chuck Jones embedded his political philosophies about the Cold War in the animated Warner Bros. series *Road Runner and Coyote,* which ran from 1949 until 1980, and that the messages contained in the cartoon meshed with the containment policy advocated by American advisor George F. Kennan. According to Chapman, the U.S. Cold War policy of containment equated to halting the expansionist ambitions of the Soviet Union. Road Runner and Wile E. Coyote embodied the two countries, and each episode communicated the theme that the aggressor would always lose the conflict. Chapman suggested Americans could identify with the consistently vigilant Road Runner who calmly deflected the Coyote's aggression. And, observed Chapman, the cartoon portrayed the Soviet Union as the Coyote: fanatical, dangerous, and ultimately self-destructive. According to Chapman, the recurring theme of the Coyote pursuing the Road Runner and destroying himself instead of his prey mirrored Kennan's belief that the Soviet Union would bring about its own undoing without U.S. military intervention.

Chuck Jones also created the character of Marvin the Martian for Warner Bros. in 1948 (Birdwell, 2001). Birdwell argued that the character and his conflicts with other Warner Bros. mainstays such as Bugs Bunny and Daffy Duck were used to criticize the Cold War, the missile crisis, the space race, and the possibility of widespread destruction, disease, and deformity that would follow a nuclear war. According to Birdwell, the cartoon conveyed the message that no one could win such a war, and that political posturing and endangering soldiers' lives was irresponsible.

Birdwell (2001) pointed out that these animated cartoons about war were significantly different from World War II animation in which Americans felt they were fighting a just war against a known enemy. Instead, he argued, the ever-present specter of a Communist invasion and Americans' inability to easily identify Communist infiltrators were reflected in the physical characteristics of the ant-like Marvin the Martian. According to Birdwell:

> Marvin is a denizen of a **red** planet, who wears a **red** shirt and sports a green helmet reminiscent of the expansionist Roman Empire. A faceless creature from Mars, Marvin reflected the perceptions of the Soviet Union many Americans held, that it was a country bent on global domination. Marvin wants more. A sneaky villain who zooms into the *mise-en-scene* by surprise, he wears sneakers festooned with red circles on the ankles. His helmet and Roman skirt are green, representing the envy he has of other planets who would compete with Mars. Armed with weapons of incredible destruction and a will to use them, he is bent on conquering the galaxy, at any cost no matter how inhospitable a planet may be [p. 34].

Birdwell also commented that Marvin's only visible facial feature was "a pair of penetrating eyes that spy on his opponent with a sense of urgency" (p. 35), and that this was an allusion to the paranoia of the times and a specific answer to the Congressional witch hunt designed to smoke out Communist influences in Hollywood.

Another Cold War cartoon, *Rocky and his Friends,* was an animated variety program created in 1958 by Jay Ward and Bill Scott that aired on Thursday evenings to an audience of children and adults (Knapp, 1996). As a political allegory, the characters and multi-episode plotlines of the show conveyed morals about American culture and the Communist threat. The title character, Rocket J. Squirrel, dressed as a World War I flying ace, symbolized the fighting spirit of Americans as well as the speed and strength of the American space program (Knapp). Bullwinkle J. Moose represented the naïveté of Americans as consumers who simply wanted a comfortable life and who took a passive stance on matters of politics. The villains of the show — Boris

Badenov, Natasha Fatale, Mr. Big, and Fearless Leader — collectively represented Communists as enemies of American peace and prosperity.

According to Knapp (1996), most storylines in the show followed the same formula: Rocky and Bullwinkle would receive some unexpected wealth or good luck, Boris and Natasha would disguise themselves to harm Rocky and Bullwinkle and steal the goods for themselves, and the scheme would backfire so that Rocky and Bullwinkle could emerge unscathed. The primary themes, Knapp argued, were warnings to an American audience preoccupied with material excess and lulled by a temporary peace between nations. Tension between the United States and the Soviet Union was a battle between good and evil in which the Communists would always try to infiltrate and sabotage the American way of life. Although good would most certainly triumph, as it did in the show, Americans had to remember the struggle was ongoing and "Americans should never let down their guard" (p. 14).

It was just this kind of rhetoric that was ridiculed in *MAD Magazine*'s "SPY vs SPY" comic strip, a black-and-white satire of Cold War espionage and superhero motifs in the 1960s (Carabas, 2007). The strip fits into this discussion of war-related messages in animated cartoons because it was reproduced in animated form as part of the *MADtv* sketch comedy show for three seasons in the mid–1990s. The cartoon was originally created by Antonio Prohías, who settled in New York City when Fidel Castro seized power in Cuba, and it centered on the causeless, ceaseless battles between a black spy and a white spy. Due to the American Congressional investigations of politically subversive comic books in the 1950s and the subsequent self-censorship of comic book publishers, Prohías used subtle cues and symbols to make his arguments appear innocuous to suspicious government officials. According to Carabas, the black-and-white drawings parodied the "us versus them" dichotomies of other cartoon heroes who wore red, white, and blue to fight menacing others, and the lack of dialogue or context demanded that readers be familiar with real-world political events and literary archetypes to discern the underlying meanings. The bird-like characters evoked and shattered the superhero/spy characterizations in other forms of Cold War rhetoric as well as the simplistic, dichotomous constructions of good and evil. As described by Carabas:

> Within the *MAD* world the fight is the status quo, and the heroes work hard to preserve it no matter what the consequences.... Their plans for reciprocal destruction, however, end up in mutual loss, in draws, or in minor, temporary victories of one or the other of the two protagonists. No final settling of the conflict occurs at the end of a strip and no final resolution of tension takes place. Moreover, no matter how extensively the two heroes injure each other, they appear unharmed and ready for action again at the beginning of the following

strip (another popular culture convention, this time used mostly in animated cartoons) [p. 15].

According to Carabas, the appearance of the female gray spy who outmaneuvers both the black spy and the white spy underscored the need for negotiating the ambiguities of the political tensions rather than forcing complex issues into artificial polarities.

Popularity of animated cartoons with mainstream audiences declined in the 1960s and were relegated to Saturday morning children's programming with very little if any propaganda related to the Korean or Vietnam wars (Raiti, 2007). Indeed, Lehman (2006) noted, the beginning of U.S. involvement in Vietnam did not spark innovation among American animators, who relied heavily on plot devices and animation techniques from the World War II era. The Vietnam-era animators generally did not make overt references to the war because they preferred stories that would not become dated in the years of television network reruns to come, Lehman noted.

However, Lehman (2006) did provide extensive illustrations of how messages about war in animated cartoons changed during the course of the Vietnam conflict. For example, the negative stereotypes and physical caricatures of Asian characters established in World War II worsened in the 1960s and 1970s as the U.S. became more entrenched in Vietnam. From 1959 to 1963, a Terrytoons cartoon series about a mouse named Hashimoto stood as a singular example of sympathetic imagery of Japan in U.S. animation because it depicted Japanese culture in a non-derogatory way, thanks in large part to the character's creator, Bob Kuwahara, a Japanese-American director (Lehman).

Vietnam also caused animators to rethink their heroes' personalities. As Lehman (2006) pointed out, the infallible Bugs Bunny of World War II gave way to an unsuccessful protagonist who sometimes defeated his enemies only to run into difficulties. According to Lehman, the U.S. cartoon *Munro* and the Japanese cartoon *Astro Boy* introduced the militaristic boy or "boy-soldier" as a new kind of protagonist to American audiences in the early 1960s, just around the same time that young U.S. servicemen were entering South Vietnam.

Like other examples of animation from the Cold War era, cartoons during the Vietnam War reflected their creators' fears of annihilation due to military escalation, nuclear weapons, and the extensive duration of the war (Lehman, 2006). Leonardo-Total Television satirized war and violence in *Underdog* by depicting guerrilla warfare techniques similar to those used by the North Vietnamese and the Vietcong, and in a separate episode, by depicting U.S. Cavalry soldiers as incompetent and unsuccessful in their imperialist attempts to kill two Native American characters, observed Lehman. In 1967, MGM's *Tom and Jerry* series featured a commentary on the cyclical, perpetual nature of violence in an episode in which the cat and mouse fought each other with blows to the head, laser weapons, and finally, a bomb. As Lehman described it, the explosion blasted them back to prehistoric times, where the characters continued their dispute while wearing leopard skins and eating bones.

Animators during the Vietnam War era were conflicted about wanting to rely on tried-and-true characterizations and storylines while making statements about war and other social issues of the times (Lehman, 2006). The last episode of Walter Lantz's *Chilly Willy* series featured a battle between the title character (a penguin) and an oil captain in which they fought with cannons and bombs, but emerged relatively unscathed. According to Lehman, "Such scenes illustrate the dilemma of studios, trying to animate traditionally militaristic activity in manners acceptable to parents of the viewers" (p. 155). By 1971, most animation was geared toward children, and television studios tried to maintain a neutral stance on the war, preferring to air less violent and more nostalgic, musical cartoons such as *Pebbles and Bamm Bamm* or *Archie's Funhouse* (Lehman).

Animated Political Commentary After the Cold War

During the 1980s and early 1990s, animated cartoons rarely featured blatant discussions of politics, though they still contained themes, stereotypical portrayals, and narrative conventions that evoked messages and sentiments about war from previous decades, either to reinforce older cultural beliefs or to spur thought about contemporary notions of war, national identity, and political responsibility.

Parenti (1992) voiced concern over the melodramatic constructions of cartoons about superheroes in the 1980s that pitted indisputably good heroes against evil alien intruders. Aside from the oversimplification of conflict, he worried about children who observed animated battles with futuristic lasers and blasters growing into voters who would unquestioningly favor "a large defense establishment with its arsenal of high-tech weaponry ready for use against foreign adversaries" (p. 170) over peaceful negotiation. Although the cartoon *GI Joe: A Real American Hero* did make frequent use of laser battles between American military forces and foreign enemies, Parenti described an occasion in which the American GI Joe team members had to cooperate with their Russian counterparts to fight Cobra, the international terrorist ring that served as the villain in nearly every episode. This storyline, noted Parenti, mirrored the thawing relationship between the United States and the Soviet Union in 1987.

But by the mid–1990s, Dobrow and Gidney (1998) found children's cartoons were still using ambiguously foreign or "non–American" accents to denote villainous characters. Specifically, cartoon villains frequently spoke with British or Slavic accents, or sometimes with American English dialects associated with groups stereotyped as having lower socioeconomic status. Dobrow and Gidney noted their surprise at the number of cartoon villains in their sample who spoke with linguistic features of Russian, Eastern European, or German cultures, an observation which they interpreted as a reflection of American biases from World War II and the Cold War years.

Woodcock (2006) selected *The Simpsons* as an animated cartoon from the 1990s and the present decade that is rich in political commentary. The fictional town of Springfield in which the show is set serves as an example of American deliberative democracy. According to Woodcock, the citizens of Springfield attend town meetings to resolve problems, and all citizens view themselves as equal participants in the democratic process. They also belong to community groups, clubs, and social networks, fostering a sense of community, and the citizens have direct access to mass media outlets such as newspapers and television for expressing their opinions (Woodcock).

In the famous "Who Shot Mr. Burns?" episode, the owner of Springfield's nuclear power facility, was depicted as a power-hungry villain bent on blocking out the sun. This could represent, as Woodcock (2006) suggested, the idea that even utopian democracies must sometimes face challenges. But viewed with an eye toward uncovering war-related messages in animated content, the evil plans of Mr. Burns suggested the dangers of dictatorial power and the ability of a tyrant to disrupt the natural order. Further, it the creators of *The Simpsons* possibly wanted to underscore the absurdity of an ideal American town centered on a nuclear power plant owned by a corporate despot and managed by bumbling workers such as Homer Simpson. This interpretation could parallel Cold War concerns about the instability of peace and the threat of nuclear weapons in the hands of those obsessed with establishing national supremacy and seemingly ignorant of negative consequences.

Japan also struggled to redefine its national culture and policies about the proper course of action for securing an enduring peace in the years after World War II and the Cold War. Fisch (2000) described a 1993 anime film, *Patlabor II*, as a blend of animation, science fiction, and war film genres that questioned Japan's future in the global political sphere and involvement with the United Nations while referencing Japan's involvement in World War II. In the film, director Oshii Mamoru implied the following: Japan had tried to divorce itself from its aggressive role in the Second World War by priding itself on avoiding military conflict in the following years, even resisting pressure to become involved in the Persian Gulf War of the early 1990s (Fisch). However, the film criticized this as a false peace built on the sacrifices of soldiers from other countries and warned that Japan would inevitably face war again if it continued to be apathetic to the problems on the world stage, and, as Fisch noted, the film was critical of American or otherwise foreign influence and sought to awaken Japan from the passivity and paralysis borne of pacifism.

Clearly, then, animated cartoons have not become an irrelevant form of media for discussions or debates about war and politics. However, Raiti (2007) was correct in pointing out the transformation of audiences, who have changed the types of cartoons they watch as well as when and where they watch them. Societal shifts have created changes in preferred aesthetics and narrative styles as well as production modes. Yet as newer types of animation and Internet-based cartoons have reflected a newfound innovation and grassroots participation in the creation of mass media messages about war, these contemporary forms often continue to closely resemble war cartoons of prior eras and political climates.

New Approaches to War-Related Animation

Raiti (2007) identified the lack of government-funded propaganda projects in recent years as a reason for commercial animation studios such as Disney ceasing creation of war-related content. Additionally, Raiti argued, globalization has attenuated nationalist identities. The most convincing reason Raiti provided for the decline in the number of animated features and series centering on war, however, was the Internet, the proliferation of media choices, and the fragmentation of a once-centralized audience. With no single mass audience for animated propaganda after the attacks on September 11, 2001, or during the War in Iraq, animation has instead manifested itself as an explanatory tool in the form of computerized graphics on news broadcasts and as a form of satire on the Internet or on cable television channels considered to be outside the conventional mainstream media (Raiti). For example, Rees (2004) used standard computer clip art images as his main characters in the comic strip *Get Your War On*, an acerbic condemnation of the wars in Iraq and Afghanistan, an animated series that began running online in 2008.

Comedy Central's *South Park* became one of the few overtly war-related cartoons on television when the show parodied Osama bin Laden and his alleged hiding spot in the caves of Afghanistan (Raiti, 2007). The creators of the show employ modern computer programs to mimic the more traditional stop-motion animation techniques of earlier cartoons. Gardiner (2005) noted the crude style of animation in *South Park* and interpreted it as reinforcing the ideology of being able to enjoy the pleasures of the world without taking responsibility for them by never growing up. In this way, the animation of *South Park* purposefully reflects the animation style of most Web-based animations, as the Internet has been a venue for unabashedly expressing controversial viewpoints that are often shunned by mainstream media outlets for legal or ethical reasons. Further, the perpetual youth and irresponsibility could be construed as commentary about the United States and its conflicts with other nations.

In the 1999 animated feature *South Park — Bigger, Longer, and Uncut*, the United States waged war with Canada, mocking earlier animated war propaganda by criticizing the Canadian accent and claiming that Canadians have "beady eyes" (Gardiner, 2005). Underlying this satire were also messages about U.S. imperialism in relation to Canada and the rest of the world (Gardiner). Further, Gardiner argued, the film "corroborate[d] United States' militarism during peacetime by turning Saddam Hussein — during the period between the first and second U.S.–Iraqi wars — into the equivalent of a Hitler with the power to subjugate the globe" (p. 55). To drive the point home with hyperbole and thus subvert it, Hussein was depicted as romantically involved with Satan, emotionally stunted, verbally abusive, and manipulative (Gardiner) — essentially worse than the devil himself.

As Andersen (2005) observed, "War is visually constructed from the mixing and remixing of media fragments past and present, (re)combined in ways to resonate with the familiar landscape" (p. 367). Further, Anderson described George W. Bush as "the first president to have become an action/adventure hero during a time of war" (p. 367) due to the shaping of his political persona in news footage to fit ideals of masculinity in fictional filmic forms. American popular culture, argued Nimmo and Combs (1980), regardless of media type, has fostered an "American monomyth" of an incorruptible hero who saves the community from the forces of evil (p. 153). Regardless of the time frame, many animated cartoons have taken this view of war, symbolically framing protagonists and antagonists in clear-cut battles over moral sanctity. But Nimmo and Combs warned of grave consequences in the political world:

> The bulk of superheroes depicted get their authority to act from translegal sources that supersede normal legal precepts. Typically, they are charismatic, pure, outsiders, and they succeed because of their moral and technological power, oftentimes by violence. They are attractive because they offer a clearcut distinction between good and evil, simplify ambiguities of life, and overcome obstacles quickly and neatly [p. 154].

Napoleon, Hitler, Lenin, and Stalin embodied these traits for their followers, with very negative results, according to Nimmo and Combs. To counter such powerful political narratives in media, active audiences are a necessity. That is, individuals must consider the possibility of layered meanings in media texts, even in seemingly innocuous animated cartoons, and evaluate the logic and veracity of claims made or morals cultivated.

Van Buren (2006) highlighted the troubling resurgence of the American monomyth in Web-based animations related to the 9/11 attacks and the War in Iraq. Venting anger, grief, and a desire for revenge, many individuals created Web-based cartoons depicting acts of cruelty against Al-Qaeda terrorists, Osama bin Laden, and Saddam Hussein, as well as Arabs and Muslims. The Internet has been treated as a more open forum for democratic expression and individualism, therefore "It is permissible, even expected, that the violence suffered by the Arab characters, and the degree of gore and sexual imagery used, far surpass the depictions of animated violence and negative stereotype that ... would be permissible today in dominant media channels" (p. 550).

Thus, according to Van Buren, the historical propaganda motif of the subhuman enemy who can be justifiably exterminated has found new life on the Internet.

Conclusion

This overview of representative research regarding war-related messages in animated films includes an implicit call to action for communication scholars to turn their attention to studying forms of media content such as animated cartoons that were perhaps discounted or overlooked in the past. Contrasting the animated propaganda of the First and Second World Wars with nationalistic and subversive commentary in the Cold War revealed a great deal of insight about cultural identity and political allegiance during and after times of military action and political tension. Even in the supposed dearth of war-related animation about other wars that occurred during or after the declared end of the Cold War, several examples were presented to demonstrate that animated cartoons are still a relevant form of political discourse about war.

Future research could explore the commonalities of animated cartoons with government-sponsored and privately developed video games about war, as many of these have direct military training and recruiting applications. Most importantly, researchers need to examine this topic from the perspective of audiences. That is, future studies of adult-child co-viewing of animated war cartoons could reveal important interpersonal or social dimensions to how mass media messages are processed. Do audiences uniformly perceive content as literal or in terms of allegorical meaning? Discussing the range of interpretations of war-related messages in animated cartoons could prove intriguing as well as enlightening for understanding how media messages could encourage or discourage the formation of certain political attitudes or behaviors.

The study of war-related messages in animated cartoons is more than a scholarly indulgence or an assessment of shallow texts suitable only for entertainment or childish diversion. Rather, it is an area worthy of attention across many disciplines and an imperative endeavor for scholars attempting to understand how humans relate to one another in times of paranoia, disorder, and conflict.

REFERENCES

Andersen, R. (2005). Gendered media culture and the imagery of war. *Feminist Media Studies, 5,* 367–370.

Barten, E., and G. Groeneveld (1994). *Van den vos Reynaerde* (1943): How a medieval fable became a Dutch anti–Semitic animation film. *Historical Journal of Film, Radio, & Television, 14,* 1994. Retrieved October 10, 2007, from Communication & Mass Media Complete database.

Bendazzi, G. (1994). *Cartoons: One Hundred Years of Cinema Animation.* Indianapolis: University of Indiana Press.

Birdwell, M. E. (2001). "Oh, you thing from another world, you": How Warner Bros. animators responded to the Cold War (1948–1980). *Film & History, 31,* 34–39.

Carabas, T. (2007). Tales calculated to drive you MAD: The debunking of spies, superheroes, and Cold War rhetoric in *Mad Magazine*'s "SPY vs SPY." *Journal of Popular Culture, 40*(1), 4–24.

Chapman, R. (2001). George F. Kennan as represented by Chuck Jones: *Road Runner* and the Cold War policy of containment (1949–1980). *Film & History, 31,* 40–43.

Dobrow, J. R., and C. L. Gidney (1998). The good, the bad, and the foreign: The use of dialect in children's animated television. *The Annals of the American Academy, 557,* 105–119.

Fisch, M. (2000). Nation, war, and Japan's future in the science fiction anime film Patlabor II. *Science Fiction Studies, 27,* 49–68.

Gardiner, J. K. (2005). Why Saddam is gay: Masculinity politics in *South Park — Bigger, Longer, and Uncut. Quarterly Review of Film and Video, 22,* 51–62.

Kim, J. Y. (2006). Critique of the new historical landscape of South Korean animation. *Animation: An Interdisciplinary Journal, 1,* 61–81.

Knapp, T. (1996). Popular political culture: Rocky and Bullwinkle and the rhetoric of the Cold War. *Journal of the Northwest Communication Association, 24,* 1–16.

Kornhaber, D. (2007). Animating the war: The First World War and children's cartoons in America. *The Lion and the Unicorn, 31,* 132–146.

Leab, D. (2005). Animators and animals: John Halas, Joy Batchelor, and George Orwell's *Animal Farm. Historical Journal of Film, Radio, & Television, 25,* 231–249.

_____. (2006). The American government and the filming of George Orwell's *Animal Farm* in the 1950s. *Media History, 12,* 133–155.

Lehman, C. P. (2001). The new black animated images of 1946: Black characters and social commentary in animated cartoons. *Journal of Popular Film & Television, 29,* 74–81.

_____. (2006). *American Animated Cartoons of the Vietnam Era: A Study of Social Commentary in Films and Television Programs, 1961–1973.* Jefferson, NC: McFarland.

MacDougall, R. (1999). Red, brown, and yellow perils: Images of the American enemy in the 1940s and 1950s. *Journal of Popular Culture, 32*(4), 59–75.
Nel, P. (2007). Children's literature goes to war: Dr. Seuss, P. D. Eastman, Munro Leaf, and the *Private SNAFU* films (1943–46). *Journal of Popular Culture, 40*, 468–487.
Nimmo, D., and J. E. Combs (1980). *Subliminal Politics: Myths & Mythmakers in America*. Englewood Cliffs, NJ: Prentice-Hall.
Parenti, M. (1992). *Make-believe Media: The Politics of Entertainment*. New York: St. Martin's.
Peters, K. M., and F. C. Blumberg (2002). Cartoon violence: Is it as detrimental to preschoolers as we think? *Early Childhood Education Journal, 29*, 143–148.
Raiti, G. C. (2007). The disappearance of Disney animated propaganda: A globalization perspective. *Animation: An Interdisciplinary Journal, 2*, 153–169.
Rees, D. (2004). *Get Your War on II*. New York: Riverhead.
Sigall, M. (2005). *Living Life Inside the Lines: Tales from the Golden Age of Animation*. Jackson, MS: University of Mississippi Press.
Van Buren, C. (2006). Critical analysis of racist post-9/11 web animations. *Journal of Broadcasting & Electronic Media, 50*, 537–554.
Ward, P. (2005). Distribution and trade press strategies for the British animated propaganda cartoons of the First World War era. *Historical Journal of Film, Radio, & Television, 25*, 189–201.
Woodcock, P. (2006). The polis of Springfield: *The Simpsons* and the teaching of political theory. *Politics, 26*, 192–199.

*Part II:
Institutional
Propaganda Messages*

ECONOMIC CONVERGENCE AND THE CELEBRATION OF MASS PRODUCTION: THE WORLD WAR II ADVERTISING CAMPAIGN TO SELL JEEPS

Kathleen German

Mass consumption has defined American society in the twentieth century, beginning with the popularity of the first assembly-line automobiles and consumer goods, reaching new heights in the demand for war material in the 1940s, and culminating in the postwar boom of the 1950s and beyond. Two primary consumers have fueled the capitalist enterprise in the United States — the federal government during wartime and civilians during times of peace. It is the point of intersection in the shift from wartime to peacetime economies or from government to civilian consumers, known as economic conversion, that is of interest in this analysis.

The potential for severe economic dislocation is enormous when industries, government, and consumers must adjust to rapid shifts in patterns of production and consumption. The end of World War II proved especially difficult because it followed several decades of economic dislocation including the turmoil at the end of World War I, followed closely by the Great Depression, and then, rapid disruption as war production escalated in the aftermath of Pearl Harbor. While historians and economists most often treat these shifts as purely physical disruptions — machines are re-tooled, workers are relocated, and raw materials are redistributed — the process also is rhetorical because human beings must be persuaded to alter their attitudes and behaviors to facilitate the dramatic economic shifts. As McCloskey (1985) argued, economics is not simply a scientific or mathematical enterprise, but "economists are poets" and storytellers engaging in the "larger conversation of humankind" (p. xiv). It is worthwhile, then, to study economics, and especially economic history, from the vantage point of the rhetorician.

A brief overview of the twentieth century, often deemed the era of consumer culture, reveals bursts of consumption during each world war as government replaced civilians as the primary consumer of industrial output in the United States. Immediately following those wars, American industry was forced to quickly return its focus to production and marketing for civilians (Snider, 1991). The economic conversion from military to peacetime spending was a major force in reshaping the economy of the United States following World War II, molding individual consumption for decades to follow. The parameters of this economic conversion established precedents that linger in the United States economy, including ritualistic divestment and the prevalence of the military-industrial complex.

As the end of World War II approached, manufacturers were challenged with the conversion of their production facilities from military hardware to civilian goods, while maintaining profits. Fearing a major economic recession like the one that followed the cessation of hostilities at the end of World War I, businesses joined together with the federal government to stimulate consumer demand to fill the gap as the military need for consumables fell. Convinced of the power of mass media because they had been proven effective in changing other behaviors of Americans during the war, government and business interests turned to media, especially film, as an important part of the solution to the problem of economic conversion (Doherty, 1993).

This is a unique juncture in United States history because it is one of the first times broad sectors of industry and government cooperated to their mutual benefit. A smooth economic transition meant continued profits for industry and limited social disruption for government agencies. The recent memory of the deep recession after World War I was the prime motivation for government to cooperate with industry to ease the transition from a wartime to a peacetime economy (Cassidy, 1989; Crump, 1989). The tentative cooperation of government and industry to maximize production from 1941 through 1945 established the fledgling relationship that continued through the remainder of the twentieth century (Koistinen, 2004).

This chapter looks at media efforts, financed by the federal government on behalf of industry, to promote consumer demand and to facilitate economic conversion. Specifically, this analysis examines the case of the Jeep as it was transformed from a weapon of war to a civilian product. *The Autobiography of a Jeep* was the centerpiece in a media campaign that also included print magazine advertisements (Simon & Marks, 2004). In order to understand the persuasive elements of economic conversion, our primary focus is on how the rhetoric of this media campaign expedited the economic conversion. A close examination of the combined media messages reveals that they exploited the foxhole values of common soldiers, redirecting those bonds of brotherhood into channels of consumption.

The primary focus of this analysis is the film, *The Autobiography of a Jeep*, produced and widely distributed to civilian and military audiences in 1943. Beginning with the film as its primary text, this chapter examines three potent, overlapping clusters of verbal and visual terms or teministic screens that dominate the advertising campaign for the Jeep — optimism, comradeship, and loyalty (Burke, 1941). These three clusters of verbal and visual terms transform the Jeep through ritualistic divestment from a weapon of war to a peacetime symbol of the Allied victory celebrated through consumption (McCracken, 1988). In other words, the Jeep is divested of its original military use and recast in a completely new role as a civilian vehicle through transcendent value clusters of optimism, comradeship, and loyalty.

We will begin with a brief history of the development of the Jeep as a military weapon, discuss the clusters of values that characterize the film produced by the Office of War Information in response to the anxieties accompanying the impending economic conversion, and draw a number of conclusions regarding the role of the mediated rhetoric of capitalist consumption in contemporary culture.

The Jeep in World War II

Prior to World War II, several small-car manufacturers had designed and produced, but failed to successfully market, small, lightweight vehicles such as the Bantam. Americans did not care for small cars, and sales stagnated. However, as a result of rapid German and Italian advances through vast tracts of territory in Europe and North Africa, the United States Army Quartermaster Corps saw the need for a smaller, all-purpose vehicle to add speed and mobility to United States armed forces (Rifkind, 1943). In the early months of 1940, the United States Army placed orders for such a vehicle with American Bantam Company of Butler, Pennsylvania. The Army also invited Willys-Overland and Ford Motor Company to submit designs because it was skeptical of Bantam's production capacity.

After rigorous field tests and alterations in specifications, the Willys-Overland general purpose vehicle, or "Jeep," design was accepted and put into production. Since Bantam Company went out of business shortly before the war, Willys-Overland was given the production contract, and Jeeps began to roll off the assembly line in early 1941. Willys-Overland plant capacity was limited, so to fill the gap, Ford was granted government contracts to build Jeeps according to Willys-Overland blueprints. By the end of 1945, 700,000 Jeeps had been manufactured and distributed at a cost of $738.74 per vehicle (Cortese, 2001; Wright, 1996).

Civilian car production ceased in February 1942, as automobile manufacturers turned their stockpiles of raw materials into tanks, airplanes, and guns (Milward, 1977; Rockoff, 1998). The concentration of production capacity of the automobile sector redirected for war production proved tremendous. General Motors, for example, built shells, bombs, fuses, navigation equipment, machine guns, artillery and anti-aircraft guns, plus engines and military vehicles. Ford mass produced bombers. Studebaker shifted to manufacturing Army trucks. Together, automobile manufacturers doubled their production capacity from 1942 through 1945, producing more than 2.5 million trucks, 50 percent of all machine guns and rifles, 60 percent of all tanks, 85 percent of helmets and aerial bombs, and much more (Moore, 1944; Seelinger 2005/2006). Between 1940 and 1945, automotive firms made almost $29 billion worth of military materials, one-fifth of the total United States wartime output (Hooks & Bloomquist, 1992; Koistinen, 2004).

As early as 1942, Willys-Overland realized that there was potential to develop a huge market for a civilian version of the Jeep at the end of the war. Civilian workers who had deferred the purchase of new automobiles because they were unavailable during wartime added to the pent-up demand, along with thousands of returning soldiers (Dumas, 1995; Sandler & Hartley, 1995). In addition, production capacity, which had more than doubled during wartime, would become available at the end of the war for civilian production. Secondary support services for an automobile-based economy were soon in place with a population shift to the suburbs requiring increased commuting, plans for a national system of interstate highways, and plenty of money to finance everything (Cross, 2000).

The design for a civilian Jeep was developed and ready for manufacture in 1945. The civilian design came with a tailgate, side-mounted spare tire, larger headlights, a keyed ignition, and an external fuel cap. Within a few years, a one-piece windscreen replaced the two-piece screen, and a taller front grille and hood were added. Later modifications such as an automatic transmission and a V-8 engine were added for driver and passenger comfort. By 1984, 16 years after Kaiser purchased the Jeep from Willys-Overland, Jeeps were manufactured in 30 countries and marketed in more than 150 countries (Fetherston,1995; Lamm, 1994; Opre, 1996; Rifkind, 1943).

A number of factors contributed to strong fears of postwar recession. Among the far-reaching effects of World War II was a military-industrial alliance that dominated mobilization for war and continued to drive the economy during the war in spite of warnings by President Eisenhower and others (Cassidy, 1989; Crump, 1989; Eisenhower, 1960; Koistinen, 2004). The military-industrial alliance operated mostly outside of government controls and, thus, proved somewhat unmanageable and unpredictable (Lynch, 1987). In addition, economists warned of danger in returning to post-war economic normalcy because of vastly expanded production capacity built during the war (Snider, 1991). The huge financial reserves in consumer-driven markets from the combined effect of high wages, full employment, and lack of consumer goods promised brisk sales but also threatened to be impossible to satisfy.

Formulating a corporate and government response to the impending end of the war occupied government and industry leaders from April 1943 onward. Haunted by memories of the severe postwar depression following World War I, many respected economists anticipated a postwar slump. They feared that industry conversion could not be accomplished quickly enough in the sectors where demand was highest, resulting in unmanageable inflation (Koistinen, 2004; Lawson, 1987). Government and industry turned to media to manipulate public attitudes and behaviors as an important part of the solution to the problem of economic conversion (Chapman, 2007; Hope, 2007). The ensuing effort to market military vehicles to civilians for work and recreation was anchored by a film-based advertising campaign intended to shape postwar public consumption and ease the transition to a civilian-propelled economy.

The Film and the Advertising Campaign

Government campaigns to limit consumption of war-critical materials like fuel, metals, and meat had been highly successful. Conservation of scarce goods, initiated early in the war, became an expression of patriotism endorsed by celebrities such as Jack Benny, Kate Smith, Bob Hope, Bing Crosby, and others. It did not matter if consumer spending dropped off because the federal government was buying from most manufacturers, guaranteeing full reimbursement of production costs plus a guaranteed 10 percent profit. American businesses continued to advertise to civilians, associating their names with patriotic conservation and advocating savings as a way to support the war effort. Fully 80 percent of business advertising expenses were tax deductible. Hilmes (2007) provided the reason civilian advertising continued during the war: "it paid to keep one's name before the public in a context of public service, even if a company had little to sell" (p. 132).

Produced and released mid-war in 1943 by the Overseas Branch of the United States Office of War Information, *The Autobiography of a Jeep* is a 9-minute black-and-white film that tells the story of the design and production of the general-purpose military vehicle commonly known as the Jeep (Simon & Marks, 2004; Wright, 1996). As typical of the "victory shorts" produced during World War II, highly talented contributors, often drafted from Hollywood, produced government messages that were intended to influence military and civilian attitudes and behaviors (Doherty, 1993). The film was produced and directed by experienced documentary filmmaker Irving Lerner, written by Joseph Krumgold, who later won Newberry Medals for his children's books *And Now Miguel* (1954) and *Onion John* (1960), and narrated by Robert Sloan as the voice of the Jeep.

In the custom of wartime business promotions, *The Autobiography of a Jeep* promotes but does not overtly sell its product. The film narrates the story of the Jeep, told by the Jeep itself, in an entertaining manner that partially disguises its purpose as an advertisement. The mood of the film expresses the mission of the Office of War Information's Overseas Branch to bolster support for the American democratic way of life to civilian and military audiences abroad by conveying facts couched in feelings of patriotism. *The Autobiography of a Jeep* was distributed to both military and civilian audiences at home and abroad and usually played with newsreels and other shorts before the main film screening.

While it is impossible to get precise numbers, it is likely that more than 90 million people saw the film before the end of the war, the typical audience figures for most of the Office of War Information victory shorts (Chapman, 2007; Hilmes, 2007). Many more subscribers to *Time, Life, The Saturday Evening Post, Collier's*, and *Look* weekly magazines saw the print advertisements. Thirteen black-and-white and two color one-page print advertisements appeared from 1944 through 1945. In early 1946, *The Saturday Evening Post* published a two-page color advertisement that consisted of a montage of 12 pictures of Jeeps working in settings around the world. This was an unusual advertisement since most ads were black-and-white, single page, and focused on United States venues. All print advertisements featured the CJ-2, the precursor to the first mass-produced civilian Jeep, the CJ2A.

Countless other readers and moviegoers recognized the Jeep in print photographs and newsreels that featured general coverage of the war. The presence of the Jeep in military advances and victories was chronicled in the newsreels and print accounts throughout the war (Alexander, 1998; Colley, 1997; Hull, 1997; Lamm, 1994). As a result, the Jeep was associated with contributing to victory. Government newsreels and print stories kept the Jeep in front of the American public for the duration of the war, in itself a huge, although indirect, advertising campaign.

Based on a close reading of *The Autobiography of a Jeep*, three clusters of words and images—optimism, comradeship, and loyalty—emerged that reflected the traits of the American soldier. In its film rendering, the Jeep was more than a military vehicle — it was an embodiment of the American spirit of rugged and practical individualism. The advertising campaign celebrated patriotism through the themes of optimism, comradeship, and loyalty that are offered in the narrative and supported by clusters of imagery that mimic repetitive form (Berthold, 1976). The next sections examine the values of optimism, comradeship, and loyalty that formed a triad engulfing the viewer in patriotism enacted through consumption.

Optimism

The National Archives catalog identifies *The Autobiography of a Jeep* as a lighthearted but important artifact in American history (Simon & Marks, 2004). This description overlooks a number of fundamental features of the film. Most important, the film expresses the myth of the American Dream. The Jeep is personified as an underdog who achieves success. This success is rooted in impending military victory and an optimistic future that echoes the materialism inherent in the American Dream.

The Jeep acquires human characteristics as a central character of the film. The entire film is narrated in first-person voice-over from the Jeep's point of view, appealing directly to the feelings and thoughts of the audience. Images of the Jeep dominate the screen space, appearing in the foreground of most frames, dominating its surroundings. Because the Jeep is the main character, humans are rarely presented onscreen. When humans are featured, they admire the Jeep or are escorted by it, while the Jeep remains the central active character in the film narrative. In the voice-over narrative, the Jeep is personified as homely and humble, uncertain of its role in the war effort. It is nervous in front of more experienced vehicles like the tank, eager to join others in the fight, proud of its contributions to the war, and increasingly confident as it surmounts difficult challenges. The tone of the narration celebrates industry and technology, symbolized by the Jeep, as critical to victory and future prosperity. The first-person narration is accompanied by third-person point-of-view camera-work that provides the viewer with perception of the Jeep's emotional state while observing it from a distance. The end result is that the viewer acts as a voyeur who both sees the object of desire and vicariously experiences its feelings. This construction heightens the viewer's identification with the Jeep as a character in the same way that viewers would experience other more typical Hollywood films of the era.

In addition to the verbal narrative, visual images reinforce the optimism of the American Dream. The Jeep tells its story against an opening montage of future highways and cities: "I come from a country of roads. A place called the United States of America where roads tie together 3,000 miles of deserts and mountains and valleys. Because of the automobile, Americans who live a hundred miles from each other are as close neighbors as the man next door" (*Autobiography*, 1943). The vast expanses in aerial shots of highways and extreme long shots of cities and horizons expose the size of the future and tap into remnants of the Frontier Myth (Turner, 1962). The images and narrative imply that mobility is critical to the American Dream.

The concluding montage of the film functions as a bookend to the introduction, reinforcing the optimistic tone of the opening through symbols of victory. In this montage, the Jeep shares General Stillwell's success in China; Winston Churchill rides in a Jeep after the victory in North Africa; and, at Casablanca, Harry Truman is driven in a Jeep after the surrender of Axis forces. This succession of images predicts the ultimate victory and resumption of the American Dream deferred at the beginning of the film.

Editing also subtly reinforces the optimism of the film. As shot length shortens, the pace of the film quickens, subtly arousing the viewer's excitement (Zettl, 1999). Longer takes typify the first half of *The Autobiography of a Jeep* as it describes the coming of war, but during the last 3 minutes, cuts occur more quickly as if in anticipation the end of the war. The ending of the film is dominated by montages and action sequences, paralleling the quicker pacing and rising excitement of the film. Thus, the film begins more slowly with the American Dream deferred, then follows the trajectory of rising action, a convention typical of most American Hollywood narratives. It concludes with an upbeat musical score and quick-paced montage of the Jeep in victory.

Throughout the film, the American Dream is defined as material growth, visualized both at the beginning and at the conclusion of the film as the expansion of cities and highways across the vastness of the nation. The Jeep is an expression of that material dream, rolled off the assembly line "one every two minutes. Thirty Jeeps an hour" (*Autobiography*, 1943). The celebration of military victory is also a celebration of material production. This spirit of material optimism resonated with the financial well-being of Americans — women and men, black and white. Average weekly wages during the war increased, along with personal savings (Milward, 1977). Optimism was firmly rooted in the rising financial status of the average American. For the first time since the onset of the Great Depression, Americans felt fiscally secure. Average weekly civilian earnings rose 93 percent from 1939 to 1944, creating consumer purchasing power at a higher level than ever before in American history (Koistinen, 2004). Although consumer purchases of durable goods such as automobiles plummeted during the war years because such goods were largely unavailable, industry continued to advertise these consumer goods (Milward,

1977). The result was pent-up demand and an expectation of satisfaction; the anticipation of military victory was expressed in real economic terms.

The growth of the United States industrial infrastructure also provided a sense of invincibility. The amount of new and expanded plant production put into place during the war years was enormous. GNP alone grew by 124 percent in just four years, with the United States producing in excess of 50 percent more than the combined output of both its allies and enemies (Koistinen, 2004). Milward (1977) argued that the war brought about "real economic changes" in social attitudes that affected consumption (p. 343). The vigorous growth of the economy enacted the American Dream in material terms. The promise of postwar consumption symbolized an easier, more secure life for white working-class families and raised the hopes of minorities, enabling them to achieve a standard of domesticity that connoted middle-class status and served as "testaments to the perseverance of the American Dream" (Hurley, 2001, p. 27). Allied victory was conceptualized in the United States in economic terms rooted in American optimism.

Comradeship

Those who have experienced combat often mention the bond that develops among the soldiers in a unit, claiming that soldiers fight, not for abstract causes or ideologies, but rather for their comrades in arms (Doherty, 1993). The bonds of brotherhood, intensified by the imminence of death, probably surpass most other human experiences. Thus, brotherhood becomes the symbolic underpinning of the World War II victory. This is a populist framework that celebrates the morality of victory through consumption. It elevates engineering and industrial output, foregrounds technical expertise, and shifts the focus from human to mechanical achievements in the war.

The narrative structure of the film duplicates the military induction process of the common soldier. The Jeep begins its story as a raw recruit, new to war and afraid of letting others down. The Jeep describes its first days in the Army: "No, I wasn't too proud of myself back there at the start when the army first looked me over" (*Autobiography*, 1943). Then, the Jeep experiences a type of boot camp indoctrination as it is put through maneuvers. The onscreen images illustrate the rigor of the field trials as the Jeep runs up inclines, splashes through creeks, and pulls larger pieces of equipment into battle.

The narrative continues as the Jeep acts, not as an inanimate piece of equipment, but as the soldier's partner: "I'll say one thing, no matter what they asked me to do, it was no worse than what my driver was ready to do himself. The American soldier and I got along fine" (*Autobiography*, 1943). The human driver remains anonymous in the middle or background of each frame. Each new sequence of actions begins with a single Jeep dominating the center of the screen frame accompanied by narration such as "I did about everything a machine could do..." or "I teamed up with General Stillwell..." that reinforces the first-person point of view.

This narrative structure reinforces the film's emphasis on the Jeep as a common soldier, placing it, like its human comrades, at every important historical moment in the war. The Jeep expresses its bond with the soldier in the final words of the film: "But the thing that makes me a success most of all is this. I made a friend. I mean the soldier. Wherever you see one of us, the other won't be far behind" (*Autobiography*, 1943).

Throughout the narration, the Jeep assumes a human voice and speaks as a participant in war, disguising its real nature as a marketed product of industry. As the film unfolds chronologically, each successive step of the story leads into the next. Each challenge of military life is confronted and overcome by the Jeep until it achieves final victory. In this way, the sequences of the film provide its form as each part prepares the viewer for the part that follows or, as Burke (1953) wrote, each part of the film provides its form in "an arousing and fulfillment of desires" (p. 124). The viewer's anticipation and satisfaction as each subsequent hurdle is overcome establishes the structure of the film and constitutes repetitive form. In the structure of the film, the postponement of the future by the intervention of war leads the viewer to expect that victory will result in the resumption of the postponed future. In most cases, when the narrative form is repetitive, the primary agent or actor is privileged. Thus, the form of the film reinforces the centrality of the Jeep. In doing so, the substance of the discourse becomes familial, stressing common ancestry and beliefs, resulting in comradeship (Burke, 1969). As a result, the repetitive form of the film itself enhances the value of comradeship and the role of the Jeep narrator.

Just as in *The Autobiography of a Jeep*, other government propaganda efforts and manufacturer advertising throughout World War II played upon the comradeship among soldiers in battle, blending personal identity with patriotism expressed through material consumption. It should come as no surprise, then, that in the aftermath of World War II, social aspirations toward better things resulted in a consumer equity forged by common dangers experienced during war (Milward, 1977). Consumption became the means by which Americans celebrated democracy. Their common experience of war received its potency from the dangers faced together.

Loyalty

In its personified film role, the Jeep bonds with its human counterpart — his pal, the common soldier. The function of the Jeep is subsumed in the friendship of the vehicle and the serviceman as the film narration claims, "I made a friend.... Wherever you see one of us, the other won't be far behind. That goes for now when we're fighting together and after the war when we'll be building together" (*Autobiography*, 1943). In this claim, loyalty derives from comradeship and is extended as future consumer behavior. The relationship of the soldier to his machine translates into a form of postwar loyalty that moves from the front line to the home front.

The depiction of the Jeep as the average American soldier — self-sacrificing, humble, homely but willing to get the job done — also places a subtle burden of gratitude on the viewer as the responsibility to remain loyal to another veteran of war. The burden of loyalty is reinforced for the viewer by the performance of the Jeep in the war. Its sacrifices create a guilt that can be expiated by sustained loyalty manifest as consumption (Burke, 1941). This guilt-redemption cycle is intensified by the film's elaboration of the trials and contributions of the Jeep. In this way, loyalty derives from comradeship as it becomes the directed future behavior of consumption.

The triad of optimism, comradeship, and loyalty comes together at the end of the film as a low-angle shot of the Jeep fills the screen, elevating the subject. The Jeep reminds the viewer of its special relationship with the soldier: "now when we're fighting together and after the war when we'll be building together. Because the rumor is going around, the Jeep is here to stay" (*Autobiography*, 1943). In this final appeal, the Jeep becomes just another soldier, returning from war ready to take up the American Dream after having patriotically served its country. The optimism for the future and comradeship of the foxhole developed in the early sequences of the film become the basis for loyalty in postwar America.

Discussion

The transition from a wartime to a peacetime economy was rocky for the auto industry because postwar sales of components of the tanks and big guns that had formed much of its wartime production were limited (Gansler, 1992; Hooks & Bloomquist, 1992; Widick, 1959). The transition of the Jeep from a weapon of war to a civilian vehicle was also problematic because it had been developed as a military vehicle rather than a family sedan. Moreover, the Jeep was restricted not only by its specialized military applications but also by public perceptions. As such, its economic value was culturally constructed (Renner, 1990; Rinehart, 1990; Sassatelli, 2007). Its transition required both a shift in the focus of the demand from government armed services to individuals but, more fundamentally, a transition in symbolic associations of the vehicle. That is, the public perception required fundamental change essential to sustain demand, and thus production and profit. Sassatelli (2007) provides the explanation: "The particular cultural politics of value which underpins the development of a 'consumer society' is thus not a natural one, it is one which requires a process of learning whereby social actors are practically trained to perform (and enjoy) their roles as consumers" (p. 11). The re-articulation of the Jeep's material use was essentially perceptual, accomplished through rhetoric. Two broad implications arise from this case of economic conversion: Ritualistic divestment based appeals to optimism, comradeship, and loyalty; and, government and industry cooperation to control economic convergence that creates a foundation for postwar collaboration.

Rhetoric of Ritualistic Divestment

When the use of consumable goods changes, this evolution is identified as ritualistic divestment (McCracken, 1988). That is, the previous meaning or use of a material possession is "transferred, obscured or confused, or even lost when goods change hands" (Lury, 1996, p. 13). In this process, the previous meaning of a product is shifted when it is transferred to another use. History offers multiple instances, such as when Camels, originally a cigarette for women, re-targeted the male consumer. Coca Cola Corporation tried, but failed, to transcend brand loyalty to the original Coke recipe, even though blind taste tests showed a distinct preference for the New Coke formula. In a similar fashion, in order to survive the economic transition to a peacetime economy, the Jeep also underwent ritualistic divestment.

Ritualistic divestment is essentially a rhetorical process facilitating economic conversion. For the Jeep, this rhetorical process was bolstered by overlapping visual and language appeals to optimism, comradeship, and loyalty. These overlapping appeals shifted its identity in a system of symbolic exchange through common denominators that conflated military and civilian, mechanical and human. Such visual and language appeals function as terministic screens through which objects of desire are perceived. These terministic screens cue behavior because they provide human beings with the symbolic means for addressing and resolving the problems they face (Burke, 1941). Thus, the celebration of victory was expressed in the orgiastic consumption of the postwar consumer boom.

Media messages are essential in the process of ritualistic divestment because they can manipulate the terministic screens through which viewers apprehend their worlds. Although the verbal text has often been considered the predominant element in such discourse, images add new dimensions of meaning to the text (Hall, 1972). Perhaps the most striking feature of our visual culture and the images that dominate it was noted by Mirzoeff (1999) as "the growing tendency to visualize things that are not in themselves visual" such as optimism, comradeship, and loyalty (p. 5). The abstract nature of images makes them ideal for transcending specific circumstances and aligning individual needs with socially desirable ends.

The effectiveness of mass media is dependent on visualization, deriving from their ability to, as W. Lance Bennett (1988) summarized, "translate the complex and multi-voiced reality of our times into another, symbolic realm of simpler images and fewer voices" (p. 14). Thus, the Jeep represents the experiences of millions of soldiers and civilians who vicariously participate in victory through multiple images of print and film — all readily available in the postwar economy. Images are particularly effective in bridging divisions between groups and across demographic differences, thereby making them a powerful tool in ritualistic divestment.

The visual element of the message is critical because it links the media text and the personal experience of the viewer (Reynolds, 1998). Thus, the visual experience forms the basis of the viewer's vicarious experience. For much of the twentieth century, the viewer's understanding of events not directly experienced has occurred largely through the images offered through media. And, images not only influence the shape of the message through clarifying, intensifying and personalizing their impact (Zettl, 1973), but also frame opinions (Whillock, 1996). In his discussion of photographs as the primary record of many events, Roy Blackwood (1983) noted that "visuals are important as conveyors of information and shapers of attitudes" (p. 710). They substitute for direct experience.

The emergence of the visual has been identified with the rise of contemporary culture and, not surprisingly, is linked to consumer culture. One reason is explained by Barthes (1972) who insisted that, "Pictures ... are more imperative than writing, they impose meaning at one stroke, without analyzing or diluting it" (p. 110). The simultaneity of the visual may even override the aural and verbal components of messages, playing the critical role in the formation of opinions and remaining in memory long after words are forgotten (Graber, 1988). If constructed in repetitive form as in *The Autobiography of a Jeep*, visual images may move the viewer from optimism and comradeship to brand loyalty.

The aftermath of World War II served to open new channels of desire and opportunities for satisfying that desire based on the enormous newfound production capacity of American industry. Patriotism expressed itself as consumerism and became a social and political force as potent as wartime armies, influencing the postwar landscape in the United States. The result is that it is critical to examine visuals as integral to the persuasive message of economic conversion by examining the powerful impact of language when it is combined with images in a context of war-infused nationalism (Aune, 2001; Korstad, 1991).

Government and Industry Cooperation to Control Economic Convergence

As already noted, the economic conversion from wartime to peacetime production was extraordinary. With peace came a transition from the production of weapons to civilian goods, resulting in a 1946-1947 economy producing at a higher level than during the years of the war (Rockoff, 1998). This was remarkable because the prospect for economic disruption was much higher in 1945 than at the end of World War I, primarily because new plant construction undertaken at the beginning of the war resulted in substantially increased production capacity. And, as Rockoff (1968) noted, "A good deal of the plant and equipment built during the war was afterwards converted to the production of civilian goods" (p. 104). Fear of winning the war but losing the peace was based on the perceived gap between the tremendous economic capacity of the United States built during the war and the inability to rapidly convert industry to meet the demand for civilian goods (Harrison, 1998).

However, within one year of the cessation of hostilities, 30 percent of United States production was converted with less than 3 percent unemployment, a record that well surpassed the traumatic conversion following World War I (Dumas, 1995). There are several reasons for limited economic disruption in the transition to peace. Because all major combatants except the United States had suffered severe damage to their economic infrastructure, there was little foreign competition for United States consumers. It was also feasible for United States companies to return to the production of prewar goods, their original manufacturing configuration prior to the war (Dumas, 1995; Sandler & Hartley, 1995). The shift in war production required little redeployment of labor, material, or production facilities because "the southern agricultural worker who moved to Detroit to build tanks stayed to build automobiles" (Rockoff, 1998, p. 100). In addition, design development and technological advances for durable goods such as airplanes and military vehicles were far-reaching in post-war years, making United States goods desirable in the global marketplace (Milward, 1977). Finally, government and industry formed a united front combining financial and persuasive efforts to smooth economic conversion.

In the conversion to a peacetime economy, one clear need was to cultivate new civilian markets and another was to develop those markets to take up the excess in production capacity (Sandler & Hartley, 1995). There were immediate applications of new technologies developed in electronics and aviation, for example, and potential outlets for durables like tank chassis in logging and other heavy industry (Lawson, 1987). However, the light military vehicle offered less opportunity for attracting civilian consumers than the more comfortable and familiar family sedan, retired during the war years. Several corporations, including Vickers, Rolls-Royce, and Boeing-Vertol, attempted to adapt military vehicles to public sector use (Sandler & Hartley, 1995). However, these corporations were unsuccessful in adjusting to changes in consumer demands and market opportunities as well as developing efficient, cost-effective methods for manufacturing products at a profit to compensate for cuts in federal defense spending.

Another barrier to economic conversion was the inferior design of many military products. American weapons like the Sherman tank, various aircraft, and small weapons were often inferior to German, Soviet, and Japanese weapons (O'Connell, 1989). Axis powers, while producing fewer materials during the war, generally produced goods that were of superior quality and design (Harrison, 1998). The American Jeep, however, was one of the exceptions. It was probably the best machinery design of the war (Lamm, 1994). Its success served to reassure Americans that they were winning the technological battle, even if this assumption was largely unfounded.

More than any other United States war, World War II provided the opportunity for government and industry to cooperate in their efforts to influence public opinion. Together, they staged successful national campaigns to communicate themes of conservation, patience, and teamwork, changing public attitudes and behaviors in dramatic ways. Corporations and advertisers donated much of the copy, graphic designs, and labor to develop more than a hundred public service campaigns that ranged from promoting victory gardens, to saving cooking fat, to selling war bonds. Government provided material, talent, and tax incentives. Civilians were urged to do without, make do, and recycle, contributing to pent-up delayed gratification of desires (Sivulka, 1998).

The war also provided an opportunity for businesses, often aided by the Office of War Information and other divisions of government, to explore persuasive campaigns. Understandably, businesses were highly motivated to frame their products in ways that would encourage consumption, especially during the transition when markets became unpredictable or unstable (Nimmo & Combs, 1983). As Ewen (1996) concluded: "War and the attendant need to stir feelings of national solidarity were, once again, supplying a state-of-the-art laboratory where business could experiment with the tools of ideological command" (p. 341).

The lessons learned by wartime propagandists smoothed the economic conversion to peacetime and laid the foundation for a greater postwar cooperation between industry and business. The Office of War Information had cooperated directly with businesses in harnessing patriotism to influence consumer behavior during the war (Winkler, 1998). And, as Ewen (1996) concluded, "Conscientiously applied, many businessmen believed, the lessons of war might carry over into the peace" (p. 341). Even before war's end, the potential relationship between government and industry was recognized. W. J. Wier (1942) of Chicago's Lord and Thomas advertising and public relations firm directly addressed the vision of America as a consumer society, linking victory and consumption in postwar society: "We can explain why the American way of life — with its bathtubs and pop-up toasters and electric refrigerators and radios and insulated homes — is worth sacrificing anything and everything not only to preserve but to take forward in a future more glorious than ever" (p. 13). World War II was a victory for consumption, for democracy expressed as capitalism, and according to one spokesperson: "the auto industry has played a central role in advancing the production and organizational frontier of industrial development" (University of Michigan-Dearborn, 2008). At the end of World War II, this role led the industrial sector into cooperation with the federal government on a scale unknown in previous decades.

Conclusion

Consumption has emerged as a critical force in historical processes, defining American society in the twentieth century and moving the United States from an agrarian nation to a consumer culture. World War II was more than a military victory; it was also a celebration of American industrial production. The economic conversion from military to peacetime spending was a major force in reshaping the economy of the United States following World War II. It enacted the celebration of military victory as material consumption for decades to follow and linked the interests of government with industry in policy and practice (Cassidy, 1989; Crump, 1989; Melman & Dumas, 1990).

The importance of effective transitions from military to peacetime economic production, and certainly vice versa, can hardly be overestimated. In World War II, the role of the government and industry in mobilizing civilians to enact patriotism through purchasing behavior was a critical part of ultimate victory, from buying war bonds that financed the military build-up to purchasing Jeeps that smoothed the return to a civilian economy. In this view, the physical process of redesigning plants and products or redeploying raw materials and laborers presents only a partial picture of the return to peace. The vital link in economic convergence is rhetorical because it is the consumer whose desires for material goods are either postponed or stimulated to facilitate the needs of government and industry.

One of the most effective campaigns during World War II, as suggested in this case study, was the transition of the Jeep from a military to a civilian vehicle. The cooperation of government and industry resulted in the sales of thousands of Jeeps at the end of the war to civilians for whom the Jeep design was never originally intended. Merging the combat values of optimism grounded in the American Dream with the comradeship and loyalty of brothers in arms, *The Autobiography of a Jeep* and the accompanying print advertisements were designed to infuse the vehicle designed for war with civilian utility. The long-term success of the campaign is obvious. Since the end of World War II, thousands of Jeeps have been sold, a tribute to the message linking consumption with conflict. The role of rhetoric, particularly the rhetoric of ritualistic divestment, is central to this process as the previous meaning of the product is shifted for a contemporary application, reinvigorating the postwar economy but, at the same time reminding us of former President Dwight D. Eisenhower's warnings about the dangers of the military-industrial complex (Eisenhower, 1960).

Scholars alert us to the troublesome growth of media images that signals a new kind of reality. In postmodern society, they argue that the image has come to replace the real. As a result, the public is often unable to distinguish between the image and reality (Baudrillard, 1983). The image becomes malleable, and the reality becomes irrelevant. Thus, a weapon designed for war mutates into a civilian vehicle. Similar transformations have occurred more recently in the wake of September 11, 2001, attacks on the World Trade Center and the Pentagon, for example, as corporate advertisers linked the purchase of their products to the practice of patriotic citizenship (Ciarrocca, 2002; Dickinson, 2005; Dumas, 1995). Such resurgence of ritualistic divestment inevitably leads us to question the foundations for the overwhelming success of 20th-century consumerism. As Sassatelli (2007) summarizes, "it is through changes in consumption we can reread the history of modernity and of the expansion of Western civilization" (p. 9). Consumption will undoubtedly continue to account for the expansion of Western culture and to shape history, both in the United States and, more importantly, on a global scale as we face shortages of fuel and food, changing environmental conditions, and continued international conflict.

REFERENCES

Alexander, J. H. (1998, November). Tracked landing vehicles proved their worth during the costly assault on Tarawa. *World War II, 13*, 146–182.

Anderson, F. D., and L. K. Prelli (2001). Pentadic cartograpy: Mapping the universe of discourse. *Quarterly Journal of Speech, 87*, 73–95.

Aune, J. A. (2001). *Selling the Free Market: The Rhetoric of Economic Correctness*. New York: Guilford.

The Autobiography of a Jeep. (1943). Office of War Information (Overseas Branch). 35mm; sw/1:1.37. National Archive and Records Administration. Transcription available from the author.

Barthes, R. (1972). *Mythologies.* New York: Hill and Wang.

Baudrillard, J. (1983). *Simulations.* New York: Semiotext(e).

Berthold, C. A. (1976). Kenneth Burke's cluster-agon method: Its development and an application. *Central States Speech Journal, 27,* 302–309.

Burke, K. (1941). *The Philosophy of Literary Form: Studies in Symbolic Action.* Baton Rouge: Louisiana State University Press.

_____. (1953). *Counter-statement* (2nd ed.). Los Altos, CA: Hermes.

_____. (1969). *A Grammar of Motives.* Berkeley: University of California Press.

Cassidy, K. J. (1989). Arms control and the home front: Planning for the conversion of military production facilities to civilian manufacturing. *Peace & Change, 14,* 46–64.

Chapman, J. (2007, February). Re-presenting war. *European Journal of Cultural Studies, 10,* 13–33.

Ciarrocca, M. (2002). Post-9/11 economic windfalls for arms manufacturers. *Foreign Policy in Focus, 7,* 210–219.

Colley, D. P. (1997, March). On the road to victory: The Red Ball Express. *World War II, 9,* 171–182.

Coontz, S. (1992). *The Way We Never Were: American Families and the Nostalgia Trap.* New York: Basic.

Cortese, R. A. (2001, February). Czech-built armor boosted the German war machine in both the East and West. *World War II, 15,* 64–67.

Cross, G. (2000). *An All-Consuming Century: Why Commercialism Won in Modern America.* New York: Columbia University Press.

Crump, J. R. (1989, Summer).The spatial distribution of military spending in the United States 1941-1985. *Growth & Change, 20,* 50–63.

Dickinson, G. (2005). Selling democracy: Consumer culture and citizenship in the wake of September 11. *Southern Communication Journal, 70,* 271–284.

Dittmar, H. (1992). *The Social Psychology of Material Possessions.* Hemel Hempstead: Harvester Wheatsheaf.

Doherty. T. (1993). *Projections of War.* New York: Columbia University Press.

Dumas, L. J. (1995). Finding the future: The role of economic conversion in shaping the twenty-first Century. In L. J. Dumas (Ed.), *The Socio-Economics of Conversion from War to Peace* (pp. 3–22). New York: M. E. Sharpe.

Eisenhower, D. D. (1960). Military-Industrial Complex Speech. *Public Papers of the Presidents,* pp. 1035–1040.

Ewen, S. (1996). *PR! A Social History of Spin.* New York: Basic.

Fetherston, D. (1995). *Jeep: Warhorse, Workhorse and Boulevard Cruiser.* Osceola, WI: Motorbooks.

Gansler, J. S. (1992, Spring). Restructuring the defense industrial base. *Issues in Science & Technology, 8,* 50–59.

Hall, S. (1972). The determinations of news photographs. In University of Birmingham Centre of Contemporary Cultural Studies (Ed.) (pp. 51–62). *Working Papers in Cultural Studies.* Birmingham, England: University of Birmingham.

Harrison, M. (1998). The economics of World War II: An overview. In M. Harrison (Ed.), *The Economics of World War II* (pp. 1–42). New York: Cambridge University Press.

Hilmes, M. (2007). *Only Connect: A Cultural History of Broadcasting in the United States.* Belmont, CA: Wadsworth.

Hooks, G., and L.E. Bloomquist (1992, December). The legacy of World War II for regional growth and decline: The cumulative effects of wartime investment on U.S. manufacturing, 1947-1972. *Social Forces, 71,* 303–337.

Hope, T. W. (2007, July/August). Photographing a war: World War II. *SMPTE Motion Imaging Journal, 116,* 287-291.
Hull, M. D. (1997, March). Hell on wheels. *World War II, 11,* 172–182.
Hurley, A. (2001). *Diners, Bowling Alleys, and Trailer Parks: Chasing the American Dream in the Postwar Consumer Culture.* New York: Basic.
Korstad, R. (1991). Smoke Signals: Cigarettes, Advertising, and the American Way of Life. *Journal of American History, 78,* 1018–1023.
Koistinen, P. A. (2004). *Arsenal of World War II: The Political Economy of American Warfare, 1940–1945.* Lawrence: University of Kansas Press.
Lawson, J. E. (1987). Civilian market opportunities for defense industry. In J. E. Lynch (Ed.), *Economic Adjustment and Conversion of Defense Industries* (pp. 155–174). Boulder, CO: Westview.
Lamm, J. (1994, June). World War II Jeep MB. *Road & Track, 45,* 149–154.
Lynch, J. E. (1987). *Economic Adjustment and Conversion of Defense Industries.* Boulder, CO: Westview.
Lury, C. (1996). *Consumer Culture.* New York: Routledge.
McCloskey, D. N. (1985). *The Rhetoric of Economics.* Madison: University of Wisconsin Press.
McCracken, G. (1988). *Culture and Consumption: New Approaches to the Symbolic Character of Consumer Goods and Activities.* Bloomington: Indiana University Press.
Melman, S., and L. J. Dumas (1990, April). Planning for economic conversion. *Nation, 250,* 509–516.
Milward, A. S. (1977). *War, Economy, and Society 1939–1945.* Berkeley: University of California Press.
Mirzoeff, N. (1999). *Visual Culture.* New York: Longman.
Moore, G. H. (1944). *Production of Industrial Materials in World War I and II.* New York: National Bureau of Economic Research.
Nimmo, D., and J. E. Combs (1983). *Mediated Political Realities.* New York: Longman.
O'Connell, R. L. (1989). *Of Arms and Men: A History of War, Weapons, and Aggression.* New York: Oxford University Press.
Opre, T. (1990, September). Fifty—and going strong. *Outdoor Life, 186,* 60–62.
Renner, M. (1990, May/June). Swords into plowshares, missiles into bicycles: The promise of economic conversion. *Utne Reader, 39,* 42–49.
Reynolds, A. (1998). Visual stories. In N. Mirzoeff (Ed.), *The Visual Culture reader* (pp. 132–147). London: Routledge.
Rifkind, H. R. (1943). *The Jeep—Its Development and Procurement Under the Quartermaster Corps, 1940–1942.* Unpublished historical report dated 1943 in NARA, Records of the Quartermaster Corps, RG-92, Entry 2116N, box 2.
Rinehart, D. (1990, February 19). From nuclear arms to candy and beer. *U.S. News & World Report, 108,* pp. 2–3, 50.
Rockoff, H. (1998). The United States: From ploughshares to swords. In M. Harrison (Ed.), *The Economics of World War II* (pp. 81–121). New York: Cambridge University Press.
Sandler, T., and K. Hartley (1995). *The Economics of Defense.* New York: Cambridge University Press.
Sassatelli, R. (2007). *Consumer Culture: History, Theory and Politics.* Thousand Oaks, CA: Sage.
Seelinger, M. J. (2005/2006, Winter). From the Jeep to the Humvee: U.S. Army light combat vehicle, World War II to present. *On Point, 11,* 8–13.
Simon, S., and M. Marks (2004). *Treasures from American Film Archives.* New York: National Film Preservation Foundation.
Sivulka, J. (1998). *Soap, Sx, and Cigarettes.* Belmont, CA: Wadsworth.

Smith, H. N. (2007). *Virgin Land: The American West as Symbol and Myth*. Cambridge, MA: Harvard University Press.

Snider, L. W. (1991, Winter). Guns, debt, and politics: New variations on an old theme. *Armed Forces & Society, 17,* 107–190.

Turner, F. J. (1962). *The Frontier in American History.* New York: Kessinger.

Whillock, R. K. (1996). The compromising Clinton: Images of failure, a record of success. In R. E. Denton & R. L. Holloway (Eds.), *The Clinton Presidency* (pp. 66–73). New York: Praeger.

Widick, B. J. (1959, March). Focus on Detroit. *Nation, 188,* 277–279.

Wier, W. J. (1942, October). Opportunity! *Printer's Ink,* 199, 13.

Winkler, A. M. (1978). *The Politics of Propaganda: The Office of War Information, 1942–1945.* New Haven, CT: Yale University Press.

Wright, R. (1996). War halts car production and changes U.S. forever. Retrieved January 18, 2008, from http://www.theautochannel.com.

Zettl, H. (1999). *Sight, Sound, Motion: Applied Media Aesthetics.* New York: Wadsworth.

"You Boys and Girls Can Be the Minute Men of Today": Narrative Possibility and Normative Appeal in the U.S. Treasury's 1942 *War Victory Comics*

James J. Kimble and *Trischa Goodnow*

The U.S. home front in World War II was no place for the faint of heart. Although they were far from the actual battlefronts, U.S. civilians at home were intimately involved in countless aspects of the war effort. Whether they were engaged in munitions work, participating in scrap metal drives, planting victory gardens, negotiating the thicket of rationing regulations, or organizing civilian defense teams, nearly every citizen was a vital part of the struggle against the Axis powers. Indeed, as the influential psychologist Gordon Allport (1942) noted early in the war, "in a democracy, every personality can be a citadel of resistance to tyranny" (p. 18).

America's children were not immune from this drive to support the war effort. The U.S. Extension Service, for example, placed city youth from across the country on heartland farms to help on the critical food front (Shultz, 1944). Leaders also drew youngsters into scrap collection work, an activity that they hoped "would arouse and instill patriotic fervor, calm fears of enemy attack, consume the excess leisure of potential miscreants, and add to the stockpiles of critical materials" (Kirk, 1995, p. 225). Younger children were also important to the cause, as when Lanham Act day care centers offered adult supervision if parents or family members were at work in a war factory (Tuttle, 1995). Despite the children's inability to fight in battle, government officials evidently viewed their youngest citizens as crucial in the prosecution of the war.

As vital as children were to the national mission on the home front, it was probably inevitable that they would become targets of opportunity for the war's largest governmental campaign, the U.S. Treasury's war bond machine (Kimble, 2006). Organized to finance a significant portion of the war as well as to bolster public morale through its ceaseless publicity, the bond operation managed to raise approximately $185 billion during the war years. Wealthier investors could purchase war bonds in amounts as high as $1,000 and, to be sure, much of the Treasury's attention focused on these potential buyers. However, the program provided a central role for younger civilians. Along with its war bonds, for instance, the Treasury produced a series of war stamps, available for only 10 cents (Kirk, 1994). The stamps could be saved by school children in a Treasury-sponsored album, to be turned in for a full $25 bond when their total reached $18.75. Such purchases were never, of course, a major part of the government's war funding. Yet, the Treasury's consistent sponsorship of the stamp campaign emphasized the importance of the youngest generation doing their part in support of the war effort.

One of the Treasury's most visible efforts to reach out to that generation appeared only eight months after the attack on Pearl Harbor. *War Victory Comics* (U.S. Treasury Department, 1942) was an unabashed attempt to convince its young readers that they should purchase war stamps in any way possible. To do so, it featured 36 pages of cartoon characters, including Superman, Blondie, and the Green Hornet, each plotting unique ways to purchase a war bond or stamp. With an initial publication run of 250,000 copies — and a second run of 250,000 more (McCarty, 1942) — the comic book was ambitious. As the "first government-sponsored comic book" (Holsinger, 1999, p. 329), it was also unprecedented. Before long, Treasury officials became quite pleased with the project's nationwide reception, calling it "one of the outstanding features of the whole War Bond campaign" (Lane, 1942, p. 15).

The evident success of *War Victory Comics* in reaching the nation's youngest readers should be of interest to those who study mediated communication in the context of war. The comic book's primary audience was thousands of miles from the war fronts and had no prospect of going to fight. The Treasury's publication, then, not only had to mediate the urgency of the battlefront to its home front audience, but it also had to convince that audience that the purchase of war securities was paramount, despite any financial or logistical hurdles. The publication was, in other words, a form of domestic propaganda, a distinction made all the more intriguing given the comic book's status as an official government document. This is even more compelling because the book targeted "Boys and Girls of America" (Morgenthau, Jr., 1942b, p. 2). The propaganda effort was specifically designed with children in mind, an audience that would possibly have little understanding of the stakes. The U.S. government production of comic book propaganda using fictional characters designed for children's consumption reveals much about the perceived urgency of the war effort *and* the lengths to which the government would go to achieve those ends.

Our aim in this chapter is to engage in a narrative and normative analysis of *War Victory Comics* and the book's various storylines. We initially build on the theory of narrative possibility, highlighting the idea that a powerful quality of stories is their ability to identify new prospective scenarios and choices of action to audience members. We then argue that *War Victory Comics* enhances its narrative rhetoric through the use of normative appeals. This perspective suggests that narratives can prompt behavioral changes by presenting normative models, characters whom we become motivated to imitate. We conclude the chapter by considering the curiously solitary nature of *War Victory Comics* on the American home front. Despite the evident success of the project in reaching out to the nation's youth, the Treasury did not produce more comic books. Although, the publication is an intriguing case study on its own, its status as a solo effort sheds important light on the U.S. government's general shift away from cartoon propaganda after 1942.

Narrative Possibility, War Stamps, and Children

War Victory Comics emerged in an environment in which comics of all sorts were a pervasive aspect of U.S. culture. With iconic characters such as Terry and the Pirates, Captain America, and Joe Palooka entertaining millions of citizens, newspaper comic strips were "the most widely read non-advertising feature among adult readers" (Barkin, 1984, p. 114). According to Muhlen's (1949) summary of surveys conducted by the Market Research Corporation of America and other commercial market and media research organizations, the percentage in army training camps was even higher. Also, 28 percent of the country's female adults said that they were regular readers. As expected, younger readers were the primary target audience for cartoonists. Indeed, approximately 95 percent of boys aged 6 to 11 read up to 15 comic books every month, while 91 percent of girls reported reading the same amount. Although comic readership rates declined for those youngsters aged 12 to 18, a surprising 80 percent still read 12 or more comic books a month.

Recognizing comics as a possible opportunity to spread vital information and ideas, the U.S. government quickly began to study the medium after Pearl Harbor. A series of early 1942 studies within the Bureau of Intelligence, for example, offered detailed analyses of war themes and references in the cartoons of home front periodicals (Barkin, 1984). Before long, the Office of Facts and Figures, the War Production Board, and (starting in the summer of 1942) the Office of War Information, were all active in the creation of various comic materials. Such activities included suggesting story lines for existing comic strips, tasking cartoonists to create images for munitions factory publications, and creation of colorfully illustrated government handbooks and manuals.

The Treasury's comic book initiative was one of the most ambitious of the government's efforts on the cartoon front. *War Victory Comics* appeared late in the summer of 1942 even as the war bond program was experiencing a potentially disastrous sales slump (Kimble, 2006). Government studies found that while the vast majority of Americans recognized the national need to stock up on war bonds and stamps, too few were actually making a purchase. According to Treasury Secretary Henry Morgenthau Jr. (1942a) the bond program enjoyed "the confidence and good will" of Americans, yet needed to "persuade people to buy War Savings Bonds willingly and enthusiastically" (p. 3). Central to the Treasury's thinking that summer, then, was a dilemma familiar to communication theorists—how to move the target audience from belief to the enactment of that belief.

The narrative patterns in *War Victory Comics*' various story lines represented a strategic attempt to show the nation's young comic book readers specific ways they could enact the purchase of war stamps. An important aspect of this approach was a persuasive strategy: "the rhetoric of possibility" (Greenbaum, 2002, p. xv). Poulakos (1984) explained that "the rhetoric of possibility labors to make its listeners envision an absent reality" even as it "addresses them in terms of their capacity to become what they are not" (p. 223). As used in narratives, suggested Kirkwood (1992), the notion of portraying the possible allows persuasive messages to show an audience "previously unsuspected ways of being and acting in the world" (p. 32). Through the use of storytelling rhetors can portray scenarios, plots, and character actions that effectively yet subtly suggest "new ways of living" (p. 32).

The Treasury's innovative comic book portrayed new possibilities to its young home front readers on at least two levels. On one level, the issue's various story lines continuously emphasized the results that a stamp purchase could make possible. War stamps and bonds, stories revealed, were the equivalent of war munitions. "A 10¢ stamp will buy three rounds of ammunition," proclaimed a cartoon officer in one panel. "Maybe," he concluded, "the lucky bullet's for Herr H." ("Your Dime's in the Army Now," 1942, p. 13). The accompanying visual illustrated a young war stamp purchaser actually firing bullets at a shocked Hitler. To reinforce the message, a nearby drawing displayed a simple equation: three oversized rifle shells on one side of an equals (=) sign and "10¢" on the other. Other drawings on the same page were nearly as literal, depicting bombs labeled "Bond" landing on the enemy, a war bond–purchased rifle slamming painfully down on the tail of a Japanese rat (p. 13). In a separate cartoon segment on the same page, an animated and life-size war stamp happily kicked Hitler in the rear (Nash, 1942). Each depiction was, in its own way, a portrayal of the possible (if figurative) outcome of a war stamp or bond purchase.

A similar approach was evident in the comic book's Green Hornet story line. In this feature, the vigilante Green Hornet and his sidekick Kato — both of radio show fame — found themselves cornered by the local police in a post office. As the gun-wielding officers rushed in, however, the masked crusader froze them by revealing that his intention at the post office was to purchase war bonds. Speaking to the stunned officials, he proclaimed that "our soldiers need *more* guns!... Our pilots need *more* planes!... Our sailors need *more* ships!... That costs money ... and here's how we can help! Buy war savings bonds and stamps" ("Green Hornet," 1942, p. 9). Here, in the words of a popular cartoon hero, the Treasury's securities were more than just an investment and more than a patriotic obligation. They became a direct means of producing more munitions for the nation's soldiers, a notion that clearly communicated to readers the vital possibilities contained within a single war stamp.

In addition to demonstrating what the purchase of a war security could make possible in the context of the war effort, *War Treasury Comics* used the rhetoric of possibility on a second level. On this level the emphasis was on depicting a number of creative strategies that readers could use to obtain war stamps and, eventually, war bonds. The book's story lines portrayed youngsters raiding their piggy banks (Young, 1942), getting paid for odd jobs in war stamps ("Smitty," 1942), finding lost change and asking parents for stamp money (Nash, 1942), using pennies given by "a generous family" who gave up "luxuries like ice cream" (Suser, 1942, p. 17), asking for war bonds as birthday presents (Byrnes, 1942), purchasing a new baseball glove (Rice, 1942), and even shining shoes on the street (Gates, 1942, p. 24). On occasion, the comic book portrayed adults being creative in obtaining war stamps and bonds, too. Dagwood Bumstead, for example, decided to break his son's piggy bank to purchase a war bond before finding that his son had already done so (Young, 1942). Winnie Winkle had another idea — asking her boss if she could take part of her salary in war bonds. As she consulted with him, the cartoonist directly addressed readers: "What about it girls? Have you started the payroll plan in your office?" (Branner, 1942, p. 7). Both children and adults, the comic made clear, should find as many ways as possible to purchase the much-needed war securities.

A particularly poignant example of the comic book's construction of possibilities appeared in the story line "A Good Idea" (Zeig, 1942). The narrative began with three children finding out from a recruiter that they were far too young to enlist in the armed forces. He informed them, however, that they could help with the war by collecting scrap newspapers. The children visited Mr. Smith, who told them that they could take away his big pile of old papers: "You're welcome to them, kids — the country needs them and you get a little money" (p. 16). Startled by this information, one of the youngsters exclaimed, "Now we can buy U.S. war stamps...!" (p. 16). The new idea was obviously exciting for the young characters who were tacitly modeling the fruits of narrative possibility. Their *eureka* moment, that is, functioned to give many of the comic book's readers a way to purchase war stamps that had not previously occurred to them. The feature's final image, a depiction of the three children celebrating their purchase of $2.40 in war stamps and scheming about ways to obtain more, would have reinforced the rewards of this enticing possibility by enhancing its perceived plausibility.

At times, *War Victory Comics* even demonstrated how some of its proposed possibilities could produce other possible purchases. Joe Palooka, for instance, first strong armed a wealthy friend into spending a tempting wad of cash on a number of war bonds, then directly advised the reader to not only find ways to purchase "lots of war stamps and bonds," but also to convince "your friends and family to save 'em, too!" (Fisher, 1942, p. 5). Another feature depicted two boys giving up their personal savings of three dollars to purchase war stamps for their mother's birthday. The final panel showed the youngsters standing proudly as she announced that the war stamps were "the nicest of my presents!" In response, her husband exclaimed, "Now *I'm* going [to go] out and buy some war savings *bonds* for all of us!" (Rice, 1942, p. 25). In these instances, the comic book attempted to convince its young readers that their creativity in scheming new ways to purchase war stamps would inevitably pay off with esteem and pride and with more purchases from their family and friends.

The Treasury's 1942 comic book was alive with narrative possibilities. It depicted the possible implications of war stamp purchases. Many panels depicted Treasury securities as the virtual equivalents of munitions and armaments. Some strips even portrayed young readers deploying the weapons themselves, as though purchasing a stamp equated personally be firing at the enemy. Moreover, *War Victory Comics* simultaneously emphasized the many possible ways that home front youth could find funds to purchase war stamps and, ultimately, trade them in for war bonds. In depicting these possibilities, the Treasury's cartoonists were effectively constructing a contingent world. Feature after feature communicated to readers that this contingency could only become a reality if the children began to make plans to purchase war stamps. If they embraced this possible course of action, the Treasury suggested, children would gain in esteem, parents would be proud, the military would have its weapons and, most importantly, the war would be won.

Normative Modeling in the Purchase of War Securities

War Victory Comics' use of narrative possibility portrayed a number of American children finding creative and unusual ways to purchase war stamps. Although these depictions might have been inspiring for many young readers across the country, they also may have appealed to the youthful desire for conformity. How many children, after all, would be comfortable behaving in exceptional and unusual ways? If the Treasury's goal was to convince "every one" of the home front's "forty million boys and girls to buy at least one ten-cent War Savings Stamp every week" (Morgenthau, 1942b, p. 2), it probably needed to do more than to construct possibilities. It needed, in a word, to depict exceptional and unusual behavior as *normal*.

An important focus of the Treasury's comic book, then, was the careful portrayal of normative models. Theorists have long been interested in the various ways that persuasive texts can serve to create positive norms (see, e.g., Rushton, 1979). Typically guided by social cognitive theory (Bandura, 2001), this strand of research suggests that when facing new social situations, humans often try to "match" the previously "modeled behaviors" they find in media portrayals (Smith, et al., 2006, p. 709). Indeed, when receivers are repeatedly exposed to such behavioral models, the matching activity "may be internalized and serve as a normative guide" (p. 709). The consistent depiction of models acting in specific ways, in this view, can act as a way of normalizing those actions. In the very moment these depictions represent a behavior as normal they effectively become social norms.

Recent work on social cognitive theory (e.g., Stern, Russell, & Russell, 2007) has suggested that one powerful means of modeling and reinforcing normative behavior is narrative communication. The various narratives in *War Victory Comics* support this suggestion. Although the book's characters were often portrayed as making exceptional behavioral choices as they struggled to attain war stamps, the Treasury consistently tried to transform these exceptional choices into socially acceptable norms. Three of the comic book's normalizing strategies are especially pertinent here.

First, *War Victory Comics* depicted a wide variety of role models with whom readers could identify and admire. The most prominent group of these role models would properly be called heroes. Superman, for example, appeared at one point in his trademark flying pose. His urgent expression emphasized the serious nature of his words: "Hurry, everyone! Your money is needed to defeat the Axis powers. Buy U.S. war bonds and stamps...!" ("Superman," 1942, p. 27). Appropriately, the panel portrayed a crowd of citizens just below the man of steel, all of them apparently rushing to follow his admonition. Elsewhere, Dick Tracy appeared in conversation with Uncle Sam, the detective smugly stating that he would be buying "*plenty*" of Treasury offerings (Gould, 1942, p. 28). Finally, a non-fictional hero — boxing champion and enlisted soldier Joe Louis — posed proudly with his recently-purchased war bond ("Buys Bond, Too," 1942). The message in each instance was clear: even heroes took the time to invest in war bonds and stamps.

The Treasury's cartoonists were careful to include a group of more down-to-earth role models as they attempted to normalize the vital quest for war stamps. Americans of all stripes appeared in the comic book with diverse profiles — young, old, rich, poor, black, and white. One of them was an attractive young businessman who held a war bond affectionately, exclaiming that "nothing looks as beautiful to me right now as this share in *freedom's fight*" (Sparling, 1942, p. 21). Skeezix and Nina, familiar characters from the Gasoline Alley comic strip, appeared to inform readers that "we give our country's enemies a jolt every pay day when we buy U.S. war stamps" (King, 1942, p. 26). Li'l Abner and a dozen or so friends from rural Dogpatch formed a parade to the post office, carrying a box of cash to purchase bonds (Capp, 1942). In each example, the comic book presented regular folks who had become motivated to purchase war stamps and, perhaps, to convince those around them to do the same. Even the appearance of screen star Shirley Temple was toned down: she was not purchasing thousands of dollars of war bonds, but humbly pasting war stamps into a booklet ("Here is Shirley Temple," 1942). In many ways the Treasury's message presented the dedicated pursuit of war stamps as socially acceptable *and* absolutely normal. Whether they were heroes or just regular folks, people across the country were evidently creating a new set of norms on behalf of the Treasury campaign.

In a second normalizing strategy, *War Victory Comics* modeled the social approval that was apparently part of the process of purchasing war securities. Character after character found their struggles to purchase war stamps or bonds received with approval, enthusiastic acclaim, and even adoration. Young (1942), for instance, illustrated Dagwood's excited approval of Baby Dumpling's initiative in using his savings to purchase war stamps, with Blondie verbally enhancing the approval with "Smart Boy" (p. 3). In another feature a father offered an infant a choice between a piece of candy and a war stamp. The baby chose the stamp, prompting the mother to exclaim proudly that "Junior catches on quick!" ("Junior," 1942, p. 10). In "A Good Idea" (Zeig, 1942), three children tried to enlist in the armed forces, but who ended up purchasing war stamps with paper recycling cash, made it clear that they had made a great choice in the eyes of their community. As one of them proclaimed, "That's smart! We help our country win the war and we also save for our future!" (p. 16). The children's delighted faces reinforced their esteem in helping win the war. Like Baby Dumpling and the anonymous infant, their choice to make a sacrifice in pursuit of war stamps was personally and socially rewarding. By emphasizing the approval and pride felt by such characters, the Treasury was reinforcing stamp purchasing as a normal and even desirable behavior.

The Treasury used a third normalizing strategy when it depicted the transformation of characters from irresponsible citizens into eager stamp and bond purchasers. The Treasury's cartoonists evidently concluded that to construct the pursuit of war securities as a vital activity, they needed to illustrate that a change in behavior was both possible and desirable. Consequently, the comic repeatedly featured characters altering their behaviors in positive ways to create a new norm. The feature "Boxcars," for example, portrayed two hobos, a father and son. Initially, the father was shocked to find his son shining shoes on the street. "Never once have we worked!" he shouted. "And now this!" The son retorted, "But I want to buy *War Savings Stamps*." "Do you know," the son continued, "if *they* win this war they'd make *slave laborers* of all of us — even us *fourth* generation hobos!" (Gates, 1942, p. 24). The father's nonverbal reaction to this retort displayed a classic illustration of transformational shock. Evidently, he soon realized the value of war stamps, because the last panel depicted the father asking a man if he would like a shoe shine.

A similarly positive transformation happened to a character in "Sweeney & Son." Here, the obviously wealthy main character, according to his wife, "used to be extravagant and squander all his dough." Her husband responded emphatically by shouting "*Them days is gone forever!*" Now, he pointed out, "I buy U.S. war bonds — yessiree — and watch my money grow!" (Posen, 1942, p. 27). Meanwhile, in the Joe Palooka story line the wealthy character Knobby was initially portrayed as a gambling spendthrift, eager to throw his money away. After being escorted by Private Polooka to the bank, however, Knobby realized the true value of war bonds. With a broad and surprised smile, he exclaimed "*Ohhh now I git it— it's a pleasure*—I'll make th' check out fer five thousand" (Fisher, 1942, p. 5). Knobby's transformation modeled, as did the positive change in the husband and in the hobo, the enthusiastic purchase of war securities by those who were initially reluctant or opposed to the idea. Such transformations spoke not only to young readers who were themselves doubtful about spending their money on war stamps, but also to youngsters who could potentially approach reluctant friends and family. Either way, the Treasury's transformational depictions helped support its normative approach.

Whether modeling the behavior of other citizens, modeling social approval, or modeling positive transformations, *War Victory Comics* engaged in strategies that helped to normalize the act of buying war stamps and bonds. This portrayal of the urgent search for war securities as normal was important because the Treasury wanted citizens to exhaust every possibility in their efforts. Simply depicting the many possibilities available to the stamp-buying public, however, was not enough. To encourage Americans to take risks, to give up necessities, and to postpone immediate gratification for the sake of the war effort meant that the Treasury's cartoonists also needed to create a new norm, one in which it was not at all unusual to scrounge in search of stamps and bonds. As a result, audiences could internalize the suggested course of action and incorporate the act of buying war bonds and stamps into their daily lives. Fittingly, as one unnamed character said, "Hey kids — all the gang in my block are buying U.S. War Stamps! How about you?" (Williams, 1942, p. 17).

Conclusions

War Victory Comics seems to have been a relative success for the U.S. Treasury in its quest to turn the popular belief that war bonds and stamps were important for the war effort into the enactment of that belief in actual purchases. Although it is impossible to isolate the comic book's specific role in the war bond program's resurgence after the summer of 1942, it is clear that Treasury officials were pleased with their cartoon salvo (Lane, 1942). Indeed, anticipating the book's success, the program's plans were to publish more issues on a quarterly basis (U.S. Treasury Department, 1942, p. 2). Yet the two subsequent comic books, dubbed *War Victory Adventures* (1943a, 1943b), were not Treasury products at all, but produced and published by the Family Comics corporation. This curious circumstance raises an important question: If the Treasury was so pleased with its initial comic book, why did it give the project up after one attempt?

In the absence of extant archival evidence, one can only speculate that the Treasury's comic initiative faltered in connection with the U.S. government's general disavowal of comics after 1942. Barkin (1984) noted that "the end of the government's formal effort to study and produce cartoon materials" was hastened by the Office of War Information's late 1942 publication of *The Life of Franklin D. Roosevelt* (p. 116). This comic book, originally intended to be distributed to Allied civilians overseas, was seized upon by U.S. Representative John Taber, one of President Roosevelt's Congressional antagonists. In remarks on the House floor, Taber called the comic book "purely political propaganda, designed to promote a fourth term and dictatorship" (as quoted in "End of a Decade," 1943, p. 36). Stung by the public criticism, OWI began to distance itself from cartoon projects altogether. By the summer of 1943 its comics division had been shuttered.

Although other government-related comic projects did not disappear completely after 1942, they were not as commonplace as one would have predicted amidst the cartoon enthusiasm at the beginning of the war. Shull and Wilt's (1987) study of animated shorts during the conflict, for example, demonstrated that after 1942 government-sponsored cartoon films declined remarkably. Barkin (1984) agreed with this observation, confirming that "from the government's point of view, the experience with comics had not been especially satisfactory" (p. 117). Thus, while the Treasury-free status of both issues of *War Victory Adventures* (1943a, 1943b) is curious in some respects, when considered in a wider context it was likely part of a larger trend.

However, the single issue of *War Victory Comics* is a valuable reminder of the importance of mediated communication in war-time, particularly of this type of communication to younger audiences. For young Americans removed from the reality of the frontlines, the government evidently saw a need early in the conflict to instill the sense of duty that could ensure victory as well as provide impetus for adults to follow their children. The war was all-encompassing and it encroached into every aspect of daily life, even for children. What better way to justify the sacrifice and process of making-do then to incorporate a sense of choice in supporting the war effort?

Just as every American citizen was encouraged to pitch in to support the war effort, the narrative and normative strategies used in *War Victory Comics* provided a rationale and a means for younger audiences to play their part by choosing to change their behaviors. Moreover, the new behaviors were visualized for audiences. Instead of being told what to do and the benefits of action, readers could actually see the actions in practice. That these acts were carried out by recognizable heroes and people like themselves only reinforced the need and desire to model the new behavior.

In the end, *War Victory Comics* was a series of diverse comic strips that constructed an overriding narrative to present possibilities that could be modeled on the home front to help win the war. In so doing, the book presented readers with palatable options for ways in which they could support the American effort. Narrative, as Fisher (1984) suggests, presents good reasons for decision making. In the case of *War Victory Comics*, the reasons presented were not only good but necessary. Ultimately, they provided a sound rationale for

America's youth to become "the minute men of today" ("You Boys and Girls," 1942, p. 6).

REFERENCES

Allport, G. (1942). The nature of Democratic morale. In G. Watson (Ed.), *Civilian Morale* (pp. 3–18). New York: Reynal & Hitchcock.
Bandura, A. (2001). Social cognitive theory of mass communication. *Media Psychology, 3,* 265–298.
Barkin, S. M. (1984). Fighting the cartoon war: Information strategies in World War II. *Journal of American Culture, 1–2*(7), 113–117.
Branner, M. (1942, Summer). Winnie Winkle. In *War Victory Comics* (p. 7). (Box 8, Folder 1). Odegard Papers, Franklin D. Roosevelt Presidential Library, Hyde Park, NY.
Buys bond, too. (1942, Summer). In *War Victory Comics* (p. 11). (Box 8, Folder 1). Odegard Papers, Franklin D. Roosevelt Presidential Library, Hyde Park, NY.
Byrnes, G. (1942, Summer). Reg'lar fellers. In *War Victory Comics* (p. 20). (Box 8, Folder 1). Odegard Papers, Franklin D. Roosevelt Presidential Library, Hyde Park, NY.
Capp, A. (1942, Summer). Lil [sic] Abner. In *War Victory Comics* (p. 7). (Box 8, Folder 1). Odegard Papers, Franklin D. Roosevelt Presidential Library, Hyde Park, NY.
End of a decade. (1943, March 15). *Newsweek,* pp. 34, 36.
Fisher, H. (1942, Summer). Joe Palooka. In *War Victory Comics* (pp. 4–5). (Box 8, Folder 1). Odegard Papers, Franklin D. Roosevelt Presidential Library, Hyde Park, NY.
Fisher, W. R. (1984). Narration as human communication paradigm: The case of public moral argument. *Communication Monographs, 51,* 1–22.
Gates, A. (1942, Summer). Boxcars. In *War Victory Comics* (p. 24). (Box 8, Folder 1). Odegard Papers, Franklin D. Roosevelt Presidential Library, Hyde Park, NY.
Gould, C. (1942, Summer). Dick Tracy. In *War Victory Comics* (p. 28). (Box 8, Folder 1). Odegard Papers, Franklin D. Roosevelt Presidential Library, Hyde Park, NY.
Greenbaum, A. (2002). *Emancipatory Movements in Composition: The Rhetoric of Possibility.* Albany: State University of New York Press.
Green Hornet. (1942, Summer). In *War Victory Comics* (pp. 8–9). (Box 8, Folder 1). Odegard Papers, Franklin D. Roosevelt Presidential Library, Hyde Park, NY.
Here is Shirley Temple. (1942, Summer). In *War Victory Comics* (p. 2). (Box 8, Folder 1). Odegard Papers, Franklin D. Roosevelt Presidential Library, Hyde Park, NY.
Holsinger, M. P. (1999). War savings stamps (home front involvement). In M. P. Holsinger (Ed.), *War and American Culture: A Historical Encyclopedia* (pp. 328–329). Westport, CT: Greenwood.
Junior catches on quick. (1942, Summer). In *War Victory Comics* (p. 10). (Box 8, Folder 1). Odegard Papers, Franklin D. Roosevelt Presidential Library, Hyde Park, NY.
Kimble, J. J. (2006). *Mobilizing the Home Front: War Bonds and Domestic Propaganda.* College Station: Texas A&M University Press.
King, F. (1942). Gasolene [sic] alley. In *War Victory Comics* (p. 26). (Box 8, Folder 1). Odegard Papers, Franklin D. Roosevelt Presidential Library, Hyde Park, NY.
Kirk, R. W. (1994). *Earning Their Stripes: The Mobilization of American Children in the Second World War.* New York: Peter Lang.
———. (1995). Getting in the scrap: The mobilization of American children in World War II. *Journal of Popular Culture, 29,* 223–233.
Kirkwood, W. G. (1992). Narrative and the rhetoric of possibility. *Communication Monographs, 59,* 30–47.
Lane, T. H. (1942, July 16). Evaluation of war bond promotion [memorandum]. (Box 8, Folder 1). Odegard Papers, Franklin D. Roosevelt Presidential Library, Hyde Park, NY.

McCarty, M., Jr. (1942, August 10). Memorandum to Mr. Fitzgerald et al. (Box 8, Folder 1). Odegard Papers, Franklin D. Roosevelt Presidential Library, Hyde Park, NY.

Morgenthau, H., Jr. (1942a, June 15). A message from the Secretary. *The Minute Man*, p. 3.

——. (1942b, Summer). Introductory letter. In *War Victory Comics* (p. 2). (Box 8, Folder 1). Odegard Papers, Franklin D. Roosevelt Presidential Library, Hyde Park, NY.

Muhlen, N. (1949). Comic books and other horrors: Prep school for totalitarian society? *Commentary, 7*(1), 80–87.

Nash, O. (1942, Summer). Nashing the Axis. In *War Victory Comics* (p. 13). (Box 8, Folder 1). Odegard Papers, Franklin D. Roosevelt Presidential Library, Hyde Park, NY.

Posen, A. (1942, Summer). Sweeney & son. In *War Victory Comics* (p. 27). (Box 8, Folder 1). Odegard Papers, Franklin D. Roosevelt Presidential Library, Hyde Park, NY.

Poulakos, J. (1984). Rhetoric, the sophists, and the possible. *Communication Monographs, 51,* 215–226.

Rice, P. G. (1942, Summer). Mom's best birthday present. In *War Victory Comics* (p. 25). (Box 8, Folder 1). Odegard Papers, Franklin D. Roosevelt Presidential Library, Hyde Park, NY.

Rushton, J. P. (1979). Effects of prosocial television and film material on the behavior of viewers. *Advances in Experimental Social Psychology, 12,* 321–351.

Shull, M. S., and D. E. Wilt (1987). *Doing Their Bit: Wartime Animated Short Films.* Jefferson, NC: McFarland.

Shultz, G. D. (1944, May). Wanted: 5,000,000 kids. *Better Homes & Gardens,* pp. 36, 94, 96–97.

Smith, S. W., S. L. Smith, K. M. Pieper, J. H. Yoo, A. L. Ferris, E. Downs, and B. Bowden (2006). Altruism on American television: Examining the amount of, and context surrounding, acts of helping and sharing. *Journal of Communication, 56,* 707–727.

Smitty. (1942, Summer). In *War Victory Comics* (p. 6). (Box 8, Folder 1). Odegard Papers, Franklin D. Roosevelt Presidential Library, Hyde Park, NY.

Sparling, J. (1942, Summer). Hap Hopper. In *War Victory Comics* (p. 21). (Box 8, Folder 1). Odegard Papers, Franklin D. Roosevelt Presidential Library, Hyde Park, NY.

Stern, B. B., C. A. Russell, and D. W. Russell (2007). Hidden persuasions in soap operas: Damaged heroines and negative consumer effects. *International Journal of Advertising, 26,* 9–36.

Suser, B. (1942, Summer). Young America helps win the war. In *War Victory Comics* (p. 17). (Box 8, Folder 1). Odegard Papers, Franklin D. Roosevelt Presidential Library, Hyde Park, NY.

Superman. (1942, Summer). In *War Victory Comics* (p. 27). (Box 8, Folder 1). Odegard Papers, Franklin D. Roosevelt Presidential Library, Hyde Park, NY.

Tuttle, W. M., Jr. (1995). Rosie the riveter and her latchkey children: What Americans can learn about child day care from the Second World War. *Child Welfare, 74,* 92–114.

U.S. Treasury Department. (1942, Summer). *War Victory Comics.* (Box 8, Folder 1). Odegard Papers, Franklin D. Roosevelt Presidential Library, Hyde Park, NY.

War victory adventures. (1943a, August). (Vol. 1, no. 2). St. Louis: Family Comics.

——. (1943b, Winter). (Vol. 1, no. 3). St. Louis: Family Comics.

Williams, J. R. (1942, Summer). Hey kids. In *War Victory Comics* (p. 17). (Box 8, Folder 1). Odegard Papers, Franklin D. Roosevelt Presidential Library, Hyde Park, NY.

You boys and girls. (1942, Summer). In *War Victory Comics* (p. 6). (Box 8, Folder 1). Odegard Papers, Franklin D. Roosevelt Presidential Library, Hyde Park, NY.

Young, C. (1942, Summer). Blondie. In *War Victory Comics* (p. 3). (Box 8, Folder 1). Odegard Papers, Franklin D. Roosevelt Presidential Library, Hyde Park, NY.

Your dime's in the Army now. (1942, Summer). In *War Victory Comics* (p. 13). (Box 8,

Folder 1). Odegard Papers, Franklin D. Roosevelt Presidential Library, Hyde Park, NY.

Zeig. (1942, Summer). A good idea. In *War Victory Comics* (p. 16). (Box 8, Folder 1). Odegard Papers, Franklin D. Roosevelt Presidential Library, Hyde Park, NY.

INSPECTING THE RHETORICAL ARSENAL: THE WAR FRAME IN NAZI GERMANY'S *DER KAMPF* AND AMERICA'S WAR ON TERROR

Roy Schwartzman

Herbert Hirsch (1995) apocalyptically predicted: "If the twentieth century is any indication, the end may result from words used to motivate, justify, and rationalize murder on a scale unprecedented in human history. Words can kill — or at least motivate a person to kill" (p. 97). In this study I examine rhetorical maneuvers that reinforce the war frame, defined as patterns and logic of discourse that configure social policy and attitudes according to the model of warfare. Ammunition for this martial mentality derives from an arsenal of rhetorical techniques revolving around the central concept of war. Two specific instances illustrate the war frame's deployment: Nazi Germany's framing of social policies as a constant struggle or battle (*der Kampf*) and the "War on Terror" adopted by the United States after 9/11. While *der Kampf* exemplified a rhetorically successful application of a war frame to social issues, specifically persecution of Jews, the War on Terror demonstrated how overextending a frame ultimately can undermine its own logical and affective grounds for support. Both cases call for ways to reflect more critically on the choice of frames to adopt, since once a frame gains momentum it may become naturalized as the default way to conceive of an issue. Faced with questions that sheer data could not answer, the frames that guide discussion can influence the possible choices of social policy. These frames help draw the boundaries of what qualifies as a legitimate or even thinkable option (Lakoff, 2002).

A frame may be conceived as an amalgamation of rhetorical devices that establish logical and normative patterns for thought and action. Frames are observable as patterns of discourse that mutually reinforce a shared interpretive schema, converging on themes that make sense of social issues (Eilders & Lüter, 2000; Scheufele, 1999). The terminology of "frame" itself helps pinpoint its role as a container or boundary designating what counts as legitimate argumentative *topoi*. Although most research on framing has concentrated on media effects (Scheufele & Tewksbury, 2007), in this essay I examine the more philosophical issue of how the construction and deployment of a specific frame in public discourse establishes the bounds of logically allowable responses and extensions to the frame's implications. One might consider this line of research as establishing the conditions for audience response rather than empirically measuring those responses.

Analysis of the war frame proceeds by examining discourse from several sources. Frames are understood best as sustained by a convergence of discourse rather than as a simple imposition of a view from a single or aggregate source such as "the media" (Scheufele, 1999). With that understanding, discursive evidence of the war frame's operation emerges from representative examples from popular newspapers, speeches and public writings of major governmental figures, and research on the social issues pertinent to the war frame.

Illustrations of how *der Kampf* operated in Nazi Germany were selected from materials appearing prior to World War II, which assured that the war terminology was not simply transferred from a literal battlefield. Items were gleaned from materials published or presented in Nazi Germany from January 30, 1933 (Hitler's accession to Chancellor) to September 1, 1939 (the onset of World War II). Every issue of *Völkischer Beobachter*, the widest circulated national daily newspaper, and *Das Schwarze Korps*, the general circulation newspaper targeted to SS members, was examined for titles that included the term *der Kampf* and its variants (such as plurals and verb forms), or terms referring to war (soldier and synonyms, weapon, names of weapons or military equipment). In addition, books and periodical articles written by so-called racial scientists, those who promulgated the theoretical grounds for anti–Semitism, were examined. Finally, the speeches and writings of Adolf Hitler and government administrators during the designated time period were included. Representative governmental discourse regarding the War on Terror derived from three major speeches President George W. Bush delivered on September 2001, as these addresses set in motion the direction public policy would take in response to the 9/11 terrorist attacks, and the USA PATRIOT Act. Additional examples were gleaned from a LexisNexis Academic search using the search strings "war on terror" and "war on terrorism" within major U.S. and world publications from September 11, 2001 to October 7, 2001 (the invasion of Afghanistan).

Der Kampf: Destiny's Modus Operandi

The noun *der Kampf* and the verb *kampfen* usually are translated as "struggle" or "battle." The terms served as "ordering concepts for the analysis of National Socialism," articulating a process that lent rationality to events (Mason, 1981, p. 39). On the personal level, struggle explained the nature of life. The process of living amounted to a process of facing and overcoming the obstacles placed in one's path. On the cosmic level, struggle operated as a law of nature. This law not only described the competition for existence, but also treated the natural world as a site where humans could assist nature by improving their ability to resist any forces that threatened their survival. The human world of struggle extended the struggle observable in nature. As Hitler (1941) proclaimed, "[W]e believe that by our struggle we are but carrying out the will of the Creator, who imbued all creatures with the instinct for self-preservation" (p. 197).

It might appear that struggle formed the central explanatory principle, a god-term worthy of worship, during the Nazi era (Gamm, 1962). This conclusion sounds plausible, but it misses the mark. Struggle itself offered little or nothing in the way of final explanations. Struggle represented the modus operandi for working out racial differences and the inevitable conflicts that would arise among races with "absolutely different" ancestry, such as Jews, and Italians or Germans ("Grundsätzliches Bekenntnis," 1938, p. 2). Any struggle remained meaningless if the battle had no wellsprings that generated conflict or objectives that justified it. The reason "struggle lay like a block of granite in the center of Hitler's *Weltanschauung*" (Blackburn, 1985, p. 67) was its importance in linking racial theories with (1) the justification of force; (2) a universally operating principle for differentiating ideas, people, and nations by quality; and (3) channeling thought along the lines of victory or defeat, which encouraged all-out effort to conquer overwhelming odds.

Once the language and concepts of warfare became commonplace, the extension to actual force would not seem drastic or unwarranted. While the discourse of struggle filled publications and speeches by prominent Nazi political figures and racial scientists, the newspaper *Völkischer Beobachter* added sections on aerial weaponry and military equipment. Beginning in January 1933, the features "Wehrpolitik und Landesverteidigung" [military policy and national defense] and "Luftfahrt, Luftschutz" [aviation and civil air defense] appeared weekly as supplements to the national edition. The focus on armaments fed the transition from symbolic to actual warfare. The following sections explain how *der Kampf* provided an important ingredient not only for the Nazi anti–Semitic agenda but also for furnishing rhetorical resources for fueling increasingly repressive social policies.

An Ongoing State of Emergency

Repressive measures became justifiable as necessary during an ongoing emergency. The emphasis on *der Kampf* helped maintain a crisis mentality, a sense of urgency that compelled action. A year before he became Chancellor, Hitler (1941) declared that "we have reached a state of general crisis" (p. 93). In effect, Hitler's pronouncement suggested that events should be interpreted in terms of struggle, so that perpetual, difficult struggle acted as a controlling metaphor through which experience would be understood. Recurrent references to struggle reinforced allied medical terminology. The "rhetoric of medical emergency: 'dangerous patients' and 'urgent cases'" (Lifton, 1986, pp. 26–27) tended to group all hereditary conditions without qualification into a single category of severe illness and, therefore, a threat to the nation's prosperity or survival. As a result, no distinction was made between those who suffered from severe physical diseases and those who were deemed less valuable [*Minderwertig*] members of society solely because of their racial characteristics.

Maintaining a "permanent state of emergency" also served a practical political function: external threats discouraged attempts to probe too deeply into the failure of Nazism to offer a definite political program (Giles, 1985). Constant struggle thus served as a palliative. If human existence consisted of endless, arduous struggle, little opportunity remained for reflecting on the miseries of life. If people had no time to think about their situation, and could not detach themselves from the "immediate struggle" to survive, they remained "untroubled by questions as to the value and interest of action" (Teilhard de Chardin, 1987, p. 151). The immediate exigency of survival took precedence over the luxury of intellectual analysis. Therefore, the ongoing need for struggle made the protection of Germany a duty for every citizen instead of a task assigned to a cadre of technical experts (Kandel, 1935).

The persistence of crises did not lessen their severity. Each year was hailed not as the year of victory, but as another year of struggle that would bring victory a bit closer. A caption to a photo of Adolf Hitler in the February 2, 1936, issue of *Das Schwarze Korps* labeled him "Adolf Hitler, the master-builder of greater Germany, the *Führer* in the new year of the German *Kampf*" (p. 13). The traditional German chant of "*Sieg heil!*" [Hail Victory] simply reaffirmed acquiescence with the goals of Nazism framed in terms of battle; it did not hail the arrival of victory itself.

War imagery and metaphors proved especially useful in the context of racial issues. Far from detached contemplation, the discourse of struggle called for action to advance the cause of racial quality. All endeavors fell within the compass of struggle. As the first two lines of an anonymous poem titled "Struggle is Life" stated, "Life amounts to struggle!—/Struggle for everything!" ("Kampf ist das Leben," 1933, n. pag.) The call to struggle placed important demands on researchers and policymakers. Political participation in struggle imitated military tactics. As an article in *Völkischer Beobachter* affirmed, the model for political action became the loyal soldier: "Alongside the armed soldier strides the political soldier" ("Neben den Soldat," 1939, p. 1). This juxtaposition highlighted a shared tactical orientation. The political soldier had to act decisively to protect the Nordic race against decay. In a similar vein *Das Schwarze Korps* included a regular section titled "The Political Soldier," which allowed readers to become part of the army of citizens struggling for the survival and prosperity of the Reich. Hitler (1941) described himself as "the soldier of my people," because he justified his actions as necessarily drastic means taken to serve the populace [*Volk*] (p. 531).

The objectives and methods of scientific investigation also were cast in military terms. Academic journals declared institutes of physics were "sites of struggle [*Kampfstätten*] for National Socialism" (Becker, 1937–1938, p. 48). Maintenance of good health fit within the militaristic framework. Hitler Youth director Baldur von Schirach (1939) stated, "You have the duty to be healthy!" (p. 135). According to von Schirach (1939), the Hitler Youth should not succumb to the temptations of alcohol and tobacco, since any poisons to the body endangered "the entire painstaking work" of cultivating the health of the nation as a whole (p. 135). Personal hygiene helped encourage proper racial hygiene, because citizens as soldiers of the Reich shouldered the responsibility to do their part in preventing any damage to national health. If other races, especially Jews, were defined as a threat, then the researcher should combat those elements just as one would combat a disease. As May (1942) noted, the "genuine researcher is also simultaneously a fighter, and, so to speak, lays the sword on the desk alongside the experimenter's tools" (p. 154).

The Receding Horizon of Victory

For the concept of struggle to spur action, victory always had to remain imminent, looming just around the next corner. Because ultimate victory never quite materialized, the extreme measures required during crisis became embedded as permanent norms. Once a struggle was won, it lost its rhetorical force. Struggle, therefore, had to continue perpetually to preserve its rhetorical value (Nelson, 1991). Failure to reach the ultimate goal of racial purity was due to lack of effort or an external force such as the pernicious influence of alien racial elements. In any case, the goal lay just ahead, reachable but never quite within grasp. Nazi educational theorist Ernst Krieck (1936) intoned, "We are the becoming which is never perfected, we are those who constantly struggle for perfection, who are wrestling for a higher goal and a final destination, again and again starting, never at the goal" (p. 34). Despite the elusiveness of perfection, hope for its attainment could not wane, because surrender to its inaccessibility would halt the struggle and make the future of a glorious Germany merely an unachievable wish. The lack of a temporally realizable terminus for struggle lends credence to the description of *der Kampf* as directed against specific enemies but not toward specific objectives (Mason, 1981). Put more pithily, "It was more important to travel hopefully than to arrive" (Peukert, 1987, p. 245).

If beauty was the aggregate essence of beautiful individuals, the scapegoat was the idealization of undesirable individuals. Jews were consistently referred to in the singular: *der Jude*. Once the unitary ideal of the Jew was concretized through the identification of inherent racial traits, each individual Jew became a more or less perfect manifestation of a racial stereotype.

Struggle could persist not for its own sake, but for the sake of promoting a single, racially unified culture [*Kultur*]. According to Kantian aesthetics, recognition of one's individual insignificance in the face of a grand totality (e.g., when faced with natural forces beyond human control) was sublime. Kant (1989) also found the process of struggle, the "ability to meet with fortitude" (p. 113) seemingly insurmountable obstacles, a sublime experience. Kant contended: "War itself ... has something sublime about it" because it demanded surrender of one's self to a greater ideal of order (pp. 112–113). Struggle carried a flexible but identifiable vision of an ultimate goal, an overarching cause that justified any sacrifice. Phrased innocuously, it could be called "Struggle for the Sake of Nordic Culture [*Kultur*]" (Almquist, 1934, n. pag.). "Nordic culture," however, elaborated into a more pernicious aspect: the imperative of reasserting the supremacy of Aryan qualities and dispositions in the face of threats to racial quality. The connection between Kantian aesthetics and Nazi racial theory appears in the work of Houston Stewart Chamberlain, a crucial precursor of Nazi ideology. Chamberlain (1912) appropriated Social Darwinism to describe the role of struggle in improving racial quality:

> The struggle which means destruction of the fundamentally weak race steels the strong; the same struggle, moreover, by eliminating the weaker elements, tends still further to strengthen the strong. Around the childhood of great races, as we observe, even in the case of the metaphysical Indians, the storm of war always rages [vol. 1, p. 276].

Kant's aesthetic devolved to the grand competition among races — a universal, unalterable, awe-inspiring process that strengthened a race by dooming others to extinction.

Hitler's struggle (*Mein Kampf*) symbolized the struggle of all Germany: to become "more and more aware of the profoundest essence of its struggle" by realizing "itself to be the purest embodiment of the value of race and personality" (Hitler, trans. 1971, p. 688). Hitler concluded the sentence with the proviso that racial doctrines called for action, not cogitation. The urgent situation demanded a *Blitzkrieg* instead of a *Sitzkrieg*. If Germany understood its racial essence and mission "and conducts itself accordingly, it will with almost mathematical certainty some day emerge victorious from its struggle" (p. 688). Only the combination of knowledge with decisive action promised the victory hailed in the salute "*Sieg heil*!"

Partially because of its purported difficulty, struggle had to continue in order to succeed. Struggle also had to persist because its cessation would shrink enthusiasm for the National Socialist movement and for racial ideas. One attractive feature Nazism offered audiences was its constant presentation of reasons to dedicate oneself to positive action (Peukert, 1987). Even if victory was declared on one front, another would emerge to fuel new enthusiasm. Hans Schemm (1934), the Bavarian minister of education, praised this attribute:

> Adolf Hitler sets up goals continuously. When one goal is reached, he sets up the next, and when the next is reached, a still more beautiful one comes, and this establishment of goals will never cease. Never will Adolf Hitler stand before his people and say: "Now we are finished. Now we have everything that we need, no more struggle and strife, now begins an easy, stagnant life." National Socialism will never be finished with struggle; it will always want to strive after something new [pp. 4–5].

National Socialism represented more a dynamic process than a static doctrine. *Bewegung* [movement], a common descriptor of Nazism, indicates its dynamism because the word is associated with physical movement as well as with a political cause. The fanatical enthusiasm Hitler frequently endorsed and sought to kindle could be sustained only if new struggles constantly loomed ahead. The masthead of *Völkischer Beobachter* included its self-portrayal as the "Battle Paper of the National Socialist Cause in Greater Germany" [*Kampfblatt der national-sozialistischen Bewegung Grossdeutschlands*]. As an article in *Das Schwarze Korps* noted, this ever-present need to face new challenges lest support for Hitler or the Nazi regime dwindle made struggle the "watchword under which men voluntarily pledge to die for their *Volk*" ("Der Kampf ist nie zu Ende," 1936, p. 11).

The call to devote everything to the struggle for national survival was justified by the ultimate goal: for "the German soul" [*Seele*] to conquer "entirely and absolutely" ("Der Kampf ist nie zu Ende," 1936, p. 11). The continuity of struggle paralleled and supported the call for all necessary measures to combat threats to national health. If the struggle had to continue until absolute victory, then actions to protect and restore racial quality should not cease until every conceivable source of danger had been eliminated permanently.

Defensive Warfare to Deflect Internal Dissent

Discriminatory and violent acts became defensive measures attributable to enemy aggression, further fueling rationale for repressive action. Internal dissent was deflected toward animosity against a common foe, thereby focusing the regime's opponents on the looming enemy instead of on the regime's repressive policies. The identification of a common foe unified audiences, so when the Jew was targeted as the enemy, the protagonists could set aside their differences (Burke, 1973). The more precisely identified the enemy was, the greater its value for rallying the populace as a whole for the sake of a "fighting movement" (Mosse, 1966, p. xxvii). The struggle against a specific opponent lent identity to the protagonist as well as the opponent. Far from defining the German as simply the antipode of the Jew, a struggle motivated audiences to seek a collective identity that would offer stability in confronting adversity. Portraying the struggle as a defensive measure struck a note of pathos, because Germany was cast in the role of victim against the unjustified aggressions of Jewry [*Judentum*].

The process of *der Kampf* was understood as a way to underscore traits associated with the Nordic soul. Racial scientists had concluded that the "Jewish spirit ... above everything else ... is focused upon its own ego," in contrast to the Nordic spirit that would sacrifice the individual for the sake of the whole (Stark, 1934, p. 207). "True" Germans had no choice as to whether they wanted to join the struggle for the sake of national existence and racial health. The Nordic racial soul demanded that individuals act according to their predispositions, and a self-centered refusal to partake in struggle would stamp the dissenter with the Jewish characteristic of egocentrism. In the Nazi mindset, victory lay in united action, not isolated and uncoordinated effort. "Struggle teaches the value of community above the interests of the ego" (von Werder, 1938, p. 4).

Members of the same race, because of their innate and unalterable linkage through shared blood-ties, offered the best potential for banding together to face forthcoming struggles. Racial comrades had an "individual character of body and soul [that] agree with each other," so dissent would be less likely in the face of a common danger (Staemmler, 1933, p. 15). Besides, since the interval or degree of difference between inferior and superior races was so great, alliances with alien races appeared impossible as well as undesirable.

The war against racial contamination maintained a defensive complexion as long as the potential for racial mixture or spreading racial influence bore the marks of a health issue. Fostering a healthy race amounted to "defensive warfare against mind and blood contamination by the Jews," so racial hygiene lived up to its name as a "cleansing process" (*Nazi Primer*, 1938, p. 78). The linkage between health and race extended a vocabulary associated with combating disease to defending against the incursions of alien races.

The War on Terror: A Fractured Frame

Martial language alone does not necessarily marshal ongoing popular support. The post–9/11 "War on Terror" demonstrated how a militaristic frame also can prove problematic for social cohesion. Several rhetorical factors enabled *der Kampf* to contribute to rallying the populace while the War on Terror fueled outrage without an outlet.

Following September 11, 2001 (9/11), the language of war was quickly and uncritically adopted throughout mainstream media, emerging as the dominant discursive frame (Levenson, 2004). Third-party commentators such as former government officials and ex-military personnel overwhelmingly urged warfare and began strategizing how to conduct it. Specific strategies were debated, but the legitimacy of the war frame received little critical attention. Logos declaring war appeared on news programs. Mainstream media "circulated discourses that assumed that the United States was at war and that only a military response was appropriate" (Kellner, 2007, p. 625). By September 16, 2001, the *Toronto Star* accepted the war as inevitable, focusing on its economic effects rather than questioning the choice of the framing itself: "Like it or not, the United States and the Western democracies are at war against international terrorism" (Carrigan, 2001, p. C2). On September 17, 2001, the *Birmingham* (England) *Evening Mail* had inaugurated a "War on Terror" category of stories.

No Sacrifice, Vague Victory

The President's public speeches after 9/11 immediately set the nation on a war footing, an agenda the news media quickly adopted and facilitated by failing to question or critically examine the frame (Levenson, 2004). Military terminology infused the President's first depiction of the attacks, which he said "were intended to frighten our nation into chaos and retreat" (Bush, 2001a). Just before quoting the 23rd Psalm, implying a righteous cause, Bush (2001a) shifted from talking about helping the victims and bringing terrorists to justice, to seeking victory, declaring that "we stand together to win the war against terrorism."

Only 16 days later, Bush's rhetoric began to reveal some of the problems in the war frame. Instead of a war that required dedication and sacrifice, Bush recommended traveling, shopping, and essentially spending away the nation's sorrows by reinvigorating commercial activity. Speaking at O'Hare International Airport amid scores of other government officials who had just completed their flights, Bush cheerily announced: "We've got quite a crowd traveling today, all of whom — all of whom are here to say as clearly as we can to the American public, get on the airlines, get about the business of America. That's got a nice ring to it, doesn't it?" (Bush, 2001c). He continued: "And one of the great goals of this nation's war is to restore public confidence in the airline industry. It's to tell the traveling public: Get on board. Do your business around the country. Fly and enjoy America's great destination spots. Get down to Disney World in Florida" (Bush, 2001c).

These remarks came while armed National Guard troops still patrolled major airports throughout the nation. Already the first fractures in the war framework crept into view. How serious could the war be if everyone simply went about their business?

The U.S. declaration of war, unlike *der Kampf*, focused on the martial mentality but not its mechanism. The War on Terror explicitly distanced Americans from any sense of sacrifice or obligation aside from the discomforts attendant to military service. The martial framework was invoked as a rallying cry, but the means to wage the war remained nebulous despite bellicose, posse-like threats to retrieve terrorist leaders dead or alive. *Der Kampf* engaged the populace in a struggle that demanded everything. The War on Terror demanded nothing outright except faith in America's ultimate righteousness. The repeated deployments of National Guard troops, for example, became objectionable not because of unwillingness to serve but because the definition of the War on Terror never set the terms of the everyday citizen's contribution to the struggle. When no sacrifices had been asked, every sacrifice seemed burdensome.

Bush's repeated calls during his September 27 speech to bring the terrorists to justice — a judicial frame — quickly gave way to war as the instrument of justice. But he also acknowledged "a new type of war" and the need for "a campaign that will have to reflect the new enemy" (Bush, 2001c). The War on Terror, however, offered neither hope nor method of achieving the "win" that President Bush promised in his speech the day of the attacks. A leading risk perception researcher wrote shortly after 9/11 that terrorism represented the most challenging risk to combat because it shattered existing models for crisis management (Slovic, 2002). Unlike environmental hazards or natural disasters, terrorist events offered no boundaries. The constant possibility of another attack warranted continual vigilance, placing everyone on a war footing with no potential for furlough. To remind viewers never to let down their guard, *Fox News* immediately and continually included a screen graphic showing the color-coded Homeland Security advisory system's terrorism threat level. Constant reminders of the threat from terrorism went beyond mere fear appeals. They signified the war must continue and may justify ever more drastic tactics.

By contrast, *der Kampf* tied ever-intensifying anti–Semitic actions and policies to observable progress in the conflict between Jews and the rest of society. Anti-Semitic measures escalated in ways that made progress seem palpable. Early legal restrictions such as the Nuremberg Laws in 1935 reduced the professional presence of Jews (Snyder, 1981). Quantifiable reductions in the numbers of Jewish professionals demonstrated that the struggle was yielding results. The persistence of the Jewish threat, however, then demanded the battle expand to additional fronts. Physical separation into ghettos would add restricted social mobility to professional restrictions already imposed. Again, escalation of the battle produced observable results: no more Jews in non–Jewish neighborhoods. Ultimately the physical eradication of Jews generated a measurable result identical to literal warfare: body counts. The terminus of *der Kampf* was approached as areas got closer to becoming totally free, or "purified," of Jews (*Judenrein*).

The War on Terror has not lent itself to benchmarks of any kind. It has remained difficult to determine the criteria for victory, much less ultimate victory itself. The War on Terror has lacked observable indicators of progress. Absent any terms of victory, no currency measured success or failure. A lull in terrorist attacks may have represented a calculated hiatus to cultivate a false sense of security. The continuing need for war without a vision for victory invites shifting the front of battle to meet the ever-changing threat. This, of course, is exactly what has happened since 9/11. The first front was Afghanistan. Then Iraq became the frontline in the War on Terror. Without consistent, tangible objectives or enemies, the War on Terror became an assault on phantoms.

Elusive Enemies

The War on Terror faced a challenge of ambiguity beyond what *der Kampf* encountered. By declaring war against the Jew, anti–Semitism could personify the aggregate of all Jews into visual and verbal images that directed hatred, fear, and dread toward a singular personification: "the eternal Jew" that would exist until exterminated. Rendering "the Jew" [*der Jude*] as singular concentrated negative imagery rather than inviting individualization of particular Jews [plural: *die Juden*] as exceptions or counterexamples. The War on Terror, however, confronted an absence of an identifiable object. Terrorism itself could be known only retroactively, after a terrorist act occurred. As for identifying terrorists, the personification of the enemy could not focus hostility if the threat itself constantly shifted.

The Nazi regime devoted substantial time, resources, and personnel to assess the so-called "ancestral proof" that established a person's genealogy and thereby one's degree of "Jewishness" (Ehrenreich, 2007). In the War on Terror, no criteria mark identity as a terrorist, thus generating generalized suspicion rather than targeted fear and hatred. If anyone could be a terrorist, none of the public health analogues employed by Nazi Germany could apply. To quarantine a population in a ghetto, for example, first required designating them, a task accomplished by rituals of physical marking such as wearing the yellow star of David.

In the War on Terror, the enemy acquired the paradoxical qualities of both invisibility and radical difference. The enemy could infiltrate anywhere, yet remained externalized as a radical "Other," utterly alien to democratic values but unrecognizable. The elusiveness of this alien, deceptive creature could justify warfare on any front with no apologies (Ivie, 2007). The amorphous nature of terrorism thwarted rhetorical iconography that could channel anger, fear, or other emotions toward "the Terrorist" as the Nazis did toward "the Jew." As Aristotle (trans. 1924) recognized in Book II of the *Rhetoric*, an emotion can be aroused only if it has an object. One cannot feel love, anger, fear, or any other emotion in the abstract; it must be directed toward someone or something.

Deflecting Dissent: Abridging Names and Rights

The War on Terror, unlike *der Kampf*, invoked an entire war frame rather than contributing a metaphor to a network of rhetorical devices. This frame generated narratives and implications that proved internally inconsistent and unsustainable. One rhetorical device that failed to buttress the frame was the strategic naming of key legislation with acronyms.

The USA PATRIOT Act illustrates the rhetorical challenges of the War on Terror. Swiftly passed on October 26, 2001, the Act bears a title that positions opponents as enemies of the state. The Act's title is an acronym for "Uniting and Strengthening America by Providing Appropriate Tools Required to Intercept and Obstruct Terrorism" Act (2001). Marcuse (1964) uncovered an ideological aspect of condensing such names into neologistic acronyms, a process he termed abridgement. Marcuse observed that abridgement concretizes complex concepts, with the foreshortened names suppressing undesired connotations. Abridged names reduce the incongruity of oxymoronic verbal juxtaposition, so that the connotations of the names' constituent terms are minimized by using acronymic shorthand. The bearer of an abridged name appears as a unified whole, so questions about the contradictory aspects of the name are less likely to arise.

Visual condensation of names into acronyms parallels a semiotic change. The original name, which has several distinct words with potentially conflicting connotations, visually reduces to a single morpheme. The visual impression of terminological unity makes the tensions between terms comprising the acronym less visible. The acronym gives the impression of verbal elements juxtaposed in complete harmony without drawing attention to the "transcending connotation" (Marcuse, 1964, p. 94) of non-institutionalized meanings that might emerge with greater emphasis on conceptuality than on mellifluous slogans. An acronym such as USA PATRIOT creates an added impression of harmony. The constituent letters blend together comfortably, their proximity uninterrupted by spacing or by periods. Other than capitalization, the acronym possesses no visual cues that it might have meanings transcending its visual unity. The acronym was presented throughout media coverage as simply the name of the bill and later the law. The popular acronym contributes to the militaristic framing of responses to terrorism. Alignment seems clarified by the name itself: patriots versus traitors. Furthermore, patriots should obediently and unconditionally support their government's initiatives.

Deconstructing the USA PATRIOT Act reveals the turmoil its name elides. The name conjures images of a new-age Minuteman (the Revolutionary War soldier, and perhaps the anthropomorphized missile), ready to respond instantly to any terrorist threat. The name of the Act also invites conflating its supporters with patriots. Since the Act was passed, especially in the Congressional debates attendant to its March 2006 renewal, almost every word of its complete title has indexed controversy. Instead of uniting the country, the Act has been a lightning rod for civil libertarians to challenge anti-terrorism practices. Clearly no acronym presents a monolithic front immune to critique. The uncritical adoption of the acronym throughout media coverage offers another example of reluctance to question frames that lay the ground for discourse.

Susan Sontag (2002b) pounced on the connection between militaristic language and expansion of government powers that could erode civil liberties. Her observations appeared only five days after the first anniversary of the 9/11 attacks, notably in an Australian rather than an American newspaper. Sontag (2002a, 2002b) recognized that the endless nature of the war on terrorism marked a sharp break from other wars. Because there could be no post-war return to normalcy, any attempts to rescind emergency government powers — warrantless wiretapping comes to mind — got discounted as a retreat, a perilous act of negligence that invited further terrorist attacks. Within the frame of war, individual liberties succumbed to more expansive government powers exercised in the name of collective security.

Reframing War

Lakoff's (2002) claims about certain kinds of frames being embedded in the mind notwithstanding, a frame requires consistent rhetorical reinforcement to become the dominant mode of reference. Frames can sustain public policy only as long as they can maintain their capacity to generate affective and cognitive associations that reinforce the frame (Schön, 1993). This generative capacity operates synchronically and diachronically, much as McGee (1980) noted with respect to ideologically charged language.

Synchronically, a rhetorically sustainable frame should comport with established conceptual vocabulary, such as prevalent metaphors and the historical context. Diachronically, a frame should draw from past cultural experiences and generate narratives that energize the force of the frame's logic. The entailments of a frame must play out consistently in the stories and metaphors operant within the frame (Kövecses, 2007).

Why the War Frame After 9/11?

Why did a war frame offer an especially attractive initial choice after 9/11? Absent a clear decision-making algorithm, people turn to heuristics, modes of rationalization that do not always obey the laws of logic or probability (Tversky & Kahneman, 1982). A heuristic is a shortcut in reasoning that enables people to arrive at conclusions or render decisions in the face of uncertainty. The war frame offered several compelling heuristics that lent simplicity and a form of logic amid uncertainty.

Shortly after 9/11, Bush activated what could be called the agonistic heuristic, simplifying intergroup relations into mutually exclusive categories of friend or foe. In his address to a joint session of Congress on September 20, 2001, Bush pronounced: "Every nation, in every region, now has a decision to make. Either you are with us, or you are with the terrorists" (Bush, 2001b). This simplistic choice eased the burden of trying to determine complex, nuanced relationships by invoking intuitively obvious principles. The law of the excluded middle affirms that something is either one thing or another. In logical notation:

A or B
~ A
B

The agonistic heuristic also appeals to the virtue of firmness, offering no equivocation in the assignment of categories. The unequivocal categorical distinction lends clarity to a situation that seemed rife with uncertainty. The agonistic heuristic necessitated clear distinctions between "us" and "them." As attention shifted from bin Laden to any potential terrorist threat, "the terrorists" became an ever murkier entity, a "them" that never acquired a stable identity to contrast with "us."

A war frame also offered the heuristic of agency, the sense of fulfillment attendant to taking action. The agency heuristic had particular attractiveness in a situation such as 9/11, when it was unclear what anyone could do aside from observe and be afraid. War metaphors offered the potential to mobilize, to invest energy in a task that might aid the war effort. This sense of personal agency could enable one to claim, "I'm doing my part." The wake of 9/11, however, offered few concrete options for positive action. The Homeland Security color codes (Department of Homeland Security, 2008) came with no clear action guides that distinguished one level of threat from another. By contrast, the Nazis treated even personal hygiene as a way to guard against alien racial incursions (von Schirach, 1939).

Finally, a powerful sense of collectivity accompanied the war footing as individual differences dissolved in the common quest to conquer the enemy. As a heuristic, collectivity used logic akin to the rule of division: whatever was right for the collective as a whole was right for the individual within that collective. The collectivity heuristic also abated the sense of isolation that could accompany a perceived threat. Reinforcing collective identity served an important role in quelling dissent, because personal disagreements waned as patriotic fervor bound individuals together for a common cause.

Alternatives to the War Frame

Reddy (1993) suggested that frames, deeply embedded, become resistant to argument because they appear necessary to the structure of thought itself. To correct a frame's pernicious influence, Reddy (1993) urged replacing one frame with another, a process that begins by finding fruitful metaphors which provide conceptual anchors as useful as those offered by the previous frame.

Richard Haass, a former State Department policy planning director and current president of the Council on Foreign Relations, recognized the disanalogies between a war on terror and a conventional war. Haass (2005, 2006) expressed concern that the war metaphor did little to counteract the recruitment of terrorists, because it provides a rather blunt policy instrument of violent and uncompromising retribution. Violence tends to beget violence, and the cycle of violence continues with each terrorist act generating a military response that often kills and maims innocent people, which fuels further anger that stimulates further terrorist attacks.

At least two alternative metaphoric frameworks could supplant the war on terror. Haass (2005, 2006) suggested using the metaphor of a disease. Like a disease, terrorism can be deadly, it seems woven into the fabric of life, and it requires care to prevent and treat. Unlike war, most disease does not invite identification of a final victory. As the resurgence of polio, malaria, and other diseases demonstrate, preventing the conditions for disease — rather than seeking utter eradication — guides policy. As a guide for policy, disease offers more nuanced options than warfare. While the terminology of war invites question only concerning its type or degree (overt, covert, total, limited, nuclear, chemical, biological, etc.), disease permits many reactions, including preventive measures. To prevent terrorism through military deterrence alone has incurred high economic and human costs — and it perpetuates the message that violence or its threat serves as the ultimate persuader. To prevent the disease of terrorism includes activating the means to "persuade young men and women throughout the world to choose an alternative career path" (Haass, 2006). The disease metaphor already contains provisions for creating conditions that would prevent its occurrence or intensification. The war metaphor invites strategizing the ways to achieve victory, not ways to avoid or minimize the war itself.

Another metaphoric alternative to a war on terror could be a quest for justice in response to the crime of terrorism. This reframing strategy parallels the move made during the war crimes tribunals after World War II, shifting from a militaristic to a judicial framing for wrongdoing. As early as September 12, 2001, a few commentators identified the terrorist attacks as international crimes against humanity that should prompt a systematic identification of responsible parties rather than a bloodlust-driven search for vengeance (Barry & Honey, 2001). These voices were drowned by rallying cries for war. After all, if the perpetrators killed themselves in the attack, who could be prosecuted?

The crime/justice frame lacks power only if it remains restricted to retributive justice. At least three other components of the crime/justice frame enable responses unaccounted for in a war frame. First, criminal justice has a wider array of proactive measures than pre-emptive military strikes. Crime-fighting, unlike war-fighting, acknowledges the crucial role of proactive measures to prevent crime. Although preventive strategies could include harsh deterrents — a point stressed within the war frame — they also include building alternative ways of expressing dissent. A crime prevention approach permits consideration of what causes violence rather than focusing mainly on the scale of reactions to violence.

Second, the criminal justice frame employs an explicit process. Warfare, at least as defended by its practitioners, does involve rules of engagement. But these rules are not publicly scrutinized or clear. Asked whether the rules of engagement would change after U.S. troops accidentally killed an Italian intelligence agent in March 2005, a military spokesperson gave the standard answer: "I can't discuss rules of engagement for operational security" (quoted in Rageh & Pitman, 2005). Furthermore, intuitively egregious violations of the rules of warfare occur often, with accompanying suitably evasive, euphemistic terminology (e.g., "friendly fire," "collateral damage"). When high-profile military blunders occur, such as the 2004 "friendly fire" killing of pro football player Pat Tillman in Afghanistan or the Blackwater Security killing of eight Iraqi civilians in September 2007, they call into question the connection between war and justice. Replacing the war frame with the frame of criminal justice automatically includes procedures for maintaining accountability. Although the fairness of criminal justice systems might invite question, the legal framework offers definite guidelines for what constitutes acceptable procedures.

Third, criminal justice can operate as a reformative as well as a retributive mechanism. While criminal justice can employ deterrence through harsh, swift, and certain punishment, it has other techniques at its disposal. A reformative approach to justice could stress intense diversionary programs to realign terrorist training programs toward other, more pro-social activities. Victim restitution offers another avenue for action, because it would align the United States with humanitarian aid programs. As these examples demonstrate, the criminal justice framework authorizes a wide array of policy options directly implied by the frame itself.

Beyond Symbolic Warfare

This study has explored how frames operate epistemologically and rhetorically, establishing the parameters for lines of thought and courses of action. Rather than focusing on how frames affect what audiences think, this analysis has concentrated on how frames can delimit the realm of the thinkable. Regarding social policy, frames set the conditions for rhetorical engagement, prioritizing certain discursive choices such as metaphors and *topoi* of discussion over others.

As their name indicates, frames are not infinitely malleable. Analysis of the war frame's modus operandi in the context of *der Kampf* in Nazi Germany and the War on Terror in post–9/11 Bush administration discourse illustrates the rhetorical resources a frame can provide for justifying social policies. The two cases demonstrate both the malleability and rigidity of frames. The terminology of *der Kampf* and its logical extensions formed a crucial component of the agonistic Nazi *Weltanschauung* that positioned an idealized icon of "the Jew" as a constant threat, enabling ever more extreme persecution to pass as necessary defensive measures. *Der Kampf* illustrated the malleable aspect of frames, their ability to integrate with families of other rhetorical devices — such as metaphoric equivalence of Jews with pestilence and disease — to provide engines for their continued usage and extension. The War on Terror, on the other hand, demonstrated that frames need not generate logical implications and metaphoric associations that sustain the frame. In this case, cross-applying the frame of warfare to a situation that admittedly violated the conditions for declaring war, muddled identification of the enemy, and lacked strategies for sustaining the struggle, stretched the credibility of the frame beyond the limits of plausibility. Unlike *der Kampf*, the War on Terror did not integrate comfortably into (1) existing cultural traditions (such as the German history of anti–Semitism), (2) entrenched metaphors that bolstered the cause (such as metaphors of pestilence and disease), or (3) historical precedents from previous armed conflicts (disanalogies with Pearl Harbor were too apparent). Boisterous bellicosity alone cannot assure a war frame's survival. At some level, the linguistically constructed context for deliberation and policy represents a choice — one that has consequences for what will count as allowable moves in thought, discourse, and action.

The war frame will continue to provide a perilous scaffold for perception and policy until replaced by other frames that can accommodate a wider range of responses to events. The Nazi inculcation of a siege mentality cast the Jewish threat as so desperate that the struggle to curb Jewish influence had to intensify. As Jews were objectified into a collective enemy, it became less plausible to do things *with* them (such as negotiate) rather than *to* them (such as relocate or eventually kill them). As for the response to 9/11, the immediate implementation of a war footing disqualified many judicial, foreign policy, and non-governmental responses as non-starters because of their presumed incompatibility with a nation-state at war.

Successful critique of any frame depends on revealing the conditionality of its core assumptions and the limits of its root metaphors. As Pinker (2007) argued in response to Lakoff (2002), frames reflect voluntary linguistic choices more than hard-wired neurolinguistic structures. The first step in preventing frames from justifying repressive or unjust social practices is to render any particular frame visible *as* a frame, as constructing discursive choices rather than as the necessary underpinning of thought itself. This revelation of conditionality, however, also requires making more visible a menu of alternative frames. Reframing the War on Terror suggests one way the task might begin. Recasting the thirst for revenge as the quest for justice or as the amelioration of a disease could activate some of the same processes of struggle that *der Kampf* sustained, but hopefully for far more morally sustainable purposes.

References

Almquist, A. (1934, 18 December). Kampf um die nordische kultur! *Völkischer Beobachter*, n. pag.

Aristotle. (1924). *Rhetorica* (W. R. Roberts, Trans.). In W. D. Ross (Trans. & Ed.), *The Works of Aristotle* (Vol. 11). Oxford: Clarendon.

Barry, T., and M. Honey (2001, Sept. 12). International crime, not war. *Foreign Policy in Focus*, 5(30), 1–2. Retrieved July 1, 2008, from http://www.fpif.org.

Becker, A. (1937–1938). Das Philipp-Lenard Institut der Universität Heidelberg. *Zeitschrift für die gesamte Naturwissenschaft*, 3, 48.

Blackburn, G. W. (1985). *Education in the Third Reich: A Study of Race and History in Nazi Textbooks*. Albany: State University of New York Press.

Burke, K. (1973). *The Philosophy of Literary Form* (3rd ed). Berkeley: University of California Press.

Bush, G. W. (2001a). *Statement by the President in His Address to the Nation*. September 11, 2001. Retrieved November 22, 2003, from http://www.whitehouse.gov/news/releases/2001/09/20010911-16.html.

———. (2001b). *Address to a Joint Session of Congress and the American People*. September 20, 2001. Retrieved November 22, 2003, from http://www.whitehouse.gov/news/releases/2001/09/20010920-8.html.

———. (2001c). *At O'Hare, President Says "Get on Board."* September 27, 2001. Retrieved November 22, 2003, from http://www.whitehouse.gov/news/releases/2001/09/20010927-1.html.

Carrigan, B. (2001, Sept. 16). Global stock-market panics rarely last long. *Toronto Star*, p. C2. Retrieved June 30, 2008, from Lexis-Nexis Academic database.

Chamberlain, H. S. (1912). *Foundations of the Nineteenth Century* (Vols. 1–2, J. Lees, Trans.). London: John Lane.

Department of Homeland Security. (2008). *Homeland Security Advisory System*. Retrieved December 24, 2008, from http://www.dhs.gov/xinfoshare/programs/Copy_of_press_release_0046.shtm.

Ehrenreich, E. (2007). *The Nazi Ancestral Proof: Genealogy, Racial Science, and the Final Solution*. Bloomington: Indiana University Press.

Eilders, C., and A. Lüter (2000). Germany at war: Competing framing strategies in German public discourse. *European Journal of Communication*, 15(3), 415–428.

Gamm, H-J. (1962). *Der Braune Kult: Das Dritte Reich und seine Ersatzreligion*. Hamburg: Rütten und Loening.

Giles, G. J. (1985). *Students and National Socialism in Germany*. Princeton, NJ: Princeton University Press.

Grundsätzliches Bekenntnis des Faschismus zur Rassenpflege. (1938, July 16). *Völkischer Beobachter*, p. 2.

Haass, R. N. (2005). *The Opportunity: America's Moment to Alter History's Course*. New York: Public Affairs.

———. (2006, August 14). An argument to jettison the metaphor "war on terror." [Radio broadcast episode]. In N. Conan (Host). *Talk of the Nation*. Washington, DC: National Public Radio. Retrieved August 1, 2008 from Newspaper Source database. Accession number 6XN200608141402.

Hirsch, H. (1995). *Genocide and the Politics of Memory*. Chapel Hill: University of North Carolina Press.

Hitler, A. (1941). *My new order* (R. de R. de Sales, Ed.). New York: Reynal and Hitchcock.

———. (1971). *Mein Kampf* (R. Manheim, Trans.). Boston: Houghton Mifflin. (Original work published 1925).

Ivie, R. l. (2007). Fighting terror by rite of redemption and reconciliation. *Rhetoric and Public Affairs, 10*, 221–248.
Kampf ist das Leben (1933, June 11–12). *Völkischer Beobachter*, n. pag.
Der Kampf ist nie zu Ende! (1936, February 20). *Das Schwarze Korps*, p. 11.
Kandel, I. L. (1935). *The Making of Nazis*. New York: Columbia University Teachers College.
Kant, I. (1989). *The Critique of Judgment* (J. C. Meredith, Trans.). Oxford: Clarendon.
Kellner, D. (2007). Bushspeak and the politics of lying: Presidential rhetoric in the "war on terror." *Presidential Studies Quarterly, 37*, 622–645.
Kövecses, Z. (2007, Spring). Studying American culture through its metaphors: Dimensions of variation and frames of experience. *Americana, 3*(1). Retrieved December 24, 2008, from http://americanaejournal.hu/vol3no1/kovecses.
Krieck, E. (1936). Die Objectivität der Wissenschaft als Problem. In *Das nationalsozialistische Deutschland und die Wissenschaft* (pp. 25–35). Hamburg: Hanseatische.
Lakoff, G. (2002). *Moral Politics: How Liberals and Conservatives Think* (2nd ed.). Chicago: University of Chicago Press.
Levenson, J. (2004). The war on what, exactly? Why the press must be precise. *Columbia Journalism Review, 43*(4), 9–11.
Lifton, R. J. (1986). *The Nazi Doctors: Medical Killing and the Psychology of Genocide*. New York: Basic.
Marcuse, H. (1964). *One-Dimensional Man: Studies in the Ideology of Advanced Industrial Society*. Boston: Beacon.
Mason, T. (1981). Intention and explanation: A current controversy about the interpretation of National Socialism. In G. Hirschfeld & L. Ketternacker (Eds.), *Der "Führerstaat": Mythos und Realität* (pp. 23–40). Stuttgart: Klett-Cotta.
May, E. (1942). Besprechung von Ph. Lenard: Grosse Naturforscher. *Zeitschrift für die gesamte Naturwissenschaft, 8*, 154.
McGee, M. C. (1980). The 'ideograph': A link between rhetoric and ideology. *Quarterly Journal of Speech, 66*(1), 1–16.
Mosse, G. L. (Ed.). (1966). *Nazi Culture* (S. Attanasio, et al., Trans.). New York: Grosset and Dunlap.
The Nazi Primer (1938). (H. L. Childs, Trans. & Pref.) New York: Harper.
Neben den Soldat der Waffe tritt der politische Soldat. (1939, July 23). *Völkischer Beobachter*, p. 1.
Nelson, E. J. (1991). "Nothing ever goes well enough": Mussolini and the rhetoric of perpetual struggle. *Communication Studies, 42*, 22–42.
Peukert, D. J. K. (1987). *Inside Nazi Germany: Conformity, Opposition, and Racism in Everyday Life* (R. Deveson, Trans.). London: B. T. Batsford.
Pinker, S. (2007). *The Stuff of Thought: Language as a Window into Human Nature*. New York: Viking.
Rageh, R., and T. Pitman (2005, March 7). Friendly fire in Iraq takes toll on U.S.–led coalition — and Iraqis. *Associated Press Newswire*. Retrieved 1 July 2008, from http://www.commondreams.org/headlines05/0307-10.htm.
Reddy, M. J. (1993). The conduit metaphor: A case of frame conflict in our language about language. In A. Ortony (Ed.), *Metaphor and Thought* (2nd ed., pp. 164–201). Cambridge: Cambridge University Press.
Schemm, H. (1934). *Deutsche Schule und Deutsche Erziehung in Vergangenheit, Gegenwart und Zukunft*. Stuttgart: Padagogische Verlangsanstalt.
Scheufele, D. (1999). Framing as a theory of media effects. *Journal of Communication, 49*(1), 103–122.
Scheufele, D. A., and D. Tewksbury (2007). Framing, agenda setting, and priming: The evolution of three media effects models. *Journal of Communication, 57*(1), 9–20.

Schön, D. A. (1993). Generative metaphors: A perspective on problem-setting in social policy. In A. Ortony (Ed.), *Metaphor and Thought* (2nd ed., pp. 137–163). Cambridge: Cambridge University Press.
Das Schwarze Korps. (1936, February 2), p. 13.
Slovic, P. (2002). Terrorism as hazard: A new species of trouble. *Risk Analysis, 22,* 425–426.
Snyder, L. L. (Ed.). (1981). *Hitler's Third Reich: A Documentary History.* Chicago: Nelson-Hall.
Sontag, S. (2002a, Sept. 10). Real Battles and Empty Metaphors. *New York Times,* p. A25. Retrieved June 6, 2008, from http://query.nytimes.com/gst/fullpage.html?res=9D01 EEDE1631F933A2575AC0A9649C8B63.
———. (2002b, Sept. 16). United States "at war" finds no time to reflect on what it won't want to see. *The Australian,* p. 13. Retrieved June 6, 2008 from Newspaper Source database. Accession number 200209161013317622.
Staemmler, M. (1933). *Rassenpflege im völkischen Staat.* München: J. F. Lehmann.
Stark, J. (1934). *Nationalsozialismus und Wissenschaft.* München: Zentralverlag der NSDAP.
Teilhard de Chardin, P. (1987). *The Future of Man* (N. Denny, Trans.). New York: Harper.
Tversky, A., and D. Kahneman (1982). Judgment under uncertainty: Heuristics and biases. In D. Kahneman, P. Slovic, & A. Tversky (Eds.), *Judgment Under Uncertainty: Heuristics and Biases* (pp. 3–21). Cambridge: Cambridge University Press.
Uniting and Strengthening America by Providing Appropriate Tools Required to Intercept and Obstruct Terrorism (USA PATRIOT) Act of 2001, Publ. L. No. 107-56 (2001).
von Schirach, B. (1939). Du hast die Pflicht, gesund zu sein! *Volksgesundheitswacht, 11,* 135.
von Werder, P. (1938, August 18). Weltkampf als politische Erziehungsform. *Das Schwarze Korps,* p. 4.

An Enduring Legacy of World War I: Propaganda, Journalism and the Domestic Struggle over the Commodification of Truth

Burton St. John III

On February 4, 2008, when Harry Landis died, there remained only one living United States veteran of World War I—107-year-old Frank Buckles. *Newsweek* reporter Tony Dokoupil (2008) wrote that unlike Britain and France, which both had preparations to honor the inevitable passing of their last World War I veterans, the United States had no plans for commemorating the war upon Buckles' death. Instead, said Dokoupil, in the United States the "first world war was slipping into the secondhand past" (p. 50). He noted that, in America, World War I was mostly forgotten. "It has no national monument on the Washington Mall ... no blockbuster film, no iconic image equivalent to soldiers' raising the flag on Iwo Jima" (p. 50).

However, when it comes to the workings of mass communication in American society, the implications of that war remain crucial. Dokoupil's (2008) observations are accurate, at least in the popular sense, and our living memory of World War I continues to fade. We need to reinvigorate our understanding of how that war contributed to key enduring foundational moments that affect communication to this day. Specifically, World War I was a crucible for the eventual rise of two industries: professionalized journalism and domestic institutionalized propaganda through the new public relations profession, a profession that supported countervailing claims in the 1920s concerning the dissemination of truth in the American public sphere.

In the decade following World War I professionalized journalism and institutionalized propaganda shaped fundamental claims to communicating and commodifying truth that influence how news is presented to us today. For example, journalists during the post–World War I period, disillusioned with their previous role in spreading domestic pro-war messages, developed principles and practices that offered safeguards against propaganda. Inspired in part by Walter Lippmann's (1922) *Public Opinion* and the concurrent rise of professional press organizations and an increasing number of academic journalism programs, journalism developed "scientific reporting" norms such as fact-based orientation, a reliance on experts and detachment from partisanship (Lee, 1937; Rosen, 1999; Schudson, 2003). These practices reflected a renewed drive within journalism for both credible truth-telling and independence. This scientific approach to journalism endures in the mainstream press because it allows news workers "to produce a description that is more accurate than any other process allows" (Ryan, 2001, p. 5).

During those same post-war years, an increasingly strategic PR industry institutionalized propaganda in the service of government, business and social causes. This happened in great part because PR practitioners made the case that they could disseminate their clients' truths that the press, left to its own devices, might not necessarily report. Many of these new public relations practitioners observed that, during the war, the U.S. Committee on Public Information (CPI) had developed systematic persuasive communication that encouraged audiences to enlist, buy bonds and be watchful of enemy spies (Ewen, 1996; Schudson, 2003; Vaughn, 1980). In fact, some key proponents of the new field of public relations like Edward Bernays and Carl Byoir developed their principles and practices while working for the CPI. These new domestic "special pleaders" had learned that truths that advanced a specific cause and/or client could be packaged and distributed in ways that would be believable to targeted audiences. As ex–CPI propagandist and public relations pioneer Edward Bernays (1925) said in an unpublished speech the new propagandists learned "they could work through the press to sell a good cause" and "keep the public sold on that cause" (p. 8). Today's public relations professionals affirm they similarly work to influence news presentation in a way that reflects their clients' truths.

The lessons that journalism and public relations professionals learned from World War I have this in common — both industries developed principles and practices that allowed them to make competing claims related to the packaging and marketing of "truths" that were deemed credible and compelling by the public. This work examines how the struggle over the commodification of truth evolved across three related developments. First, it briefly examines the post war press's sense of disillusionment with the CPI's propaganda. Second, it demonstrates how journalists, in industry anti-publicity bulletins of the 1920s, attempted to protect newspaper credibility in the face of the rising public relations profession. Third, it explores how, during the 1920s, PR practitioner Edward L. Bernays tried to rehabilitate propaganda by maintaining it provided fresh truths to the public. Additionally, this work briefly discusses how this struggle over commodifying truth presents lingering concerns about propaganda's role in news content today.

Post-War Press Disillusionment with CPI Propaganda

When the Committee on Public Information (CPI) was established on April 13, 1917, just one week after the United States' declaration of war with Germany, the Woodrow Wilson Administration conceived it as an organization that would encourage American coalescence behind the war effort. Public sentiment about going to war against the Central Power countries (Germany, Austria-Hungary, Turkey and Bulgaria) was, at best, mixed. After the German sinking of the American ship *Lusitania* in May 1915, the United States witnessed the emergence of militaristic and patriotic groups that wanted to counteract the Central Powers (Hofstadter, 1955). At the other extreme were peace radicals who urged the United States to observe the destruction that had already occurred during the Great War and to realize that the conflict was the result of tragic missteps by autocratic regimes (Hasian, 1998). Public opinion was polarized and conflicted about entering the war. Americans had many reasons to be ambiguous, including persistent isolationism, pacifism and a sense of social and cultural links to Germany (Hofstadter, 1955; Sullivan, 1996).

According to historian John Morton Blum (1956), President Wilson had a vision that Americans, properly informed and motivated, would support a "war to end war, a war to make the world safe for democracy, a people's war" (pp. 132–133). This Wilsonian ideal reflected the progressive movement's belief that, if the public was induced to conform to the war effort, by war's end American society would find more opportunities for social reform (Ford, 2008). When H. G. Wells (1914) wrote, "The ultimate purpose of this war is propaganda, the destruction of certain beliefs and the creation of others" (p. 98) he touched upon the Wilsonian vision that the post-war world would bring a new era of democratic cooperation. However, obtaining this ideal was contingent on two factors. First, the American public must know about the rightness of the cause. Second, the citizenry needed to embrace sacrifice to support the war.

Wilson appointed as head of the CPI George Creel, a former muckraker who had worked for newspapers in Kansas City and Denver. Creel (1920) was keenly aware that public opinion was a muddled mixture of uncertainty, pacifism and hawkish extremism. He believed the best way to rally support and overcome indecisiveness and opposition was through aggressive publicity of the war aims. The CPI, Creel said, was a "plain publicity proposition" designed to sell the need for the war (p. 4). To garner widespread support, he said, the CPI needed to practice an advocacy that would avoid perceived or actual concerns about silencing dissenting viewpoints. According to Ponder (1999), Creel issued the following in a memo to Wilson: "The suppressive features of the work must be so overlaid by the publicity policy that they will go unregarded and unresented. Administrative activities must be dramatized and staged, and every energy exerted to arouse ardor and enthusiasm" (p. 93).

The CPI's efforts were of a scale never seen before in a modern democracy. Propaganda materials that encouraged proper citizen behavior (enlist and serve, buy bonds) and avoid undermining the war (conserve resources, watch what you say, turn in potential spies) appeared in schools, stores, factories, and churches. More relevant to this review is the extent to which the CPI successfully penetrated newspaper columns in the United States. The *Creel Report* (1920) indicated that the News Division's weekly war reports went out by mail to 12,000 daily newspapers, resulting in an estimated 6,000 columns of CPI-influenced news stories. CPI newswire propaganda served another 2,000 newspapers, and this material showed up in about 12,000 newspaper columns each week (p. 14). The News Division also sent out more than 6,000 distinct news releases during the war which, according to CPI estimates, were published in approximately 20,000 newspaper columns per week (Creel, 1920, p. 50; Mock & Larson, 1939, p. 68). In one instance, Creel claimed that by seven months into the war every newspaper in California had already received the equivalent of six pounds of CPI propaganda materials — enough information for 1,200 columns (Ponder, 1999, p. 96).

The News Division also published the *Official Bulletin*, the first nationwide state-supported newspaper in America, and sent it to newspapers throughout the country, achieving a peak wartime circulation of 118,000 (Creel Report, 1920, pp. 63–67; Mock & Larson, 1939, p. 68; Ponder, 1999, p. 97). The CPI Division of Syndicate Features sent stories to newspapers that went beyond facts to examine the racial, social and financial aspects of the war (Vaughn, 1980). This service reached a newspaper circulation of 12 million, said the CPI and, assuming that two people read each paper, it was likely that "one-fourth of the people in this country had access to our syndicate stories" (Creel Report, 1920, p. 75). The CPI also established an American Alliance for Labor and Democracy which held hundreds of community meetings across the country and obtained 10,000 columns of newspaper coverage (Jackall & Hirota, 1995). The CPI's efforts spawned more than 50 loosely-affiliated government press bureaus, inundating the press with war-related propaganda (Ponder, 1999).

The CPI was more than simply prodigious; it was also the epitome of self-assuredness regarding the virtues of American involvement in the Great War. The idealism and apparent sincerity behind the CPI's propaganda messages reflected what many citizens truly believed. Many Americans had, at a minimum, a notion that Germany pursued the war for evil and selfish motives and that the United States was engaged in a noble effort to right a wrong. The CPI "simply took over a whole range of rehearsed responses and exploited them to the hilt" (Buitenhuis, 1976, p. 142). The CPI exaggerated the citizenry's often-vague impressions and amplified them into portrayals of America as "the savior against the aggressor, the liberator against the tyrant, the citizen-soldier against the cruel murderer" (Hollihan, 1984, p. 255). The CPI rhetoric appealed to this pro-war sensibility. Additionally, its messages were helpful to journalistic news construction. Throughout the war, journalists found a sense of mission and purpose — even honor — in working with the CPI to sell World War I (Leonard, 1995). In fact, a 1918 Pulitzer Prize was awarded to *Louisville Courier Journal* editor Henry Watterson for two pieces he wrote in April 1917 in support of the war effort (Callaway, 1918).

However, shortly after the war's end, news workers realized that, by working with the propagandists, they had tainted the news with "large-scale lying" (Irwin, 1936, p. 4). In fact, journalists' growing disenchantment with their complicit transmittal of propaganda was also part of a wider societal realization. Although Wilson's CPI was designed to stimulate war support through education, Americans were increasingly convinced that the government had overstepped its bounds. It had used the press to bombard the public with propaganda, colluded with the press to censor information and had abused individuals and institutions for the will of the state (Blum, 1956; Buitenhuis, 1976; Tobin & Bidwell, 1940; Vaughn, 1980).

A formerly-compliant press fulminated; concerned that propaganda was expanding in post-war America. John Dewey (1918) noted shortly after the war that "propaganda disguised as ... news" had been used by the U.S. government to mold public sentiment and, he wondered, "whether the word 'news' is not destined to be replaced by the word 'propaganda'" (p. 216). Journalist Will Irwin (1919), a former CPI employee, wrote that the CPI had become so adept at shaping the news that, even in peacetime, editors and reporters, along with their readers, could be unwitting victims of more propaganda. A journalism text from the 1920s conceded that the war's most pronounced effect on journalism "has been in respect to propaganda — its early complacency in regard to it; its later acceptance of the role which it was asked to play" (Flint, 1925, p. 142). Nelson Crawford (1924), author of a journalism ethics text, opined, "The problem of propaganda is serious," made manifest by the war, and press credibility is threatened by reporters who are failing "to seek out news and have given most space to persons who would furnish them with typed copies of speeches" and other pre-packaged material (pp. 160–162).

Journalist Walter Lippmann, who had participated in overseas propaganda efforts aligned with the CPI, wrote in the *New Republic* in 1919 that the nation was "saturated with propaganda." The country found itself "in the face of aggravated problems without any source of information that it can really trust, and without leaders to interpret events," he wrote. What was needed, he said, was "trustworthy news, unadulterated data, fair reporting [and] disinterested fact" (p. 319). Scholar Leon Flint (1925) noted that others extended on Lippmann's call to journalistic arms. For example, Eric Allen, Dean of Oregon's School of Journalism, observed:

> Worse than the material disorganization following on the war ... is the menacing power of propaganda.... I think that the greatest and most dangerous problem before the American people today is "shall propaganda, or the independent voices of trained journalists, speaking their own honest, unbiased ideas ... uninfluenced by fear or favor, reach the public ear?" [quoted in Flint, p. 142].

Journalistic Truth and the American Newspaper Publishers Association's Anti-Publicity Bulletins

In the 1920s, due in great part to its disillusionment with its earlier entanglement with CPI propaganda, journalism began to develop a professionalism that would allow news workers to rehabilitate press credibility. One of the key articulators of this movement was Lippmann (1922), whose *Public Opinion* advocated a more rationalist approach for the gathering and reporting of news. He observed that the war had shown journalists that unchecked experts could lead a democratic society into an ill-advised effort. There is no democratic mass that can prevent against such an abuse, he wrote. But journalism can provide a route to moderating the power of authority by encouraging news workers to report in an objective style, focusing on facts contextualized by experts. Lippmann advocated that the reporter learn from the scientist's detached posture of observation. Effectively employing an objective stance called for the news worker to be detached, ferret out the facts and force experts to assert their claims against counterclaims. This scientific approach was necessary because "the press is a servant and guardian of institutions," and can best serve society "based on a system of analysis and record" (pp. 363–364).

Lippmann's emphasis on a scientific, facts-based approach to journalism resonated with the press. Shortly after publication of *Public Opinion*, Nelson Crawford (1924) wrote that "newspaper men ... do hold, theoretically at least, the doctrine that the dissemination of objective facts is the primary ... function of the press" (p. 36). William Gibbons (1926), in his newspaper ethics book, observed that "it is the first duty of the press to present a truthful mirror of life" and, therefore, the "reporter's job is to get the plain, simple facts" (pp. 16–17). Journalists worked to restore their profession by taking this truth-centered orientation and formalizing principles and practices in the newsroom. This move toward professionalism was reflected in the rise of national and state press associations that emphasized codes of ethics and news workers assisting universities in creating more journalism courses.

Newspaper owners also were determined to protect the industry's integrity. The American Newspaper Publisher Association (ANPA) used its Anti-Publicity bulletins to guard the financial model of the newspaper by exposing publicists' efforts to get free space in newspapers. The ANPA, formed in 1887, began its Anti-Publicity Bulletins in 1908 under the direction of general manager Lincoln Palmer. By the end of the World War I, and throughout the 1920s, the ANPA sent the bulletin to more than 500 daily newspapers (Emery, 1950, p. 133). Prior to World War I, the bulletin kept a tight focus on guarding the newspaper advertising model by highlighting the intrusion of publicity materials into news space. However, after the war, it gradually provided a forum for journalists to speak about how domestic propaganda undermined professional journalism's ability to claim it provided credible, objective news accounts. The release entitled "French Government to Control News!" (1922) claimed that the burgeoning public relations industry threatened the veracity of news, saying:

> The press agent ... is gradually strengthening his position as a controller of news sources. He is establishing himself more firmly as guard for political and business leaders. Canned statements are becoming the sole diet of what was, and should be, an independent press, a self-controlled interpreter of public sentiment [p. 73].

Vigilance against propaganda is the key, according to the bulletin. It is essential for a newspaper to ensure the integrity of the news room by exercising caution concerning the deluge of publicity material in the press, wrote J. N. Heiskell (1927) of the *Little Rock Gazette*. Heiskell noted that "No publisher of sincerity and intelligence will have any difficulty in identifying that proferred publicity" which attempts to fill up news pages with information that reflects the prerogatives of the "lords of business" (p. 702). In another bulletin, an unidentified news worker from *The Washington (D.C.) Evening Star* detailed how the paper modeled such watchfulness and enhanced its credibility with its readership. According to the bulletin, *The Star* made sure that publicity agents did not work through the newspaper's advertising or business offices to win assurances of publication; instead, all space-seekers had to appeal directly to an editor. Whole sections of the paper became cleansed of publicity.

> We have found that we have been able to improve our papers by eliminating all space grafting publicity and making our columns contain real news. The reader reaction has been gratifying.... We eliminated factory and automobile handouts.... As a consequence ... reader interest and attention is more closely confined to the section than before.... We have won the reputation of being "hard-boiled" in press agent circles, but on the other hand, repeated commendation of our readers has justified our right to make *The Star* what all newspapers should be, a *News* paper ["*The Washington Evening Star*'s Secret of Success," 1929, p. 162].

Not satisfied with simply increasing newspaper awareness of the threat of rising domestic publicity, the bulletin sporadically provided its readers with examples of the press pursuing confrontational resistance. One of the bulletin's more explicit counter-publicity tactics focused on reprinting correspondence journalists had written to the clients of publicity campaigns. In 1924, in a letter addressed to the National Association of Farm Equipment Manufacturers (NAFEM), an ANPA member listed all the people the NAFEM had paid to ensure the free news insert made it to the news room — the copywriter, the engravers, the typesetters, the paper and ink suppliers and the postal delivery personnel. Why, then, asked the letter writer, "should you expect us to spend our money to get your message across to the farmer?" The message to the NAFEM, and other would-be propagandists, is clear, said the writer; "this idea that a newspaper can be used for propaganda was exploded long before the great war" ("Get to the Press Agent's Boss," 1924, p. 16).

The bulletin also revealed the inner workings of press agents, by reprinting publicity plans put together for clients in areas like engineering, life insurance and the tea industry. Under a banner "extra" headline, a 2-page exposé detailed how the Inter-Ocean Syndicate attempted to sell its publicity services with a pledge to potential clients that "if we do not deliver the circulation guaranteed, you do not pay" ("Full Account of How It's Done," 1923, pp. 580–581). Another public relations machination it often spotlighted was the press agent's threat to withhold advertising if a newspaper failed to run publicity pieces as news. For example, a front-page article on a national baseball week publicity campaign exposed a confidential letter from promotional managers to their space-seekers that advised "if the sporting editor does not show an inclination to mention [this particular] week and you are advertising in his paper, a request to the advertising department usually will result in a 'must' order that a story on the event be run" ("Read This and Weep," 1924, p. 125).

Occasionally, the bulletin sponsored "Newspaper Thrift" weeks designed to encourage members to bundle all free publicity materials and send them to the bulletin's office. After its Thrift Week in January 1928, the ANPA reported that its 500 member papers received 65 tons of propaganda materials from January 17 to January 23. The report promised the following: "These bids for free advertising space average about 200 a week per member ... [or 5,200,000 publicity items a year], and the postage on which is well in excess of $100,000 per annum" ("65 Tons of Free Advertising," 1928, p. 13). The bulletin identified periodicals, motion picture producers, radio outlets, the automobile industry and government agencies as the chief generators of "urgent news releases" (p. 13).

Clearly, the bulletin provided additional impetus to press's economic argument against the rise of domestic propaganda. But there were more than financial exigencies going on here. The ANPA bulletins, by advocating awareness of the rise of domestic propaganda and vigorous, often-confrontational countermeasures, served as both a reflection and amplification of journalism's post-war drive for professionalism. Furthermore, the bulletin acted as a self-policing vehicle for the larger motive behind the press professionalization movement — the assertion that journalism was a serviceable product because it offered truths in its pages. As the bulletin demonstrated, publishers and journalists were concerned about their industry's credibility; the more newspapers used propaganda the more they faced the very real threat that their key commodity — truth — would no longer be a selling point. The bulletin stridently maintained newspapers would face increasing difficulty affirming their marketing of reality unless news workers refused the "news" advances of the expanding PR field.

As the ANPA Anti-Publicity Bulletins of the 1920s show, the press had learned from its experience with World War I domestic propaganda that journalism's distinctive asset — truth-telling — was now under assault in the American public sphere by the rising PR industry. The bulletin was well aware of the professional press's assertions that they worked from a more clear-eyed, objective posture. However, the bulletin's chief concern was to encourage a journalistic call to arms about an emerging obstacle. Domestic propaganda penetrated news columns through the emergence of "near journalists," special pleaders who increasingly played the role of news authorities who offered prepackaged information and sources of commentary ("The Reds, Big Business and Ivy Lee," 1926, p. 141). For the bulletin, the more news rooms found the near journalist useful, the more the press was potentially imperiling journalism's attempts to rebuild its stature as a reliable product in the U.S. marketplace. If news workers did not resist the space-seeking propagandist, the bulletin proclaimed, newspapers would face mounting difficulty marketing themselves as viable truth-tellers to news consumers.

Edward L. Bernays and Propaganda's Pro-Social Truths

As journalistic cynicism toward propaganda helped propel its professionalization in the 1920s, Edward L. Bernays extolled a seemingly counterintuitive message — propaganda can serve as a pro-social force that could benefit American society. Bernays' perspective immediately garnered attention as his contemporaries considered him a trailblazer for the new field of public relations. Many scholars and PR professionals continue to rank him as a pioneer of public relations. Over six decades, Bernays grew a thriving practice, wrote or edited six books focused on public relations and propaganda, published innumerable articles, and taught the first college-level public relations course.

However, in 1918, when Bernays left the CPI's export division at the age of 27, he had not yet articulated his own definition of propaganda. In fact, before the war, he had been chiefly engaged as a press agent for musical acts. Bernays' (1923) *Crystallizing Public Opinion* set out to re-define publicity as the new field of public relations. In this book, Bernays developed and demonstrated the thesis that the PR person serves as an interpreter between a client and its many publics. He also began to make the case that propaganda benefits society by representing a minority, or dissenting, perspective. These minority views were often resisted by the public, he claimed. Bernays was influenced by Lippmann's observations that crowds often focused on pre-established stereotypes. This, argued Bernays, was why the masses often suppressed new visions offered by marginalized groups. Propaganda is a purposeful, directed effort to overcome this "censorship of the group mind and the herd reaction" (p. 122).

Although Bernays' book did not set out primarily to define propaganda, in the years after its 1923 publication he began to elaborate on his argument that propaganda was pro-social because it elevated various minority voices into the public sphere of a democratic-capitalist state. One of the first documented examples of this claim was a speech he gave in 1925, "Crystallizing Public Opinion for Good Government," before a group of public policy advocates and civic leaders. He urged his audience to re-think how they promoted their pro-social causes in a society that is fractured by many "group cleavages." In the American marketplace of ideas, efforts to improve health, housing, schools and transportation need to be thought of as concepts that are sold as commodities, he said. Propaganda sells ideas as products. It attaches symbols to proposals, making them less abstract and more marketable. Propaganda also creates circumstances to dramatize novel concepts, highlight their importance, and garner the attention of newspapers. The press, he said, was vitally important because newspaper coverage can re-translate these pro-social ideas so that they "become fact with [the] power to influence large bodies of people." Bernays ended the speech by exhorting the audience to recognize that "a minority group, understanding the technique of reaching the public mind, can 'sell' a good cause to the public and keep the public 'sold' on that cause."

Propaganda, to Bernays (1927a), was essential for achieving progress in the modern democratic society. He maintained business interests needed propaganda to assert their concerns within a marketplace of ideas dominated by other powerful interests who are already using propaganda. The democratic-capitalist society hums with new schemes, designs and competitive counter-proposals; the public relations professional advances his client's fresh perspectives by taking his client's vision and breathing "the breath of life into [the] idea and mak[ing] it take its place among other ideas and events" (p. 76).

Arguing against the post-war view that propaganda was deceitful, Bernays (1927b) asserted that effective propaganda must have, at its core, the truth. But, it is more than that. It is also about shaping or creating events to demonstrate that truth. He acknowledged that propaganda works on the emotions of the masses because "prejudices, notions and convictions are used as a starting point" to take the audience to a "passionate adherence to a given mental picture" (p. 151). However, despite this manipulative aspect, propaganda is not inherently bad, he asserted. The same emotional appeals that the KKK use can also be used by charities for good causes. Therefore, society's discerning minority, who can see innovative routes for societal progress, should use propaganda to elevate their proposals, products and services into the mainstream.

Several of Bernays' (1929) unpublished works drafted in the mid– to late–1920s attempted to build an expansive and cohesive case for pro-social propaganda. The arguments in these undated drafts highlighted four main ideas. First, individuals want to pursue happiness. Second, individuals are embedded within, and influenced by, the crowd, an entity which cannot be trusted to adequately judge what leads its members towards happiness. Third, the crowd's limited capacity to ascertain the best route toward happiness is best addressed through propaganda, which exposes the masses to new, beneficial perspectives. Fourth, the new PR professional, who understands how to create circumstances, is the individual best able to commodify these emerging ideas, products and services and convey them to various mass audiences through the news media.

Bernays' (1928), *Propaganda*, was a compendium of his 1920s articles and unpublished drafts and speeches and it claimed that a thriving democracy needed propaganda's ability to surface multiple minority perspectives. Without propaganda to deliver to the public the truths held by these minority views, the masses could not coalesce around new ideas and civilization's progress would stall. In this way, propaganda encouraged progress because it accounted for "not merely ... the individual, nor even the mass mind alone, but also and especially the anatomy of society, with its interlocking group formation and loyalties" (p. 28).

By the end of the 1920s, Bernays still proclaimed that propaganda was an essential force that enabled a wider realization of truths in American society. In one of Bernays' last published essays of that decade, he attempted to counter critic Everett Dean Martin's arguments that propaganda rested in untruths. In an unpublished portion of the piece, he maintained that the propagandist is a seeker of truth, even if that truth is centered within the interest and knowledge of a client. Bernays (1929) wrote:

> Are truths necessarily antagonistic to private facts? Truths are not antagonistic to special pleading, nor are truths the property of an academic mind, or reformers or limited to circumscribed circles only. "The truth shall make them free." But how can the truth be made clear to 120 million people if it is not done by a definite technique? [p. 5].

Although these words never made it into the article, they reveal that Bernays wrestled with a core challenge to his claim that propaganda surfaced truth. Although Bernays did not mention it as an example of a "circumscribed circle," the press, through professional principles and practices concurrently claimed that it was the source for truthful renditions. Bernays' awareness of journalism's truth claims were implied in his assertion that propaganda articulated "private truths" as opposed to the facts-oriented public truths that was the purview of the professionalizing press. Although Bernays deleted these passages from his proposed piece, they show that, almost a decade into his claim of pro–social propaganda, he struggled against the backdrop of a press that claimed it knew how to present truths more accurately.

The Commodification of Truth and Implications for Today's News

Not surprisingly, the press was highly skeptical of Bernays' claims that propaganda served a social good by offering unacknowledged truths. News workers often saw the pro-social rhetoric of Bernays as simply fresh rationales for professional persuaders to flood the press with publicity about their clients and manipulate journalists into providing coverage. But, behind this guardedness was the press worker's concern that Bernays' attempts to legitimate propaganda would undermine journalism's move toward autonomy and credibility. This was evident in an *Editor & Publisher* editorial, "Bernays Tells Us How" (1928), that appeared just months before the publication of *Propaganda*. The piece criticized Bernays for a speech at Cornell in which he partially justified the creation of events because they help provide news copy to newspapers. It read:

> The Bernays doctrine is of course the keystone of the publicity arch, though few of its practitioners have the temerity to utter it so boldly. There is no limit or definition to "affecting circumstances," nor is the press agent bound by strict construction of "before they happen." If he makes them news, it concerns him very little if they never happen [p. 32].

This concern about who is "affecting circumstances" is a vital part of the commodification of truth tussle in the 1920s between the professionalizing journalism industry and the nascent PR field. The press maintained that, through its adoption of facts-oriented reporting and use of experts for context, it now provided more reliable accounts of the day's events. The professional practice of objectivity and its related work routines also had the extra added benefit of safeguarding newspaper columns against further propagandist manipulations. The ANPA reinforced such thinking through hundreds of anti-publicity bulletins that asserted the refusal of publicity materials was crucial if news rooms were to protect the press's integrity and economic viability.

The emergent PR occupation, however, maintained that it provided other vital information that the public needed to know — products, services and viewpoints that the public would not necessarily see represented in news stories without the helping hand of the propagandist. Bernays took that assertion even further and maintained that the press, left to its own devices, reflected a detachment, ignorance and inertia similar to that of the crowd. He claimed that journalism was not equipped to surface minority group perspectives and initiatives. Rather than wait on the press to address this deficiency, the propagandist, he maintained, was the one equipped to help these groups conceptualize and then communicate the assets they offered society. Bernays' efforts ultimately were problematic, as his attempts to cast propaganda as a beneficent force were ill-timed, often vaguely conceived, and weighed down with elitist tones (Cutlip, 1994; Ewen, 1996; Olasky, 1987). News workers of the 1920s reacted to claims that PR could commodify truths by accelerating the development of professionalized journalism.

The legacy from this post-war struggle between professionalized journalism and the nascent PR occupation is a conundrum that affects the mainstream press to this day. An underexplored lesson from both industries' truth arguments in the 1920s is that the PR industry developed the strategic and tactical capacity to provide propaganda as a technical and conceptual aid to journalists "finding" the truth. This happened, in large part, because professional journalism's emphasis on objective accuracy biased story development toward institutionalized sources that could provide data, facts and experts.

There is ample evidence that this unintended link between professional journalism and PR began to crystallize throughout the 1920s. In 1924 and 1925, said a U.S. Senate committee on banking and currency, pure oil promoters paid a publicist "$1,000 for getting printed 228 stories in 111 newspapers with 12,540,000 circulation in 67 cities" (Lee, 1937, p. 464). In 1925, a national magazine reported that, in one state, 90 percent of the newspapers were running editorials in favor of the state power company provided solely by a PR firm (Olasky, 1987, p. 42). Two years later, Arthur W. Page, AT&T's Vice-President of Public Relations, speaking at an internal conference, noted that about half of the news content of the *New York Times* came from PR sources (Griese, 2001, p. 107).

By 1928, the Federal Trade Commission began an investigation of utility company public relations and determined that American newspapers regularly used propaganda. Journalist George Seldes (1935) spent one month reviewing the first ten volumes of the FTC's report and found the utility industry claimed 80 percent of the American press used their propaganda (p. 83). Psychologist Leonard Doob (1935), reflecting on the post-war growth of domestic PR in the United States, cited instances where some editors received hundreds of press releases a week, with the total copy sometimes exceeding all the content of one daily edition. Editors claimed they used only about 10 percent of these materials, and this claim, according to Doob, only encouraged PR persons to enhance and refine their ability to meet news reporters' needs. It would be "plain nonsense" to say that newspapers were free of propaganda, wrote Doob (pp. 186–187, 334).

Professional journalism in the first decade after the war already developed an unanticipated synergy with propaganda — objectivity's call for facts contextualized by experts had the unintended effect of promoting news worker reliance on propagandists. Today, the irony of journalism's continuing assertions that it commodifies truth is that its objectivity stance contributes to a persistent, if unintended, preference for PR sources and propaganda materials. *Newsweek's* Dokoupil (2008) accurately stated that World War I has, at least in a popular sense, slipped into a "secondhand past" (p. 50). However, the ramifications of that war linger in a very important arena. Propaganda during the Great War laid the foundation for the advent, in the 1920s, of a rhetorical skirmish between two commercial industries that claimed purview over the truth. Journalism and PR appeared to be on parallel tracks, both emphasizing a distinct ability to surface truths and then sell those accounts in the market. Those two tracks, however, had already begun to blur within

10 years of the war's end. So, when it comes to the news we receive today, World War I has left us an enduring quandary. The modern press persists in its claim that it gives the news consumer truth based on a journalistic frame of objective and accurate reporting. However, the substance within that journalistic construct — data, facts and expert commentary — is often the product of trained PR professionals. Propaganda continues to provide its own truths through a spot within the journalistic frame.

References

Bernays, E. (1923). *Crystallizing Public Opinion.* New York: Horace Liveright.
_____. (1925, November). *Crystallizing Public Opinion for Good Government.* Speech presented at the National Municipal League, Pittsburgh, PA, Bernays papers, Box I: 422.
_____. (1927a, January 26). A public relations counsel states his views. *Advertising and Selling,* pp. 76–77.
_____. (1927b, April). The minority rules. *The Bookman,* pp. 150–155.
_____. (1928). *Propaganda.* New York: Horace Liveright.
_____. (1928, June). *Propaganda and Impropaganda.* Speech presented in Rochester, New York. Bernays papers, Box I: 422.
_____. (1929). *Our Debt to Propaganda.* Bernays papers, Box III: 57. Unpublished manuscript.
Bernays tells us how (1928, February 25). *Editor & Publisher,* p. 32.
Blum, J. M. (1956). *Woodrow Wilson and the Politics of Morality.* Boston: Little, Brown.
Buitenhuis, P. (1976). The selling of the Great War. *The Canadian Review of American Studies, 7*(2), 139–150.
Callaway, J. (1918, June 13). Colonel Watterson and the Pulitzer Prize. *Macon (GA) Daily Telegraph,* p. 4.
Crawford, N. A. (1924). *The Ethics of Journalism.* New York: Alfred A. Knopf.
Creel, G. (1920). *How We Advertised America.* New York: Harper and Brothers.
The Creel Report (1920) *Complete Report of the Chairman of the Committee on Public Information.* New York: Da Capo.
Cutlip, S. (1994). *The Unseen Power: Public Relations. A History.* Hillsdale, NJ: Lawrence Erlbaum.
Dewey, J. (1918, December 21). New paternalism: Molding public opinion. *The New Republic, 17,* 216–217.
Dokoupil, T. (2008, February 18). The war we forgot. *Newsweek,* p. 50.
Doob, L. (1935). *Propaganda: Its Psychology and Technique.* New York: Henry Holt.
Emery, E. (1950). *History of the American Newspaper Publishers Association.* Minneapolis: University of Minnesota Press.
Ewen, S. (1996). *PR! A Social History of Spin.* New York: Basic.
Flint, L. N. (1925). *The Conscience of the Newspaper: A Casebook in the Principles and Problems of Journalism.* New York: D. Appleton.
Ford, N. G. (2008). *The Great War and America: Civil-military Relations During World War I.* Westport, CT: Praeger Security.
Free publicity. Wake up. (1922, October 7). *Bulletin-Free Publicity,* p. 731.
French government to control news! (1922, February 28). *Bulletin-Free Publicity,* p. 73.
Full account of how it's done: Inter-Ocean Syndicate activities revealed (1923, September 27). *Bulletin-Free Publicity,* pp. 580–581.
Get to the press agent's boss. (1924, January 17). *Bulletin-Free Publicity,* p. 16.

Gibbons, W. F. (1926). *Newspaper Ethics: A Discussion of Good Practice for Journalists.* Ann Arbor, MI: Edwards Brothers.
Griese, N. L. (2001) *Arthur W. Page: Publisher, Public Relations Pioneer, Patriot.* Atlanta: Anvil.
Hasian, M. A. (1998). Freedom of expression and propaganda during World War I: Understanding George Creel and America's Committee on Public Information. In *Free Speech Yearbook* (pp. 48–60). New York: NCA.
Heiskell, J. N. (1927, November 10) Why give it away? *Bulletin-Free Publicity,* p. 702.
Hofstadter, R. (1955). *The Age of Reform: From Bryan to F.D.R.* New York: Vintage.
Hollihan, T. (1984). Propagandizing in the interest of war: A rhetorical study of the Committee on Public Information. *The Southern Speech Communication Journal, 49,* 241–257.
Irwin, W. (1919, December). An age of lies: How the propagandist attacks the foundation of public opinion. *Sunset, 43,* 23–25, 54–56.
Irwin, W. (1936). *Propaganda and the News or What Makes You Think So?* New York: Whittlesey House.
Jackall, R., and J. M. Hirota (1995). America's first propaganda ministry: The Committee on Public Information during the Great War. In R. Jackall (Ed.), *Propaganda* (pp. 137–173). New York: University Press.
Leonard, T. C. (1995). *News for All: America's Coming-of-Age with the Press.* New York: Oxford University Press.
Lee, A. M. (1937). *The Daily Newspaper in America.* New York: Macmillan.
Lippmann, W. (1919, November 12). Unrest. *The New Republic, 20*(258), 315–322.
_____. (1922). *Public Opinion.* New York: Macmillian.
Mock J. R., and C. Larson (1939). *Words That Won the War: The Story of the Committee on Public Information, 1917–1919.* Princeton, NJ: Princeton University Press.
Olasky, M. (1987). *Corporate Public Relations: A New Historical Perspective.* Hillsdale, NJ: Lawrence Erlbaum.
Ponder, S. (1999). *Managing the Press: Origins of the Media Presidency: 1897–1933.* New York: St. Martin's.
Rosen, J. (1999). *What Are Journalists For?* New Haven, CT: Yale University Press.
Read this and weep. (1924, April 12). *Bulletin-Free Publicity,* p. 125.
The reds, big business and Ivy Lee. (1926, April 8). *Bulletin-Free Publicity,* p. 141.
Ryan, M. (2001). Journalistic ethics, objectivity, existential journalism, standpoint epistemology and public journalism. *Journal of Mass Media Ethics, 16,* 3–22.
65 tons of free advertising! (1928, February 9). *Bulletin-Free Publicity,* p. 13.
Schudson, M. (2003). *The Sociology of News.* New York: W.W. Norton.
Seldes, G. (1935). *Freedom of the Press.* Indianapolis: Bobbs-Merrill.
Sullivan, M. (1996) *Our Times: America at the Birth of the Twentieth Century* (abridged). New York: Scribner.
Tobin, H. J., and P. W. Bidwell (1940). *Mobilizing Civilian America.* New York: Council on Foreign Relations.
Vaughn, S. (1980). *Holding Fast the Inner Lines: Democracy, Nationalism and the Committee on Public Information.* Chapel Hill: University of North Carolina Press.
The *Washington Evening Star's* secret of success in keeping free advertising from its news columns. (1929, December 20). *Bulletin-Free Publicity,* p. 162.
Wells, H. G. (1914). *The War That Will End War.* London: Duffield.

/ Part III:
Effects of News Coverage*

Coverage of the Iraq and Afghanistan Wars in Business Magazines: The Profit and Economy of U.S. War and Policy

Karen Rohrbauck Stout

Businesses that provide the military with goods and services can profit from war. Other companies, however, can lose revenue because of war. It is reasonable to expect, therefore, that U.S. business media publications will address issues related to war, military action, and policy in order to inform and even warn readers about the business-specific or economy-wide effects of war. This study was designed to ask the general question, *how do business media publications represent the relationship between business and war?* The study describes, through qualitative content analysis, how three business media publications (i.e., *Business Week*, *Forbes*, and *Inc.*) address business revenues and economic forecasts in regard to U.S. military action and foreign policy in the Middle East over a six-year time period. To date, no examinations of business media in relation to U.S. war efforts has been conducted.

Justification

Business Magazines Under Examination

The three magazines under study were *Business Week* (hereafter referred to as *BW*), *Forbes*, and *Inc.*, which are circulated worldwide. In 2004–2005, they had combined subscriptions of approximately 3,341,429. *BW* had a 2004

North American and worldwide circulation of 1,281,429 (Business Week Advertising Information, 2005), while *Forbes* and *Inc.* had North American and worldwide circulations of 1.4 million (Forbes Advertising Information, 2005) and 660,000 respectively (Internet Public Library, 2008). Circulation does not account for potential readership, however, as issues are often read by multiple people (i.e., in waiting rooms and libraries). *Forbes*, for example, estimated in 2005 that it had 5.19 readers per copy (Forbes Advertising Information, 2005).

According to the demographic profiles of readers presented on the publications' websites, the primary audience addressed by these magazines (i.e., CEOs, managers, entrepreneurs, and other business leaders) was wealthy, educated men with influence in business and politics. For example, *Forbes* reported that 71 percent of readers were men with annual incomes over $206,000. Its readers "fund the economy, move markets, and are responsible for the direction of their organizations" (Forbes Advertising Information, 2005, paragraph 2). *Inc.* targets entrepreneurs and small business owners, so its demographic profile included college-educated males who earned incomes between $35,000 and $149,000 (Inc. Advertising Information, 2005). Whether in large businesses or small, readers of these business media are influential as they construct organizational policies that affect millions of workers across the U.S. and the globe.

Because of their organizational leadership and wealth, readers also likely exert political influence through lobbying, campaign contributions, and interpersonal relationships with government officials and politicians. According to a *BW* survey of readers, sampled government leaders identified involvement with "defense and national security" professionally (30.9 percent) or personally (50.3 percent) and with "legislative/governmental policy" professionally (31 percent) or personally (53.5 percent) (Business Week Advertising Information, 2005, paragraph 5). Such business leaders are uniquely positioned to shape U.S. policies regarding war and peace in the Middle East. Therefore, the media they consume shape and reflect the motivations and perceptions of their own communities and of the communities with which they have contact.

While targeting a similar audience, these magazines differ from each other in terms of ownership and editorship. *BW* is owned by the McGraw-Hill Companies, which is a publicly traded corporation and a parent company for several organizations. These include an educational publishing and multi-media learning company, a collection of television stations, Standard and Poor's investment rating services, JD Power and Associates, as well as publishing, networking, and conference planning services for the construction, energy, aviation, and defense industries (McGraw-Hill Companies,

2008). Stephen J. Adler is the editor-in-chief of *BW*, was the deputy managing editor of the *Wall Street Journal*, wrote and edited three books, and was named one of the 100 most influential business journalists (Wikipedia.org, 2008). John Byrne is *BW*'s executive editor and wrote for *BW* for many years. He was also editor-in-chief of *Fast Company* and authored eight books (Business Week.com Author Bios, 2008).

Forbes magazine is published by Forbes Inc., which is primarily owned by the Forbes family. Forbes Inc. also publishes several other magazines, maintains Forbes.com, and produces business-related conferences. Malcolm (Steve) Forbes, Jr. serves as President, CEO, and editor-in-chief of Forbes, Inc. and was a two-time self-funded Republican Presidential candidate (Yahoo! Finance, 2008). Casper Weinberger served as the chairman and publisher of *Forbes* and was a regular commentator until his death. Weinberger was a lawyer, politician, Cabinet member (for Presidents Nixon and Reagan, including Secretary of Defense), chairman of the Federal Trade Commission, and vice president and chairman of Bechtel (Associated Press, 2006).

Inc. was sold by creator Bernie Goldhirsh to Gruner + Jahr in 2000. In 2005, Joe Mansueto purchased and combined *Inc.* and *Fast Company* to create Mansueto Ventures (Burlingham, 2005). John Koten is editor-in-chief of *Inc.*, and served in various editorial capacities for *Worth*, the *Wall Street Journal*, and *Smart Money* (Boston Business Journal Staff, 2002). Jane Berentson is editor and served in various editorial positions at the *Wall Street Journal*, *Real Simple*, *The American Lawyer*, and *Worth* (Inc. 500, 2008). While these magazines may share a similar audience, they are clearly different in their ownership and executive editorial staff. Such differences are likely to be evident in magazine content and perspective.

The Relationship Between Business and War

A variety of research has examined the rhetoric surrounding the "War on Terror," the Gulf War, the current Iraq War, and September 11 (e.g., Hindman, 2004; Hutcheson, Domke, Billeaudeaux, & Garland, 2004; Noon, 2004; Ryan, 2004; Todorov & Mandisodza, 2004). Research found that the metaphor "this war is business" was used by the U.S. and allies to justify foreign intervention in Kosovo (Kuusisto, 2002). But to date, no research has addressed business media rhetoric in relation to the Iraq or Afghanistan wars since September 11, 2001.

Several major corporations and countless small companies contribute to U.S. military efforts as they develop defense, aerospace, and information technologies used in war. Some of these new developments become important to private industry and U.S. consumers' lives and broaden the potential reach of these companies. These commercial entities have the capability to earn significant profit, benefiting them as well as the U.S. economy. Since October 2006, for example, Lockheed Martin and Northrup Grumman have received over $46 billion and $29 billion respectively in U.S. government contracts (The Military-Industrial Complex, 2008). As these companies employ Americans, such contracts pay salaries that fund local economies. "The truth about war is that it is a business, a centre of profit for the suppliers of war materials and for those who reap the benefits of resources acquired or controlled" (West, 2006, p. 2). Deen (2003) pointed out that the initial 14-day attack on Iraq employed 8,700 bombs, 3,000 missiles, 36 Tomahawk missiles, and millions of rounds of ammunition. These munitions had to be replaced in military supplies, estimated to cost "billions of dollars — giving a tremendous boost to the U.S. military industry, which has been on the skids since the last Gulf War in 1991" (p. 1).

War, however, is expensive and can harm the economy. As an example, the first national debt was created after the Revolutionary War, and grew significantly after the Civil War, World War I, and World War II. Cost overruns, corruption, waste, and loss contributed to this debt (Folsum, 2006). Further economic harm can come through skyrocketing commodity prices and inflation, which results in fearful consumers who cut back on personal spending. Such outcomes, often coupled with the uncertainty of war, can lead to nervous investors and a sluggish economy, as companies withhold expansion or hiring efforts. Such concerns were evident in March 2003 and were "troubling downside risks for the economy" affecting business hiring and investment ("Second-half Pickup," 2003, p. 68). Further hidden company costs can include changes in employee staffing (as workers become soldiers) and training replacement employees (like "Rosie the Riveter"). Additionally, manufacturing resources may be diverted or rationed, resulting in purchasing and production modifications for military efforts. Finally, government defense spending diverts money that could be used elsewhere.

During the Iraq and Afghanistan wars and ongoing occupations, defense spending rose sharply. $661 billion was spent between 2001 and early 2007, with President Bush asking for an additional $141.7 billion in emergency supplemental funding for 2008. These totals surpass the cost of the Vietnam War (Tyson, 2007). Much of the money spent in Iraq and Afghanistan paid for goods or services from independent contractors. By 2008, news reports forecast the number of private contractors in Iraq at 190,000 and that 20 percent of Iraq war funding went to such companies. At that rate, it was estimated that $100 billion would be paid to such companies by the end of 2008 (Fisher, 2008).

Growing war costs estimates are influenced by "cost-plus" contracting, which guarantees contractors a 3 percent profit on expenses. This government approved billing procedure provides a financial incentive to inflate bills (Taibbi, 2007). Unfortunately, many U.S. military personnel who have acted as "whistle-blowers" to egregious billing and other related contractor corruption have been reprimanded, demoted, or transferred. Further, the government has not prosecuted any cases of fraud, nor sued for breach of contract, although such evidence has been found (Taibbi, 2007).

Controversy began early in the contract awarding process as U.S. based companies, rather than international companies or non-profits, overwhelmingly won government contracts. Halliburton and Bechtel were expected to be prominent contract recipients as they and only a few other companies were invited to make bids (Bhatia, 2005; Fogarty, 2003). Further controversy centered on invited bidders' campaign contributions to Republican political candidates and clear political connections between contract awardees and members of the Bush administration (Bhatia, 2005; Fogarty, 2003). Other concerns include lacking oversight and accountability for the 25,000 to 30,000 private security personnel (Fisher, 2008) and the contractor employees who outnumber U.S. troops in Iraq (Taibbi, 2007).

These controversies demonstrate that there is great profit to be earned during wartime. However, business media war mongering for the sake of potential corporate profits would likely seem distasteful to many business magazine readers. Conversely, pessimistic attitudes about warfare also could be worrisome. As a result, business media editors and authors must manage a variety of considerations when developing war-related stories. Therefore, the following research questions were posed:

RQ 1: What differences in article coverage exist based on the *magazine of origin*?

RQ 2: How are U.S. business *profit gains or losses* addressed in business publication articles?

RQ 3: How is the impact of U.S. *economic growth or loss* addressed in business publication articles?

Methodology

This study examined articles published in *BW*, *Forbes*, and *Inc.* between September 2000 and September 2006. *BW*, *Forbes*, and *Inc.* were selected for sampling because of their high circulation rates, the nature of their audiences, and because all issues during the six-year sample frame were available at local university and public libraries. Further, the focus and content was relatively consistent among these three magazines, which was important as many similar magazines addressed personal finance issues more heavily.

A purposive sampling method was used to find appropriate articles for coding. Research assistants examined each magazine issue cover-to-cover to find articles with content (evident by titles, stories, pull-out quotes, and captions) that addressed the U.S. military or military activities and war in Iraq and Afghanistan specifically and the Middle East generally. They also were to sample articles addressing terror/terrorism and oil, but only if these articles related to U.S. domestic or foreign policy. Articles had to be at least one column in length and could be editorials. This resulted in 85 articles sampled, which were photocopied and numbered. Two research assistants each received approximately half of the sample for coding.

The coding scheme was designed to answer the study's RQs. One coding sheet was used for each article. Research assistants coded for three categories: 1) magazine name, 2) business profit gains/losses, and 3) U.S. economic growth. Additional data not discussed in this paper were collected for analysis.

Coders took note of the publication (i.e., *BW, Forbes, Inc.*) for each article. These data were collected in order to demonstrate any differences in con-

---

Magazine: _____
Issue / Date: _____
Journalist/Author: _____
Page #: _____

- Look at headlines, body text, captions, and sidebars for both news and editorial content.
- Do not examine ads, cartoons, letters to the editor, or other non-journalistic elements.
- Fill out one coding sheet per article. Code the writing (i.e., voice of the journalist, *nor* individual source as it refers to American military action as directed by the President and Executive Branch, military officials/leaders, Dept of Defense, etc.
- If the author indicates disagreement between any of these groups, please indicate below.
- Do **not** code articles or references to troops and common members of the military.
- **Remember to also fill out the back of this sheet.**

circle one per set	When discussing American military actions or policies, [except troops] does the journalist...	Record key phrases or quotes that illustrate/support your answers to the adjacent questions
+ o −	predict any business profit gains ignore profit impact (or predict neutral impact) predict any business profit losses	
+ o −	predict any US economic growth ignore US Economic impact (or predict neutral impact) predict any US economic loss	
+ o −	predict positive outcomes for humanity/ positive morality avoid predicting outcomes for humanity/ neutral morality predict negative outcomes for humanity/ negative morality	
+ o −	indicate support re: Executive policies & decisions indicate neutrality re: Executive policies & decisions indicate dissent re: Executive policies & decisions	
circle one	Does the author articulate or identify primarily with: U.S. national self-interests or concerns Iraqi national interests or concerns Global/shared human interests or concerns	
Y N	Does the author indicate dissent or disagreement between the President & military leaders (e.g., Pentagon, DoD, etc)? If so, indicate who disagrees: _____	

tent focus, or editorial bias among the three magazines. This information was compared to other data collected.

The category *business profit gains/losses* represented evidence that indicated a relationship between U.S. military action/policy and business *profits*. Such articles could include stories about companies with increased income due to military contracts or increased consumer sales due to fears of war or military activities. Articles concerning *losses* could, for example, address business costs associated with increased security constraints or decreased sales due to consumer anxiety. Language had to address specific companies or specific industries. Coders were to indicate revenue gain as positive (+) or loss as negative (-). They were instructed to code articles as neutral/ignore (o) if article authors provided an even amount of both negative and positive comments or ignored the topic all together. Handwritten comments explained whether article was "neutral" rather than "ignore." Coders also provided examples of statements to support their coding decisions.

The category *U.S. economic growth/loss* represented evidence regarding the impact of war and military action/policy on the U.S. *economy*. Articles coded into this category could address, for example, a variety of economic factors including changes in Gross Domestic Product, inflation, and trade deficits because of U.S. war efforts or the rebuilding of Iraq. Additionally this category represented the impact on an aggregate of industries, including widespread patterns of employee staffing or domino-like effects of profit/loss among associated industries (e.g., among manufacturing, transportation, consumer sales). Coders did not code for any impact on the global economy. They were to indicate positive impacts on the U.S. economy (+) where optimistic growth was expected in areas (e.g., hiring, trade balances, and decreased commodity costs) and negative impacts (-) where pessimistic expectations were expressed (e.g., layoffs, trade deficits, inflation). Issues of consumer anxiety affecting sales could also be coded into this category, but such examples had to relate to an aggregation of companies or industries. Coders again could indicate articles as neutral/ignore (o) with handwritten comments again expounding the difference. Handwritten comments also explained general coding decisions.

Two research assistants read each assigned article completely to code for these categories by reading at the manifest and thematic levels. The units of analysis in this study were phrases and sentences in the articles. Research assistants were carefully trained and given a detailed instruction sheet regarding the coding scheme. Several meetings were held throughout the coding process to ensure the coders understood their task.

One coding assistant entered data into SPSS, and the author checked each entry for accuracy. The author calculated frequencies and cross-tabulations for the three categories.

Frequencies

	Magazine
BW	51
Forbes	25
Inc.	9

	Profit
Gain	17
Loss	4
Neutral	6
Ignore	58

	Economy
Gain	3
Loss	4
Neutral	4
Ignore	74

Cross-Tabulations

	Magazine		
	BW	Forbes	Inc.
Profit			
Gain	8	5	4
Loss	1	2	1
Neutral	3	1	2
Ignore	39	17	2
Economy			
Gain	2	0	1
Loss	3	1	0
Neutral	2	1	1
Ignore	44	23	7

Reliability Check

Two reliability checks were conducted assessing each category. The first reliability check demonstrated 100 percent reliability on all three categories. At the second check, 100 percent reliability was achieved on *magazine of origin* and *business profit gains/losses*. While *U.S. economic growth* dropped slightly to 88 percent, it was still within acceptable range.

Results

To answer RQ 1, frequencies of *magazine of origin* were calculated. *BW* provided the most articles in the sample at 51 (60 percent), *Forbes* 25 (29.4 percent), and *Inc.* 9 (10.6 percent). Because *BW* and *Forbes* publish weekly and bi-weekly, these magazines have more "time" each month (in terms of publication space) to address topics in greater breadth and depth on a quicker publication schedule. This inflates the perception they are more focused on U.S. policy and war-based topics. Other differences existed between the magazines, however.

BW was the only magazine that addressed war-based issues prior to September 11, 2001, as it published five articles related to military recruiting, the defense industry as a poor investment option, Saddam Hussein manipulating oil production/sales, and Exxon's profitability linked to global relations. *BW* published 32 articles from September 11, 2001, to May 1, 2003, when President Bush declared victory over Saddam Hussein. These articles emphasized specific businesses (like expansion due to federal contracts), technologies (expected to improve military effectiveness), or industries (like the impact of war on the oil industry). During the occupation (May 1, 2003, until September 2006), however, *BW* coverage diminished to 14 articles over more than three years' time. This shows that as the occupation continued, *BW*'s coverage did not.

A heightened state of war was not evident in *Forbes*' coverage, as only seven of its 25 articles were published between September 11, 2001, and May 1, 2003. Its coverage (of 18 articles) was greatest during the occupation. Thirteen articles were editorials (many written by Casper Weinberger and Steve Forbes) addressing topics such as funding Iraqi reconstruction and improvements to Iraqi quality of life. Other editorials addressed U.S. foreign policy beyond Iraq, as authors addressed lacking global support for U.S. foreign policy and the growing threats of North Korea and Iran. Titles such as "Mushrooming Crisis" and photographs of a nuclear mushroom cloud or a Hitler-like pose of Iranian President Mahmoud Ahmadinejad with arms raised emphasized the insistent rhetoric: "Alas, the White House has done next to nothing to prepare and persuade the U.S public of the possible need for stern measures [with Iran].... European-style diplomacy (a mechanism for doing nothing) is no longer viable" (Forbes, 2006, p. 23). These articles framed for readers the necessity of an aggressive U.S. approach and the failure of diplomacy. Such editorials embedded among business and economic concerns served to teach readers about necessary and acceptable viewpoints regarding the U.S.'s foreign policy and its "place" in the world.

Inc.'s coverage was almost evenly split during the two timeframes of war and occupation. Economic issues were emphasized in the early stages of the occupation, with coverage dwindling over time. As *Inc.*'s audience consisted primarily of small business owners and entrepreneurs, its topics addressed their concerns, such as companies desiring or obtaining federal contracts for new technologies and the impact of war on issues like security or consumer sales. *Inc.*'s focus was clearly more on business and economic issues, bypassing direct comments on U.S. war and policy or global relations.

The three magazines also differed in article authorship. *BW*'s coverage was practically evenly split between news stories and editorials (26 and 25 respectively), while *Forbes* clearly had more editorials (16 out of 25) and *Inc.* clearly had more news stories (7 out of 9). Considering the topic of *Forbes*' editorials, *Forbes* was clearly more concerned with "spinning" perceptions of the Iraq War and occupation as successful, despite isolation and opposition from global allies, and of the U.S. need to focus on North Korea and Iran as immanent threats.

RQ 2 asked about how U.S. military action and policy influenced *business profits/losses*. Most articles (58 or 68.2 percent) ignored this issue. Six (7.1

percent) indicated neutral effects, as they balanced the possibility of profit and loss within the same article. Seventeen (20 percent) indicated that businesses would profit. Most articles predicting business profits came during Iraqi occupation and were written by journalists (not commentators). Some of these articles addressed oil company profits. For example, one article concerned lifted trade embargos against Libya to provide access to new oil sources for U.S companies. Overwhelmingly, however, articles addressed increased profits due to war or technological developments.

Most *profit* articles concerned specific companies with increased sales due to fears of war and terrorism (e.g., of safety items like gas masks), or that received military contracts or federal grants to develop new technology helpful to the military. These new technologies, for example, included a type of bandage that could be used on the front lines to stop bleeding, drone technology that could go into battle rather than soldiers, computer technology to improve surveillance, and medicinal antidotes to respond to bio-terrorist attacks. One journalist detailed such hope for profit in the story of a blimp company that lobbied the military to use blimps for surveillance (despite historical problems with blimp technology). Such technology was expected to increase the efficiency and effectiveness of war, implying such advancements could make war quick and decisive with few casualties.

Huge growth and revenue was assured if companies could develop a technology useful to the military. Many articles addressed companies' dubious assets or inventions and how lobbying or political connections spared the companies from financial demise. One such article was titled, "It's who ya know: Chris McCormack wanted in on the rebuilding of Iraq. Fat chance, given his company's shaky finances and unproven technology. Until his lobbyists zeroed in on what could be a $1B government contract" (Wherry, 2003, p. 78). Such contracts assisted in expansion to commercial markets, like "Case study: The problem: DefenseWeb's technology was a big hit with the U.S. military. Was it time to target Corporate America?" (Kurtz, 2004, p. 56). This company was "on track to triple revenue this year" (p. 58). Articles concerning the potential for profit, regardless of technological quality or executives' business acumen, provided an inspirational picture for growing and inventive companies that could develop products useful for military activities.

Of the 17 articles that addressed *business profit gains*, two addressed controversial government contract decisions that lead to specific companies profiting. These two articles justified such behavior as necessary for expediency and cost efficiency. One article titled, "Desert Storm: All is fair in war and Defense Department contracting" (Swibel, 2004, p. 91) addressed the awarding of a large government contract regardless of a conflict of interest.

The illegal contract was justified as the company provided the technology at a significantly reduced price than competitors. The second article (published four days after President Bush declared victory over Saddam Hussein) identified companies that received early contracts to rebuild Iraq and how/why those decisions were made. Throughout, criticisms of "secret" decisions was countered with justifications based on expanding existing contracts for work to begin immediately (i.e., rather than wait through a bureaucratic process) or experience (e.g., Bechtel's experience in Arabic-speaking countries or Halliburton's experience in the Gulf War). An "ends justify the means" perspective was evident throughout the article, which justified questionable decision-making and dismissed negative perceptions that may result.

Only four articles (4 .7 percent) indicted that war led to revenue *losses*, all of which were published soon after September 11. Article topics addressed the impact of terrorism on sales in specific industries, like increased oil prices hurting transportation industries or fears of war damaging consumer confidence. Another addressed companies suffering financial losses because they failed to take security measures. One article conveyed several stories of small business owners who were military reservists called to serve in the Middle East and the impact on their businesses. A pullout quote demonstrated a lack of compassion evident throughout the article: "If their business withers, tough luck. Like good grunts, they have to suck it up" (Gray, 2004, p. 30), which was surprising, as *Inc.* targets small business owners. Language such as "grunt" implies a division of management and labor, which should not be convoluted. Unlike the *profit* articles that focused on only one business per article, the *loss* articles addressed several businesses with challenges in each story. Further, by detailing security failures or collapsing businesses because owners did not "suck it up," authors put the responsibility for losses on business owners and managers. The business failure is *their* failure. Such rhetoric serves to warn readers to manage differently, to learn from others' mistakes.

RQ 3 concerned *U.S. economic gains and losses*. As a whole, most articles (74 or 87.1 percent) ignored this topic. However, articles coded into this category associated U.S. economic health with U.S. business profitability and the length of the Iraq War. In other words, a short war with Iraq would allow U.S. businesses to get back to normal operations, prompting economic growth. *BW* published seven articles addressing economic concerns, while *Forbes* and *Inc.* only minimally addressed the economy by publishing two articles each. This is particularly interesting as *Forbes* had more articles in the sample than *Inc.*

Three (3.5 percent) articles indicated possible *positive* effects on economic growth and stimulus. Articles indicating economic gain often addressed negative economic concerns and continually refuted them. An example article was titled, "The storm before the calm: Might war with Iraq spur economic growth? And what will it mean for small companies?" (Mead, 2003, p. 86). The author wrote, "While I would never support waging war to stimulate the economy,... a short war leading to Iraqi reconstruction and re-entry into world oil markets is more likely to signal the beginning of a new boom than another recession" (p. 88). He listed examples of wars that were followed by economic booms, in part due to low energy prices. He recognized that budget deficits due to war could be "ruinous," but then denigrated "doom spinners" who worried about war cost estimates nearing $200 billion, which he thought were high. The author was sure the war would be short and inexpensive. He also denigrated specific economists who warned the economy would suffer if oil prices went beyond $40/bbl and gas, $2/gallon. "Thankfully, they are wrong," he said. In retrospect, *he* was wrong. Oil prices climbed in 2004 from $40/bbl to approximately $145/bbl in the summer of 2008, although prices have decreased ("Crude Oil Prices in 2007 dollars," 2007; Energy Information Administration, 2008). Gas prices have been over $2/gallon since 2006 and reached average highs over $4 in the summer of 2008 (Energy Information Administration, 2008). This article and the other *positive* economic articles clearly presented a message that anxiety about the economic outcome of the Iraqi war was unwarranted. But these articles, published early in the conflict, also failed to recognize the protracted deployment of U.S. troops, which has resulted in a mounting deficit. Further, the Iraqi insurgency has made producing Iraqi oil impossible, which has led OPEC to limit oil production thereby driving up energy costs worldwide (Emmott, 2007). Authors' assurances of economic stimulus were entirely based on an abbreviated war.

Four (4.7 percent) articles (three published soon after September 11) indicated a variety of *negative* economic effects. One concern was that a lengthy war would result in soaring energy costs, which would have a trickle-down effect. For example:

> Any (oil) price increase has devastating effects on the U.S. economy. Each dollar increase in the per-barrel price of oil trims airline margins by half a percentage point and cuts profits.... Consuming 45 billion gallons of fuel a year, truckers are vulnerable, too; ... the pain has a widening circle [Fisher & Cook, 2001, p. 66, 68].

Further, the prospects of war and possible continued terrorism would hit consumer confidence "hard" and result in shaky investment markets (Mandel, Coy, & Symonds, 2001, p. 30). Finally, concerns about government and military "spending restraints [going] out the window" would result in "fiscal profligacy and, ultimately, harm the economy" (Magnusson, Woellert, &

Gleckman, 2001, p. 34). While these concerns came immediately after September 11, the dire consequences seem in hindsight more accurate than the positive economic reassurances discussed earlier.

Four (4.7 percent) articles (published between 2001 and 2003) indicated *neutral* effects as they evenly weighed positive and negative economic predictions. Neutral articles were of two formats. In one type, a variety of people with differing viewpoints were juxtaposed against each other. In several cases, authors countered (and discounted) well-credentialed economists' analyses of widespread negative economic impacts of war with opinions from business executives who were concerned only with specific costs (e.g., security concerns upsetting transportation costs). In a similar article, written prior to President Bush's State of the Union speech where he introduced his war plan, a variety of business leaders were quoted for their perspectives on the impending war. The author argued, "Business executives insist that indecision over Iraq is leading them to put off investment and hiring; ... war jitters are hurting growth — which [Bush] views as another reason to get on with it" (Dwyer, Walczak, Dunham, Crock, Arndt & Reed, 2003, p. 35). One executive wanted to "get this [war] over with one way or another" (p. 36). While some business leaders expressed concern about the war and economy, the authors undermined the arguments. For example, "In reality, the idea that war worries are undermining the economy is overstated. A string of other [economic] woes is retarding growth" (p. 36).

In the second type of *neutral* article, one source compared factors that could influence the economy. An interview with a former Federal Reserve governor balanced such factors: "In the event of a quick and decisive war, the impact in the following quarter would be negative, but afterward the economy would do better." He pegged the U.S.'s chances at a "benign" war outcome at 40 percent to 60 percent, but renewed terrorism or continued hostilities would result in "a lot of really bad things" for the economy (Inc. Staff, 2003, p. 43). Discussion of a "malignant" war and its likelihood did not occur. The ambiguity of this and similar statements disguised the realities of war and the possible harmful effects on not only the economy but on those involved in enacting war. It portrayed, however, an optimistic impression of war as "quick and decisive" that allowed business leaders to get back to business.

Conclusion

This analysis demonstrates that the business media under investigation represented a clear relationship between war and business profitability and that economic concerns were based on the length of war. War-based business topics established for readers what the relevant issues were, while the written and visual texts likely reflected and shaped human perceptions and motives related to politics and war.

Clearly some companies were expected to financially benefit from war. Those that lost revenue because of war were blamed for failure to plan or because of attempting to manage dual interests (i.e., business and military service). Such personal responsibility in maintaining profit in a time of war obscures the relationships of businesses to the U.S. and global economies. Further, such assertion of responsibility shifts the burden of blame from those who declare and support war to U.S. businesses that become additional casualties of war.

Many pro-profit articles described companies obtaining government contracts or grants as they offered technological advancements (e.g., bandages that stop bleeding, drones that replace soldiers) for efficient and effective war. These articles connoted harmless, bloodless battles with quick recoveries. Such rhetoric emphasized a factory-like vision of improving productivity and minimizing expense. By aiding the U.S. military in its goals, these primarily small companies were financially rewarded for their efforts. Therefore, these articles do not appear to address war-profiteering, but rather war-enabling.

While the business of war was constructed as achievable for small and growing businesses in these articles, the stories of large corporations garnering huge contracts were ignored and obscured. So were the stories of corruption and greed that have inflated war costs (Fogarty, 2003; Taibbi, 2007; Winslow, 2004). During times of war, profits for companies with military contracts can soar as high as 1,800 percent beyond their non-war profits (Butler, 1974). These exorbitant profits cannot solely be based on increased sales, but are likely due, at least in part, to greed, inflated prices, and corruption. The brief acknowledgement and justification for the contract-awarding process did not address the paucity of attention to large corporations garnering huge grants. Were such grants not "news"? Gushing over huge contracts and profits for a few companies could seem like war-mongering and reveal the system of profit available for only a few. Clearly stories of corruption and greed were available during the time frame of this study, and surely, such stories were "news." By failing to investigate the businesses (and their military/government relationships) that the business media are supposed to represent, these magazines obscured and, indeed, concealed war-profiteering.

When it came to issues of the U.S. economy, the overall message from the magazines under study was confused and confusing. Predictions of economic growth or recession were relatively even and discussions of war-related issues (e.g., the economic impact of a growing national deficit, or deaths and casualties of soldiers) were absent. Predictions of "benign" war outcomes at 60 percent to 40 percent disguised the reality that the U.S. had a 50–50 chance of "malignant" outcomes. Such predictions and obfuscations presented war in a positive light. Such messages were reinforced by economists' expectations for a "quick and decisive" war. Further, by emphasizing business concerns as justification for the President to "get this over with," moral and humanitarian issues related to war were ignored. Additionally, such language equated war with production schedules and business plans, making war seem as simple as changing factory locations or upgrading production equipment. While these may be perspectives business executives understand, they are far from the realities of war.

The Iraq and Afghanistan wars have been far from "quick and decisive." Continued occupation has resulted in a mounting national deficit, increased energy costs, and, when combined with other U.S. and global factors, resulted in a recession. It is clear in retrospect that the economic "doom spinners" addressed in articles were correct, and their dismissal by authors was surprising. By obscuring the economic impact of war for U.S. businesses, these magazines failed to provide the information necessary for readers to make decisions they could trust.

Clearly, war is good for some businesses. But war is the business of soldiers, and some career soldiers say it is best to keep business out of it. Many military commanders did not support the war in Iraq, either advising against it or resigning because of it (West, 2006). Historically, many commanders have spoken against the relationship between war and profit. Major General Smedley Butler, one of the most decorated soldiers in U.S. history, said, "War is a racket. It always has been. It is possibly the oldest, easily the most profitable, surely the most vicious. It is the only one international in scope. It is the only one in which the profits are reckoned in dollars and the losses in lives" (Butler, 1974, p. 1). Most famously, President Eisenhower warned about the power of the business-war relationship and popularized the phrase "military industrial complex" in the process. He warned that liberty and democracy are at stake:

> A vital element in keeping the peace is our military establishment; ... we have been compelled to create a permanent armaments industry of vast proportions.... This conjunction of an immense military establishment and a large arms industry is new in the U.S. experience.... We recognize the imperative need for this development. Yet we must not fail to comprehend its grave implications. Our toil, resources and livelihood are all involved; so is the very structure of our society. In the councils of government, we must guard against the acquisition of unwarranted influence, whether sought or unsought, by the military-industrial complex. The potential for the disastrous rise of misplaced power exists and will persist [Eisenhower, 1961, Section 4 paragraph 1].

President Nixon also warned of the power of this financial relationship. He argued, "short of changing human nature, therefore, the only way to achieve a practical, livable peace in a world of competing nations is to take the profit out of war" (Nixon, 1983, p. xx).

The "military industrial complex" connotes the relationship between those who declare and manage war (i.e., government and military) and those with commercial interests in supplying and sustaining war (i.e., producers of goods and services). Media outlets are commercial interests that are influenced by war. War news reports influence ratings that influence advertising revenues, which may be paid for by corporations in the defense industry. Further, media owners, creators, and broadcasters have vested personal interests in the defense industry, military, or government, or may be significant political donors (e.g., Klinenbert, 2005; NewsMeat, 2008). Therefore, the military industrial complex is shaped by language, perception, and meaning created by the media. The media have been called the "fourth estate," which indicates their role in safeguarding the public interest by serving as watchdogs of governmental activities. This role is complicated, however, by commercial interests that benefit and support war. For U.S. business media, this watchdog role is particularly complicated as some readers would likely benefit from a careful eye guarding their interests, while other readers clearly benefit from a watchdog asleep at his post.

Limitations

While this study demonstrates how *BW*, *Forbes*, and *Inc.* addressed U.S. policy in the Middle East, its claims are not generalizable to the broader business media market. The demographic profile of *Inc.*'s readers also demonstrated difference from the significantly more affluent readers of *BW* and, in particular, *Forbes*. Audience differences likely affects the type of articles published in *Inc.*, accounting for its smaller portion of the sample.

Future Directions for Research

Future research on this topic should examine how other business or economic publications, such as the *Wall Street Journal* or *The Economist*, address U.S. military action and policy in relation to the conflict in the Middle East. As these publications vary from those sampled here (e.g., *WSJ* is a daily publication, *The Economist* addresses more global issues), a variety of methodological considerations must be made. Future projects may sample only one publication thoroughly to maintain consistency. Broadening the sample to include non-business (e.g., *Newsweek*, *Time*) and progressive business and economic publications (e.g., *Left Business Observer*, *Progressive Populist*) would provide a comparative balance to the magazines in this study.

As the Iraq occupation is ongoing, it also would be helpful to continue this data analysis over time. It also would be useful to conduct a similar analysis during other periods of war, such as the Vietnam War and the first Gulf War. Examinations of business media in relation to U.S. war and policy across time are warranted.

This sampling process resulted in a number and variety of articles for analysis. It would be valuable to reanalyze these articles by topic. Patterns clearly existed in topics like those related to oil (e.g., ownership, profitability, production), security (e.g., surveillance challenges, civil liberty concerns), technology (e.g., development of, promise of military efficiency), and U.S. foreign policy (e.g., in relation to North Korea, Russia, Iran), and these patterns could be compared to other article data, such as date of publication. Additional areas for analysis could include references to the global economy.

Summary

This study undertook a qualitative content analysis of three top business magazines (*BW*, *Forbes*, and *Inc.*) from September 2000 to September 2006. The audience for these magazines is influential in society and the U.S. business community. The articles analyzed revealed that war was expected to benefit some U.S. companies, while the companies expected to reap the greatest benefits were not discussed. Economic evaluations of war were contradictory, as negative evaluations of war's impact on the economy were dismissed. As a variety of military leaders and U.S. presidents have warned about the relationship between profit and war, the findings of this study demonstrate rhetoric that supports the profitability and obscures the reality of war.

Author's note: This essay was funded with a grant from Research and Sponsored Programs, Western Washington University. The author would like to acknowledge Drs. Anna Eblen and Michael Karlberg for co-authoring a pilot study for this project. I would also like to thank my research assistants Jessica Jewett, Shannon Reed, Taylor Stockton, Luke Ware, and Kate Wallis for their assistance in data collection and analysis.

References

Associated Press (2006, March 28). Former Defense Secretary Weinberger dies. *MSNBC Web site.* Retrieved March 1, 2007, from http://www.msnbc.msn.com/id/12050783/.

Bhatia, M. (2005). Postconflict profit: The political economy of intervention. *Global Governance, 11,* 205–244.

Boston Business Journal Staff (2002, September 9). John Koten named editor of Inc. magazine. *Boston Business Journal.* Retrieved November 14, 2008, from http://www.bizjournals.com/boston/stories/2002/09/09/daily4.html.

Burlingham, B. (2005, September). The anatomy of a sale — ours. *Inc.com Web site.*

Retrieved November 14, 2008, from http://www.inc.com/magazine/20050901/anatomy-of-sale-1.html.
Business Week Advertising Information (2005). *Reader Survey Results and Circulation Table.* Retrieved October 10, 2005, from http://www.businessweek.com/advertising.htm.
Business Week.com Author Bios (2008). *Author Info: John A. Byrne.* Retrieved November 14, 2008, from http://www.businessweek.com/bios/John_A._Byrne.htm.
Butler, S. D. (1974). *War Is a Racket.* New York: Revisionist Press. (Original work published in 1935.)
Crude oil prices in 2007 dollars (2007). *WTRG Economics Web site.* Retrieved September 3, 2008, from http://www.wtrg.com/prices.htm.
Deen, T. (2003, April 3). There's no business like war business. *Commondreams.org Newscenter Web site.* Retrieved July 6, 2007, from http://www.commondreams.org/headlines03/0403-01.htm.
Dwyer, P., L. Walczak, R. S. Dunham, S. Crock, M. Arndt, and S. Reed (2003, February 3). Can he close the deal? *Business Week, 3818,* 34–36.
Eisenhower, D. (1961). *Farewell Address to the Nation.* Dwight D. Eisenhower Presidential Library and Museum Web site. Retrieved July 6, 2007, from http://www.eisenhower.archives.gov/speeches/farewell_address.html.
Emmott, B. (2007, March/April). The price of oil. *Foreign Policy, 159,* 47–48.
Energy Information Administration (August 27, 2008). *Spot Crude WTI Prices & U.S. Regular Gasoline Prices.* Retrieved September 3, 2008, from http://tonto.eia.doe.gov/oog/info/twip/twip.asp.
Fisher, D., and L. Cook (2001, November 12). The Prize. *Forbes, 168*(12), 64–68.
Fisher, W. (2008, September 6). One fifth of Iraq funding goes to private contractors. *Alter Net Web Site.* Retrieved September 11, 2008, from http://www.alternet.org/waroniraq/97834/one_fifth_of_iraq_funding_goes_to_private_contractors_/.
Fogarty, T. A. (2003, March 26). Companies bid on rebuilding Iraq. *USA Today,* B03.
Folsom, B. W., Jr. (2006, August). Our economic past: Our presidents and the national debt. *Foundation for Economic Education Web Site.* Retrieved September 11, 2008, from http://www.fee.org/publications/thefreeman/article.asp?aid=5603.
Forbes Advertising Information (2005). *Forbes Circulation Information.* Retrieved October 11, 2005, from http://www.forbesmedia.com/forbes/borbdemo.php.
Forbes, S. (2006, January 9). Mushrooming crisis. *Forbes, 177*(1), 23.
Gray, T. (2004, November), Priority: Company halted. *Inc., 26*(11), 29–30.
Hindman, D. B. (2004). Media system dependency and public support for the press and president. *Mass Communication & Society, 7,* 29–42.
Hutcheson, J., D. Domke, A. Billeaudeaux, and P. Garland (2004). U.S. national identity, political elites, and a patriotic press following September 11. *Political Communication, 21,* 27–50.
Inc. 500 (2008). Jane Berentson editor, *Inc.* magazine. *The 25th Annual Inc. 500 Conference Web site.* Retrieved November 14, 2008, from http://www.globalexec.com/inc500/speakers.php?lname=Berentson Inc.
Advertising Information (2005). *Subscriber information.* Retrieved October 11, 2005, from http://inc.com/advertising.htm.
Inc. Staff (2003, January). Readers' questions. War: Who is it good for? *Inc., 25*(1), 42–43.
Internet Public Library (2008). *Entrepreneurship Magazine Information.* Internet Public Library Web site. Retrieved October 10, 2007, from www.ipl.org/div/serials/browse/bus33.00.00/.
Klinenbert, E. (2005, February 24). Beyond "fair and balanced." *Rolling Stone, 968,* 36–38.
Kurtz, R. (2004, October). The problem: DefenseWeb's technology was a big hit with the U.S. military. Was it time to target Corporate America? *Inc., 26*(10), 56–57.

Kuusisto, R. (2002). Heroic tale, game, and business deal? *Quarterly Journal of Speech, 88*, 50–68.
Magnusson, P., L. Woellert, and H. Gleckman (2001, October 1). Suddenly, Washington's wallet is open. *Business Week, 3751*, 34.
Mandel, M., J., P. Coy, and W. Symonds (2001, October 1). Rethinking the economy. *Business Week, 3751*, 28–33.
Mead, W. R. (2003, March). The storm before the calm. *Inc., 25*(3), 86–91.
NewsMeat (2008). *Hall of Fame — "The Media": Federal Campaign Contributions Since 1978.* Retrieved September 6, 2008, from http://www.newsmeat.com/media_political_donations/.
Nixon, R. (1983). *Real Peace.* Boston: Little, Brown.
Noon, D. (2004). Operation enduring analogy: World War II, the war on terror, and the uses of historical memory. *Rhetoric & Public Affairs, 7*, 339–366.
Ryan, M. (2004). Framing the war against terrorism. *Gazette: The International Journal for Communication Studies, 66*, 363–382.
Second-half pick up (2003, March). *ABA Banking Journal, 95*(3), 68.
Swibel, M. (2004). Desert Storm. *Forbes, 174*(4), 91.
Taibbi, M. (2007, September 6). The great Iraq swindle. *Rolling Stone, 1034*, 62–75.
The McGraw-Hill companies (2008). *McGraw-Hill Company Descriptions.* Retrieved November 14, 2008, from http://www.mcgraw-hill.com/index.html.
The Military-Industrial Complex (2008). *The Military-Industrial Complex Leaderboard Since 10/30/06.* Retrieved September 11, 2008, from http://www.militaryindustrialcomplex.com/contracts-leaderboard.asp.
Todorov, A., and A. N. Mandisodza (2004). Public opinion on foreign policy: The multilateral public that perceives itself as unilateral. *Public Opinion Quarterly, 68*, 323–349.
Tyson, A. S. (2007, February 6). Bush's defense budget biggest since Reagan Era: Iraq, Afghanistan spending top Vietnam War. *The Washington Post*, A6.
West, J. (2006, November 14). The truth about war: It's a for-profit business. *Znet Web site.* Retrieved June 8, 2007, from http://www.zmag.org/znet/viewArticle/2756.
Wherry, R. (2003, June 9). It's who ya know. *Forbes, 171*(12), 78–79.
Wikipedia.org (2008, September 15). *Stephen J. Adler.* Retrieved November 14, 2008, from http://en.wikipedia.org/wiki/Stephen_J._Adler.
Winslow, L. (Executive Producer). (2004, June 23). *News Hour with Jim Lehrer* [Television broadcast]. Washington, DC: Public Broadcasting Service.
Yahoo! Finance (2008). *Forbes Inc. Company Profile.* Retrieved November 14, 2008, from http://biz.yahoo.com/ic/44/44195.html.

"NEW MEXICO'S ALWAYS BEEN PATRIOTIC AND LOYAL TO THE COUNTRY": UNCRITICAL JOURNALISTIC PATRIOTISM IN WARTIME

David Weiss

In this chapter, I use the theory and methods of critical linguistics (Fowler, 1991; Fowler & Kress, 1979; Hodge & Kress, 1993) to analyze "N. M. [New Mexico] Plays a Large Role in Iraqi Engagement" (Linthicum & Romo, 2003), a pro-war feature story that ran on the front page of the *Albuquerque Journal* on March 30, 2003, the twelfth day of U.S. combat operations in Iraq. The story's tone of uncritical patriotism offered a sharp contrast to the daily protests, bumper stickers, "No War" yard signs, and other highly visible expressions of anti-war sentiment on abundant display in the Albuquerque community—outcries that were not merely visible but practically inescapable, and yet virtually ignored by the local media.

I was attracted to the Linthicum and Romo piece precisely because of its apparent innocence. The article did not state a position on the war, nor did it report on developments in the conflict. On its surface, it was merely a human-interest feature story: an unassuming survey of New Mexicans' participation in and attitudes, unanimously positive, toward war efforts past and present. As I dug into the specific lexical and grammatical choices made by its authors, the article struck me as more powerful and revealing, in its own way, than many of the hard news reports and opinion pieces on offer during the Iraq War's early days. Here was a piece of journalistic writing whose very subtlety was, paradoxically, the source of its power: an easily dismissible "local color" puff piece, and thus precisely the sort of reportage that normalized and naturalized both war and pro-war sentiment even as it declined to offer an explicit argument or point of view. As such, it seemed to me, "N. M. Plays" practically screamed out for critical attention and, in particular, for the sort of micro-level analysis offered by critical linguistics, a methodological framework developed specifically to reveal and critique ideological bias and other manifestations of imbalances of power encoded, whether consciously or unconsciously, in the very nuts and bolts of grammar: word choice, tense, voice, and sentence structure.

Criticizing the Press's War Coverage

While few writers to date have undertaken linguistic analyses of the U.S. media coverage of the war, there has certainly been no shortage of criticism. Indeed, within weeks of the launch of combat operations in Iraq, cultural and social critics began offering their assessments not only of the government's and military's actions, but also of the press's coverage. The critical consensus that emerged — at least, after the "honeymoon" period, which included the fall of Baghdad and the president's tragically inaccurate May 2003 "Mission Accomplished" declaration — was consistent and clear. Observers from all corners excoriated the U.S. mainstream media for their failures to serve as "watchdogs": their inability or unwillingness to provide truly independent reporting, their reluctance to scrutinize or even express skepticism regarding Bush Administration claims about the war's necessity and inevitability, and their homogeneously pro-war (or, at least, pro–Administration and anti-dissent) coverage of the issues.

During the years since the U.S. began its war in Iraq, the publication of books criticizing the press's complicity with White House's pro-war communications has turned into a cottage industry, spawning various bestsellers (e.g., Boehlert, 2006; Katovsky & Carlson, 2003; Massing, 2004; Miller, 2004; Rampton & Stauber, 2003; Rich, 2006; Schechter, 2003; Solomon & Erlich, 2003; Thomas, 2006), monographs and edited collections (e.g., Allan & Zelizer, 2004; Artz & Kamalipour, 2005; Dadge, 2006; Hoskins, 2005; Kamalipour & Snow, 2004; Kuypers, 2006; Mirzoeff, 2005; Rutherford, 2004), and academic journal articles and book chapters critically analyzing (and in most cases, skewering) the practices and performances of the press (e.g., Dardis, 2006; Edwards & Cromwell, 2004; Kull, Ramsay, & Lewis, 2003–04; Mermin, 2004; Mooney, 2004; Porpora & Nikolaev, 2008; Ravi, 2005; Ryan, 2006; Seib, 2005; Snow & Taylor, 2006; White, 2005; Williams, 2004).

To varying degrees and in varying ways, all these scholarly books and articles, like the more commercial publications, argued that "the American media failed to ask the tough questions of an Administration that seemed determined to go to war" (Dadge, 2006, p. 1). And while most of the academic critics were somewhat more measured (or, at least, slightly less rabid) in tone than the commercial writers, their arguments and findings were no less troubling. Indeed, it would be fair to say that the scholarly inquiry was united in its charge that mainstream press coverage in the United States, at the very least, "suffer[ed] from a lack of balance and context required for comprehension of the most serious of political issues, [leaving] Americans confused about the reasons for invading Iraq and unable to offer informed consent in response to the current occupation" (Fraley, 2007, p. 434).

In retrospect, such failures should not be entirely surprising. Even if the producers and disseminators of news in the United States do not necessarily have an overt political agenda, they do not operate in a vacuum. The national media "are influenced by the overall political environment in which they exist [and are] inextricably linked to the broader sociopolitical environment in which they operate [thus reflecting] the position of dominant national actors and institutions" (Dimitrova, Kaid, Williams, & Trammell, 2005, p. 35). Such "environmental" influence on the press is particularly strong during times of war. Newspapers, especially, are "rooted firmly in a national ethos," so they are susceptible to being caught up in the tension "between patriotism and the professional practices of truth telling, sensitivity, fairness in presenting different sides of the story, and critical examination of official accounts" (Ravi, 2005, pp. 45–46). As Ravi observed in his examination of the "flawed journalistic practices" that characterized U.S. coverage of the war and the Administration's justifications for it, "this is a time when the press is under close scrutiny from critics who are dissatisfied either that the press is not patriotic enough or that there is too much of a home-side type of reporting and not enough questioning of official sources" (p. 46).

Some media scholars representing the "too much of a home-side" argument took particularly strong, often controversial positions. Consider, for example, Herman's (2004) summary of the situation in his essay "Normalizing Godfatherly Aggression":

> The U.S. propaganda system has normalized and even put a very good face on its government's straightforward aggression against — and conquest and colonial occupation of — a small distant country.... In the case of the 2003 Iraq invasion and conquest ... the media cooperated beautifully in pushing these propaganda themes [and] collaborated fully in these various charades ... conform[ing] to the party line [pp. 176, 180].

Even so, much of the scholarship on the mainstream media's Iraq coverage avoided leveling such serious charges and in many cases steered clear of the term "propaganda" entirely, opting instead to dissect the media's performance in terms of agenda-setting theory (Christie, 2006; Lee, Maslog, & Kim, 2006) or constructs such as "spiral of silence" that focus on the muting or marginalizing of dissent (e.g., Artz, 2005; Couldry & Downey; 2004; Jensen, 2005; Porpora & Nikolaev, 2008; Ravi, 2005; Reese, 2004).

Another important stream of academic Iraq War media criticism took as its foundation the theoretical notion of framing, a continually hot topic in mass communication scholarship. For better of worse, framing is itself a contested concept. Indeed, virtually all of the scholars analyzing the media's framing of the Iraq War[1] note that there is no single accepted definition of the term. Still, many took as their foundation Entman's (1993) popular definition: to frame is to "select some aspects of a perceived reality and make them more salient in a communicating text in such a way as to promote a particular problem definition, causal interpretation, moral evaluation, and/or treatment recommendation" (p. 52). A good deal of the extensive Entman-inspired work on Iraq War media framing was conducted by Dimitrova and her colleagues. Building on Entman's (1993) general concept and applying it to war coverage specifically, Dimitrova, et al. (2005) pointed out that "in a case of war, the media can select to focus on the destruction of war as opposed to freedom or tyranny, can frame the event as an invasion versus attack, can emphasize the victims versus invaders, and can highlight a positive versus negative attitude toward the war" (p. 26). Guided by this general insight, Dimitrova and her colleagues developed over the course of several articles a list of the specific frames found in the media's Iraq War coverage. Chief among them were the *military conflict frame* (stories that place emphasis on military involvement, conflict, or action in Iraq, focusing on troops), the *violence-of-war frame* (emphasis on the destruction caused by war), and the *human-interest frame* (emphasis on the personal stories of the human participants in the war, with more "soft news" focus on the plight of involved parties).[2]

Dimitrova (2006) and her colleagues (Dimitrova & Stromback, 2005; Dimitrova, et al., 2005) applied their framing taxonomy in a series of quantitative content analyses that determined which frames were used at various times, by various media outlets, and in various countries. They found, for example, that U.S.–based Internet news sites "focused more heavily on the military conflict, human interest, and media self-coverage [frames] while the responsibility frame was more common for international sites" (Dimitrova, et al., 2005, p. 22); that the frames used on the *New York Times*'s web site varied over time (Dimitrova, 2006); and that Swedish newspapers used the responsibility frames and anti-war protest frames more frequently than U.S. newspapers, which relied more heavily on the military conflict frame (Dimitrova & Stromback, 2005). In a similar study, Carpenter (2007) applied the

Dimitrova taxonomy and found that "elite" U.S. newspapers used the military conflict and violence of war frames more than "non-elite" U.S. newspapers, whose Iraq stories focused more on human interest coverage.

Such studies provided a macro-level understanding of the media coverage of the Iraq War as they identified framing trends and patterns across time and place. However, as a result of the nature of such scholarship, the tendency of which was to sort and content-analyze massive numbers of news stories in terms of competing framing categories, almost no insight was gained into what *constitutes* the frames. As pointed out by Wolfe, Swanson, and Wrona (2008), who conducted a rare, in-depth semiotic analysis of Iraq War news articles: "While it seems unfalsifiable to say that "media frames" help journalists construct news texts and help audiences comprehend them, content analysis does not and cannot explain how news words and images, considered both separately and in tandem, fashion the frames that frame theorists claim to be so influential" (p. 42).

Put another way, surprisingly little scholarship published to date has journeyed *inside* the frames, analyzed *how* they are constructed, or focused on their specific textual and visual contents. In fact, other than the Wolfe, et al. (2008) investigation, which analyzed the words and photographs used in two news stories posted on MSNBC's web site during February 2005, the only other micro-level analysis of Iraq War journalistic content I have found is Lule's (2004) study of the metaphors used on NBC's *Nightly News* broadcasts during the six weeks immediately preceding U.S. operations in Iraq (February 5–March 19, 2003) to describe the "march toward war."

My own analysis journeys inside the frame, the human-interest frame, with its emphasis on "soft" news and personal stories used at the very beginning of the war, a time when mainstream media coverage was virtually uniformly supportive (or, at least, uncritical) of the Bush Administration's actions in Iraq. Although not a semiotic analysis per se, my investigation ultimately shares some of semiotic theory's goals: "to describe the meanings texts make by asking such questions as 'What are the observable signifiers in the chosen texts?' and 'What are the signifieds that these signifiers suggest?'" (Wolfe, et al., 2008, p. 43). By exploring and analyzing in highly specific terms the textual content (signifiers) of a human-interest article published by an organ of what Boehlert (2006) would call the "lapdog press," I clarify how a war story's news frame was constructed *and* how its ideological make-up was enacted. I reveal how this construction and enactment served to guide readers toward a preferred position on the war and Americans' participation in it: one of uncritical patriotism.

Context and Synopsis

"N. M. Plays a Large Role in Iraqi Engagement," written by *Albuquerque Journal* staff writers Leslie Linthicum and Rene Romo, appeared on Sunday, March 30, 2003. During this early period of the war, national and global attention were firmly fixed on events in Iraq; moreover, tensions between the proponents and opponents of the war were fiercely pronounced, even if those tensions were not always reflected in the mainstream media's coverage (Boehlert, 2006; Dadge, 2006; Rutherford, 2004). Reflecting—and, arguably, reinforcing—*Journal* readers' interest in the war, the article begins on the paper's front page (p. A1), where it is accompanied by three other war-related pieces: "Iraq: 'We Will Use Any Means,'" "4 Killed in Suicide Bombing," and "U.S. Troops Get First Mail Call on Front."

Although placed on the front page of the newspaper, "N. M. Plays" is a feature story rather than a so-called "hard" news story.[3] Rather than providing breaking bulletins from the battlefront, the article supplements the hard news to which it is adjacent by recounting a series of anecdotes about New Mexicans and New Mexico–based institutions involved in war efforts past and present. Among other topics, "N. M. Plays" discusses the provenance of the F-117A Nighthawks used to bomb Baghdad (New Mexico's Holloman Air Force Base), the home of the F-16 pilots that attacked Iraqi tanks (New Mexico's Cannon Air Force Base), the testing location of the Patriot missiles used in Iraq (New Mexico's White Sands Missile Range), and the number of New Mexicans enrolled in the National Guard. At the same time, the article also puts 21st-century military-supportive New Mexico in historical context. It includes a conversation with an 83-year-old New Mexican veteran of World War II ("New Mexico's always been patriotic and loyal to the country," the Albuquerque resident is quoted as saying), mentions the number of New Mexicans who died in Japanese prison camps during World War II, and quotes a former state historian who lauded New Mexicans' ready participation in both the Mexican-American and Spanish-American Wars. Given these foci, "N. M. Plays" also exemplifies what Dimitrova (2006) categorizes as the journalistic human-interest frame, in which emphasis is placed "on the personal stories of the human participants in the war" (p. 80).

Additionally, "N. M. Plays" serves as an example of "non-elite newspaper" journalism, a category that has received relatively little attention by scholars of Iraq War media coverage, despite non-elite papers' large aggregate reach (Carpenter, 2007). Whereas elite newspapers serve a national geographic area, non-elite publications such as the *Albuquerque Journal* concentrate on statewide coverage and have circulations well below that of their elite counterparts.[4] Moreover, the *Journal*—and, by extension, the "N. M. Plays" article—

manifests other, more important characteristics of non-elite newspapers. While elite newspapers have been found to present more balanced coverage of controversial issues (Lacy, Fico, & Simon, 1991), non-elite newspapers "cover local issues to set themselves apart from elite newspapers [and therefore] promote the status quo by producing stories that reflect the United States' viewpoints" (Carpenter, 2007, p. 763). Non-elite newspapers are more likely to rely on local sources at the state level as well as non-official sources, and such limited access "may affect the accuracy and diversity of reports stemming from non-elite papers" (Carpenter, p. 765). In addition to the use of non-official sources typical of non-elite newspapers' articles, "N. M. Plays" *does* include quotes from players on the national political stage, including Governor Bill Richardson (D–N.M.), U.S. Representative Heather Wilson (R–N.M.), and the commander of the New Mexico National Guard. Even so, "N.M. Plays" serves as a representative non-elite, human-interest feature story published during wartime and as an opportunity to explore in depth how such a story promoted and contributed to a particular, elite-preferred point of view about a controversial war, a world event with local as well as national and international ramifications.

However, as is true of any newspaper story, in "N. M. Plays," it is not merely the article's topics and themes that convey its ideological standpoint, an uncritically pro–U.S., pro-war position. The standpoint is also communicated via the *way* those topics and themes are developed grammatically, syntactically, and lexically — in the very guts, so to speak, of the article's content. Considering simultaneously both the form and the content of the article allows for a critical reading that can bring us inside a journalistic frame and allow us to see how, precisely, a piece of pro-war journalism works to encourage and contribute to the more generalized, and often unreflexive, patriotism that is preferred by government elites during wartime.

Critical Linguistics

In my analysis of the *Albuquerque Journal* article "N. M. Plays," I use the tools of critical linguistics, the theoretical and methodological framework originally developed by Fowler and Kress (1979) to which more recent forms of critical discourse analysis are indebted. The purpose of all critical discourse scholarship, including critical linguistics (henceforth "CL"), is to reveal and critique ideologically biased points of view and other instantiations of power imbalances that might otherwise remain hidden, particularly in those discourses in which power is encoded only covertly, if at all (Fairclough, 1995; Fairclough & Wodak, 1997; Meyer, 2001; van Dijk, 1997; van Leeuwen, 2005, 2008; Wodak, 2001). The distinguishing operating assumption of CL, specifically, is that "features of the grammatical form of a text are seen as meaningful choices from within the possibilities available in grammatical systems" (Fairclough & Wodak, 1997, p. 263), choices that are both reflective and constitutive of ideological bias.

In their foundational essay "Critical Linguistics," Fowler and Kress (1979) made these bold theoretical claims about their new approach to the analysis of discourse:

> Syntax can code a world-view without any conscious choice on the part of a writer or speaker. We argue that the world-view comes to language-users from their relation to the institutions and the socio-economic structure of their society. It is facilitated and confirmed for them by a language use which has society's ideological impress. Similarly, ideology is linguistically mediated and habitual for an acquiescent, uncritical reader who has already been socialized into sensitivity to the significance of patterns of language. Any text, then, embodies interpretations of its subject, and evaluations based on the relationship between source and addressee.... To generalize further, there are social meanings in a natural language which are precisely distinguished in its lexical and syntactic structure and which are articulated when we write or speak. There is no discourse which does not embody such meanings [p. 185].

Further, CL's founders argued, social and/or ideological content of written and spoken discourse is not exclusive to, or isolable from, specific utterances. Rather, in a coherent discourse, we systematically exercise options from sets of linguistics alternatives, such that "the total and interacting effect of these [options] carries a meaning over and above that of the items and processes in isolation" (Fowler & Kress, 1979, p. 186). As a critical and political scholarly approach, CL is concerned primarily with understanding the components and processes of speech that produce and reproduce power relationships at both the personal and institutional level and is thus often used to analyze legal and governmental documents as well as mass-mediated texts. In these forms, particularly, language is often used "to manipulate people, to establish and maintain them in economically convenient roles and statuses, to maintain the power of state agencies, corporations, and other institutions" (Fowler & Kress, p. 190). Wartime journalism, as exemplified by the *Albuquerque Journal*'s "N. M. Plays" article, represents a particularly insidious use of language to manipulate people and maintain institutional power. Consequently, I find the theoretical and methodological orientations of critical linguistics particularly helpful in elucidating the workings of such manipulation and power maintenance.

Content Analysis

The methodology of critical linguistics involves painstaking examinations of individual elements of speech: sentences, phrases, words, and even parts of words, such as suffixes. As Fowler and Kress (1979) argued, "It is only when we acknowledge the meaning carried by the items themselves that linguistic form can be demonstrated to be a realization of social (and other) meaning" (p. 188). To make the application of their theory pragmatically useful Fowler and Kress provided the "aspirant in critical linguistics" a methodology in the form of a checklist. On the checklist are those grammatical structures that "are particularly likely to be revealing" ideologically (p. 197). The checklist items of greatest relevance to my analysis of the "N.M. Plays" article are:

1. "Transitivity": the types of predicates that occur in a text as well as the types of entities that perform actions.

2. "Modality": terms that express the writer's attitude toward his or her subject matter.

3. "Transformations": lexico-syntactic derivations that allow a writer to shift the reader's focus in the direction desired by the writer. (p. 198)

Along with their checklist, however, Fowler and Kress also offered a caveat: "There is no predictable one-to-one association between any one linguistic form and any specific social meaning.... Different features and processes must be related to one another" (p. 198). Bearing this caution in mind, I analyze "N. M. Plays" in terms of its individual linguistic structures as well as the relationships among them. In so doing, I hope to make clear how, precisely, the micro-level linguistic choices made by the article's authors reveal, constitute, and promote a particular ideological orientation toward the Iraq War *and* to military operations in general.

The Grammar of Transitivity

In traditional linguistics, *transitivity* refers to the distinction between transitive and intransitive verbs: between those that can take a direct object (e.g., **assassinate, destroy, prefer**) and those that can not (e.g., **smile, fall, elapse**) (Trask, 1993). In the critical linguistics framework, however, transitivity is far more value-laden, referring to the elements of a sentence that reveal the speaker's or writer's point of view regarding the agency of the person or entity performing an action, experiencing a state, or going through a process (Barker & Galasinski, 2001; Fowler & Kress, 1979; Halliday & Hasan, 1985). The syntactic unit that encodes this information is the predicate, typically a verb or adjective, which serves as the "action" component of a sentence. Critical linguistics considers how predicates are structured and used, and asks the following: "Who, if anyone, benefits from the action?"; "What other circumstances attend on the event and how are they connected to it?"; and especially "What *kinds* of entities perform actions?" (Fowler & Kress, 1979, p. 199). When inanimate entities, abstractions, or organizations are attributed agency by a speaker or writer, such attribution relieves actual individual humans of responsibility for their actions, and this act of relief reveals and stakes out an ideological position. Bearing this in mind, consider the following textual elements from "N. M. Plays":

Inanimate subjects (agents). Inanimate subjects occur with great regularity in the article, beginning with the lead sentence: "The **opening salvos** in the war against Iraq came from **F-117A Nighthawks** streaking through the night sky...."[5] As is the case in the opening sentence, most of the article's inanimate subjects are weapons or other military equipment: "**The F-16s** that are flying over infantry troops and taking out enemy tanks"; "**the so-called 'stealth' fighters' mission** ... almost devastated Saddam Hussein"; "**the PAC-3** has performed better than its predecessor"; "**the Patriot** later targeted a U.S. F-16, but **the fighter** destroyed its radar dish"; and "**PAC-3 batteries** ... have shot down eight of 10 Iraqi Scud missiles." What is striking about such constructions is the overall impression they create: that of an exciting world in which jets and missiles and missions "streak," "destroy," "devastate," "drop bombs," and "shoot down" things of their own accord, conveniently relieving living, breathing military members, and, specifically, members of the *United States* military, of the responsibility for these actions. This deflection of human agency, and thus of responsibility, is particularly notable in the rare sentence in which Linthicum and Romo bring up a topic of embarrassment for the U.S. war management team: "The military, however, is investigating why **the PAC-3** recently targeted two friendly aircraft — including the accidental downing last Sunday of a British Royal Air Force Tornado GR-4 aircraft."

Indeed, it is certainly more palatable, and pro–American, in such a situation to find a missile, not a person, in the U.S. armed forces to blame for "targeting" and "downing" an allied jet (and the unidentified, unmentioned humans inside it). Such attribution of agency to inanimate objects reaches unparalleled heights in this pair of sentences: "**The F-16s** that are flying over infantry troops and taking out enemy tanks? Many of **their** pilots live and train in Clovis." In "N. M. Plays," then, Linthicum and Romo have created a narrative world in which jets not only have agency but in which "*their* pilots" are mere objects that are possessed, and not (subjective) people who do the possessing.

Although Fowler and Kress (1979) discuss only inanimate sentential *subjects*, I found two sentences in "N. M. Plays" in which the reporters use inanimate sentential or clausal *objects*. The referents of these objects are (equipment operated by) Iraqis, but not Americans: "F-16s ... flying over infantry troops and taking out **enemy tanks**" and "bombs dropped by F-117A Nighthawks on **targets**." Presumably the *Albuquerque Journal*'s readers find it less offensive to visualize F-16s (but not "their" pilots) "taking out" *tanks* than to imagine them "taking out" the soldiers inside them. It is certainly less graphic to drop bombs on "targets" than on the people there situated, and such a method of framing these military events certainly discourages a critical or anti-patriotic stance on the part of the article's readers.

Abstract subjects (agents). Even more frequent than sentences headed by inanimate subjects in "N. M. Plays" and, arguably even more powerful in their contribution to the article's overarching tone of uncritical patriotism, are those headed by abstract subjects, including the headline, "**N.M.** Plays a Large Role in Iraqi Engagement." Among the many sentences in "N. M. Plays" in which abstract subjects are ascribed agency are the following: "Through accident and design, **New Mexico** has played a premier role in the first week and a half of fighting the war in Iraq"; "**Both tradition and economy** have converged to bring New Mexicans into the military in numbers disproportionate to the population"; "**the successes and hardships of battle in this war** unfold live on television"; "**Military tradition** here dates back to before New Mexico became a state. **That tradition** ... [has] given military service a badge of heroism and a family tradition to follow..."; "**Having several Air Force bases and national laboratories that develop weapons** puts military careers in young people's minds or attracts soldiers to New Mexico"; and "**the incident** showed that ... the maintenance company may be in harm's way." The net effect of this overuse of abstract subjects is the creation of a discursive world in which (American, New Mexican) people are relieved of causal agency in acts of war. In their places mere abstractions take up the responsibility. How can anyone oppose a war not enacted by agentive humans?

Linthicum and Romo also use abstract nouns in their story's subheads to powerful effect. "Badge of **Heroism**," "Family **Tradition**," and "**Help** from Home" are the phrases that head the various sections of the article. These abstractions, perhaps more than any of those used in the article's sentences, paint a particularly positive picture of New Mexican military-related attitudes and practices. They are subheads, and thus unanchored to any named agent even as they are set apart from the article's text and made more prominent through the use of larger, bolder type. They contribute powerfully to the overall pro-military tone of the article.

Organizations as subjects. This final item in the transitivity section of Fowler and Kress's (1979) checklist is also abundantly represented in "N. M. Plays." Among the more representative examples: "**their [New Mexico's reserves] units** are playing key roles"; "**the military**, Wilson said, 'has been one of the most egalitarian organizations"; and "**the base** [White Sands Missile Range] has made important contributions to the effort through the testing of many of the weapons used by the Army, Navy, and Air Force."

Unlike those sentences headed by inanimate subjects (most of which conveniently divert responsibility for violence from unnamed human agents), these sentences with organizational and other collective subjects all celebrate their accomplishments, attributing, in other words, a sort of generalized or diffused group agency even while masking the identities of the groups' members, for good or bad. If "the military" is portrayed as an "egalitarian organization," then the anti-egalitarian actions of (some) specific individuals in the military are rendered unimportant or non-existent. If "the base" is credited with making "important contributions," then the actual people responsible lose the opportunity to be credited, while those base members who did not "contribute" get to bask in the reflected glory of those who actually did something. In any case, the use of U.S. organizations as subjects dehumanizes (or, possibly, super-humanizes) those persons truly responsible for the actions described and, in so doing, renders them immune from criticism or judgment, thus foreclosing the possibility of reader reaction that is anything but prowar or patriotic.

The Grammar of Modality

In the CL framework, constructions that convey *modality* "express speakers' and writers' attitudes toward themselves, toward their interlocutors, and toward their subject-matter, their social and economic relationships with the people they address, and the actions which are performed via language" (Fowler & Kress, 1979, p. 200). A news article's modality markers, then, are among the most important components of its framing. Among the linguistic manifestations of modality on the CL checklist most revealing of the ideological bias in "N. M. Plays" is the use of personal pronouns, particularly a first-person plural pronoun.

"**We**" appears with great frequency in the article's numerous quotations. It conveys the values of the speakers interviewed by Linthicum and Romo and, by extension, those of the reporters, who decide which sources are interviewed in the first place and which quotations are included in an article. According to Fowler and Kress (1979), while the referent of **I** is almost always unambiguously the speaker of an utterance, "the plural form **we** displays the added complexity that the source claims to speak of and for himself and on behalf of someone other than himself" (p. 201). Using **we**, then, can allow a speaker or writer to be deliberately vague about who is included or excluded from reference (Lakoff, 1990; Marmaridou, 2000).

In many "N. M. Plays" quotations, **we** (or **us**) is inclusive, "implicat[ing] the addressee in the content of the discourse and ... therefore, ostensibly, more intimate and solidary" (Fowler & Kress, 1979, p. 202). Consider the following: "'New Mexico's always been patriotic and loyal to the country,' said

Agapito Silva, an 83-year-old World War II veteran living in Albuquerque. 'Any time there's a war, **we've** got a lot of people there'"; "'**We** serve,' Wilson said"; and "'**We** have more guardsmen here than Arizona, which has a much higher population,' Horn said. '**We** have a high ratio of folks in the National Guard....'" Each of these quoted speakers uses **we** to speak for himself or herself *and* presumably all New Mexicans, a use that creates the "superficial impression of solidarity and involvement" with not only the immediate addressees (the reporters) but by extension, all New Mexican readers of the *Journal*. If "we" (that is, all New Mexicans, or all readers of the article) share in the experience of "serving" and sending "our" citizens to any war, then presumably "we" are also implicated in the pro-war sentiments described in the article. Again, the implicature of "we" subtly — and repeatedly — contributes to the foreclosing of any standpoint that might perceive of marching off to war as something other than "patriotic and loyal."

Transformations

One of CL's most powerful tools is its analysis of "transformations." Borrowing a central idea from traditional generative grammar (Chomsky, 1957, 1965), CL argues that a sentence's so-called surface structure (i.e., the syntax of an actual spoken or written utterance) is in fact a "transformation" or derivation of its so-called deep structure, its putative underlying form.[6] The specific syntactic transformations Fowler and Kress (1979) considered to be "particularly rewarding" in CL analysis are *nominalization* and *passivization* (p. 207). "N. M. Plays" abounds with such "transformed" structures. These are among the most important contributors to the article's promotion of an uncritically patriotic standpoint toward the U.S. military operations in Iraq.

Nominalizations. A nominalization is a noun or noun phrase that has been transformed or derived from an underlying verb or adjective; e.g., "leadership" from the verb "to lead." As Fowler and Kress (1979) point out, nominalizations create the impression of impersonality and detachment because they delete references to participants; often, both subject and object are invisible and thus incapable of taking responsibility or of being objects of critical scrutiny. Consider these participant-, modality-, tense-, and/or attitude-obscuring nominalizations and resulting objectifications in Linthicum and Romo: "N. M. plays a large role in Iraqi **engagement**" (headline); "People like Silva, watching the **successes** and hardships of **battle** in this war unfold live on television..."; "White Sands Missile Range personnel are not involved in **combat** or support missions in Iraq, but the base has made important **contributions** to the effort through the **testing** of many of the weapons..."; "The effectiveness of 1-ton 'bunker buster' bombs ... in the war's opening **attack** on Baghdad was tested..."; "the accidental **downing** ... of a British [jet]"; service members from Fort Bliss "might not expect to see heavy **action** in wartime"; an American group was "caught in an **ambush**"; and "The incident showed that in **a conflict** ... the maintenance company may be in **harm**'s way."

By using nominalizations such as **engagement, testing, downing,** and **ambush,** any suggestion of agentive subjects doing something is removed — and with it, the possibility of critical evaluation. The same effect is achieved through the use of other nouns that, while not nominalizations of verbs, are also the names of actions, such as **war, mission, salvo,** and **effort.** If **war** is merely some *thing* that exists independently in the world or some natural *state of being*, then killing is transformed from an acted (and therefore agent-requiring) process into a static (and therefore agentless) object — and, as a result, violence and war are naturalized (Boaz, 2005).

Passivizations. A passive construction is one in which "an intrinsically transitive verb is construed in such a way that its underlying object appears as a surface subject, its underlying subject being either absent or expressed as an oblique noun phrase" (Trask, 1993, p. 201).[7] Critical linguists note that passivizations allow a writer to "emphasize ... thematic priorities, to emphasize what a text is 'about' even when the [subject is], strictly speaking, semantically subordinate. [With passivization], chunks of the utterance are moved about so as to focus our attention, and to direct our perception, in certain ... complex ways." (Fowler & Kress, 1979, pp. 209–210). Passive structures in which the underlying subject is absent are particularly problematic, and revealing of a writer's ideological intention, because agency is either re-assigned or stripped away completely.

Virtually all of the passivizations in "N. M. Plays" elide the underlying subject. Among the most important are the following: "A high ratio of folks in the National Guard ... **are being deployed**"; "The effectiveness of 1-ton 'bunker buster' bombs ... **was tested** at White Sands"; "The bombs, which explode at a **desired** depth ... **are used** against heavily fortified targets"; "The PAC-3, the **much-publicized** defensive weapon **deployed** around command centers ... **was also tested** at White Sands"; "Some of the batteries **have been reported** to be moving with troops toward the front lines"; "Eight [members of the 507th Maintenance Company] **were unaccounted for**"; and "The F-16s ... **were used** to attack airfields, military production facilities and Scud missile sites." Such passives make it difficult for the reader to visualize, and even more difficult to critically evaluate, the violent and otherwise troubling military actions described because they fail to provide information about the *persons* performing (or even observing) them. A critical linguist must ask: *Who* deployed these troops? *Who* tested the "bunker buster" bombs? *Who* uses them against heavily fortified targets? *Who* reported that the missile batteries are moving toward the front lines? And most important, *who* used F-16s to attack airfields? The obvious answers (specific individuals in the U.S. military) are conveniently left unstated, allowing Linthicum and Romo to create, and invite readers to enter, a narrative world in which people are deployed by no one in particular, bombs are dropped of their own accord, and no actual (U.S. military) humans are held morally accountable. The article's one passive construction in which the agent is specified, "the effectiveness of the 'bunker buster' bombs **dropped by F-117A Nighthawks**," uses an *inanimate* agent. Even when the bomb droppers are identified, they are jets and not persons (who might be subject to scrutiny). Human actors are syntactically invisible and thus relieved of responsibility.

Discussion

I entered the frame used to structure a specific artifact of early Iraq War journalism, explored how its human-nature frame was lexically and syntactically constructed, and uncovered those ideological components of the article that reinforce the status quo and guide readers toward a preferred view of (the) war and its participants. I applied the theories and methods of critical linguistics precisely because "N. M. Plays" does *not* overtly advocate a position on the war in Iraq or offer an explicit argument in support of the Administration's military actions. Rather, the article instantiates a more insidious form of ideological persuasion, as its authors work within the human-interest frame rather than the military conflict frame (Dimitrova, 2006) and therefore focus primarily on the actions and opinions of individual citizens who have professional and emotional ties to the military and its causes. Moreover, in their interviews with ordinary citizens and elected officials, Linthicum and Romo avoid raising sensitive issues or asking hard questions about the costs of war. They choose, instead, to elicit ostensibly neutral or positive evaluations of military involvement, and they syntactically structure their observations in ways that naturalize those evaluations. CL, uniquely, provides tools that allow a discourse analyst to tease out precisely how such naturalization is accomplished.

Media are not and can never be neutral. If indeed the media "work ideologically by disseminating the ideas and world-views of the ruling class" (McQuail, 2000, p. 76), as Marxist and neo–Marxist media critics have long claimed, then specific media texts are particularly useful, visible, and widely available windows into ruling-class ideological bias. As Hodge (1979), an early critical linguist and colleague of Fowler and Kress, observed, "newspapers inevitably give only a partial version of the world. They select, reorder, transform, distort, and suppress ... caus[ing] systematic bias of content" (p. 157).

These influences do not occur in a vacuum. As Hodge and Kress (1993) later noted, "meaning does not exist unless there are people who make it happen, in a process where those who *receive* texts (readers, listeners, viewers) engage in an activity which produces its own distinctive kinds of meaning, without which no text would have any social effect" (pp. 174–175). Further, as scholars of the press's framing of war have pointed out, any nation's media "are influenced by the overall political environment in which they exist [and reflect] ... the position of dominant national actors and institutions" (Dimitrova, et al., 2005, p. 35). Newspapers in particular, observed Ravi (2005) are "rooted firmly in a national ethos" (p. 45). The media, then, can not be held solely responsible for the ideological tendencies prevalent in a society at any given time. Still, as Boaz (2005) noted in her essay on war and public policy framing in international media, "public opinion on foreign policy and national security initiatives is directly related to the media's efficacy in naturalizing violence and creating the perception of national and global insecurity. As such, the type of media information to which ... citizens had access is directly linked to public support for war in Iraq" (p. 350).

I considered the "type of media information" available to the readers of a large, albeit "non-elite," American newspaper, and I analyzed the very phrases, words, and parts of words used in the construction and framing of that information, much of which (re)inforced the "naturalizing [of] violence" identified by Boaz (2005). Although the political/ideological bias of "N. M. Plays" might have been relatively easy to identify even without using the tools of critical linguistics, the micro-analysis that the CL framework provided made the slant inescapably clear. The breadth and depth of the pro-military, pro-war bias of the article's writers (and, by extension, the *Albuquerque Journal*) were illuminated, as was the successful construction of the human-interest frame through which the story's messages were filtered.

At the time of the article's publication (March 2003), public sentiment about America's involvement in the Iraq war was starkly, at times even violently, polarized. Yet the content and tone of "N. M. Plays" reflected none of the country's or the state's division of feelings about the issue, feelings that were observable from even the most cursory glance at the dueling bumper stickers in Albuquerque parking lots. Rather than bowing to journalistic objectivity, the piece revealed a pro-war stance that pandered to New Mexico's large military presence through its boasting about New Mexico's "contributions" to military efforts past and present.

Punctuated by subheads such as "Badge of Heroism," "Family Tradition," and "Help from Home," Linthicum and Romo's article endorsed, and even glorified, New Mexico's and New Mexicans' military participation without raising the possibility that war might *not* be a force of unalloyed good. Moreover, the article never acknowledged the existence of people (in New Mexico or elsewhere) who opposed war in general or the Iraq War in particular. In its aim to reflect, and perhaps even magnify, the degree of pride that (some) New Mexicans had in their state's pro-military tradition, the article never allowed for the possibility that not all New Mexicans are proud of the high profile the military-industrial complex enjoys in their state. Linthicum and Romo did not acknowledge the visible and vocal anti-war movement which, at the time of publication, was daily making its presence known on the streets of Albuquerque and Santa Fe, and they did not express regret about lives lost in Iraq.

Applying CL theory and methods adds to the understanding of the ideology underlying and motivating "N. M. Plays" and to an appreciation of the construction and subtle power of human interest framing which naturalizes violence and war as it draws our attention to the following:

1. overuse of inanimate and abstract subjects, allowing us to see how the manipulation of transitivity contributed to a world-view in which (American military) humans are not accountable for violence and death;

2. skillful use of the ambiguous pronoun we, creating the impression of inclusion and solidarity necessary for successful recruitment of an audience to a speaker's or writer's cause;

3. overwhelming frequency of nominalizations, lexical transformations that discursively reduced aggressive military actions to abstract entities, states, or self-perpetuating events; and

4. tactical use of passivizations, which made the agents behind violent actions disappear from view, effectively relieving the unnamed actors of moral obligation or responsibility.

A CL-based analysis allows for clear and specific identification of the components of the news frame and, therefore, the components of the ideological position of an article representative of locally focused, imbalanced, pro-war, human-interest-driven, non-elite journalism prevalent during the early days of combat operations in Iraq (Carpenter, 2007; Dimitrova, et al., 2005), a type of journalism harshly judged by many commercial and scholarly critics in the years since. By specifically, mechanically, and systematically examining the details of the Linthicum and Romo article's linguistic structure, it was easy to see how the pro-war media bias, instantiated in language, contributed to the pervasive marginalizing of opposing views concerning the war (Edwards & Cromwell, 2004; Porpora & Nikolaev, 2008; Ravi, 2005).

Almost two decades before "framing" became a *sine qua non* of media criticism, CL's Fowler and Kress (1979) made an observation that anticipated many of the concerns of contemporary framing theorists. In written discourse, they argued,

Chunks of the utterance are moved about so as to focus our attention, and to direct our perception, in certain ways.... Our attention and the sequence in which we decode are here being directed, manipulated, in complex ways; and any analysis of discourse needs to be responsive to these processes [p. 210)].

In the case of an article such as "N. M. Plays," casual readers were exposed to (and possibly persuaded by) the point of view of the article's writers and editors, a point of view that, not incidentally, happened to be similar to that of most of the nation's government and military elites at the time. "N. M. Plays," with its uncritical look at (some) New Mexicans' attitudes toward war, reinforced these dominant positions, accepting and presenting the Administration's pro-war message as not only beyond question but, in fact, the only possible stance.

During the spring of 2003, a time when anti-war sentiment was suppressed, condemned, or marginalized in both mediated and interpersonal discourse, such uncritically pro-war journalism further contributed to the bolstering of the status quo, a typical function of non-elite journalism, and thus the muting of dissent. Beyond the importance tacitly given to the article by the *Albuquerque Journal*'s editorial decision to position it as front-page "news," the subtlety of its authors' linguistic structures made the mechanics of such muting nearly undetectable and therefore all the more insidious. Surely, "N. M. Plays" was not the only such article foisted upon American newspaper readers during the early days of U.S. military operations in Iraq.

Notes

1. Representative studies of the framing of Iraq War coverage focus upon issues such as: types of frames, which were used, by whom, when, and why (Boaz, 2005; Christie, 2006; Dimitrova, 2006; Dimitrova, et al., 2005; Luther & Miller, 2005; Pfau, et al., 2004; Schwalbe, Keith, & Silcock, 2008); cross-cultural comparisons of news frames (Dardis, 2006; Dimitrova, et al., 2005; Dimitrova & Stromback, 2005; Herber & Filak, 2007; Lee, Maslog, & Kim, 2006; Lewis, 2004; Ravi, 2005; Willnat, et al., 2006); and the differences between frames used by elite U.S. media and those used by non-elite U.S. media (Carpenter, 2007).

2. My descriptions here paraphrase and consolidate the descriptions of the frames that appeared in Dimitrova (2006, p. 80), Dimitrova, et al. (2005, p. 32), and Dimitrova & Stromback (2005, p. 409).

3. As the Associated Press's *Guide to News Writing* points out, features "aim to give readers pleasure and entertainment along with information, ... supplement the straight news content in timely and topical ways, ... illuminate events, offer perspective, explanation, and interpretation, ... and tell people about people" (Cappon, 2000, p. 95).

4. The *Albuquerque Journal*'s circulation of approximately 150,000 makes it New Mexico's largest newspaper, but places it only 84th in the United States (Audit Bureau of Circulation, 2008). By contrast, each of the top three "elite" newspapers boasts a circulation in excess of 1,000,000.

5. In this section, when quoting from "N. M. Plays" I will **boldface** the words that are the focus of a given analysis.

6. For example, the surface-structure interrogative *"Is John here?"* would be analyzed as a transformation of the deep-structure declarative *"John is here."*

7. In *Jane was fired*, the underlying subject is absent, but in *Jane was fired* **by Tom**, the underlying subject (Tom) is expressed as an oblique noun phrase (i.e., as neither the construction's subject nor direct object).

References

Allan, S., and B. Zelizer (Eds.) (2004). *Reporting War: Journalism in Wartime.* London: Routledge.

Artz, L. (2005). Political legitimacy, cultural leadership, and public action. In L. Artz & Y. R. Kamalipour (Eds.), *Bring 'Em On: Media and Politics in the Iraq War* (pp. 7–21). Lanham, MD: Rowman & Littlefield.

_____, and Y. R. Kamalipour (Eds.) (2005). *Bring 'Em On: Media and Politics in the Iraq War.* Lanham, MD: Rowman & Littlefield.

Audit Bureau of Circulation. (2008). Top 100 newspapers in the United States. Retrieved August 6, 2008, from http://www.infoplease.com/ipea/A0004420.html

Barker, C., and D. Galasi_ksi (2001). *Cultural Studies and Discourse Analysis: A Dialogue on Language and Identity.* London: Sage.

Boaz, C. (2005). War and foreign policy framing in international media. *Peace Review, 17,* 349–356.

Boehlert, E. (2006). *Lapdogs: How the Press Rolled Over for Bush.* New York: Free Press.

Cappon, R. J. (2000). *The Associated Press Guide to News Writing* (3rd ed.). Stamford, CT: Thomson Learning/ARCO.

Carpenter, S. (2007). U.S. elite and non-elite newspapers' portrayal of the Iraq War: A comparison of frames and source use. *Journalism & Mass Communication Quarterly, 84,* 761–776.

Chomsky, N. (1957). *Syntactic Structures.* The Hague: Mouton.

_____. (1965). *Aspects of the Theory of Syntax.* Cambridge, MA: MIT Press.

Christie, T. B. (2006). Framing rationale for the Iraq War: The interaction of public support with mass media and public policy. *International Communication Gazette, 68,* 519–532.

Couldry, N., and J. Downey (2004). War or peace? Legitimation, dissent, and rhetorical closure in press coverage of the Iraq war build-up. In S. Allan & B. Zelizer (Eds.), *Reporting War: Journalism in Wartime* (pp. 266–282). London: Routledge.

Dadge, D. (2006). *The War in Iraq and Why the Media Failed Us.* Westport, CT: Praeger.

Dardis, F. E. (2006). Military accord, media discord: A cross-national comparison of U.K. vs. U.S. press coverage of Iraq War protest. *International Communication Gazette, 68,* 409–426.

Dimitrova, D. V. (2006). Episodic frames dominate early coverage of Iraq War in the NYTimes.com. *Newspaper Research Journal, 27,* 79–83.

_____, Kaid, L. L., A. P. Williams, and K. D. Trammell (2005). War on the Web: The immediate news framing of Gulf War II. *International Journal of Press/Politics, 10,* 22–44.

Dimitrova, D. V., and J. Stromback (2005). Mission accomplished? Framing of the Iraq War in the elite newspapers in Sweden and the United States. *Gazette: The International Journal for Communication Studies, 67,* 399–417.

Edwards, D., and D. Cromwell (2004). Mass deception: How the media helped the government deceive the people. In D. Miller (Ed.), *Tell Me Lies: Propaganda and Media Distortion in the Attack on Iraq* (pp. 210–214). London: Pluto.

Entman, R. (1993). Framing: Towards clarification of a fractured paradigm. *Journal of Communication, 43,* 51–58.

Fairclough, N. (1995). *Critical Discourse Analysis: The Critical Study of Language*. London: Longman.

_____, and R. Wodak (1997). Critical discourse analysis. In T. A. van Dijk (Ed.), *Discourse as Social Interaction* (pp. 258–284). London: Sage.

Fowler, R. (1991). Critical linguistics. In K. Malmkjær (Ed.), *The Linguistics Encyclopedia* (pp. 89–93). London: Routledge.

_____, & Kress, G. (1979). Critical linguistics. In R. Fowler, B. Hodge, G. Kress, & T. Trew (Eds.), *Language and Control* (pp. 185–213). London: Routledge & Kegan Paul.

Fraley, T. (2007). A Century of Media, a Century of war; The War in Iraq and Why the Media Failed Us; Killing the Messenger: Journalists at Risk in Modern Warfare [book reviews]. *Journalism & Mass Communication Educator, 61*, 433–435.

Halliday, M. A. K., and R. Hasan (1985). *Language, Context, and Text*. Oxford: Oxford University Press.

Herber, L., and V. F. Filak (2007). Iraq War coverage differs in U.S., German papers. *Newspaper Research Journal, 28*, 37–51.

Herman, E. (2004). Normalizing godfatherly aggression. In D. Miller (Ed.), *Tell Me Lies: Propaganda and Media Distortion in the Attack on Iraq* (pp. 176–184). London: Pluto.

Hodge, B. (1979). Newspapers and communities. In R. Fowler, B. Hodge, G. Kress, & T. Trew (Eds.), *Language and Control* (pp. 157–174). London: Routledge & Kegan Paul.

Hodge, R., and G. Kress (1993). *Language as Ideology* (2nd ed.). London: Routledge.

Hoskins, A. (2005). *Televising War: From Vietnam to Iraq*. London: Continuum.

Jensen, R. (2005). The problem with patriotism: Steps toward the redemption of American journalism and democracy. In L. Artz & Y. R. Kamalipour (Eds.), *Bring 'Em On: Media and Politics in the Iraq War* (pp. 67–83). Lanham, MD: Rowman & Littlefield.

Kamalipour, Y. R., and N. Snow (Eds.) (2004). *War, Media, and Propaganda: A Global Perspective*. Lanham, MD: Rowman & Littlefield.

Katovsky, B., and T. Carlson (2003). *Embedded: The Media at War in Iraq*. Guilford, CT: Lyons.

Kull, S., C. Ramsay, and E. Lewis (2003–04). Misperceptions, the media, and the Iraq War. *Political Science Quarterly, 118*, 569–598.

Kuypers, J. (2006). *Bush's war: Media Bias and Justifications for War in a Terrorist Age*. Lanham, MD: Rowman & Littlefield.

Lacy, S., F. Fico, and T. Simon (1991). Fairness and balance in the prestige press. *Journalism Quarterly, 68*, 363–370.

Lakoff, R. T. (1990). *Talking Power: The Politics of Language*. New York: Basic.

Lee, S. T., C. C. Maslog, and H. S. Kim (2006). Asian conflicts and the Iraq War: A comparative framing analysis. *International Communication Gazette, 68*, 499–518.

Lewis, J. (2004). Television, public opinion, and the war in Iraq: The case of Britain. *International Journal of Public Opinion Research, 16*, 295–310.

Linthicum, L., and R. Romo (2003, March 30). N. M. plays a large role in Iraqi engagement. *Albuquerque Journal*, pp. A1–A2.

Lule, J. (2004). War and its metaphors: News language and the prelude to war in Iraq, 2003. *Journalism Studies, 5*, 179–190.

Luther, C. A., and M. M. Miller (2005). Framing of the 2003 U.S.–Iraq War demonstrations: An analysis of news and partisan texts. *Journalism & Mass Communication Quarterly, 82*, 78–96.

Marmaridou, S. S. A. (2000). *Pragmatic Meaning and Cognition*. Amsterdam: John Benjamins.

Massing, M. (2004). *Now They Tell Us: The American Press and Iraq*. New York: New York Review Books.

McQuail, D. (2000). *McQuail's Mass Communication Theory* (4th ed.). London: Sage.

Mermin, J. (2004). The media's independence problem. *World Policy Journal, 21,* 67–71.
Meyer, M. (2001). Between theory, method, and politics: Positioning of the approaches to CDA. In R. Wodak & M. Meyer (Eds.), *Methods of Critical Discourse Analysis* (pp. 14–31). London: Sage.
Miller, D. (Ed.) (2004). *Tell Me Lies: Propaganda and Media Distortion in the Attack on Iraq.* London: Pluto.
Mirzoeff, N. (2005). *Watching Babylon: The War in Iraq and Global Visual Culture.* London: Routledge.
Mooney, C. (2004, March/April). Did our leading newspapers set too low a bar for a preemptive attack? *Columbia Journalism Review,* pp. 28–34.
Pfau, M., M. Haigh, M. Gettle, M. Donnelly, G. Scott, D. Warr, & E. Wittenberg (2004). Embedding journalists in military combat units: Impact on newspaper story frames and tone. *Journalism & Mass Communication Quarterly, 81,* 71–88.
Porpora, D. V., and A. Nikolaev (2008). Moral muting in U.S. newspaper op-eds debating the attack on Iraq. *Discourse & Communication, 2,* 165–184.
Rampton, S., and J. Stauber (2003). *Weapons of Mass Deception: The Uses of Propaganda in Bush's War on Iraq.* New York: Tarcher/Penguin.
Ravi, N. (2005). Looking beyond flawed journalism: How national interests, patriotism, and cultural values shaped the coverage of the Iraq War. *International Journal of Press/Politics, 10,* 45–62.
Reese, S. D. (2004). Militarized journalism: Framing dissent in the Gulf Wars. In S. Allen & B. Zelizer (Eds.), *Reporting War: Journalism in Wartime* (pp. 247–265). London: Routledge.
Rich, F. (2006). *The Greatest Story Ever Sold: The Decline and Fall of Truth from 9/11 to Katrina.* New York: Penguin.
Rutherford, P. (2004). *Weapons of Mass Persuasion: Marketing the War Against Iraq.* Toronto: University of Toronto Press.
Ryan, M. (2006). Mainstream news media, an objective approach, and the march to war in Iraq. *Journal of Mass Media Ethics, 21,* 4–29.
Schechter, D. (2003). *Embedded: Weapons of Mass Deception: How the Media Failed to Cover the War on Iraq.* Amherst, NY: Prometheus.
Schwalbe, C. B., B. W. Solcock, and S. Keith (2008). Visual framing of the early weeks of the U.S.–led invasion of Iraq: Applying the master war narrative to electronic and print images. *Journal of Broadcasting & Electronic Media, 52,* 448–465.
Seib, P. (2005). Hegemonic no more: Western media, the rise of Al-Jazeera, and the influence of diverse voices. *International Studies Review, 7,* 601–615.
Snow, N., and P. M. Taylor (2006). The revival of the propaganda state: U.S. propaganda at home and abroad since 9/11. *International Communications Gazette, 68,* 389–407.
Solomon, N., and R. Erlich (2003). *Target Iraq: What the News Media Didn't Tell You.* New York: Context.
Thomas, H. (2006). *Watchdogs of Democracy? The Waning Washington Press Corps and How It Has Failed the Public.* New York: Scribner.
Trask, R. L. (1993). *A Dictionary of Grammatical Terms in Linguistics.* London: Routledge.
van Dijk, T. A. (1997). Discourse as interaction in society. In T. A. van Dijk (Ed.), *Discourse as Social Interaction* (pp. 1–37). London: Sage.
van Leeuwen, T. (2005). *Introducing Social Semiotics.* London: Routledge.
———. (2008). *Discourse and Practice: New Tools for Critical Discourse Analysis.* New York: Oxford.
White, A. (2005). Truth, honesty, and spin. *Democratization, 12,* 651–667.
Williams, G. (2004). Watchdogs or lapdogs? Media, politics, and regulation: The U.S. experience. In D. Miller (Ed.), *Tell Me Lies: Propaganda and Media Distortion in the Attack on Iraq* (pp. 195–203). London: Pluto.

Willnat, L., A. Aw, N. N. Hamdy, Z. He, V. Menayang, M. T., K. La PorteSanders, and E. Tamam, (2006). Media use, anti–Americanism, and international support for the Iraq War. *International Communication Gazette, 68,* 533–550.

Wodak, R. (2001). What CDA is about: A summary of its history, important concepts, and its developments. In R. Wodak & M. Meyer (Eds.), *Methods of Critical Discourse Analysis* (pp. 1–13). London: Sage.

Wolfe, A. S., J. Swanson, and S. Wrona (2008). What the American people deserve from American journalism during wartime: A First Amendment view abetted by semiotic analysis. *Journalism Studies, 9,* 38–56.

Embedded Reporting and Audience Response: Parasocial Interaction and Perceived Realism in Embedded Reporting from the Iraq War on Television News

M. F. Casper and *Jeffrey T. Child*

Operation Iraqi Freedom began with a bang on March 19, 2003. The media relayed the military name for the attack, and "Shock and Awe" became a household term. What was sold by the Bush administration as a brief and relatively painless process became a long struggle. The human and financial cost of the war and the ongoing conflict in Iraq continue to grow (Calbreath, 2008; Kumar, 2006; "Post February 2006 displacement in Iraq," 2008). The reputation of the United States and the American people has been tarnished and international relationships irrevocably damaged (Kagan, 2004; Kull, Ramsay, & Lewis, 2003–04; Nisbet, Nisbet, Scheufele, & Shanahan, 2004; Nye, 2004). Public support has been a significant issue throughout the war, and a battle for public opinion has been waged from the White House, primarily through the strategic use of media reports (Fritz, Keefer, & Nyhan, 2004).

At the inception of the war (May 30–June 1, 2003) 67 percent of those polled trusted the Bush administration about the presence of weapons of mass destruction in Iraq ("USA Today/Gallop Poll," 2008). Belief that Saddam Hussein had a direct link to the September 11, 2001, terrorist attacks rose in 2003 from 42 percent in February to 45 percent in March and was at an all-time high of 53 percent in early April, just over two weeks from the initial attacks against Baghdad ("CBS News Poll," 2008). In August 2003, 46 percent of those polled said the result of the war was worth the cost, including the cost in American lives (Rosen Jr. & Wolf, 2005), and 75 percent approved of the job Bush was doing in Iraq ("ABC News/Washington Post Poll," 2007).

Opinions have shifted dramatically since 2003. In 2008, 58 percent said they did not believe that Saddam Hussein was linked to the September 11, 2001, attacks ("CBS News Poll," 2008), 53 percent said the Bush White House deliberately misled them about weapons of mass destruction ("USA Today/Gallop Poll," 2008), 65 percent said they disapprove of the way Bush is handling Iraq ("CBS News Poll," 2008), and 64 percent said that the Iraq war was not worth the cost ("CBS News Poll," 2008).

Several things were taking place in the media in the lead up to the war. Television news took on fresh importance and gained persuasive power in the turmoil and public upheaval of post–9/11 America. The American public relied on television news for information and help in understanding the attacks. Pubic interest led to increased consumption of news media and increased trust in media and political figures (Fritz, et al., 2004).

News media carried enormous influence in post–9/11 America. American mainstream press, including television news, regained respectability after a decline in public opinion in the 1990s following accusations of liberal bias (Eisman, 2003; T.-T. Lee, 2005; Sutter, 2001). According to a September 24, 2001, Associated Press poll, 90 percent of Americans said the news media's coverage of the World Trade Center attacks was good or excellent (Eisman, 2003). Even sources normally critical of news media gave the coverage excellent ratings. There was "a widespread belief that the American news media changed in the wake of September 11" (Eisman, 2003). This rise in media repute helped to build public trust in the news, even as information from governmental sources became increasingly ambiguous and sensationalized (Fritz, et al., 2004).

The American public was exposed to a new form of news coverage during a period of increased public trust in the media throughout the early days of the Iraq war. Reporters were "embedded" with military units and reported live from their positions, relaying images and actions as they saw them, without time for editing or fact checking. For the television viewer at home, embedded reports provided a view into a world most could hardly imagine. Embedded reports broadcast evocative scenes and intimate, spontaneous commentary as audiences accompanied journalists into battle via helmet cams and night vision lenses. The American people became witness to how a high-tech war was carried out through images of young heroes and their weapons silhouetted against dusky skies and bittersweet commentaries on hope and home.

Embedded reporting has been widely criticized by journalists and scholars alike as biased, as military propaganda, as lacking in objectivity and context, as narrow in perspective and scope, and as undermining to the international reputation of the United States (Berry, 2004; Campbell, 2003; Edwords, 2003; Jackson & Stanfield, 2004; Shadid, 2004). Despite such criticisms, little research has moved our understanding of the effects of embedded reporting systematically forward. The current investigation tests for differences in viewers' levels of parasocial interaction and perceived realism as a result of watching either a traditional or embedded news report. Analysis controlled for television affinity, general attitudes about news credibility, and news viewing habits as potential confounding variables (Gaziano & McGrath, 1986; Jackson & Stanfield, 2004; Rubin, 1981; Vivian, 2005). Such research is vital given the use of embedded news reports as wartime framing devices.

Traditional Versus Embedded News Reporting of the War

American audiences are conditioned to respond to a traditional television news format, in which information is broken down into carefully scripted segments delivered to the audience through a newscaster (McCombs, Danielian, & Wanta, 1995). Summaries and contextualization of news stories by journalists and newscasters provide oral captions to the images shown (Hall Jamieson & Kohrs Campbell, 2006). Reporters, camera crews, and the location of news bureaus influence the content of news coverage (Sutter, 2004). The newscaster, the format, the placement of the story, and even the tone of the stories surrounding it, impact how audiences interpret information and create meaning (Greenberg & Pascual-Leone, 2001; Robinson, 1995).

Unless a viewer identifies with the topic being covered, watching a traditional newscast is unlikely to generate a feeling of connection to the events reported (Lippmann, 1922; McLeod, Pan, & Rucinski, 1995; Price & Oshagan, 1994; Sood, 2002). As newscasts report what has already taken place, the viewer sees past events that he or she cannot influence, reducing or removing exigency (Gerbner, 1994). While the television itself provides a sense of inclusion, or electronic intimacy, through the viewer's proximity to the screen and the direction in which the action takes place, the viewer maintains a passive role (Borchers, 2002). However, direct interaction can be simulated through the norms of the newscast, in which the newscaster looks into the camera and addresses the viewer directly (Isotalus, 1998). Audience members who feel personally engaged by what they see are more affected by the images shown (Cortese, 1999; Greenberg & Pascual-Leone, 2001; Lippmann, 1922; Phillips, 1997; Wellner, 2002). Emotionally impactful images and news stories have been found to elicit physiological responses such as increased heart rate and respiration (Newhagen, 1998).

Embedded television news reports differ from traditional television news reports in several ways. Events are reported as they happen, rather than in past tense (Gerbner, 1994). Embedded TV reporting uses episodic framing rather than thematic framing, personalizes stories and focuses on the activities at hand without providing broader contextual understanding (Pfau, et al., 2005). Reporters are often on the move, rather than standing facing the camera. Scenes may be recorded through a "helmet-cam," a small camera mounted on a helmet worn by the reporter, rather than being filmed by a cameraman. Unexpected noises, shouts, and motions confuse the moment while the reporter narrates live from the scene. Reporters use conversational language, rather than the scripted formalized speech used in traditional television news reporting. Embedded television news reporting appears both spontaneous and instantaneous, giving the viewer the opportunity to act as a participant in the event, rather than observe an event that has already occurred (Campbell, 2003; Edwords, 2003).

Elements Affecting Audience Perceptions of News Reporting

Television affinity and perceptions of news credibility are potential factors that might influence audience perceptions (Gaziano & McGrath, 1986; Jackson & Stanfield, 2004; Rubin, 1981; Vivian, 2005). Audiences do not mindlessly absorb information and attitudes from television news. Interpretation of television news and news events are impacted by various elements, including: viewers' existing perceptions; level of trust in television news; perceived realism; and expectations of news format and content.

Existing perceptions effect audience beliefs of what is reported (Fishbein & Ajzen, 1975; Greenberg & Pascual-Leone, 2001; Kull, et al., 2003–04; Lippmann, 1922; McCombs, et al., 1995; Robinson, 1995). Audience members judge the reality of media texts by relating and comparing media information to their own lives and experiences (Bussell & Greenberg, 2000; A. Hall, 2003). Perceived realism influences social judgments, thereby influencing audience members' understandings of their own lived experiences (Bussell, 2001; Bussell & Greenberg, 2000; A. Hall, 2003).

Busselle and Greenberg (2000) state "Research into social reality construction has demonstrated that individuals who judge the television they watch as more realistic are more likely to be influenced by that content" (p. 251). This sense of realism influences social understandings, feelings of efficacy, emotion, and attitudes (Busselle & Greenberg, 2000). A variety of concepts related to perceived realism have emerged, including social realism and identity (Busselle & Greenberg, 2000). These concepts involve perceptions that television content is similar to life in the real world, the extent to which content is incorporated into life or to which viewers involve themselves in content elements (Busselle & Greenberg, 2000, p. 257).

Narrative consistency increases perceptions of realism, as do compelling visuals and relatability to real-world experiences (A. Hall, 2003). This means that a viewer may believe that content is "real life," incorporate media information into his or her life through attitude or behavior changes or further involve themselves with the content (e.g., talk to others about the content, gather more information about the content). In essence, the viewer responds to television content in a manner similar to how he or she might respond to lived experience.

Trust, or lack of trust, in the television news also figures into the audience's willingness to believe what they are observing (Jones, 2004; Wellner, 2002). Hall (2003) found that audiences relied on information from media sources that they saw as trustworthy to evaluate the plausibility and typicality of other media texts. Familiarity with television news broadcast formats allows audiences to relax critical interpretation. Security in the familiar leads to interpretive generalizations and less attentive viewing (Cook, 2001), while information seeking and perceived news realism lead to active involvement (Rubin & Perse, 1987).

Television news follows a formulaic arrangement (Borchers, 2002; Hall Jamieson & Kohrs Campbell, 1983, 2006; Pfau, et al., 2005). Unless a story is extraordinarily shocking or emotional in content, or a viewer has a personal stake in the story shown, the viewing audience remains objective and somewhat disengaged with the material it is viewing (Rubin & Perse, 1987). While a person watching the evening news may express sympathy for Katrina survivors, unless she has a personal stake in what she sees (i.e., her own experience in the hurricane or having family or friends who are hurricane victims) or the images are particularly horrific, she does not engage on an emotionally reactive level (Campbell, 2003; Rubin & Perse, 1987). Audiences that feel personally engaged by what they see are more affected by the images shown (Cortese, 1999; Greenberg & Pascual-Leone, 2001; Lippmann, 1922; Phillips, 1997; Wellner, 2002). Emotionally impactful images and news stories have been found to elicit physiological responses such as increased heart rate and respiration (Newhagen, 1998).

The novel format of embedded television news reporting may affect audience perceptions of information differently than the clearly mediated reports of traditional newscasts. If traditional television news formats lulls audiences into passivity, then embedded television news reports may provide a sense of exigency that moves them out of passivity. Since the format is less familiar, viewers may feel that they are witnessing an event first-hand, in a seemingly unmediated manner. Such participation may provoke an emotional response in the viewer, which may cue cognition, rather than passivity (Bilandzic, 2006; A. Hall, 2003; Isotalus, 1998). In turn, viewers may evaluate what they have witnessed differently than they evaluate traditional reporting.

Without passivity, emotional response is likely to contribute to audience evaluations of realism. The viewer's perceived presence within the action may form a parasocial relationship with the reporter and the events seen. This also may be impacted by a person's already existing assumptions about television news. Each of these factors may change audience evaluation of the newscast. Therefore, we propose:

H_1: Controlling for overall perceptions of television news credibility and television news viewing habits, individuals will perceive embedded reporting newscasts to have greater realism than traditional newscasts.

The potential effect of embedded reporting on the perceptions and understandings of audience members leads to questions of levels of interaction and perceived presence. While the difference in format may stimulate audiences to perceive embedded television news reports to have greater realism than traditional news reports, the increased level of interaction also may lead to perceptions of presence and intimacy. Such perceptions could further influence audience reactions to and understanding of embedded news reports.

Parasocial Interaction and Audience Perceptions

Parasocial interaction blurs "the distinction between mass media and interpersonal interaction" (Sood, 2002, p. 168). Television provides a false intimacy with its audience (Borchers, 2002; Nacos, 2003). This false intimacy is the basis for parasocial interaction with a person in the media (Isotalus, 1998). Isotalus (1998) describes parasocial interaction as a blurring of parasocial relationship and simulated interaction (p. 178). Parasocial relationship is an audience member's perception of a relationship or intimacy with a person in the media (Sood, 2002). Simulated interaction is an audience member's perception of interpersonal interaction with a person in the media (Isotalus, 1998). Interpersonal communication can be simulated by the presenter looking into the camera and speaking directly to the viewer, by behaving as if there is no screen between the presenter and the viewer, or by acting as if the viewer is a third party in a conversation (Isotalus, 1998, pp. 176–177).

Audiences relate to television on different levels. When the level of interaction is at a micro-level, audiences are more likely to experience an individual relationship with television actors and make decisions based on this perception (Borchers, 2002). Television messages, and the manner in which they are presented, affect audience interaction. McLeod, Pan, and Rucinski (1995) describe this process, noting: "Mass media initiate cognitive and affective activities within individuals through messages attributes, including: (1) content, that is, main themes, concepts, ideas; (2) appeals to fear, joy, reasoning, and so on, and (3) textual and visual structures" (p. 66).

Embedded reports from the Iraq war have been found more positive toward the military than traditional news reports, and contain textual and visual structures framed from the media participant's perspective. Pfau, et. al. (2005) found that embedded reporting provided positive relational cues through interviews with military personnel. Textual structures of embedded reporting include the use of the words "I," "we," and "us," which include both the reporter and the viewer in the events as they view them. Traditional reporting uses third-person language such as "he" or "she" and "they" or "them," which underscores the distance between the viewer and the event (Gerbner, 1994). The elements contained in embedded reporting may increase its persuasive influence and lead to expression of the opinions formed in either active ways (discussion, voting) or passive ways (contemplation, interest) (Price & Oshagan, 1994). Furthermore, textual structures may increase parasocial interaction by simulating interpersonal communication, including the viewer in the scene (ignoring the barrier of the screen), and including the viewer as a third party in the conversation.

Presence is experiencing virtual objects as if they were physically present to be touched or seen (K. M. Lee, 2004). The ability of audience members to relate to people on television can extend into perceived presence, in which the audience member feels as if she is physically with the other person. Humans are socialized to interact with one another. When audience members experience other people through the media, they do so in the same manner that they might experience the physical presence of another person (Isotalus, 1998, K. M. Lee, 2004). Bilandzic (2006) relates that audience members are transported into the scene, and

> ...assume a point of view from within the narrative, which creates immediacy to the presented events and emotions. Rather than using our own relevance structures to interpret the context, we adopt the relevance structure of the characters in the story whose points of view we share. This is consistent with the notion of identification in the sense of adopting the point of view of a character in a narrative, which is characterized by a loss of self-awareness [p. 337].

Transportation into a narrative, whether real or fictional, eliminates counterargument and increases persuasiveness of media messages (Bilandzic, 2006). According to Bilandzic (2006), "...transportation might influence beliefs and attitudes because it creates a mediated experience that closely resembles a personal one" (p. 338). Embedded reporting provides opportunities to both build virtual relationships and experience virtual presence with media actors, increasing the potential for simulating "real world" experiences and relationships, as well as persuasive outcomes. This may produce long-term effects such as "...stronger attitudes, thus more persistent, more resistant to counterpersuasion, and more predictive of behavior" (p. 347).

Embedded television news reporting places audience members in the role of participants, altering the manner in which messages may be processed by viewers. Therefore, viewers may be more likely to believe they are seeing a true version of reality. Vicarious participation within the embedded reporting broadcast increases the likelihood that viewers will form a parasocial affinity with embedded reporters. Therefore, we propose:

H_2: Controlling for television affinity and television news viewing habits, audience members will have a stronger parasocial interaction with embedded television news reporters than with traditional television news reporters.

Method

Participants

Participants for this sample were undergraduate students enrolled at a medium sized Midwestern university ($N = 191$). Data collection occurred during the fall 2004 semester. Participants were recruited through campus e-mail and provided with a hyperlink to a computerized survey.

From the sample, 85 participants (44.5 percent) watched a clip of an embedded news broadcast report, and 106 participants (55.5 percent) watched a clip of a traditional news broadcast report. Upon initiating the questionnaire, participants were randomly assigned to one of two different types of news clips. Overall, the 18 to 22 year-old group was the largest age group sampled at 148 participants (77.5 percent). There also were 15 participants (7.9 percent) from 25 to 30 years old, 7 participants (3.7 percent) from 31 to 36 years old, 14 participants (7.3 percent) from 37 to 45 years old, 6 participants (3.1 percent) from 46 to 55 years old, and 1 participant (0.5 percent) from the 56 to 65-year-old age group. No significant differences in age groups existed among the two media clip types, $\chi^2(5, N = 191) = 7.238, p = .204$.

Overall, 105 participants (55.6 percent) were women, and 84 participants (44.4 percent) were male. There were not significant differences in the proportion of men and women who watched either media clip type, $\chi^2(1, N = 189) = 0.154, p = .694$.

Sample participants also indicated their level of education. In all, 120 individuals (62.5 percent) indicated they had completed some college. Fourteen participants (7.3 percent) had completed high school, and 57 participants (30 percent) had completed an associate degree or more education. Education completed was not significantly different among participants who watched either media clip type, $\chi^2(6, N = 191) = 2.159, p = .905$.

Television viewing habits were not significantly different among participants who watched either media clip type, $\chi^2(4, N = 191) = 4.399, p = .355$. Overall, 134 participants (70.2 percent) reported watching 0 to 2 hours of television a day, 49 participants (25.7 percent) watched 3 to 5 hours daily, six participants (3.1 percent) watched 6 to 9 hours daily, and two participants (1 percent) watch 10 hours or more a day.

Television news viewing habits were significantly different among participants who watched the two media clips, $\chi^2(4, N = 191) = 11.907, p = .018$. There were more weekly news watchers among participants who watched the embedded reporting media clip than among those who watched the traditional news media clip. News viewing patterns were controlled for as a covariate due to the differences in viewing habits by participants who watched each clip. From the sample, 76 participants (39.8 percent) indicated occasionally watching the news, 53 participants (27.7 percent) watched the news daily, 38 participants (19.9 percent) watched the news weekly, 20 participants (10.5 percent) watched the news multiple times a day, and four participants (2.1 percent) indicated they never watched the news.

Procedures

The study was conducted online and accessed by participants through a hyperlink to a computerized survey. Once the link was selected, a media clip of either an embedded or a traditional television news report was played. Participants were randomly assigned to watch one of two reporting clips and then answer a questionnaire. The questionnaire was the same for participants who watched either media clip of embedded television news reporting or traditional television news reporting.

Media clips. The clips selected for the study were chosen from a NBC news broadcast that took place on March 24, 2003. The news clips were chosen for their similarities in an effort to reduce differences other than the type of reporting technique being used. Both clips came from the same news station and the same news broadcast to eliminate any potential bias toward a particular news program or event in Iraq. Both clips contained male reporters to eliminate any potential gender bias. To eliminate content bias, both clips pertained to the Iraq war and were specifically related to the ground battles taking place in Iraq. Both clips dealt with ground battles and troop movements and contained images of tanks. Both contained other scenes related to the story, such as images of soldiers.

Reporter Jim Miklaszewski narrated the 59-second traditional reporting clip while standing in front of the Pentagon. He wore a suit and tie and glasses. His news clip contained images of tanks, a press conference held by General Tommy Franks, night images of bombings, troops lying on the ground with their weapons aimed in front of them, more tanks, and closed with Miklaszewski in front of the Pentagon.

Reporter David Bloom reported from the top of a tank with the U.S. Army's 3rd Infantry Division in Iraq in the 75-second embedded reporting clip. He was dressed in what appeared to be military fatigues and a flack jacket, and he wore a headset over his ears. Throughout most of the clip, he was standing with his legs inside the tank and his head and torso exposed. He also was shown sitting on the tank with one of his legs dangling inside. His news clip was shot at night, and contained scenes of troops sitting in the sun and standing near transport vehicles, a map detailing the proposed routes to Baghdad, and disabled Iraqi anti-aircraft guns.

Survey structure. The survey was constructed to begin with questions specifically about the clip viewed by the participant, then more generalized information about the amount of time individuals watched television and the news, and finally the survey ended with demographic questions. Placing the questions relating to the news clip immediately after it had been viewed allowed for recording initial audience responses to the clips. Participants evaluated the perceived realism of the information discussed in the television news report and their overall parasocial interaction for each television reporter directly after viewing the TV news clip they were randomly assigned to watch (Rubin, 1981; Rubin, Perse, & Powell, 1985).

Once these items had been completed, the participant was cued to go to a new page. The first set of items was about television affinity (Rubin, 1981). After completing this section, participants were instructed to think about the news program that they were most familiar with when answering the remaining items. The items assessed participants' overall perceptions of news credibility (Gaziano & McGrath, 1986). Demographic questions included participants' age, biological sex, education level, television viewing patterns, and news viewing patterns.

Measures

Perceived realism scale. Participants answered five items relating to the media clip they watched and perceptions of reality from the reporting. The perceived realism scale was developed by Rubin (1981, 1985). The scale items answered by participants all related to the specific news broadcast clip viewed by the participants. Each item was on a five-point Likert scale. The five items were averaged to provide a perceived realism measure. The perceived realism measure maintained strong reliability ($M = 2.96$; $SD = .70$; $\alpha = .78$).

Parasocial interaction scale. Participants also answered a 13-item parasocial interaction scale. The parasocial interaction scale was developed by Rubin, Perse, and Powell, (1985). The items were all on a five-point Likert scale. The parasocial interaction measure maintained strong reliability among participants from the sample ($M = 2.86$; $SD = .58$; $\alpha = .84$).

Television affinity scale. Participants also answered five items assessing their overall affinity for television in general. The television affinity scale was developed by Rubin (1981). The items were all on a five-point Likert scale. Participants answered items relating to the importance of watching television in day-to-day life. The television affinity scale measure maintained strong reliability ($M = 2.14$; $SD = .88$; $\alpha = .88$).

Television news credibility scale. Participants responded to 12 items on a five-point semantic differential scale indicating their general attitudes toward television news reports in general. The news credibility scale was developed by Gaziano and McGrath (1986). The news credibility measure maintained excellent reliability ($M = 3.38$; $SD = .62$; $\alpha = .83$).

Results

A one-way analysis of covariance (ANCOVA) was conducted to test the first hypothesis. The independent variable, newscast clip type, included two levels: an embedded newscast report and a traditional newscast report. The dependent variable was an individual's perception of realism with overall perceptions of television news credibility and television news viewing habits as the covariates. A preliminary analysis evaluating the homogeneity-of-slopes assumption indicated that the relationship between the covariates and the dependent variable (the three-way interaction) did not differ significantly as a function of the independent variable, $F(2, 177) = 0.74$, $MSE = 0.44$, $p = .48$, partial $\eta^2 = .008$.

The ANCOVA results indicate a significant main effect for the type of news clip on perceived realism, $F(1, 179) = 10.11$, $MSE = 0.44$, $p = .002$, partial $\eta^2 = .05$. The strength of relationship between the newscast clip type and an individual's perception of realism was moderate, as assessed by a partial η^2, with the newscast clip type accounting for 5 percent of the variance of the dependent variable, holding constant overall perceptions of television news credibility and television news viewing habits. The covariate of television news credibility significantly influenced perceived realism of the news clip ($F[1, 179] = 16.42$, $MSE = 0.44$, $p < .001$, partial $\eta^2 = .08$), while the covariate of new viewing habits did not significantly influence perceived realism ($F[1, 179] = 2.73$, $MSE = 0.44$, $p = .100$, partial $\eta^2 = .02$). Hypothesis one was supported. Individuals who watched the embedded newscast report rated it significantly more real to life (adjusted $M = 3.15$; unadjusted $M = 3.14$) than individuals who watched the traditional newscast report (adjusted $M = 2.84$; unadjusted $M = 2.85$), while controlling for overall perceptions of television news credibility and television news viewing habits.

A one-way analysis of covariance (ANCOVA) was conducted to test the second hypothesis. The independent variable of newscast clip type was examined in relationship to an individual's level of parasocial affinity, while controlling for overall perceptions of television affinity and television news viewing habits as the covariates. A preliminary analysis evaluating the homogeneity-of-slopes assumption indicated that the relationship between the covariates and the dependent variable (the three-way interaction) did not differ significantly as a function of the independent variable, $F(2,177) = 0.22$, $MSE = 0.31$, $p = .80$, partial $\eta^2 = .002$.

The ANCOVA results revealed a significant main effect for the type of television news clip and parasocial affinity, $F(1, 179) = 11.96$, $MSE = 0.31$, $p = .001$, partial $\eta^2 = .06$. The strength of relationship between the newscast clip type and an individual's perception of parasocial affinity was moderate, as assessed by a partial η^2, with the newscast clip type accounting for 6 percent of the variance of the dependent variable, holding constant overall perceptions of television affinity and television new viewing habits. Neither of the two covariates of television affinity ($F[1, 179] = 3.23$, $MSE = 0.31$, $p = .074$, partial $\eta^2 = .02$) nor television news viewing habits ($F[1, 179] = 1.93$, $MSE = 0.31$, $p = .166$, partial $\eta^2 = .01$) significantly influenced parasocial affinity as main effects. Hypothesis two was supported. Individuals experienced significantly stronger parasocial affinity for the embedded television reporter (adjusted $M = 3.03$; unadjusted $M = 3.03$) than the traditional television newscast reporter (adjusted $M = 2.75$; unadjusted $M = 2.74$), while controlling for overall perceptions of television affinity and television new viewing habits.

Discussion

Results of the current study demonstrate the ubiquitous nature of parasocial interaction and perceived realism as constructs, by examining differences of these two important areas of research in relation to traditional and embedded television news reporting. Therefore, the current study allows us to move beyond common criticisms of embedded television news reports (Berry, 2004; Campbell, 2003; Edwords, 2003; Jackson & Stanfield, 2004; Shadid, 2004), to a deeper understanding of the mechanisms of television media influence, which may be why distrust abounds for the embedded television news reporting style.

A test of the first hypothesis relating to higher perceptions of realism with watching embedded reporting versus traditional reporting found that participants who watched the embedded reporting clip perceived them as more realistic than participants who watched the traditional media clip, while controlling for different perceptions of television news credibility in general and television news viewing habits. This demonstrates that the perception of realism was related to the clip viewed itself, rather than reflecting participants' existing predispositions towards television news reports.

Higher parasocial interaction was found in participants who watched the embedded reporting clip than in participants who watched the traditional media clip, while controlling for differences in television affinity and television news viewing habits. This demonstrates that parasocial interaction was related to the clip viewed itself, rather than a mere reflection of participants' existing affinity toward television viewing.

Study results demonstrate the inherent power of television news reporting as important framing devices given that embedded television reporting results in more relatable parasocial evaluations from television audiences about reporters who provide more realistic portrayals and accounts of wartime proceedings. We argue that these combined affects due to the method of television reporting style may also increase the likelihood that television viewers will believe information consumed by embedded television reporters is more truthful and accurate.

Implications

Television news reporting methods affect audience interpretation of what is seen and what it means (Borchers, 2002; Robinson, 1995). Examining television news reporting methods may help generate better understanding of the process of opinion formation and the role of television news in public relations and public diplomacy. The U.S. military's willingness to include embedded reporters in their ranks reflects an understanding of embeds' potential for developing public support (Hiebert, 2003). While public support assists the military in its goals, it does not reflect the democratic requirements of news reporting. In fact, the illusion of unedited information and the immediacy of audience response is couched within the careful control of the military (Jackson & Stanfield, 2004).

The persuasive nature of embedded reporting seems particularly relevant as it relates to the population surveyed. One hundred forty eight participants (77.5 percent), were 18 to 24 years of age, which is also an age range heavily recruited for military enlistment. When the 15 participants between 25 to 30 years old are included, 85.4 percent of the total sample is within standard military recruitment ranges. Embedded reporting may serve as a recruitment tool as war and deployment are made to seem both real and immediate, seemingly removing the veil of war to reveal the heroic face of the troops beneath.

Embedded reporting was used during the initial phase of Operation Iraqi Freedom when the need for public support for the war was high. The need for public support leveled off over time, and embedded reporting became less and less evident. Once Baghdad fell and the war was declared to be over, embedded reports became virtually non-existent, dropping from over 600 embeds during the March 2003 invasion to 114 embeds in October 2005 when Iraqis went to the polls to ratify a new constitution (R. Hall, 2006; "Number of embeds drops to lowest level in Iraq," 2006).

When placed within the context of the war, the influence of embedded reporting could help to explain why the absence of weapons of mass destruction was not an issue in public support. Information related to weapons of mass destruction was reported using traditional methods, while the heroic efforts of the American soldier were experienced through embedded reports. Weapons or no weapons, the American public supported the people they identified with (Kull, et al., 2003–04).

Limitations, Future Research, and Conclusion

This study examined one clip of traditional television news reporting and one clip of embedded television news reporting. The limited nature of these clips may have affected viewer's interactions with the reporters. Participants in the study were primarily representatives of younger audiences. Future research might explore how embedded news reporters affect older audiences.

Future research might be better served by using longer clips, or multiple clips, for examination. Increasing audience heterogeneity and representativeness of the sample could lead to greater insights into diverse audience segments and reference groups beyond the primarily military-aged sample of the current study. The impact of viewing patterns on perceptions of immediacy and truth is an area that needs further examination. Future research focused on older audiences may reveal differing views of embedded reports. In addition to variations in audience and clips, the clips themselves might provide insight into American culture.

The manner in which embedded television news reporting was used and the sequence of its use lends credibility to claims that embedded television news reports of the second Iraq war functioned as governmental and military propaganda (Edwords, 2003; Hiebert, 2003). Such criticisms, coupled with the demonstrated influence of embedded reporting, call for an examination of embedded television news reporting as propaganda.

In this study, participants' perceptions of television affinity and television news credibility were controlled for in examining levels of perceived realism and parasocial interaction for two different types of news reports. The study supports that embedded television news reporting results in significantly higher levels of perceived realism and parasocial interaction, independent of pre-existing levels of television news credibility, television affinity, and news viewing habits. This demonstrates that embedded television news reporting affects audience perceptions of immediacy and parasocial interaction, increasing the likelihood that viewers will believe what they see is a true and accurate representation of events. However, immediacy and parasocial dynamics do not necessarily mean the viewer has a better overall understanding of what she is seeing. In fact, the lack of cohesive captioning usually present in television news makes the overall messages harder to comprehend. It simply means that the viewer experiences the television broadcast as real and immediate, which, in the minds of viewers, often translates into truth.

References

ABC News/Washington Post Poll. (2007). Sept. 4–7. Retrieved April 13, 2008, from http://www.pollingreport.com/iraq2.htm.

Berry, S. J. (2004, Fall). CBS lets the Pentagon taint its news process. *Nieman Reports, 58*, 76–79.

Bilandzic, H. (2006). The perception of distance in the cultivation process: A theoretical consideration of the relationship between television content, processing experience, and perceived distance. *Communication Theory, 16*, 333–355.

Borchers, T. A. (2002). *Persuasion in the Media Age*. Boston: McGraw Hill.

Busselle, R. W. (2001). Television exposure, perceived realism, and exemplar accessibility in the social judgment process. *Media Psychology, 3*, 43–67.

_____, and B. S. Greenberg (2000). The nature of television realism judgments: A reevaluation of their conceptualization and measurement. *Mass Communication & Society, 2*(2&3), 249–268.

Calbreath, D. (2008, March 30). Financing Iraq war is taking toll on economy. *San Diego Union Tribune*, F1.

Campbell, D. (2003). Representing contemporary war. *Ethics & International Affairs, 17*(2), 99–108.

CBS News Poll. (2008). March 15–18, 2008. Retrieved April 12, 2008, from http://www.pollingreport.com/iraq.htm.

Cook, G. (2001). *The Discourse of Advertising* (second ed.). London and New York: Routledge.

Cortese, A. J. (1999). *Provocateur: Images of Women and Minorities in Advertising*. Lanham, MD: Rowman & Littlefield.

Edwords, F. (2003, July/August 2003). The issue at hand. *The Humanist, 63*, 1.

Eisman, A. (2003). The media of manipulation: Patriotism and propaganda—mainstream news in the United States in the weeks following September 11. *Critical Quarterly, 45*(1–2), 55–72.

Fishbein, M., and I. Ajzen (1975). *Belief, Attitude, Intention and Behavior*. Reading, MA: Addison-Wesley.

Fritz, B., B. Keefer, and B. Nyhan (2004). *All the President's Spin: George W. Bush, the Media, and the Truth.* New York: Touchstone.

Gaziano, C., and K. McGrath (1986). Measuring the concept of credibility. *Journalism Quarterly, 63,* 451–462.

Gerbner, G. (1994). Instant history, image history: Lessons from the Persian Gulf War. In R. F. Fox (Ed.), *Images in Language, Media and Mind* (pp. 123–140). Urbana, IL: National Council of Teachers of English.

Greenberg, L. S., and J. Pascual-Leone (2001). A dialectical constuctivist view of the creation of personal meaning. *Journal of Constructivist Psychology, 14,* 165–186.

Hall, A. (2003). Reading realism: Audiences' evaluations of the reality of media texts. *Journal of Communication, 53*(4), 624–641.

Hall Jamieson, K., and K. Kohrs Campbell (1983). *The Interplay of Influence: Mass Media and Their Publics in News, Advertising, Politics.* Belmont, CA: Wadsworth.

____, and ____. (2006). *The Interplay of Influence: News, Advertising, Politics, and the Internet.* Belmont, CA: Thomson Wadsworth.

Hall, R. (2006, November 6). Number of embedded reporters in Iraq at "terrible" levels. *The Nation* Retrieved April 20, 2008, from http://www.cnsnews.com/ViewNation.asp?Page=/Nation/archive/200611/NAT20061106b.html.

Hiebert, R. E. (2003). Public relations and propaganda in framing the Iraq war: A preliminary review. *Public Relations Review, 29*(3), 243–255.

Isotalus, P. (1998). Television performance as interaction. *Nordicom Review, 19*(1), 175–183.

Jackson, P. T., and J. R. Stanfield (2004). The role of the press in democracy: Heterodox economics and the propaganda model. *Journal of Economic Issues, XXXVIII*(2), 475–482.

Jones, M. C. (2004). Voters lack trust in an age of disillusionment. *Brand Strategy,* 12–13.

Kagan, R. (2004). America's crisis of legitimacy. *Foreign Affairs, 83*(2), 65–79.

Kull, S., C. Ramsay, and E. Lewis (2003–04). Misperceptions, the media, and the Iraq war. *Political Science Quarterly, 118*(4), 569–581.

Kumar, D. (2006). Media, war, and propaganda: Strategies of information management during the 2003 Iraq war. *Communication and Critical/Cultural Studies, 3*(1), 48–69.

Lee, K. M. (2004). Presence, Explicated. *Communication Theory, 14*(1), 27–50.

Lee, T.-T. (2005). The liberal media myth revisited: An examination of factors influencing perceptions of media bias. *Journal of Broadcasting & Electronic Media, 49,* 43–64.

Lippmann, W. (1922). *Public Opinion.* New York: Free Press.

McCombs, M., L. Danielian, and W. Wanta (1995). Issues in the news and the public agenda: The agenda-setting tradition. In T. L. Glasser & C. T. Salmon (Eds.), *Public Opinion and the Communication of Consent* (pp. 281–300). New York: Guilford.

McLeod, J., Z. Pan, and D. Rucinski (1995). Levels of analysis in public opinion research. In T. L. Glasser & C. T. Salmon (Eds.), *Public Opinion and the Communication of Consent* (pp. 55–85). New York: Guilford.

Nacos, B. L. (2003). Terrorism as breaking news: Attack on America. *Political Science Quarterly, 118*(1), 23–31.

Newhagen, J. E. (1998). TV news images that induce anger, fear, and disgust: Effects on approach-avoidance and memory. *Journal of Broadcasting & Electronic Media, 42*(2), 265–276.

Nisbet, E. C., M. C. Nisbet, D. A. Scheufele, and J. E. Shanahan (2004). Public diplomacy, television news, and Muslim opinion. *Harvard International Journal of Press/Politics, 9*(2), 11–37.

Number of embeds drops to lowest level in Iraq. (2006, October 15). Retrieved April 20, 2008, from http://www.editorandpublisher.com/eandp/news/article_display.jsp?vnu_content_id=1003254981.

Nye, J. S., Jr. (2004). The decline of America's soft power. *Foreign Affairs, 83*(3), 16–20.

Pfau, M., M. M. Haigh, L. Logsdon, C. Perrine, J. P. Baldwin, R. E. Breitenfeldt, et al. (2005). Embedded reporting during the invasion and occupation of Iraq: How the embedding of journalists affects television news reports. *Journal of Broadcasting & Electronic Media, 49,* 468–487.
Phillips, B. J. (1997). Thinking into it: Consumer interpretation of complex advertising images. *The Journal of Advertising, XXVI*(2), 77–87.
Post February 2006 displacement in Iraq [Electronic (2008) Version]. *International Organization for Migration Emergency Needs Assessments Bi-Weekly Report,* 1–21. Retrieved April 1, 2008 from http://www.uniraq.org/documents/Iraq_Displacement_Assessments_March.pdf.
Price, V., and H. Oshagan (1994). Social-psychological perspectives on public opinion. In T. L. Glasser & C. T. Salmon (Eds.), *Public Opinion and the Communication of Consent* (pp. 177–216). New York: Guilford.
Robinson, G. J. (1995). Making news and manufacturing consent: The journalistic narrative and its audience. In T. L. Glasser & C. T. Salmon (Eds.), *Public Opinion and the Communication of Consent* (pp. 348–369). New York: Guilford.
Rosen Jr., B., and C. Wolf (2005, Oct/Nov). Public diplomacy: Lessons from King and Mandela. *Policy Review,* 63–80.
Rubin, A. M. (1981). An examination of television viewing motivations. *Communication Research, 8,* 141–165.
_____, and E. M. Perse (1987). Audience activity and television news gratifications. *Communication Research, 14*(1), 58–84.
_____, _____, and R. A. Powell (1985). Loneliness, parasocial interaction, and local television news viewing. *Human Communication Research, 12,* 155–180.
Shadid, A. (2004, Summer). The Iraq experience poses critical questions for journalists. *Nieman Reports, 58,* 54–60.
Sood, S. (2002). Audience involvement and entertainment-education. *Communication Theory, 12,* 153–172.
Sutter, D. (2001). Can the media be so liberal? The economics of media bias. *Cato Journal, 20,* 431–451.
_____. (2004). News media incentives, coverage of government, and the growth of government. *The Independent Review, VIII*(4), 549–567.
USA Today/Gallop Poll. (2008). CNN opinion research corporation poll. Feb. 21–24, 2008. Retrieved April 12, 2008, from http://www.pollingreport.com/iraq.htm.
Vivian, J. (2005). *The Media of Mass Communication* (7th ed.). Boston: Pearson Education.
Wellner, A. S. (2002, February). The female persuasion. *American Demographics, 24,* 24–30.

PRINCE HARRY AND THE AFGHANISTAN MEDIA BLACKOUT

Terri Toles Patkin

Journalists spend their careers in pursuit of information. They pursue leads, interview people, and sometimes even put their lives on the line to get a story. It would take an extraordinary event for a journalist to voluntarily decline to publish newsworthy, accurate, and timely information. For a journalist to advocate censorship would be like a dentist advocating tooth decay. So it was remarkable when not just one reporter, but an entire nation of journalists, conspired to block information from the public for almost three months. This chapter examines the ethical questions surrounding the media blockade of Prince Harry's military service in Afghanistan and the public's response to it, with particular attention to the BBC's evaluation of the media's ethical obligations.

A Prince's Tale

For 10 weeks in the winter of 2007-2008, Britain's Prince Harry — third in line for the throne — quietly served as a member of a combat unit on the front lines in Afghanistan. The 23-year-old officer's responsibility was to link ground and air forces in Helmand Province, only a few yards from Taliban outposts. His deployment was top secret, and the British press did everything it could to keep it that way (Gillan, Tran, & Walker, 2008).

Harry Wales (the surname he and his brother William use in circumstances requiring one) served as a Cornet (equivalent to an American Second Lieutenant) with the Joint Tactical Air Control in the Household Cavalry Regiment Battlegroup, known as the Blues and Royals. After graduating from Sandhurst with training as a tank commander in 2006, Harry retrained as a battlefield air controller (Associated Press, 2008b). His duties in Afghanistan included calling in air strikes and air support, assuring bombing accuracy, and averting friendly fire incidents (CNN, 2008). A handful of Ministry of Defense officials and Harry's family were the only ones informed about his deployment. Some generals and Harry's close friends were not told that he had left the country (Associated Press, 2008a; Gammell, 2008; Gillan, et al., 2008; Stelter & Lyall, 2008).

Bob Satchwell, the executive director of the Society of Editors in England, at the request of the Ministry of Defense, brokered a top-secret agreement with journalists to keep the news out of the headlines in an effort to protect both Harry and his fellow soldiers. The deal—voluntary on the part of the media—was that a small number of reporters would receive access to the Prince in Afghanistan as long as they held the story until the military decided it would be safe to release the information. More than 100 outlets, including all the British media, participated, as did Reuters, the Associated Press, and CNN (Gammell, 2008; Gillan, et al., 2008; Panja, 2008; Stelter & Lyall, 2008). Harry completed 10 weeks of a planned four-month tour, from December 24, 2007, to February 29, 2008, before the news was irrevocably leaked (Gillan, et al., 2008).

On February 28, 2008, American Internet journalist Matt Drudge broke the news on his popular web site, *The Drudge Report*, at 10:32 in the morning. Actually, Harry's presence in Afghanistan had been revealed earlier by the Australian women's magazine *New Idea* on its website on January 7 and again a week later in the January 15 edition of its print magazine (Gammell, 2008), but the story received little attention. After Drudge broke the story, Australian readers roundly condemned *New Idea* in online comments (Gammell, 2008), and 78 percent of Australians said in a poll that they thought it was wrong for the media to have leaked the news (Squires, 2008). A German women's magazine, *Frau Im Spiegel*, also ran a piece titled "Harry in Iraq?" during the last week of February, and *Bild* ran a piece on February 27 (Gammell, 2008; Stelter & Lyall, 2008). However, all these pieces were largely ignored as being questionable celebrity gossip. At first, Drudge cited *Bild*, but he soon deleted that information and called his story a "world exclusive" (Riviera, 2008; Stelter & Lyall, 2008).

Immediately following Drudge's revelation, the worldwide press blackout was lifted, and photos and interviews were released. Within a few hours, the British Ministry of Defense announced that Harry would be shipped back to England several weeks early for his own safety and that of his colleagues. The prince apparently enjoyed his time away from the limelight, joking to reporters that he had been a "normal person" during the blackout (BBC News, 2008).

After the story broke, PR professionals, propagandists and just about everyone else instantly began to spin the story to suit their own agendas. The British Army blamed "foreign media" for irresponsible journalism without consulting the Ministry of Defense (Riviera, 2008). Sir Richard Dannatt, chief of the General Staff and head of the British Army, contrasted Drudge's leak with the "highly responsible attitude" that cooperating media outlets had shown in entering into an "understanding" with the military about coverage of Harry's deployment (Gillan, et al., 2008).

Harry was praised by British leaders as a fine example of a responsible younger generation prepared to take on serious security tasks. Prime Minister Gordon Brown said the country owed the Prince a debt of gratitude and that everyone in Britain was proud of his service (BBC News, 2008). For his part, Harry was said to be bitterly disappointed at having his tour cut short (Riviera, 2008), particularly since an earlier deployment to Iraq the previous year had been cancelled due to security concerns.

Media Ethics and the Blackout

The Harry-Afghanistan blackout raised ethical concerns for many journalists. Although unusual, this media blackout was not unique. Until recent years, it was routine for the press to bow to the censorship demands of the military, and vital information was sometimes not released until well after a conflict had ended. Even in today's media-saturated environment, journalists occasionally keep quiet about the movements of important public figures, as when President Bush made a surprise holiday visit to troops in Iraq in 2003, and no report was made until Air Force One was heading back home (Stelter & Lyall, 2008).

The decision regarding what information to release and when can be a difficult and complicated one. Journalism is, in many ways, an exercise in competing loyalties. The journalist must balance loyalties arising from shared humanity, loyalties arising from professional practice, loyalties arising from employment, and loyalties arising from the media's role in public life (Patterson & Wilkins, 2007). Often these loyalties can exert strong competing pressures. The Harry story touches on several of these of these. Professional practice might push a journalist to publicize the story, while concerns for the personal safety of a fellow human being might push the same journalist to hold the information; one's employer might want to wait on publication while the pressures of the media marketplace encourage going to press rapidly.

Journalists do on occasion withhold information. They may wish to avoid harm to others or anticipate some advantage by holding publication to a later date (Day, 2006). Despite potentially virtuous motivation, however, such a decision invariably leads to a diminished public trust in the particular journalist or news outlet once the information is ultimately revealed, and perhaps a greater suspicion concerning journalism in general. The compromises journalists make are constant and motivated by a variety of factors. According to Poniewozik (2003), "Reporting is full of noble and not-so-noble compromises. You keep troop movements secret. You leave certain subjects off limits in order to secure an exclusive with a certain ingénue. You don't ask a question that's begging to be asked — so you'll get called on at the next press conference. You do it out of decency or out of caution or, you tell yourself, to build the capital and relationships to tell the truth and damn the consequences ... someday" (p. 92). A central concern in this case was the decision to withhold not only information specific to the story, but also contextual information that would clue in audience members to the very existence of a blackout. The public may well accept the concept that reporters cannot release the particulars of a battlefield situation when reporting from a war zone, but audience members may have a general expectation that they at least will be informed of the existence of the war zone. Reporters must carefully tread the fine line between discretion and censorship.

In Harry's case, he simultaneously occupies the position of individual soldier (a status usually too obscure to merit any media coverage at all) and celebrity member of the Royal family (fair game for continual and often intrusive reporting). As a public figure, Harry enjoys less privacy than the ordinary citizen, and the question of journalistic discretion in selecting when and what to report about his activities takes on larger meaning (Bugeja, 2008; Leslie, 2004).

The Society of Editors viewed its actions as simply exercising discretion in limiting the information that was revealed, balancing social utility against the possible harm to the subject himself as well as to others. This case was not seen by the British media as an exercise in secrecy — intentional concealment in order to prevent others from learning, possessing or using information (Bok, 1983) — because the intent was always to publicize the information once Harry's safety was no longer potentially compromised. Indeed, journalists are taught that they have a duty to withhold confidential information from third parties under certain circumstances. According to Day (2006), these may stem from an express promise on the part of the journalist (e.g. to keep information off the record), from a legal requirement (e.g., doctor-patient privilege), or from a sense of loyalty (e.g., a public relations firm protecting the best interest of a client). In this case, the express promise on the part of British media emerged from a sense of loyalty to both the Royal Family and the military. And the Society of Editors most definitely did not view the blackout as deceptive. Deception in the news includes fabrication or exaggeration or information as well as reporter self-misrepresentation in order to obtain a story (Knapp, 2008). The rules of engagement always were that reporters agreeing to the blackout merely kept silent rather than affirmatively lying about Harry's presence in Afghanistan while he was on duty. Had Harry managed to find a nightclub in Kabul on his day off, for instance, it would have been fair game for media coverage. For his part, Harry played along with the media blackout, and took no risks that his presence in Afghanistan would be revealed.

There are almost as many professional codes of ethics for journalists as there are news outlets. One comprehensive code that is commonly subscribed to is that of the Society of Professional Journalists. The group's 2008 Code of Ethics emphasizes both the thorough pursuit of truth and maintenance of the journalist's credibility through professional integrity. It includes the following overarching tenets: *Seek Truth and Report It, Minimize Harm, Act Independently,* and *Be Accountable* (Society of Professional Journalists, 2008). Some of these were adhered to closely in this instance; others were not.

Seek Truth and Report It includes commitments to accuracy, objectivity, sensitivity, identification of sources whenever possible, avoiding distortion of images and headlines, being as open as possible in news gathering, eschewing plagiarism, and recognizing the difference between news and advertising (Society of Professional Journalists, 2008). The Harry blackout partially fulfilled this tenet. The reporters sought truth but delayed in reporting it. Journalistic truth strives for an ideal of objective accuracy. Whether objectivity emerges from the facts reported or from the process by which those facts are gathered, the question remains: which intersubjective truth does one communicate? Bugeja (2008) asserted, "Journalists should strive for *full disclosure* in a news report ... including all available facts and providing impartially a complete a truth as possible. They should avoid partial disclosure, the omission of facts and details that might bias an assignment or cast it in an improper light or context" (p. 110). In short, transparency of the reporting process is to be achieved. In retrospect, this occurred following the Harry incident, but not during the time frame of his actual deployment in Afghanistan.

The ethical obligation to *Minimize Harm* includes showing compassion for those affected negatively by news coverage, sensitivity in interviewing and photographing subjects, protecting the privacy of private individuals, showing good taste and avoidance of appealing to lurid curiosity, protecting the identity of juveniles or victims of sex crimes, and balancing a criminal suspect's fair trial rights with the public's right to be informed (Society of Professional Journalists, 2008). Clearly, this was a major factor in Harry's case. Day (2006) argued, "Battlefield coverage is particularly vulnerable to accusations of inaccurate reporting, a result in part of heavy dependence upon military sources of information, the inherent complexities of modern military operations, and the rapid pace of battlefield engagements that is antithetical to journalistic reflection and perspective" (p. 86). Reporting on Harry's presence could have brought harm both to him personally and to the other soldiers serving in his unit. According to Riviera (2008), Harry's nickname among his peers was the "Bullet Magnet" (paragraph 24). Fears that he would draw fire or be captured were emphasized in several articles. Indeed, the Taliban went on record saying that they knew that Harry was in Afghanistan and were said to be gunning for "an important chicken," aiming to capture or kill the prince, according to Mullah Abdul Karim, a Taliban officer (quoted in Edwards, 2008, paragraph 2).

The ethical obligation to *Act Independently* means that journalists should avoid conflicts of interest, refuse gifts or associations that could compromise integrity or damage credibility, and deny favored treatment to advertisers and special interest groups (Society of Professional Journalists, 2008). One might argue that, as a Royal, Harry received special treatment that could lead to a conflict of interest for journalists in a competitive marketplace. On the other hand, since all British media signed on to the blackout agreement, that conflict was confined to the less immediate competition of the international media — and indeed, it was a non–British outlet that ultimately broke the story.

Finally, journalists should *Be Accountable* to their audience members and to one another. This includes explaining news coverage, admitting mistakes and correcting them promptly, exposing ethical lapses of the news media, and abiding by high ethical standards at all times (Society of Professional Journalists, 2008). Certainly, the post-event coverage managed this element well, but one might argue that the blackout itself violated this tenet of the Code of Ethics rather dramatically.

The BBC's Analysis of the Blackout

The British Broadcasting Corporation (BBC) is a major player in the multifaceted British media market, and it played an important role in shaping discussions of media ethics relating to the blackout of the Harry-in-Afghanistan story. BBC editor Jon Williams (2008) pointed to many universal journalistic ethical guidelines, such as those outlined in the Society of Professional Journalists' Code, in his online defense of the BBC's decision to participate in the news blackout, but most strongly emphasized the *Minimize Harm* theme. He noted that a news blackout, while unusual, was not unique, and that similar embargoes have occurred in cases of kidnappings or hostage-takings in the past (paragraph 2). The British media formally agreed with the

Ministry of Defense that they would not speculate on nor report about the Prince's deployment in order to reduce the harm to him and to others; in return, reporters would be given access to him to gather material for later publication. They would remain silent, but would not deceive the audience. Williams expressed surprise that the agreement lasted as long as it did, and ended the editorial by reassuring readers that no other voluntary agreements of the sort were currently in place, promising audience members that "there's nothing else we're not telling you" (paragraph 10).

The BBC's own multifaceted Code of Ethics focuses on the following values: *Truth and accuracy, Impartiality and diversity of opinion, Editorial integrity and independence, Serving the public interest, Fairness, Privacy, Harm and offence, Children,* and *Accountability* (BBC, 2008). Of the 634 points listed on the A–Z index of Editorial Guidelines (several of which have subcategories ranging from one or two points to as many as 41 specific guiding principles), none specifically address the secrecy of a Harry-type agreement. The only types of disguised identities listed in the Code of Ethics include those of criminals, innocent citizens caught on tape, people who could be targets for terrorists, or those from whom it would be difficult to obtain consent such as persons with brain damage.

The BBC Code emphasizes the avoidance of misleading audiences through the distortion of known facts, presenting invented material as fact or knowingly doing anything misleading. The Harry blackout certainly misled the audience about his whereabouts through a lack of coverage. At the same time, however, the BBC Code protects the private behavior of public officials (which could include Harry if one were to stretch the definition of official) unless that behavior raises broader public issues, and it strongly protects the vulnerable. The section of the Code of Ethics on war reporting states that war reporting should include information that lets the audience know that reports are censored or monitored, or "if we withhold information, and explain, wherever possible, the rules under which we are operating" (BBC, 2008, paragraph 3). The BBC's behavior post-blackout closely conforms with its self-imposed Code of Ethics, but the blackout itself could be interpreted either positively or negatively. Truth and accuracy are central values in the BBC Code; the Code explicitly places accuracy as more important than speed of breaking a story. The BBC also promises to deal fairly and openly with the audience as part of its accountability to them.

Williams (2008) paralleled the limited coverage of Harry's deployment to cooperating with the police in kidnapping cases. For example, the authorities may request that the media withhold information in order to ensure the safety of the victim while the abduction is under way. In return, the police promise to update the media regularly and reveal the full story when lives are no longer at risk. By using this model, the journalistic community in Britain was able to rationalize the delayed coverage — no doubt aided by their unprecedented access to Harry during the blackout.

Audience Understanding of Media Motivation for the Blackout

But do audience members and professional journalists share the same understanding of ethical imperatives in covering war? Did the British public share journalists' perceptions that withholding information about Harry's deployment was an ethical obligation? Members of the BBC's audience, for the most part untrained as journalists and holding a naïve layperson's understanding of journalistic ethics, responded in an online forum to editor Jon Williams's (2008) defense of the network's decision to participate in the media blackout. The degree to which audience members' response paralleled of the professional journalist's code of ethics is examined here through an exploratory qualitative content analysis of the 854 unique responses left on the BBC website in the week following the surfacing of the blackout. Multiple codings were permitted for each individual's posting, and sequential duplicate codings were permitted in cases where the writer emphasized the point by beginning a new paragraph.

Support of the Blackout

Of 854 total comments, just over a quarter (225, or 26 percent) were general positive statements in support of the media's blackout of information. These included commendations to the BBC, and wide-ranging remarks about common sense and social responsibility. The question of harm and the need to balance multiple pressures was mentioned by several respondents. Audience members also echoed Williams' (2008) points about accountability and seeking truth. Paradoxically, the blackout actually increased some audience members' trust in the media. For example, one respondent wrote:

> I can't understand those people who think the blackout agreement was wrong. I'm pretty sure they'd feel otherwise if they had family or friends out in Afghanistan (as I do). This wasn't about colluding with the government, lying to the public, pandering to the Royal Family or anything else. It was about protecting lives.

Some readers (32 comments, or almost 4 percent of responses) were so enthusiastic about the concept of a news blackout that they suggested extending the blackout concept to include other celebrities, particularly the Royal Family.

Opposition to the Blackout

Few respondents on the BBC board were opposed to the media blackout. Only 27 comments (3 percent) expressed opposition to the media blackout, although an additional 58 comments (6.8 percent) mentioned decreased trust in the media and concerns that other information was being kept from the public. Parallels to Nazi propaganda were made, and concerns about censorship were expressed, with some audience members positing the existence of a broader conspiracy, as did this one:

> There's nothing else we're not telling you." By telling the public about an event that has happened and was not initially reported, how can you possibly expect anyone to believe the quoted line above? Even if it was true, there's no doubt it won't be true for long. There have always been issues that have not been reported in the media for long periods of time, and indeed, some issues that somehow never saw the light of day. Carry on being deluded Britain. Your government has your best interests at heart. Honestly. Because they said so. So it has to be true.

More virulent anti–Royal or anti–Harry sentiment was expressed in 36 comments (4 percent). Statements that Harry didn't deserve special treatment or that Buckingham Palace exerted too much influence in the decision were included here. Clearly, this incident joins a number of actions relating to the Royal family that are of continuing concern to some audience members:

> I understand that this is an action that's mutually beneficial to the Royals and the BBC, but not to those serving with Harry. At the end of the day, it looks like a mockery put into place to grant a pampered boy one of his greatest wishes. Being born into privilege in this day and age means that he cannot have everything he wants, not the other way around, surely??!!

It's Complicated

Ironically, a fair number of the responses were accompanied by anti–BBC or anti-media remarks even as the writer praised the media blackout of the Harry information. Ninety-five general anti-media comments were made, accounting for just over 11 percent of the responses. Concerns that the media blackout led to increased profits or other benefits for the media were included here, as were calls for time limits on any future media blackouts. One reader said:

> Let's not become moist-eyed about the British media; if there is anything viler than the political animal, that specimen is the news hound. The journo shoves microphones into the faces of bereaved persons, torments ordinary people, wallows in the salacious details of female rape and murder and pretend that we require him to do all this in the name of freedom of information. When not hounding largely decent though imperfect public servants out of office, he can

be found selling his granny on street corners; he never lets the truth get in the way of a good story. How amusing it is to see the hack in a state of moral outrage. Now he knows how the rest of us feel.

Another 11 percent of responses (95 comments) attacked "foreign media," especially the *Drudge Report* and *New Idea Magazine*, for breaking the story. Some of these came from Americans, who apologized for the leak and assured others that Drudge does not represent mainstream media coverage in the United States, such as this one:

> I would also note that it would be unfair to lump much of the American media together with Drudge. I am sure that many of our mainstream news outlets such as CBS, ABC, and NBC, etc. would have been quite content to keep this quiet until the Ministry of Defense said otherwise.

Certainly, CNN, as a participant in the blackout, would agree. Other comments simply addressed the increasingly-unpopular war on terror and British involvement in hostilities rather than focusing on media ethics:

> Great! We help the Yanks out in their pointless posturing and enter a ridiculous and unwinnable war against an idea, suffer hundreds of casualties — often from the gung ho American forces in 'friendly fire' incidents, and this is how we're repaid.

Safety of the Soldiers

The ethical obligation for journalists to minimize harm appears to be very well-understood by the BBC audience. Harry's safety and that of his fellow soldiers was mentioned in 105 comments (12 percent), with the safety of soldiers being the primary theme. Another 47 comments (5 percent) expressed positive sentiment about the bravery and service of soldiers in general:

> The BBC and the British media were right to hold back on this information. No we don't have a 'right to know' if it puts Harry and others at risk. Whatever we feel about the war, a war it is, and therefore appropriate secrecy is vital, and this was appropriate!

Support for Harry

A surprising result from the audience response involved Harry's personal career plans. Harry's use of his military training and his commitment to his career was mentioned positively in 64 (7 percent) comments. Many of these remarks focused on Harry's personal career ambitions, in effect recasting him as an average young man rather than a privileged member of the Royal Family. These remarks tended to be very personal, viewing Harry as a private individual who simply wants to go to work every day without being harassed by the media. This was not a factor in the media blackout decision for journalists, but appears to have been an important consideration for at least some audience members, such as this one:

> Harry might be a royal, but he deserves the same rights as everyone else, including privacy, and the right to work a job.

Many audience members apparently experienced a change of heart regarding Prince Harry once his activities in Afghanistan were revealed. Where previous media coverage had constructed an image of him as a playboy and partygoer, articles about his military service made some audience members perceive him as more mature and serious. In 70 comments (8 percent), BBC audience members said they saw Harry in a positive light as a result of the media blackout, with some describing him as a proud symbol of Britain:

> MOST IMPORTANTLY, my sincere thanks, congratulations, and highest respect to Prince Harry. He is showing himself to be a true leader and deserving of the title "Prince." Your entire nation is rightly very proud of him. One hell of a guy....

Indeed, Harry's conduct in Afghanistan is said to have been exemplary, with Harry being fully involved with operations and running the same risks as other soldiers (Gillan, et al., 2008).

Disconnect Between Audience and Journalists

The strongest agreement of the BBC audience members with professional journalists was associated with the *Minimize Harm* component of the Code of Ethics of the Society of Professional Journalists. An intuitive understanding that reportage would have endangered Harry exists, but an even stronger concern for the safety and security of his colleagues was expressed. In fact, while 20 comments mentioned Harry's safety alone, more than twice as many (47) mentioned the safety of his fellow soldiers with no mention of Harry whatsoever, and an additional 38 comments discussed the joint safety of Harry and his colleagues.

Some of the anti-media comments followed the *Minimize Harm* theme as well, criticizing the media for often acting like paparazzi and sticking cameras and microphones into people's faces indiscriminately, despite the fact that the media did not behave in this way either during or after the Harry blackout. The penchant for Royal gossip and tabloid journalism appears to foster what some BBC audience members consider to be a harmful environment for British society.

Other than the clause about being open about newsgathering, the ethical tenet of *Seek Truth and Report It* was not reflected in many of the comments. It may speak well for the British press that many of the audience members appear to accept the truthfulness of reporting as a given, or it may mean something else entirely. No one mentioned that some of the gossip column leaks included inaccurate information. It was suggested that Harry was in Iraq, rather than Afghanistan, on at least one occasion prior to Drudge's breaking of the story.

Similarly, the ethical obligation to *Act Independently* did not receive much attention from readers, other than a handful of conspiracy-style remarks concerning the erosion of trust in the media exacerbated by the blackout. The sense, however, was that the writers did not give particularly high marks for credibility to either the press or the government before the blackout, and the Harry news embargo merely strengthened their opposition.

For the ethical tenet that journalists should *Be Accountable*, results were mixed. Several readers praised the BBC for its handling of the blackout and reassured editors that no apology for keeping secrets was necessary; a smaller number criticized the media for what they perceived as an ethical lapse.

Many of the comments of audience members expressed concern with broader social ethical problems, such as the nation's involvement in war, but less interest in issues specifically related to journalistic ethics. The enthusiastic support for Harry's pursuit of a career appeared to center largely on his interpersonal achievements. Perhaps Brits who watched him grow up, lose his mother, and make foolish adolescent choices were delighted to see a more mature, responsible Harry. Other remarks revealed the Republican-Royalist tensions in Britain today. For these audience members, Harry's special treatment in the news blackout took on larger symbolic meaning relating to the role of the Royal Family in the British sociopolitical system. Broader concerns about the war on terror and Britain's place in the international coalition were also exposed in comments about Harry.

Explaining the Disconnect: The Making of a Hero

The difference between the audience response and the journalistic response to the Harry blackout signals the differing orientations the two groups hold towards the process of newsgathering. Journalists, print or electronic, are behind the scenes, facilitating the connection between events as they unfold and the audience at home. They are in the business of balancing conflicting ethical demands, especially in wartime, as they see the big picture. The audience, on the other hand, exists in a more-or-less passive relationship to the events that journalists bring to them. They must rely on these gatekeepers to uphold ethical standards and to provide complete and accurate information to the public. At the same time, the magic of contemporary media is that the audience feels as if we are hidden in Goffman's (1959) backstage region, privy to the secret lives of celebrities. Media create a false sense of intimacy by turning public and private inside out, integrating the real with the synthetic, offering us vicarious intimacy in an increasingly isolated world (Cerulo, Ruane, & Chayko, 1992). It replaces the journalist's "right to know" with the immediate gratification of the audience's "want to know" (Leslie, 2004). The fact that, even before Drudge's report, the very first news outlets to break the story of Harry's presence in Afghanistan were celebrity gossip media (i.e., *New Idea* and *Frau Im Spiegel*) provides an ironic twist to the controversy, and one that echoes news coverage of Harry's own mother, Princess Diana.

Those journalists who chose to keep Harry's presence in Afghanistan were protecting his physical well-being, as well as that of his comrades. Those who chose to violate the blackout saw Harry as a "virtual" being, a celebrity, almost a fictional character. The new and improved post-blackout Harry turned the celebrity nightclub-crawling Prince Harry into the heroic Cornet Wales. Harry Wales has become more of an "ordinary bloke," a sincere young man just like the other chaps in the pub, and less of a privileged, idler dilettante. He tells the *Telegraph* that he doesn't miss much of anything from England while in the field: "I honestly don't know what I miss at all: music, we've got music, we've got light, we've got food, we've got (non-alcoholic) drink.... No, I don't miss booze, if that's the next question" (Telegraph, 2008, paragraphs 8–9). At least one audience member responded to this shift in identity.

> I commend Prince Harry for the highly admirable commitment he has shown to this alternate character Harry Wales, the soldier.

The news blackout served to transform Harry from celebrity to hero. As described by Boorstin (1961), "The hero was distinguished by his achievement; the celebrity by his image or trademark. The hero created himself; the celebrity is created by the media. The hero was a big man; the celebrity is a big name" (p.61). The Harry of the tabloids — carousing drunkenly with his buddies — metamorphosed into the soldier-prince protecting his homeland and bravely doing his duty without regard to personal safety. Absurdly, all it took was a media blackout to push Harry Wales into the spotlight as a prime candidate for future warrior-king.

References

Associated Press. (2008a). Media withheld Prince Harry's deployment to Afghanistan for months. Retrieved March 22, 2008 from http://www.foxnews.com/story/0,2933, 334249,00.html.

Associated Press. (2008b). Prince Harry on Afghan front line. Retrieved March 22, 2008 from http://www.msnbc.msn.com/id/23391374/.

BBC. (2008). *Editorial Guidelines.* Retrieved July 9, 2008 from www.bbc.co.uk.
BBC News. (2008). *Harry withdrawn from Afghanistan.* Retrieved March 22, 2008 from http://news.bbc.co.uk/2/hi/uk_news/7270743.stm.
Bok, S. (1983). *Secrets: On the Ethics of Concealment and Revelation.* New York: Random House.
Boorstin, D. (1961). *The Image: A Guide to Pseudo-Events in America.* New York: Harper and Row.
Bugeja, M. (2008). *Living Ethics Across Media Platforms.* New York: Oxford University Press.
Cerulo, K.A., J. M. Ruane, and M. Chayko (1992). Technological ties that bind: Media-generated primary groups. *Communication Research* 19(1), 109–129.
CNN. (2008). *Prince Harry heads home from Afghanistan.* Retrieved March 22, 2008 from http://cnn.com/2008/world/asiapcf/02/29/prince.afghanistan/index.html.
Day, L. (2006). *Ethics in Media Communication* (5th ed.). Belmont, CA: Wadsworth.
Edwards, R. (2008). *Taliban 'knew' Prince Harry was in Afghanistan.* Retrieved March 22, 2008 from http://www.telegraph.co.uk/news/main.jhtml?xml=/news/2008/03/03/nharry203.xml.
Gammell, C. (2008). *How the Prince Harry blackout was broken.* Retrieved March 22, 2008 from http://www.telegraph.co.uk/news/main.jhtml?xml=/news/2008/02/28/nharry2128.xml.
Gillan, A., M. Tran, and P. Walker (2008). *Prince Harry secretly serving in Afghanistan.* Retrieved March 22, 2008 from http://www.guardian.co.uk/uk/2008/feb/28/military.afghanistan.
Goffman, E. (1959). *The Presentation of Self in Everyday Life.* Garden City, NY: Doubleday Anchor.
Knapp, M. (2008). *Lying and Deception in Human Interaction.* Boston: Pearson.
Leslie, L. (2004). *Mass Communication Ethics: Decision Making in Postmodern Culture* (2nd ed.). Boston: Houghton Mifflin.
Panja, T. (2008). *Britain's Prince Harry serving combat duty in dangerous region of southern Afghanistan.* Retrieved March 22, 2008 from http://media.www.iowastatedaily.com/media/storage/paper818/news/2008/02/29/AssociatedPress/Britains.Prince.Harry.Serving.Combat.Duty.In.Dangerous.Region.Of.Southern.Afghan-3243065.shtml.
Patterson, P., and L. Wilkins (2007). *Media Ethics: Issues and Cases* (6th ed.). Boston: McGraw Hill.
Poniewozik, J. (2003, April 28). The trouble with sitting on the story. *Time*, p. 92.
Riviera, G. (2008). *Prince Harry's ordered home from Afghanistan.* ABC News. Retrieved March 22, 2008 from http://abcnews.go.com.
Society of Professional Journalists. (2008). *Code of Ethics.* Retrieved March 25, 2008 from http://www.spj.org/ethicscode.asp.
Squires, N. (2008). *Australian magazine broke Prince Harry story.* Retrieved March 22, 2008 from http://www.telegraph.co.uk/news/main.jhtml?xml=/news/2008/02/28/wdrudge328.xml.
Stelter, B., and S. Lyall (2008). Prince Harry and the secret kept by Fleet Street. *New York Times*, March 1. Retrieved March 24, 2008 from http://www.nytimes.com/2008/03/01/business/media/01harry.html?scp=2&sq=harry+afghanistan&st=nyt.
Telegraph. (2008). *Prince Harry speaks about life in Afghanistan.* Retrieved March 22, 2008 from http://www.telegraph.co.uk/news/main.jhtml?xml=/news/2008/02/28/nharry428.xml.
Williams, J. (2008). *News black-out.* Retrieved March 22, 2008 from www.bbc.co.uk/blogs/theeditors/2008/02/news_blackout.html.

Part IV:
Future

CYBERWAR: THE FUTURE OF WAR?

Brett Lunceford

When Estonian officials decided to remove Soviet war monuments from their capital in 2007, local Russians rioted and looted in protest. But the battle also took place online. An article in *The Economist* described the cyber-attacks: "Some have involved defacing Estonian websites, replacing the pages with Russian propaganda or bogus apologies. Most have concentrated on shutting them down. The attacks are intensifying.... At least six sites were all but inaccessible, including those of the foreign and justice ministries" ("A Cyber-riot," 2007, p. 55).

Although these events seem relatively minor, such actions trouble the distinction between the physical world and the digital realm in the information age and raise questions concerning the potential for cyberspace to become an electronic battlefield.

> NATO has been paying special attention. "If a member state's communications centre is attacked with a missile, you call it an act of war. So what do you call it if the same installation is disabled with a cyber-attack?" asks a senior official in Brussels. Estonia's defense ministry goes further: a spokesman compares the attacks to those launched against America on September 11th 2001 ["A Cyber-riot," 2007, p. 55].

The full implications of information warfare are still being considered, but it seems that in an increasingly connected world such disruptions will become progressively more severe in impact.

The threat of hackers breaking into electronic systems has existed for quite some time, but the nature of the threat has evolved. In 1989, the Air Force Satellite Control Network System Program Office for Sustaining Engineering (1989) issued a pamphlet titled *The Hacker Threat* that portrays hackers more as a nuisance than as a terrorist threat. Hackers are no longer seen as simply a nuisance. They are now potential terrorists or enemy combatants with the ability to destroy computerized systems from the relative anonymity of the ether. With the shift to an information economy comes the possibility that information can be used as a weapon, especially as the military becomes increasingly dependent on electronic communication systems and cryptography. McLuhan, Fiore, and Agel (1967/1996) prophetically declared that "real total war has become information war" (p. 138).

In this essay, I consider the potential for digital warfare to function as an appendage to traditional warfare. Cyberwar encompasses not only warfare against communication systems, but also warfare mediated through communication systems. Communication systems have always been a primary target in warfare, but now the attacks come not only from missiles but also from within the system. Moreover, the lines between citizen and enemy are no longer clearly demarcated. Individuals can do the work of armies in the digital realm through the use of programs and automation. Taking the battle into cyberspace allows an attacker to evade physical surveillance and disconnect from the body — possibilities inconceivable in industrial-age warfare. Communication systems are no longer simply the means by which one organizes forces in battle or wins the hearts and minds of the people — these systems are now part of the battlefield itself.

Defining Cyberwar

The practice of warfare is ever-evolving, often spurred on by combatants who attempt to use technological advances to achieve military superiority over those who lack that technology. For example, White (1962) suggested that the invention of the stirrup forever altered the nature of warfare, allowing for the possibility of mounted shock combat (pp. 1–38). Rothstein (2007) traced an evolution in American warfare strategies from massive land forces that were then coupled with naval forces and air power, through the advent of network-centric warfare (NCW) (pp. 277–278).

Modern military forces have evolved considerably from horse-mounted warriors. However, technologies tend to build on the past, augmenting previous practices rather than replacing them altogether. For example, despite its primitive origins, the infantry is still an important component of modern warfare, especially in the case of irregular warfare and guerrilla warfare where NCW may not be as effective (see Betz, 2006). Artillery and machinery, cast in the forge of the industrial age, continue to play an essential role in warfare. However, it is clear that the dawning of the information age will significantly influence the future of warfare (for theories concerning the information society, see Bell, 1999; Castells, 2000; Schement, 1989; Schement & Curtis, 1997; Toffler, 1980, Webster, 1995). Communication systems are already an essential component of increasingly technologized warfare (see Schleher, 1999; Vakin, Shustov, & Dunwell, 2001).

Cyberwar is difficult to define, as it is sometimes used interchangeably with the terms netwar, information warfare, electronic warfare, cyberterrorism, hacking and net-centric warfare. Yan and Wang (2006) explained that "NCW is not only a campaign idea but also a campaign system ... centralizing command, control, communication, computer, intelligence, surveillance, and reconnaissance (C^4ISR), electronic warfare, information warfare, campaign support, and firepower system altogether, making [up] an information network system" (p. 121). Alexander (2008) provided this definition of cyberwar: "Cyberwar (CW) can be defined as a subset of the electronic order of battle (EOB) encompassing all operations that either attack computer systems and networks or defend against attacks, by aggressors, on friendly systems and networks" (p. 78). Arquilla and Ronfeldt (2001) defined netwar as "an emerging mode of conflict (and crime) at societal levels, short of traditional military warfare, in which the protagonists use network forms of organization and related doctrines, strategies, and technologies attuned to the information age" (p. 6). This is one of the more tailored definitions in that it accounts for the shifting ideologies that underlie modern warfare and recognize that the protagonists are no longer mainly agents of the state. It suggests that "these protagonists are likely to consist of dispersed organizations, small groups, individuals who communicate, coordinate, and conduct their campaigns in an internetted manner, often without a precise central command" (p. 6).

Cyberwar may be only one tactic among many in the practice of modern warfare, but it marks an important shift. The ideas of NCW, information war, electronic warfare, netwar, and cyberwar all point to a changing, increasingly digitized battlefield — a battlefield that is much more difficult to define in terms of civilian and military space. Brenner (2008) explained how the advent of cyberspace has brought about a significant shift in the ability to wage war, observing that "giving non-state actors access to a new, diffuse kind of power, cyberspace ends nation-states' monopolization of the ability to wage war and effectively levels the playing field between all actors" (p. 404). Arquilla and Ronfeldt (2001) also observed that "many — if not most — netwar actors will be nonstate, even stateless" (p. 7).

Although warfare is no longer the sole prerogative of the nation state, the kinds of warfare that can be waged by non–nation-state actors remain limited. In addition to isolated, but significant acts of terrorism, such as those performed on September 11, 2001, the potential exists for widespread disruption through infiltration of electronic networks. The cost of attacking another individual, group, or even nation-state in cyberspace is significantly lower than the cost of waging a similar attack in physical space. But the virtual and the physical have become intertwined, and attacks on the digital realm can ripple out into physical space. Nations and organizations that rely heavily on information technology systems are most vulnerable to cyberattacks (Gompert, Lachow, & Perkins, 2006, pp. 54–55).

It is now possible to distill some principles of cyberwar. First, *cyberwar is decentralized.* Cyberwar can be waged by small networks of individuals using sophisticated technology. Attacks can come from anywhere in the world with little warning. Second, *cyberwar mainly takes place in and through cyberspace.* As networks become increasingly important, they also become a more prominent target. During a hearing before the House Committee on Science, U.S. Congressman Bart Gordon stated,

> Networked information systems are key components of many of the Nation's critical infrastructures, including electrical power distribution, banking, finance, water supply, and telecommunications.... But we know that many international terrorist groups now actively use computers and the Internet to communicate, and they are clearly capable of developing or acquiring the technical skills to direct a coordinated attack against networked computers in the United States [*Cyber security: U.S. vulnerability,* 2005, p. 14].

Gordon underscored the potential for non-state actors to engage in attacks through digital space rather than physical space and the vulnerability of networked systems.

Third, *cyberwar exploits the interconnection between physical space and cyberspace.* Cyberwar is a product of the information age. Alexander (2008) noted that "with the increasing use of semi- and fully autonomous robotic surrogates for the soldier-in-the-loop in the battlespace, the cyberdomain is being exploited as a command and control interface with unmanned aerial vehicles (UAVs), unmanned underwater vehicles (UUVs) and battlefield robots" (p. 82). The interconnection between physical space and digital space makes it possible to engage in warfare remotely, thereby reducing risk to personnel. But anything that can be controlled remotely is vulnerable to intrusion or interference.

Considering the Future of Cyberwar Through Current Practice

In considering the future of cyberwar, it is illustrative to consider where we are presently. For the moment, I will propose an alternate definition of cyberwar: *cyberwar is the use of information technology to further the ends of warfare*. I recognize that this is a broad definition, but broadening the scope of cyberwar allows for an exploration of some of the more mundane elements of cyberwar. With this definition, cyberwar encompasses the areas of communications, propaganda and psychological operations, funding operations, and intelligence. We will consider each, in turn.

Communications

Information technologies allow for an unprecedented ability to communicate in battle. One can communicate with friendly forces or intercept enemy communications to gather intelligence. Because of the importance of secrecy in tactical communications, cryptography has long been an important element of wartime communications, and information technologies provide new ways of encrypting messages (Gordon, 1981, pp. 14–25). Although early uses of cryptography were mainly in the hands of the government, it is increasingly used by the general public as well. This has altered the balance of power between the state and non-state actors. For example, cryptography has been used by those who fight against oppressive regimes (Jones, Kovacich, & Luzwick, 2002, p. 394). Cryptography also has been used by terrorist organizations to keep their transmissions secret, but the use of code can be decidedly lo-tech. Fielding (2004) reported that

> Al-Qaeda members have relied on simple encryption in ordinary e-mail exchanges. The September 11 hijackers, for example, while communicating between Europe and America, renamed the World Trade Center as the "faculty of town planning." Capitol Hill was the "faculty of law" and the Pentagon was the "faculty of fine arts." The date for the attack was also referred to openly in a simple code [p. 14].

Steganography is another way that information technologies allow for encryption. Steganography hides confidential information within another file. For example, a map can be embedded within another image or a document may be embedded within an mp3 music file. Most any digital file can be used to hide another digital file. For example, Polish researchers "were able to transmit 1.3Mbits of data in one direction during a 9-minute telephone call using the method, which relies on dropping bits into audio streams while retaining enough quality to make the call session useful to participants" ("Researchers Encode Secret Messages," 2008, p. 2). Thus, even wiretapping is no longer enough — one must consider the possibility that the message is embedded within the medium itself, rather than the spoken word that travels through the medium.

Steganography has clear benefits for terrorism and non-state sponsored attacks. Kolata (2001) reported that steganography "was used by recently apprehended terrorists who were planning to blow up the United States embassy in Paris. The terrorists were instructed that all their communications were to be made through pictures posted on the Internet" (p. F1). Other reports have suggested that Osama bin Laden has used cryptography and steganography in communications to operatives (Cha & Krim, 2001; Murphy, 2001). With steganography the casual observer sees only an image or hears a sound file. Only the intended recipient understands that there is a message within the file. Gary Gordon, vice president of digital forensics technology for WetStone Technologies, stated, "It's so insidious, you don't even know there is any communication going on" (quoted in Murphy, 2001, p. 5C).

As with most encryption schemes, the technology for resisting steganalysis is becoming more sophisticated. Liu and Liao (2008) proposed a method of embedding information within a JPEG image that resists several of the major attacks on steganography. This, coupled with the fact that steganography will easily hide an encrypted file, allows for a secure file to be hidden in plain sight. Thus, even if one can recognize that the file employs steganography, which may become more difficult as methods become increasingly sophisticated, the interceptor must then also break the encryption of the hidden file.

Impeding Enemy Communications

Information technologies can be used to impede an opponent's ability to disseminate their message. One example of silencing others can be found in the use of denial of service (DOS) attacks. At its most basic, a denial of service attack is overloading a server through the use of a zombie network or a script. Some hacktivists refer to this as a "virtual sit-in," because the effect is similar (Lane, 2003; Wray, 1999). Those who wish to enter cannot because the server is essentially full.

Denial of service attacks can also be used as a means of hackstortion, holding the server hostage unless demands are met (Conley, 2000). In 1999, a hacker collective called the electrohippies launched a denial of service attack against the World Trade Organization (WTO) during the WTO conference in Seattle. This provided an opportunity to raise consciousness concerning the actions of the WTO and allowed those who opposed the WTO to voice their arguments (DJNZ & Action Tool Development Group, 2000, pp. 7–8). Electronic Disturbance Theater also used this tactic to engage in politically motivated denial of service attacks on behalf of the Zapatista movement in Mexico (Lane, 2003; Wray, 1999).

The defacement of websites is another way that cyberwarriors can silence another's message while simultaneously disseminating their own.[1] A striking example of this took place on Sunday, September 13, 1998, when the *New York Times* website was hacked by a group of hackers called HFG, or H4ckIng for Girl13s (Hacking for Girlies). The hack was a belated response to a 1994

New York Times article by John Markoff (1994) that portrayed Kevin Mitnick, a hacker, as a danger to society. However, Markoff was no mere beat reporter. Three years before writing the article for the *Times*, he had published a book that discussed Mitnick in great detail (Hafner & Markoff, 1991). By the time the hack occurred, Markoff had written another book and a screenplay describing Mitnick's capture and arrest (see Chappelle, 2000; Shimomura & Markoff, 1996). Thus, many hackers blamed Markoff for the demonization of Mitnick. The timing for the hack was well thought out. Kenneth Starr had just published his report to Congress concerning President Bill Clinton and Monica Lewinski. To regain control of the site, the *New York Times* had to take the site offline for most of the day. Bernard Gwertzman, editor of the *New York Times* on the Web, called it "the equivalent of somebody blowing up a press" (quoted in Noack, 1998, p. 55).

Propaganda and Psychological Operations

Information technologies also are used to disseminate propaganda. Ellul (1965) defined propaganda as "a set of methods employed by an organized group that wants to bring about the active or passive participation in its actions of a mass of individuals, psychologically unified through psychological manipulations and incorporated in an organization" (p. 61). According to Ellul, propaganda is too large an undertaking to be performed by one person. But, as information technologies have become more widespread it is now possible for individuals and small groups to disseminate messages and silence others.

According to Bernays (1928/2005), propaganda is about the management of an image, or "interpreting enterprises and ideas to the public, and ... interpreting the public to promulgators of new enterprises and ideas" (p. 63). One way this is done is through the use of websites. Dallal (2001) described how Hizballah has adapted their messages specifically for the Internet and how they have managed their image both through linking and as participants in a digital war against Israeli hackers. Even anarchists are organizing and using the Internet for damage control when they receive unfavorable news coverage related to anti-globalization protest actions (Owens & Palmer, 2003).

Terrorists, in particular, seem adept at using Internet communications as a way to gain attention from traditional mass media. For example, a communication from Osama bin Laden may be released on the Internet, then picked up by Al-Jazeera, and subsequently broadcast by CNN and other major U.S. news outlets. Of course, this requires some kind of interest in the message whether because of interest in the individual speaking—bin Laden, for example—or from a shocking display, such as the videotaped beheadings of Westerners (Colarik, 2006, pp. 50–51). Wagner (2005) wrote, "Along with satellite television, the web has turned out to be the preferred medium for dissemination of terrorist 'information,' including news, propaganda, and other data that the terrorists would like to make available" (p. 21).

Terrorist organizations also have used websites as a tool to recruit potential members. Coll and Glasser (2005) reported,

> The Saudi Arabian branch of al-Qaida launched an online magazine in 2004 that exhorted potential recruits to use the Internet: "Oh Mujahid brother, in order to join the great training camps you don't have to travel to other lands," declared the inaugural issue of Muaskar al-Battar, or Camp of the Sword. "Alone, in your home or with a group of your brothers, you too can begin to execute the training program" [p. 10A].

Such an approach disseminates information much more efficiently than meeting in physical space while making it more difficult to identify who has taken part in such trainings. Sympathizers who may have been unable to participate due to lack of financial means or inability to travel can learn how to function as al-Qaida operatives where they already live. This allows for a wider, more diffuse network of potential operatives.

Funding Operations

In addition to disseminating information and recruiting potential operatives and sympathizers, information technologies also provide new ways to fund a group's or individual's actions, such as money laundering, especially through wire transfers (Shaffer, 2005; Wagner, 2005, pp. 22–23). The advantages of such a use of wire transfers are readily apparent, especially when conducted through non-mainstream bank entities. Transactions can be done anywhere in the world without being physically present.

Like other uses of information technology, money laundering can also be used in the service of mundane crime. A group of eleven hackers was indicted in 2008 for stealing over 40 million credit card numbers from various locations by breaking into computer systems and installing "sniffer" programs that gathered the data. They then encoded these onto blank cards and withdrew cash from ATM machines. CNN reported that the hackers "used anonymous Internet-based currencies to conceal and launder their proceeds, as well as channeling funds through bank accounts in Eastern Europe" ("Justice," 2008, paragraph 12). It is not difficult to see how terrorist organizations or other non-state opponents could employ similar methods to bankroll their activities.

Intelligence Gathering and Data Use

One area of cyberwar in which the government has a distinct advantage is intelligence gathering, especially in the use of data mining (Last, 2005). Seifert (2004) describes the core components of data mining as "the ability to collect and combine, virtually if not physically, multiple data sources for the purposes of analyzing the actions of individuals" (p. 463). According to Seifert, "Data mining consists of more than collecting and managing data, it also includes analysis and prediction" (p. 464). But, as Seifert and Relyea (2004) observed, centralized databases provide "a rich target for hackers" (p. 403). When hackers gain access to these databases, they can gather considerable information, whether that information is intelligence concerning the plans of their enemies or simply the ability to engage in identity theft. Identity theft is the collateral damage of cyberwar. It is relatively unlikely that an individual will be targeted for identity theft. Rather, hackers tend to work in aggregates. Such information can be gathered in many ways. For example, at the University of California, Berkeley someone simply walked into an unlocked office and left with a laptop containing Social Security Numbers and information on over 98,000 former graduate students and applicants (Burress, 2005). On a more financial note, CardSystems, a credit card processing company, improperly kept data which resulted in 40 million credit card numbers being compromised, including the security check code that is supposed to deter fraudulent use (Dash, 2005). Savvy criminals can even buy information. ChoicePoint sold access to 145,000 consumer records to thieves who presented themselves as small business owners (Zeller, 2005).

All of these examples demonstrate the potential for groups and individuals to use financial and personal information that the affected individuals may not have even known existed. These digital activities may also spill over into physical space. In her discussion of identity theft, McCue (2005) stated, "After 9/11, it became painfully obvious that the highjackers had easily obtained the false credentials necessary to move throughout the many systems that require identification" (pp. 53–54).

Viruses as Weapons

There are ways that cyberwar could theoretically be waged by exploiting code flaws in software. One such way is through the use of a computer virus. Computer viruses have been around since at least 1983, when Fred Cohen invented what is generally considered to be the first computer virus (Jones, et al., 2002, p. 498). Viruses, worms, and other malware are a concern to many because of our reliance on information technology. Hughes and DeLone (2007) argued that discourse concerning viruses range from dangers that are "widely touted, by the media, the government, and others" to a "growing chorus of voices criticizes this position for being based on an irrational fear of what often turns out to pose little to no real threat" (p. 92). Hughes and DeLone's study suggests that both sides have an element of truth to them (p. 93).

Although the impact of computer viruses can be significant, assessment of actual cost of damages varies widely. For example, Colarik (2006) stated that the Love Bug virus reportedly caused $3–15 billion in damages worldwide (pp. 86–87). Hinde (2000) reported the estimate at $100 million to $10 billion in worldwide damages, but observed, "Now that looks a pretty accurate estimate! This compares to Computer Economics' estimate that $12.1 billion in damages were incurred worldwide due to viruses in all of 1999" (p. 408).

Although viruses could be used for warfare, perhaps the threat is overstated. Most security breaches come not from external hackers, using viruses and other tools, but from employees or former employees. Perry (2006) reported that the "DTI Information Security Breaches Survey found that the average cost to large businesses of a major security incident was more than $170,000—and 87 percent of them had experienced a breach," but that the threat from the inside of an organization is considerably higher than threats from the outside (p. 11). Perry concluded, "Whatever the true cost, internal threats certainly cost millions more every year than losses from viruses or spyware" (p. 11; see also, "IP Theft Costs," 2003, p. 3).

Although viruses receive a lot of press and are highly visible when they occur, combatants are more likely to exploit existing flaws in the software or use other programs to gain access to the network. Viruses work mainly as a way to temporarily disable a network and would therefore remain useful from the perspective of cyberwar, but in a more limited capacity than the fear surrounding them would indicate. Combatants may be more interested in keeping the network open, especially if they wish to intercept enemy communications. Moreover, viruses are difficult to control once they are released and may hinder friendly systems as well as those of the enemy.

Cyberwar as an Appendage to Conventional Warfare

Where cyberwar has the greatest chance of impact is as an appendage to conventional warfare. Arquilla and Ronfeldt (2001) explained that

> netwar is not simply a function of 'the Net' (i.e., the Internet); it does not take place only in "cyberspace" or in the "infosphere." Some *battles* may occur there, but a *war's* overall conduct and outcome will normally depend mostly on what happens in the "real world"—it will continue to be, even in information age conflicts, generally more important than what happens in cyberspace or the infosphere [p. 11].

Cyberwar's power, in part, comes from the ability of non-state actors to take the battle to a more level playing field in cyberspace. Oxblood Ruffin (2000), a member of the hacker collective Cult of the Dead Cow, argued,

"Where a large physical mass is the currency of protest on the street, or at the ballot box, it is an irrelevancy on the Internet.... Programs make a difference, not people" (paragraph 18). Separating the programs from the people implies a significant shift in warfare and protest.

The possibilities of electronic systems to alter the balance of power between the nation state and groups of citizens can be found in the study of social movement protest actions in which protesters use technology to integrate digital strategies with physical action. Kahn and Kellner (2004) explained that social movements are becoming increasingly technologically savvy, with members using cell phones, personal digital assistants (PDAs), global positioning systems (GPS), laptops, wireless internet access, and engaging in actions such as wardriving and blogging to disseminate their message. The anti-globalization movement in particular has made significant use of new media as a way to forward its goals and enhance its protest actions (e.g., DeLuca & Peeples, 2002; Juris, 2005; Kahn & Kellner, 2004; Van Aelst & Walgrave, 2002).

Rheingold (2002) suggested that individuals can be brought together as "smart mobs" through a mixture of technologies such as mobile phones, wireless Internet, text messaging systems, and blogging. According to Rheingold, smart mobs "cooperate in ways never before possible because they carry devices that possess both communication and computing capabilities" (p. xii). In one striking example, Rheingold called President Joseph Estrada of the Philippines, who had just had his impeachment proceedings stopped by supporters, "the first head of state in history to lose power to a smart mob" (p. 157). According to Rheingold,

> Tens of thousands of Filipinos converged on Epifanio de los Santas Avenue, known as "Edsa," within an hour of the first text message volleys: "Go 2EDSA, Wear blck." Over four days, more than a million citizens showed up, mostly dressed in black. Estrada fell. The legend of "Generation Txt" was born [Rheingold, 2002, pp. 157–158].

The diffusion of mobile technologies such as cellular phones, wireless internet, text message systems (SMS) and interconnected devices such as personal digital assistants (PDA) and global positioning system (GPS) units allow groups to function as united bodies, especially when combined with websites generating RSS (Really Simple Syndication) feeds which provide constantly updated information from a centralized location. Such technologies are important when opposing a militarized police force equipped with tactical communication systems and help to shift the balance of power. Although the end result in Rheingold's example — physical protest — is similar to previous social movement actions, the means by which it is conducted and organized have become more efficient, more tactical.

Concluding Postscript

As I wrote this conclusion, Russia and Georgia were locked in a conflict that included both physical attacks and cyber attacks. Don Jackson, director of threat intelligence for SecureWorks, explained that "in the run-up to the start of the war over the weekend, computer researchers had watched as botnets were 'staged' in preparation for the attack, and then activated shortly before Russian air strikes began on Saturday" (quoted in Markoff, 2008, paragraph 15). In an illustration of how difficult it is to trace the protagonists in cyberwar, Markoff (2008) reported, "Exactly who was behind the cyberattack is not known" (Paragraph 8). It seems that cyberwar is not the future of war; cyberwar is now just another component of modern warfare. Thus, the future of war is likely to be an age old story — the violent deaths of men, women, and children as people continue to march to the battlefield. Cyberwar only expands the battlefield and allows more people to enter.

Note

1. Website defacement is quite common. For example, in the week ending August 2, 2008, Zone-h, a cyber security site, reported 9,717 website defacements. This is only a representation of defacements that were reported. For up to date information on website defacements, view the attack archive at www.zone-h.org.

References

A cyber-riot. (2007, May 12). *The Economist*, p. 55.
Air Force Satellite Control Network System Program Office for Sustaining Engineering (1989). *The Hacker Threat*. Washington, DC: Air Force Satellite Control Network System Program Office for Sustaining Engineering.
Alexander, D. (2008). Cyberwar comes of age. *Military Technology, 32*(3), 78–85.
Arquilla, J., and D. F. Ronfeldt (2001). The advent of netwar (revisited). In J. Arquilla & D. F. Ronfeldt (Eds.), *Networks and Netwars: The Future of Terror, Crime, and Militancy* (pp. 1–25). Santa Monica, CA: Rand.
Bell, D. (1999). *The Coming of Post-Industrial Society: A Venture in Social Forecasting* (Special anniversary ed.). New York: Basic.
Bernays, E. L. (2005). *Propaganda*. Brooklyn, NY: Ig. (Original work published 1928.)
Betz, D. (2006). The more you know, the less you understand: The problem with information warfare. *Journal of Strategic Studies, 29*, 505–533.
Brenner, S. W. (2007). "At light speed": Attribution and response to cybercrime/terrorism/warfare. *Journal of Criminal Law & Criminology, 97*, 379–475.
Burress, C. (2005, March 29). Berkeley / Cal issues alert about stolen laptop computer / It contains 98,000 Social Security numbers — notifications to warn of identity-theft risk. *San Francisco Chronicle*, p. B1.
Castells, M. (2000). *The Rise of the Network Society* (2nd ed.). Oxford: Blackwell.
Cha, A. E., and J. Krim (2001, September 19). Terrorists' online methods elusive; U.S. agencies seek experts' help in tracing encrypted messages. *The Washington Post*, p. A14.
Chappelle, J. (Director). (2000). *Track Down* [Motion picture]. United States: Dimension Home Video.

Colarik, A. M. (2006). *Cyber Terrorism: Political and Economic Implications.* Hershey, PA: Idea Group.
Coll, S., and S. B. Glasser (2005, August 7). Jihadists make Web base for recruiting, training. Ease, portability boost movement. *Journal-Gazette,* p. 10A.
Conley, J. (2000). Outwitting cybercriminals. *Risk Management, 47*(7), 18–26.
Cyber Security: U.S. Vulnerability and Preparedness: Hearing Before the Committee on Science, House of Representatives, 109th Cong., 1 (2005).
Dallal, J. A. (2001). Hizballah's virtual civil society. *Television & New Media, 2,* 367–372.
Dash, E. (2005, June 20). Lost credit data improperly kept, company admits. *New York Times,* p. A1.
DeLuca, K. M., and J. Peeples (2002). From public sphere to public screen: Democracy, activism, and the "violence" of Seattle. *Critical Studies in Media Communication, 19,* 125–151.
DJNZ, & Action Tool Development Group of the electrohippies collective (2000, February). *Occasional Paper No. 1: Client-Side Distributed Denial-of-Service: Valid Campaign Tactic or Terrorist Act?* Retrieved January 30, 2006, from http://www.fraw.org.uk/ehippies/papers/op1.pdf.
Ellul, J. (1965). *Propaganda: The Formation of Men's Attitudes* (K. Kellen & J. Lerner, Trans. 1st American ed.). New York: Knopf.
Fielding, N. (2004, August 8). Al-Qaeda betrayed by its simple faith in high-tech. *Sunday Times,* p. 14.
Gompert, D. C., I. Lachow, and J. Perkins (2006). *Battle-wise: Seeking Time-Information Superiority in Networked Warfare.* Washington, DC: Center for Technology and National Security Policy, National Defense University Press.
Gordon, D. E. (1981). *Electronic Warfare: Element of Strategy and Multiplier of Combat Power.* New York: Pergamon.
Hafner, K., and J. Markoff (1991). *Cyberpunk: Outlaws and Hackers on the Computer Frontier.* New York: Simon & Schuster.
Hinde, S. (2000). Love conquers all? *Computers & Security, 19,* 408–420.
Hughes, L. A., and G. J. DeLone (2007). Viruses, worms, and Trojan horses: Serious crimes, nuisance, or both? *Social Science Computer Review, 25,* 78–98.
IP theft costs overtake virus losses. (2003). *Computer Fraud & Security, 2003*(6), 3.
Jones, A., G. L. Kovacich, and P. G. Luzwick (2002). *Global Information Warfare: How Businesses, Governments, and Others Achieve Objectives and Attain Competitive Advantages.* Boca Raton, FL: Auerbach.
Juris, J. S. (2005). The new digital media and activist networking within anti-corporate globalization movements. *The Annals of the American Academy of Political and Social Science, 597,* 189–208.
Justice: Hackers steal 40 million credit card numbers. (2008, August 5). *CNN.com.* Retrieved August 6, 2008, from http://www.cnn.com/2008/CRIME/08/05/card.fraud.charges/.
Kahn, R., and D. Kellner (2004). New media and internet activism: From the "battle of Seattle" to blogging. *New Media & Society, 6,* 87–95.
Kolata, G. (2001, October 30). Veiled messages of terror may lurk in cyberspace. *New York Times,* p. F1.
Lane, J. (2003). Digital Zapatistas. *TDR: The Drama Review, 47,* 129–144.
Last, M. (2005). Using data mining technology for terrorist detection on the web. In M. Last & A. Kandel (Eds.), *Fighting Terror in Cyberspace* (pp. 41–62). Hackensack, NJ: World Scientific.
Liu, C.-L., and S.-R. Liao (2008). High-performance JPEG steganography using complementary embedding strategy. *Pattern Recognition, 41,* 2945–2955.
Markoff, J. (1994, July 4). Cyberspace's most wanted: Hacker eludes F.B.I. pursuit. *New York Times,* pp. A1, A36.

Markoff, J. (2008, August 12). Before the gunfire, cyberattacks. *New York Times*. Retrieved August 14, 2008, from http://www.nytimes.com/2008/08/13/technology/13cyber.html.
McCue, C. (2005). Data mining and predictive analytics: Battlespace awareness for the war on terrorism. *Defense Intelligence Journal, 13*(1&2), 47–63.
McLuhan, M., Q. Fiore, and J. Agel (1996). *The Medium Is the Massage: An Inventory of Effects*. San Francisco, CA: HardWired. (Original work published 1967.)
Murphy, K. (2001, October 11). Hidden messages used to plan attacks? *The Charleston Gazette*, p. 5C.
Noack, D. (1998, September 19). Hack attack sends chill through news Web sites. *Editor & Publisher, 131*, 14, 55.
Owens, L., and L. K. Palmer (2003). Making the news: Anarchist counter-public relations on the world wide web. *Critical Studies in Media Communication, 20*, 335–361.
Oxblood Ruffin. (2000, July 17). *Hacktivismo*. Retrieved November 17, 2008, from http://w3.cultdeadcow.com/cms/2000/07/hacktivismo.html.
Perry, S. (2006). Network forensics and the inside job. *Network Security, 2006*(12), 11–13.
Researchers encode secret messages in VoIP calls. (2008). *Network Security, 2008*(7), 2.
Rheingold, H. (2002). *Smart Mobs: The Next Social Revolution*. Cambridge, MA: Perseus.
Rothstein, H. S. (2007). Less is more: The problematic future of irregular warfare in an era of collapsing states. *Third World Quarterly, 28*, 275–294.
Schement, J. R. (1989). The origins of the information society in the United States: Competing visions. In J. L. Salvaggio (Ed.), *The Information Society: Economic, Social, and Structural Issues* (pp. 29–50). Hillsdale, NJ: Lawrence Erlbaum.
Schement, J. R., and T. Curtis (1997). *Tendencies and Tensions of the Information Age: The Production and Distribution of Information in the United States*. New Brunswick, NJ: Transaction.
Schleher, D. C. (1999). *Electronic Warfare in the Information Age*. Boston: Artech House.
Seifert, J. W. (2004). Data mining and the search for security: Challenges for connecting the dots and databases. *Government Information Quarterly, 21*, 461–480.
Seifert, J. W., and H. C. Relyea (2004). Do you know where your information is in the homeland security era? *Government Information Quarterly, 21*, 399–405.
Shaffer, Y. (2005). Analysis of financial intelligence and the detection of terror financing. In M. Last & A. Kandel (Eds.), *Fighting Terror in Cyberspace* (pp. 105–116). Hackensack, NJ: World Scientific.
Shimomura, T., and J. Markoff (1996). *Take-down: The Pursuit and Capture of Kevin Mitnick, America's Most Wanted Computer Outlaw — by the Man Who Did It*. New York: Hyperion.
Toffler, A. (1980). *The Third Wave*. New York: William Morrow.
Vakin, S. A., L. N. Shustov, and R. H. Dunwell (2001). *Fundamentals of Electronic Warfare*. Boston, MA: Artech House.
Van Aelst, P., and S. Walgrave (2002). New media, new movements? The role of the internet in shaping the anti-globalization movement. *Information Communication & Society, 5*, 465–493.
Wagner, A. R. (2005). Terrorism and the internet: Use and abuse. In M. Last & A. Kandel (Eds.), *Fighting Terror in Cyberspace* (pp. 1–28). Hackensack, NJ: World Scientific.
Webster, F. (1995). *Theories of the Information Society*. London: Routledge.
White, L., Jr. (1962). *Medieval Technology and Social Change*. Oxford: Oxford University Press.
Wray, S. (1999). On electronic civil disobedience. *Peace Review, 11*, 107–111.
Yan, T., and B. Wang (2006). Grid architecture model of network centric warfare. *Journal of Systems Engineering and Electronics, 17*, 121–125.
Zeller Jr., T. (2005, March 5). Release of consumers' data spurs ChoicePoint inquiries. *New York Times*, p. C2.

About the Contributors

M. F. Casper is an assistant professor in the Department of Communication at Boise State University. She teaches public relations and public relations support courses that explore the social impact, historical, ethical and theoretical contexts of mass media and public relations. She has presented her work at local, regional, and national conferences both individually and collaboratively and has published in *Health Communication, Feminist Media Studies, Journal of the Speech Communication Association of Puerto Rico*, and *Advertising in Developing Countries*.

Jeffrey T. Child is an assistant professor in the School of Communication Studies at Kent State University. His research interests include exploring the impact of new communication technologies in interpersonal and family contexts. He has presented his research at multiple conferences from world, international, national, and regional communication associations. His articles have appeared in *Management Communication Quarterly, Communication Education, Communication Quarterly, Journal of Intercultural Communication Research, Health Communication, Qualitative Research Reports in Communication*, and *Communication Research Reports*.

Koji Fuse is an assistant professor of journalism at the University of North Texas. His research areas include cross-cultural communication, public opinion, and war and media.

Kathleen German is a professor in mass communication at Miami University. She has been active at regional, national, and international levels in the communication discipline and has published work on the basic course in public speaking, rhetorical criticism, media criticism, and American Indian studies. She is working with World War II documentary film.

Trischa Goodnow is an associate professor of speech communication at Oregon State University. Her primary area of research is visual rhetoric. She has published in *Visual Communication Quarterly, The Journal of the Northwest Communication Association* and *The Handbook of Visual Communication*. She is the chair of the Visual Communication Division of the National Communication Association, vice president of the Northwest Communication Association, and the editor of the *Journal of the National Parliamentary Debate Association*.

Paul M. Haridakis is an associate professor of communication studies at Kent State University. He conducts research in media uses and effects, law, public policy, new communication technologies, sports media, and media ethics. His recent work has focused on First Amendment issues related to the regulation of content in various media such as the Internet and television and the regulation of communication during wartime.

Barbara S. Hugenberg is an assistant professor of communication studies at Kent State University. She conducts research in the areas of sports organizations, gendered sports fandom and instructional communication. Her recent research has focused on NASCAR fandom, the NASCAR organization, the politics of fandom, and gendered media coverage of the Indy Racing League. Other research interests include rhetorical criticism of the political message strategies of Barry Goldwater, George W. Bush and Sandra Day O'Connor.

James J. Kimble is an assistant professor of communication at Seton Hall University. He researches domestic propaganda, war rhetoric, and visual imagery. His book *Mobilizing the Home Front: War Bonds and Domestic Propaganda* was published by Texas A&M University Press in 2006. Other research has appeared in *Women & Language*, *Rhetoric & Public Affairs*, *Southern Communication Journal*, *Great Plains Quarterly*, and the *Quarterly Journal of Speech*. He is a distinguished honor graduate of the U.S. Army's Chaplain Center and School and has been recognized by the National Communication Association with the Gerald R. Miller dissertation award and the Karl R. Wallace award for outstanding scholarship in rhetoric and public discourse.

Richard A. Lee has more than 30 years of experience in journalism and public relations and is communications director for the Hall Institute of Public Policy—New Jersey. He also teaches media, government and communications courses at Rutgers University and Mercer County Community College, and is working on a Ph.D. in media studies at Rutgers. Before joining the Hall Institute, he was a deputy director of communications for two New Jersey governors. As a journalist, Rich held a variety of jobs ranging from political reporter to rock music critic. He continues to work in both fields. His recent activities include authoring chapters on public policy issues for two books published by the Hall Institute, as well as serving as an expert advisor for Enslow Publishers.

Brett Lunceford is an assistant professor of communication at the University of South Alabama. His research interests focus primarily on the intersection of new technologies and political action. His research projects examine politically motivated hacking and the social consequences of new technologies.

James E. Mueller is an associate professor of journalism at the University of North Texas. His research areas include political communication, journalism history, and media management. He is the author of two books: *Towel Snapping the Press: How George W. Bush Learned to Play with Journalists* (2006) and *Tag Teaming the Press: How Bill and Hillary Clinton Work Together to Handle the Press*.

Wesley J. O'Brien is an associate professor in the Department of Media Studies at Southern Connecticut State University. He teaches courses in film, film music, masculinities, visual literacy and mediated persuasion. These are also his principal research interests.

Terri Toles Patkin is a professor of communication at Eastern Connecticut State University.

Burton St. John III is an assistant professor of communication at Old Dominion University. He also completed journalism and public affairs studies at the Department of Defense's Information School in Indianapolis in 1979. His background features 15 years of public relations experience for the U.S. Postal Service. His academic work has appeared or is forthcoming in *Public Relations Review*, *The Communication Review* and the *Journal of Mass Media Ethics*. He is a co-chair of research for the AEJMC's Civic and Citizen Journalism Interest Group.

Roy Schwartzman is a professor of communication studies at the University of North Carolina at Greensboro. A winner of the National Communication Association Outstanding Dissertation Award, his research interests include the rhetoric of science and technology, figurative language, and Holocaust studies. A former Holocaust Educational Foundation fellow, he coordinates the AfterWords Project, which collects, disseminates, and analyzes resettlement stories of Holocaust survivors. He is the author of *Fundamentals of Oral Communication* (Kendall/Hunt, 2007).

Rekha Sharma is a doctoral candidate in the School of Communication Studies at Kent State University. Her research interests include news and politics as well as political messages in non-traditional news or entertainment contexts. A dissertation regarding the uses and gratifications of online information related to government conspiracy theories is under way.

Karen Rohrbauck Stout is an associate professor of communication at Western Washington University. Her primary interests are in organizational communication and communication education. She has authored numerous articles on power relationships in organizations and social communities, as well as the impact of technology on educational processes. She is a past president of the Northwest Communication Association.

Stanley T. Wearden is the Dean of the College of Communication Studies at Kent State University. His research interests include changing patterns of media use, audience perceptions of digital media, Web credibility, television news accuracy, and media ethics. His administrative focus is on fostering interdisciplinary research collaboration among faculty in related but traditionally separate disciplines.

David Weiss is an assistant professor of media studies at Montana State University Billings. His research interests include popular culture, critical linguistics, and the intersections of U.S. political and religious discourse. He has published in *Popular Communication* and *The Howard Journal of Communications*. Before returning to academia, he spent two decades as an advertising agency executive in New York City.

Index

advertisement 97
advertising campaign 94, 96, 97, 98, 145
al-Qaeda 57, 87, 242
alien registration act 8, 11, 15
allied powers 5
alternative media 24, 25, 27, 31
animated films 76, 77, 79, 87
anti-military 71
anti-war messages 31, 35, 67
anti-war protests 11, 12, 26, 35
anti-war rhetoric 5
anti-war sentiment 5, 72
atomic bomb 53
automobile 92, 95, 99, 105
axis powers 5, 99, 106, 112, 119

Bataan death march 52
Battle of Iwo Jima 62, 50, 52, 54
Bin Laden, Osama 85, 87, 139, 243, 244
Bolshevik Revolution 79
boot camp 100
Bush, George W. 24, 86, 127, 134, 135, 139, 142, 167, 168, 171, 174, 176, 184, 187, 205, 206, 224

cartoons 75–88, 113, 114, 115, 116, 121, 122
Castro, Fidel 81
censorship 81, 156, 222, 224, 225, 230
Central Intelligence Agency (CIA) 79
Churchill, Winston 99
Civil War 167
Clinton, William 24, 63, 244
Cold War 7, 9, 10, 11, 12, 13, 75, 79, 80, 82, 84, 87
Columbia radio research project 5
Committee on Public Information *see* CPI
commodification of truth 147, 148, 158, 159
Communication Studies 1, 4, 7, 9, 16
Communism 8, 14, 16, 28, 31, 79
conscription *see* draft

CPI 148–152, 156
credibility 7, 44, 143, 149, 152, 153, 155, 158–159, 207, 208, 214, 215, 216, 217, 218, 219, 226, 233
critical linguistics (CL) 183, 184, 189, 190, 191, 194, 195, 197, 198, 199
Cuba 9, 81
cyberattack 241, 249
cyberterrorism 240

demonization 57, 70, 244
Desert Storm 65, 173
dissent 133, 137, 140, 141, 184, 186, 200
domestic propaganda 113, 153, 155
draft 4, 24, 34, 37, 72, 100

economic convergence (conversion) 92, 93, 94, 96, 103, 104, 105, 106, 107
Eisenhower, Dwight D. 96, 108, 178
electronic warfare 240
elite media 187, 188–189
embedded journalists 13, 16, 62, 64, 205–214, 216–219
enemy 28, 44, 62, 116, 117, 133, 136–137, 143, 202, 239, 247; portrayals of 11, 29, 30, 57, 78, 80, 87
espionage 81
Espionage Act 4, 11, 15
ethics/ethical practices 16, 61, 86, 153, 222, 224, 226–234

fantasy theme 42, 43
fantasy theme analysis 41, 43–46, 52–54
Fascism 77
Fear appeals 6, 7, 10, 136
First Amendment 5
flag 41, 42, 46, 48, 53, 58, 61, 62, 69, 70, 147; desecration 11, 36
folk singers 26
framing 14, 86, 126, 127, 134, 138, 139–143, 186, 187, 193, 194, 198, 199, 207, 208, 217

257

freedom 36, 53, 60, 62, 69, 119, 186
freedom of speech 11, 16

globalization 85, 244, 248
Great Depression 92, 99
guerrilla warfare 82
guerrillas 30, 31

hackers 238, 239, 243, 244, 245, 246, 247
Hero 41, 44, 45, 46, 47, 48, 49, 57, 58, 59, 61, 63, 64, 66, 71, 72, 81, 82, 83, 86, 116, 119, 122, 206, 233, 234
heroism 29, 45, 57, 59, 60, 63, 64, 65, 66, 69, 71, 72, 193, 198
Hitler, Adolf 6, 78, 86, 115, 116, 127–132
Hollywood 34, 42, 45, 49, 50, 57, 71, 72, 80, 97, 98, 99
homeland security 135, 140; *see also* national security
House Un-American Activities Committee 8, 15
human-interest frame 186, 187, 188, 197, 198
Hussein, Saddam 86, 87, 171, 174, 192, 205, 206

ideological bias 184, 189, 190, 194, 197, 198
imperialism 54, 60, 86
indoctrination 6, 51, 100
induction *see* draft
information society 239–240
institutionalized propaganda 147, 148
insurgent 57
intelligence 6, 77, 240, 242, 245, 246, 249
Internet 13, 14, 15, 85, 86, 87, 186, 223, 240, 241, 243, 244, 245, 247, 248
Iraq War 13, 14, 63, 64, 65, 66, 67, 71, 76, 85, 87, 136, 164, 166, 167, 169, 172, 174, 175, 178, 183–200, 206, 211, 213, 219

Johnson, Lyndon 12, 27, 29, 34, 35
journalism, professionalized 147, 148, 159
journalistic patriotism 183

Kaiser 76
Kaiser (jeep) 95
der Kampf 126–137, 142, 143
Kennedy, John F. 12, 27, 28
Korean War 7, 10, 14, 15, 16, 82

Lenin, Vladimir 86
lexical and grammatical choices 183
Library of Congress 5, 6
loyalty 8, 94, 97, 98, 101–102, 103, 104, 108, 225

mainstream media 25, 26, 27, 29, 85, 86, 134, 148, 159, 184, 185, 187, 188, 206, 231

materialism 98
McCarthyism 8
media coverage 11, 12, 13, 14, 15, 27, 29, 33, 138, 184, 187, 188, 225, 226, 231, 232; *see also* news coverage
media effects 2, 3, 4, 5, 6, 7, 9, 10, 12, 14, 15, 127, 207, 212, 216
media portrayals 11, 57, 78, 83, 118, 151, 217
media violence 10, 12
metaphor 29, 59, 64, 67, 129, 137, 139, 140, 141, 142, 143, 166, 187
military-industrial complex 93, 95, 96, 100, 108, 167, 178–179, 199
mobilize 3, 5, 6, 95, 107, 140
morale 6, 42, 76, 113
morality 52, 59, 60, 64, 65, 66, 71, 72, 86, 178, 186, 199, 231

Napoleon 86
narrative possibility 112, 114, 117, 118
national security 16, 165, 198; *see also* homeland security
National Socialism 128, 130, 132
nationalism 78, 105
Nazi 57, 78, 79, 128, 130, 131, 132, 133, 137, 140, 142, 143, 230
Nazi Germany 78, 126, 127, 137, 142
Nazism 129, 132
netwar 240, 247
new public relations 147, 148
news coverage 25, 27, 31, 206, 207, 226, 227, 234, 244; *see also* media coverage
news reporting 16, 25, 27, 29, 30, 152, 159, 161, 184, 185, 205–219, 225, 226, 227, 228, 233
newspaper credibility 149
9/11 *see* September 11, 2001
Nixon, Richard 166, 179
normative appeals 112, 114
nuclear power 13, 84
nuclear war 8, 53, 79, 80, 141
nuclear weapons 82, 84

Office of War Information 6, 8, 94, 96, 97, 106, 115, 121

pacifism 85, 149, 150
patriotism 42, 49, 69, 77, 96, 97, 98, 101, 104, 106, 107, 183, 185, 187, 189, 193; *see also* journalistic patriotism
peacetime 86, 92, 93, 94, 102, 103, 105, 106, 107, 151
Pearl Harbor 78, 92, 113, 114, 143
Persian Gulf War 13, 59, 63, 85, 166, 167, 174, 180
persuasive texts 118
political movements 35, 37

POW 24, 43
Princeton radio research project 5
prisoners of war *see* POW
privacy 225, 226, 228, 232
propaganda film 76, 77
protest 11, 13, 14, 15, 26, 32, 33, 35, 183, 238, 244, 248
protest movements 34
pro-war sentiment 184, 195
psychological warfare 79
public opinion 5, 6, 11, 13, 26, 37, 148, 149, 150, 152, 156, 198, 205, 206
public relations *see* new public relations
public support 24, 198, 205, 217, 218

racism 35, 53, 78
Reagan, Ronald 63, 68, 166
Republican Guard 57, 60, 64
Revolutionary War 29, 138, 167
rhetoric 5, 13, 72, 81, 94, 103, 108, 114, 115, 116, 129, 134, 137, 151, 158, 166, 172, 174, 177, 180
rhetorical vision 42, 43, 44, 45, 48, 52, 53, 54
ritualistic divestment 93, 94, 103–105, 108
Rockefeller Foundation 5
Roosevelt, Franklin 42, 121, 122

scientific reporting 148
Second Persian Gulf War *see* Iraq war
secrecy 225, 228, 231, 242
Sedition Act 4
September 11, 2001 14, 15, 58, 61, 63, 69, 76, 85, 87, 108, 126, 127, 134, 135, 136, 138, 139, 140, 143, 166, 171, 172, 174, 175, 205, 206, 238, 240, 242, 246
social movements 11, 14, 248
social norms 118
Stalin, Josef 86
stereotypes 77, 82, 84, 87, 131, 156
surveillance 15, 16, 64, 173, 180, 239, 240
symbolic convergence theory 44, 45, 54

technology 1, 60, 71, 98, 173, 174, 180, 239, 241, 243, 245, 246, 248
television violence 10, 12
terministic screens 94, 103
terrorism 14–16, 127, 134–138, 140, 141, 169, 173, 174, 175, 176, 240, 242
terrorist 15, 76, 83, 87, 127, 134, 135, 136, 137, 138, 139, 140, 141, 173, 205, 228, 238, 239, 241, 242, 243, 244, 245
Third Reich 38
torture 42, 47, 59, 60, 68
training 6, 7, 28, 64, 69, 77, 87, 114, 142, 222, 231, 245
transformational Depictions 121
Truman, Harry 99

United Nations 84
U.S. Constitution 3, 4
United States Information Agency (USIA) 9, 15, 17, 27
USA PATRIOT Act 127, 137, 138

value clusters 94
veteran 24, 47, 64, 65, 67, 102, 147, 188, 195
"Victory shorts" 97
Vietnam War 7, 9, 10–12, 13, 14, 15, 24–38, 58, 59, 61, 64, 71, 79, 82, 83, 167, 180
Voice of America (VOA) 8, 15, 17

War on Terror 14, 126, 127, 134, 135, 136, 137, 138, 140, 141, 142, 143, 166, 231, 233
War Savings Bonds 115, 116, 117
War Stamps 113, 114–118, 119, 120, 121
wartime research 1–17, 166
Wilson, Woodrow 99, 149, 150, 151
World War I 2, 4, 6, 11, 75, 76, 80, 87, 92, 93, 96, 105, 147, 148, 151, 153, 155, 160, 161, 167
World War II 5 6, 7, 8, 10, 11, 16, 28, 49, 53, 54, 58, 66, 72, 75, 76, 77, 78, 82, 84, 87, 92, 93, 94, 95, 97, 100, 101, 104, 106, 107, 108, 112, 127, 141, 167, 188, 195

www.ingramcontent.com/pod-product-compliance
Ingram Content Group UK Ltd.
Pitfield, Milton Keynes, MK11 3LW, UK
UKHW041934140426
5217IPUK00014B/475